THEC

A READER

THEORIES OF FEDERALISM: A READER

Edited by
Dimitrios Karmis
and
Wayne Norman

palgrave
macmillan

First published in 2005 by
PALGRAVE MACMILLAN™
175 Fifth Avenue, New York, N.Y. 10010 and
Houndmills, Basingstoke, Hampshire, England RG21 6XS
Companies and representatives throughout the world.

PALGRAVE MACMILLAN is the global academic imprint of the Palgrave Macmillan division of St. Martin's Press, LLC and of Palgrave Macmillan Ltd. Macmillan® is a registered trademark in the United States, United Kingdom and other countries. Palgrave is a registered trademark in the European Union and other countries.

ISBN 0–312–29580–4
ISBN 0–312–29581–2 (paperback)

Library of Congress Cataloging-in-Publication Data

Theories of federalism: a reader / co-edited by Dimitrios Karmis and Wayne Norman.
p. cm.
Includes bibliographical references and index.
ISBN 0–312–29580–4—ISBN 0–312–29581–2 (pbk.)
1. Federal government. I. Karmis, Dimitrios. II. Norman, W.J.

JC355.T454 2005
321.02—dc22 2004053380

A catalogue record for this book is available from the British Library.

Design by Newgen Imaging Systems (P) Ltd., Chennai, India.

First edition: February 2005

10 9 8 7 6 5 4 3 2 1

Printed in the United States of America.

Transferred to digital printing in 2006.

To our parents:
Marie Lemienx Karmis and Paul Karmis; Valerie and
Jack Norman

Contents

About the Editors

Dimitrios Karmis is Assistant Professor of Political Studies at the University of Ottawa. He works in the fields of Political Theory, Comparative Politics, and Canadian Politics. His research focuses on the normative dimensions of federalism, the politics of identity, the politics of language, citizenship education, and democracy in diverse societies. He has published on these subjects in numerous books and journals, including *Ethnic and Racial Studies*, the *Canadian Journal of Political Science*, and *Politique et sociétés*. He is currently working on a book tentatively titled *Between Nationalism and Cosmopolitanism? Reassessing the Potential of Normative Theories of Federalism in the Modern World.*

Wayne Norman is McConnell Professor of Business Ethics at the Université de Montréal. He has published widely on federalism, secession, nationalism, multiculturalism, including reference articles on these subjects in the *Routledge Encyclopedia of Philosophy*, the *Blackwell Companion to Applied Ethics*, the *Oxford Handbook on Practical Ethics*, and the *Encyclopedia of the Philosophy of Law*. He is the author of *Taking Freedom Too Seriously?* (New York, 1991), and co-edited *Citizenship in Diverse Societies* (Oxford, 2000) with Will Kymlicka, and *Canadian Political Philosophy* (Oxford, 2001) with Ronald Beiner. His next book will be called *Negotiating Nationalism: Nation-building, Federalism, and Secession in the Multinational State.*

Acknowledgments

Johannes Althusius, *Politica*, edited and translated by Frederick S. Carney (Indianapolis: Liberty Fund, 1995), chap. I, sections 1–33, pp. 17–25. Reprinted by permission of the publisher.

Samuel Pufendorf, *De Jure Naturae et Gentium Libri Octo*, edited by James Brown Scott and translated by C.H. and W.A. Oldfather (Oxford: Clarendon Press, 1934), volume II, book VII, chap. V, sections 2–3 and 13–22, pp. 1,024–1,025 and 1,038–1,054. Reprinted by permission of the publisher.

Montesquieu, *The Spirit of the Laws*, translated by Thomas Nugent (New York: The Colonial Press, 1900), volume I, Book IX, chaps. 1–3, pp. 131–133.

Jean-Jacques Rousseau, "Statement of St. Pierre's Project" and "Criticism of Saint Pierre's Project for Perpetual Peace," in *A Lasting Peace through the Federation of Europe*, translated and edited by C.E. Vaughan (London: Constable and Company, 1917), pp. 36–39, 57–91, and 92–112.

Immanuel Kant, "Toward Perpetual Peace," in *Practical Philosophy*, translated and edited by Mary J. Gregor (Cambridge: Cambridge University Press, 1996), sections 8:348–8:357, pp. 322–328; sections 8:365–8:368, pp. 334–337; sections 8:376–8:380, pp. 343–347. Reprinted by permission of the publisher.

Alexander Hamilton, John Jay, and James Madison, *The Federalist* (New York: The Colonial Press, 1901), paper II, pp. 5–7; paper IX, pp. 38–43; paper X, pp. 44–51; paper XV, pp. 72–79; paper XVII, pp. 85–89; paper XXXIX, pp. 205–211; paper LI, pp. 284–288.

John C. Calhoun, "On the relation which the States and General Government bear to each other [The Fort Hill Address]," in *The Works of John Calhoun*, volume VI: *Reports and Public Letters of John Calhoun*, edited by Richard K. Cralle (New York: D. Appleton and Company, 1855), pp. 59–76.

Alexis de Tocqueville, *Democracy in America*, translated by Henry Reeve (London and New York: Longmans, Green, and Co., 1889), volume I, pp. 150–172.

John Stuart Mill, "Of Federal Representative Governments," in *Considerations on Representative Government* (London: Everyman Library, 1910).

Pierre-Joseph Proudhon, *The Principle of Federation*, edited and translated by Richard Vernon (Toronto: University of Toronto Press, 1979), sections 1, 6–9, 11, pp. 5–8, 36–49, 50–53, 67, 70–71. Reprinted by permission of the publisher.

Harold Laski, "The Obsolescence of Federalism," *The New Republic* (May 3, 1939), V. 98, pp. 367–369.

Altiero Spinelli and Ernesto Rossi, "The 1944 Ventotene Manifesto: Towards a free and united Europe" reprinted with the kind permission of the European Federalist Movement. The complete text is available at www.federalunion.org.uk.

Robert Schuman, "Declaration of 9 May 1950: The Schuman Plan for European Integration."

Franz L. Neumann, "Federalism and Freedom: A Critique," in *Federalism: Mature and Emergent* edited by Arthur W. Macmahon (Garden City, New York: Doubleday & Company, 1955), pp. 44–57. Permission to reprint kindly granted by Michael Neumann, literary executor of Franz Neumann's estate.

Pierre Elliott Trudeau, *Federalism and the French Canadians* (Toronto, Macmillan, 1968), pp. 191–196. Permission to reprint kindly granted by Marc Lalonde, literary executor of P.E. Trudeau's estate.

Ronald L. Watts, adapted from "Examples of Partnerships," in *Beyond the Impasse* edited by Guy Laforest and Roger Gibbins (Montreal: Institute for Research in Public Policy). Permission to reprint granted by the IRPP and the author.

Alfred Stepan, "Federalism and Democracy: Beyond the U.S. Model," *Journal of Democracy*, 10: 4 (October 1999), pp. 19–34. Permission to reprint granted by Johns Hopkins University Press.

Will Kymlicka, "Federalism, Nationalism and Multiculturalism," adapted from "Federalismo, Nacionalismo y Multiculturalismo," *Revista Internacional de Filosofia Politica*, 7 (1996), pp. 20–54, with kind permission of the author.

Richard Bellamy and Dario Castiglione, "Building the Union: The Nature of Sovereignty in the Political Architecture of Europe," *Law and Philosophy*, 16 (1997), pp. 421–445. Permission to reprint granted by Kluwer Academic Publishers B.V.

Ferran Requejo, adapted from "Cultural Pluralism, Nationalism and Federalism: A Revision of Democratic Citizenship in Plurinational States," *European Journal of Political Research*, 35 (1999), pp. 255–286. Permission to reprint granted by Kluwer Academic Publishers B.V.

We are grateful to Bryn Williams-Jones, Alex Sager, Junichiro Koji, Jean-François Caron, and Julie Bernier for research assistance; and to Rainer Bauböck, Richard Bellamy, Michael Burgess, Josep Costa, Alain-G. Gagnon, Will Kymlicka, Guy Laforest, and Daniel Weinstock for helpful advice along the way.

Introduction

1

The Revival of Federalism in Normative Political Theory

Dimitrios Karmis and Wayne Norman

In its most general sense, federalism is an arrangement in which two or more self-governing communities share the same political space. Citizens of federal states (or superstates, as in the case of the European Union) are members of both their subunit (sometimes called a province, canton, land or, confusingly, a state) and the larger federation as a whole. For a number of largely unrelated reasons, interest in both the theory and practice of federalism has exploded in the years following the collapse of Communism in Europe.

Of course, the implosion of Communist rule in the technically federalist Soviet Union and Yugoslavia led to the creation of new, more democratic federal states in Russia, Bosnia, Serbia-Montenegro, as well as federal-like arrangements in other successor states like Macedonia and the Ukraine, not to mention the short-lived post-Communist federation in Czechoslovakia. The 1990s also saw federalization in Belgium and Spain; attempts to radically reform the federal constitutions in Canada, Switzerland, and Australia; and more recently discussions have begun in earnest about the potential of federalism for the United Kingdom and Italy, and even (somewhat imprudently) for Afghanistan and Iraq. Throughout this period there have also been significant steps toward European integration—both in terms of "deepening" the nature of union, and in "broadening" the membership by admitting new member states—and this has led to open debates about the possibility of a European federation.[1]

These have also been very exciting times for the *theory* of federalism. For one thing, all of the political developments just mentioned have gone hand-in-hand with debates about why and how these federal reforms should (or should not) take place. Other motivations for political theorists to explore federalism, often for the first time, derive from the tremendous amount of attention they have paid in recent years to what we might call the challenges of citizenship in diverse societies.[2] Many political leaders and political theorists have seen federal arrangements as one of the best options available to reconcile such apparently paradoxical trends as the expansion of regional trading blocks, globalization, the reemergence of minority-nationalist movements, and the multiplication of identity-based demands. At the very least, federalism is seen as an attractive alternative to secession in multinational states, not to mention to the interethnic violence that sometimes accompanies secessionist movements. In political theory, the federal idea has been increasingly visible in the major debates about cultural diversity, nationalism, liberalism, citizenship, justice, and stability. More specifically, theoretical discussions have focused on overlapping themes such as federalism and nationalism, federal citizenship, federalism and identities, federalism and democracy, asymmetrical federalism and justice, and federalism and secession.

All of this interest in the theory and practice of federalism contrasts strikingly with the much more muted concern for these issues from the mid-1960s to the late 1980s. During that period European integration proceeded at a glacial pace, federal constitutions in newly liberated former colonies in the developing world disappeared almost as soon as they had been ratified, and political theorists generally wrote as if the frontiers of their discipline coincided with those of the centralized nation-state.

Despite the revival of interest recently, there has still been surprisingly little published about the theory of federalism from a primarily *normative* perspective; that is, from the perspective of evaluating and recommending institutions, and not merely explaining or comparing them. There are, of course, a tremendous number of recent volumes—especially collections of readings—on federalism; but these tend to focus on historical and comparative issues, or on normative concerns specific to a particular federal state.[3] Apart from the book you are currently reading, there exists no anthology of the classics of federal theory. There have been literally hundreds of texts collecting classic readings in the history of thought about the unitary nation-state; but not one that follows the parallel history of thought about the diverse, federal state (and this despite the fact that several A-list philosophers, such as Rousseau, Kant, and J.S. Mill, contributed to both traditions). There are some excellent recent books showing a serious preoccupation with the history of federal ideas. But as secondary sources, these studies necessarily present the history of federalist theory through their authors' particular intellectual prisms. And they tend to concentrate either on one type of federal theory or on the theories specific to a few authors or to a geographical area.[4]

This volume is, to the best of our knowledge, the first-ever anthology of theories of federalism with readings from the Renaissance to the present day. The emphasis throughout is on normative arguments: on the advantages or disadvantages of federal and confederal arrangements compared to those of unitary states; and on the relative merits of various proposals to improve particular federations or confederations. Because of the pragmatic or consequentialist[5] structure of many of these arguments, most of the readings also develop empirical arguments drawing on the full range of political science subfields: from political sociology, political economy, and constitutional studies, to comparative politics and international relations. There are also readings, both contemporary and historical, that attempt to clarify conceptual issues.

This general introduction is divided into four parts. In part I, we provide a brief overview of the conceptual history of the key components of the language of federalism. In part II, we argue in favor of a cautious approach concerning the potential of federalism in divided societies. As noted already, federalism has increasingly been presented as an institutional panacea in states characterized by the plurality of identities. The rationale behind this claim is obvious: federalism is a pluralist political solution that aims to reconcile divergent but overlapping identities; so it may offer hope for societies characterized by such pluralism.[6] While we agree that federalism is *potentially* a pluralist political theory, historically speaking, it has also easily supported antipluralist or "monistic" political projects. An awareness of these monistic tendencies of the federal tradition therefore is a prerequisite to any successful attempt at building a pluralist theory of federalism. In part III of this introduction we propose some basic principles of multinational federalism. Finally, in part IV, we briefly introduce the structure of the volume.

1. The Language of Federalism in the Eighteenth and Nineteenth Centuries

Historical texts can never be accurately understood without some knowledge of the contexts in which they were written. In the case of pre-twentieth-century writings on federalism, two contextual and closely interrelated terminological points seem particularly germane. First, the passage from the American Articles of Confederation of 1781 to the innovative Constitution of 1787 is the critical event that led to the now conventional distinction between confederation and federation.[7] Second, eighteenth- and nineteenth-century writings interchangeably used the terms federation and confederation.[8] This latter clarification needs to be addressed first.

We now typically think of confederations as much "looser" unions than federations. The defining nature of this "looseness" has been characterized in various ways. Some theorists will be inclined to call an arrangement a "confederation" instead of a "federation" if, for example, the subunits (or member states) have a right to veto all changes to the constitution or basic treaty, if they can exit unilaterally, or if they are clearly the primary locus of their citizens' identity and political loyalty. However, as Ronald Watts suggests, the key characteristic of confederations is that their "common government is dependent upon the constituent governments, being composed of delegates from the constituent governments."[9] By most contemporary definitions, the European Union is mostly a confederation, while Argentina, Canada, India, Nigeria, and the United States of America are clear examples of federations. The distinction has not always been seen this way, and it is important to take note of the evolution of these terms when we are reading texts from different historical periods.

"Confederation," "federation," and most of the other key components of the contemporary version of the language of federalism are derived from the Latin *foedus*, which means an alliance among individuals or collectivities aiming at the promotion of both specific and common interests.[10] English, French, and American dictionaries of the eighteenth and nineteenth century provide evidence that confederation and federation were initially used as synonyms. According to Martin Diamond, in eighteenth- and early nineteenth-century English dictionaries, "federalism meant [. . .] exactly what we mean now by confederalism: 'a sort of association or league of sovereign states' ".[11] The main French dictionaries of the time give similar results. In the *Dictionnaire de l'Académie française*, though the word *fédération* appeared later than *confédération*, both terms were defined in exactly the same way. For example, the 1798 edition defines *fédération* in the following way: "Alliance, union. See confederation"[12] (our translation). In the *Dictionnaire de Trévoux*, both terms refer to loose alliances of independent states whose main purpose was military and whose common endeavors rested upon the good faith of their members.[13] Definitions were not significantly different in nineteenth-century French dictionaries. The only major difference is with the inclusion of a reference to the Jacobin critique of federalism.[14] Even the first American dictionary defines both confederation and federation as a "compact" or "league" between "states or nations." Moreover, in both cases, the United States of America is given as an example.[15]

The passage from the American Articles of Confederation of 1781 to the innovative Constitution of 1787 is the key event that led to the now conventional distinction between confederation and federation. In fact, the *conceptual* distinction between these two types of political systems was established much earlier than the *terminological* distinction. As early as 1787–1788, Alexander Hamilton, John Jay, and James Madison were able to clearly identify the distinctive characteristics of the new proposed constitution. In their newspaper commentaries to bring about the ratification of the constitution in the state of New York, they contrasted that constitution with both the Articles of Confederation and what they called a "national Constitution."[16] In *Federalist* XXXIX, the authors argue that the proposed constitution is neither a "confederacy of sovereign States," like the Articles, nor a pure "consolidation of the States." According to them, it "is, in strictness, neither a national nor a federal Constitution, but a composition of both" (here we see them using "federal" and "confederal" interchangeably to mean what we now mean by "confederal").[17] For example, they argue that the constitution is federal in its foundation, but that it creates a national government as it relates to the operation of its powers. On the one hand, the constitution is federal in its foundation because its ratification "is to be given by the people, not as individuals composing one entire nation, but as composing the distinct and independent States to which they respectively belong. [. . .] Each State, in ratifying the Constitution, is considered as a sovereign body, independent of all others, and only to be bound by its own voluntary act."[18] On the other hand, the constitution creates a national government in the sense that the powers of that government operate "on the individual citizens composing the nation" rather than "the political bodies composing the confederacy."[19]

Hamilton, Jay, and Madison devoted much effort to emphasizing the defects of previous confederations. In their opinion, creating a government of the Union of citizens—rather than a federal government designed merely to represent the interests of the states—was essential to better protect order, security, and property. The American Articles of Confederation of 1781 had not created such a government. Such words as "federal government" or "central government" did not appear in the Articles, which made clear that the confederation had no existence when the states were not formally meeting together through what was called the "united states in Congress assembled" (note that "united states" is in lower case letters).[20] According to John Adams, that Congress was "not a legislative assembly, nor a representative assembly but only a diplomatic assembly," each of the states exercising the sort of powers associated with an independent government.[21] As Tocqueville noted a few decades later, the Constitution of 1787 made a major innovation by creating a government "served by its own civil and military officers, by its own army, and its own courts of justice."[22] What is important to note here is that the framers of the Constitution of 1787 decided to continue to use the older federal vocabulary even though they knew that they had radically reformed the political system of the United States. Most significantly, they decided to use the term "federal government" rather than "national government" or "central government."[23] Whether or not they kept using the language of federalism for political reasons (i.e., to avoid alienating those happier with the previous arrangement), the framers had introduced a conceptual distinction between two different types of federal arrangements[24] that would later develop into the current distinction between federation and confederation.

These two clarifications on the evolution of the language of federalism are important for several reasons. First, they help us to avoid basic mistakes while reading pre-twentieth-century writings on federalism. Second, they partially explain why the American model of federalism has so often been used as an example by other countries and by scholars: it is the original version of a radically new type of federal system. And third, they inform us about a major change in the federal tradition. From the late 1780s on, the federal tradition evolved into two very different—and often opposed—schools or traditions of political thought: one dominated by the evolving American model; and the other continuing the older, and increasingly neglected, confederalist tradition. In fact, for Thomas Hueglin, it would be more accurate to talk about two traditions. According to him, *The Federalist* "was a deliberate and radical break with that tradition [the federal tradition constituted by previous confederations]."[25] While it is not obvious that Hamilton, Jay, and Madison broke so radically with the federal tradition of the time,[26] Hueglin rightly points out that *The Federalist* misinterpreted Montesquieu.[27] More generally, he rightly implies that the gradual evolution and domination of the American model of federalism has led to the neglect of important ideas of the (original) federal tradition.[28]

2. A Cautious Approach to the Pluralism of the Federal Tradition

What reasons are there for political communities to federate? Why might the citizens in an independent state want to join with other states in a confederation or a federation? Why might those in a unitary state (say France or Japan) want to loosen the reigns of the central government and create provincial governments with sovereign rights to govern in certain policy jurisdictions? Why should the members of self-governing political communities within federations (such as Quebec within Canada) wish to remain in the federation rather than secede and form their own unitary state? The answers to questions like these form the core of a normative theory of federalism.

Throughout much of the history of federalist thought—sometime explicitly, sometimes implicitly—the answer to the basic question "Why federate?" has been because it gives a self-governing political community the best of both worlds: the advantages of being a relatively small, homogeneous polity, along with the advantages of being part of a stronger, more secure larger state or alliance; while at the same time avoiding some of the worst disadvantages of being either too small or too large. For much of modern history, the advantages of being part of a larger state or empire were primarily military, although economic arguments have always been important. The advantages of small communities have generally been seen in terms of more effective democratic or republican self-government. As we shall see, this "best of big, best of small" argument was an important one for theorists as different as Montesquieu and the authors of *The Federalist* in the eighteenth century, to Tocqueville and Mill in the nineteenth century, and even to the founders of what would be called the European Union in the twentieth century.

More recently, as we hinted at the outset, a new twist on this old argument pattern has become one of the principal rationales for creating, reforming, or reinforcing federations. The new argument concerns the way in which federal arrangements can facilitate multiple and overlapping cultural identities. In these terms, a small, relatively homogeneous cultural or religious community can preserve and promote much of its unique identity within a federal subunit, while nevertheless enjoying the advantages of being part of a larger, more economically powerful state or superstate. And given the fact that ethno-cultural and ethno-religious groups tend to overlap in any given territory, federalism holds out the possibility that these different communities can share states in which members have multiple identities and affiliations and look to different orders of government to assure the flourishing of their identities and to facilitate peaceful relations between groups. This, at any rate, is the theoretical promise. One can look to a few examples where this works fairly well in practice (Switzerland is everyone's favorite example), as well as more contested examples that may show the dangers of either (a) attempting to reconcile different cultural communities within a federal arrangement, or (b) of not doing it correctly. Different interpretations of what might have happened in a democratic Yugoslavia, as well as what did happen when the

Yugoslav federation dissolved, are used by both supporters and critics of the new federalist solution to the challenges of cultural pluralism.

We would now like to raise a certain "scholarly caution" about the most enthusiastic theories of federal pluralism. This caution is based on our reading of the history of federalist thought, which, as it turns out, has been less receptive to pluralism than is often supposed. To put it bluntly, there have been a lot more "monistic" than "pluralistic" theories of federalism in the history of thought. Such a monistic tendency characterizes not only Hamilton, Jay, Madison, and their followers. It also characterizes authors that better fit Hueglin's "countertradition" of federalism,[29] namely John Calhoun and Pierre-Joseph Proudhon. At least part of the explanation for this tendency, of course, is that problems of identity and cultural pluralism have never been as prominent in any aspect of political theory as they have been in recent years. So in adapting older traditions of federalist theory to deal with the fact of identity pluralism in contemporary societies, we must recognize that we are often trying to get these political arrangements to do things they were not, in some sense, originally designed to do.

Pluralism is a highly contested concept in need of clarification. In its descriptive meaning, pluralism refers to the fact that contemporary states are characterized by a growing plurality and diversity of collective identities (identities based on culture, ethnicity, language, class, gender, religion, sexual orientation, disabilities, profession, hobbies, and so on) and by a growing political expression of that plurality and diversity (new human rights, group rights, advocacy groups, political parties, NGOs, media and communication strategies, etc.). A pluralist political theory is based on a view of citizenship that advocates sensitivity not only to a plurality of monistic identities, but also to identities that are inherently plural, that is to say, shared identities. To take a tragic example, a pluralist political theorist recommending new arrangements for Yugoslavia when the Communist regime fell would have advocated something that took seriously not only the identities of citizens who identified themselves primarily as Serbs or Croats, say, but also for the many who identified themselves as simultaneously part Serb, part Croat, and part Yugoslav (and so on for all of the other overlapping identities in that former state).

One might argue that the issue of the plurality and diversity of political identities is inherent to the language of federalism. The very fact of an alliance among collectivities has two basic implications. First, citizens come to belong formally to two collectivities: they continue to be part of one of the constitutive entities, while becoming members of the alliance itself. Second, they *might* come to supplement their primary sense of belonging by an allegiance to the alliance. In other words, they might develop a dual sense of belonging. In the case of an alliance of alliances—what Proudhon called a "confederation of confederations"[30]—citizens might develop an even more plural or shared sense of belonging. So what we call a federal identity may be defined as a dual or plural identity that both generates and reflects the duality or plurality of political levels characteristic of federal systems.[31]

Most political theories in the modern era have been monistic, not pluralistic in this sense. The modern domination of monistic conceptions of identity is deeply rooted in the Enlightenment's rigid opposition between patriotism and nationalism, on the one hand,[32] and cosmopolitanism, on the other. For example, although they do not stand on the same side of the barricade, writers like Rousseau and Voltaire both implied that men could not love their *patrie* (roughly, their nation) and humankind at the same time. Rousseau could not accept the possibility of a genuine pluralistic, cosmopolitan engagement. For him, "it seems that the feeling for humanity is dissipated and weakened by being extended over the whole Earth [. . .]. Interest and commiseration must be limited and compressed in some way to make them active."[33] Those who pretend to be cosmopolitan, Rousseau speculated, simply "feign to love everybody so that they have the right to love no one."[34] Voltaire sarcastically agreed with Rousseau on the exclusive nature of patriotism: "it is sad that in order to be a good patriot, one has often to be the enemy of mankind."[35] But he "was certain that the idea of *nation*, as well as that of *patrie*, would be erased from the repertoire of the 'men of reason,' who believed in cosmopolitanism."[36] For various reasons, many classical theorists of federalism did not break with this monistic language of identity: you had to identify either with your own group, or with all of humankind. There was no room in this picture for diverse, shifting, overlapping affiliations and identities.

The issue of identity in federal systems gained importance with the advent of the American model of 1787. With the establishment of a real central government, the new constitution institutionalized two potentially strong political poles of allegiance.[37] Despite interpretive disagreements, early leading theorists of this form of federal system, like the authors of *The Federalist* and Tocqueville, generally agreed on its main innovative features: it created both a federal government with an unmediated executive capacity to intervene in its own spheres of jurisdiction and distinct citizenship rights and obligations attached to that level of government. However, these theorists did not support the idea of a dual identity. Two reasons may explain their monism. First of all, they often depicted the United States as the repository of "one nation" or "one united people"—from which were excluded Blacks and Aboriginal peoples—because of its low level of linguistic, ethnic, and cultural diversity.[38] In other words, we may think that they did not seriously consider the idea of a dual identity because they did not conceive the United States as a multinational or multiethnic federation. Second, the authors of *The Federalist* and, later, Tocqueville shared common assumptions about the greater strength of allegiances to states, and this led them to focus almost exclusively on the reinforcement of the federal government as a pole of allegiance. According to Publius (the collective pseudonym of Madison, Hamilton, and Jay), "it is a known fact in human nature that its affections are commonly weak in proportion to the distance or diffusiveness of the object"[39] and "many considerations [. . .] seem to place it beyond doubt that the first and most natural attachment of the people will be to the governments of their respective

States."[40] For Tocqueville, "the Union is a vast body, which presents no definite object to patriotic feeling."[41] To be sure, Publius and Tocqueville did not go as far as Rousseau and Voltaire in dismissing the possibility of a dual allegiance.[42] But the important fact is that strong assumptions about the "natural" attraction to one pole of allegiance led them to consider the two poles as naturally and continuously conflicting with each other—one's gain is always at the expense of the other—and prevented them from a serious exploration of the features and possibilities of a dual identity. Such a "competitive" conception of dual identity may easily amount to negating the viability of duality.[43]

Monistic conceptions of very different sorts are even more apparent in the great nineteenth-century theorists of federalism, John Calhoun, John Stuart Mill, and Pierre-Joseph Proudhon. All of them recognized the problems that arise from diversity, but in different ways they were more interested in controlling diversity than in enabling it to flourish, so to speak. According to the antebellum Southern statesman, Calhoun, "the great diversity of language, pursuits, situation and complexion" are the source of the formation of "great many communities." "Between these there is the same tendency to conflict [. . .] as between men individually; and even stronger—because the sympathetic or social feelings are not so strong between different communities, as between individuals of the same community. [. . .] Self-preservation is the supreme law, as well with communities as with individuals."[44] Calhoun's interpretation of constitutionalism, and of the American Constitution in particular, aimed at giving to the major collective interests of each country (excluding noncitizens such as Blacks) the "right of self-protection."[45] Being a Southerner supporting slavery, he focused most of his attention on the protection of the economic interests of the South and left little room for shared allegiances in his interpretation of the American Constitution.

Mill famously believed that "[f]ree institutions are next to impossible in a country made up of different nationalities." He argued that "[a]mong a people without fellow-feeling, especially if they read and speak different languages, the united public opinion, necessary to the working of representative government, cannot exist. The influences which form opinions and decide political acts are different in different sections of the country."[46] Accordingly, he recommended either mono-national states, with the assimilation of national minorities like the Breton, the French Basques, and the Welsh,[47] or federations between culturally similar populations that are likely to behave as one nation.[48]

The French utopian thinker, Proudhon, is often thought of as one of the pioneers of a more pluralistic approach to federalism and to political theory more generally (sometimes referred to as "integral federalism"). After all, his federalism was largely a response to the Jacobin homogenizing principles of "nationality" and "unity" conceived of as the source of an absolute, indivisible and immutable power over large and artificial political entities like the nation-state.[49] So, while in some passages Proudhon may speak of the federal principle as the way to a world in which "nationality will cease to be exclusive" and individuals will be allowed "to become citizens of several *patries*" on the sole conditions of residence and will,[50] his obsessive fear of Jacobinism led him to argue that geographical, ethnographic, and historical criteria make *cities* the "true" nations[51] and that the federal government must be a "subordinate function" without executive capacity.[52] In sum, Proudhon ends up supporting something very close to the pre-1787 model of (con)federalism and this prevents him from thinking about the federation itself as an additional pole of allegiance.

Much of the twentieth century was equally unkind to the idea of pluralistic federalism. Two developments in the aftermath of the First World War tarnished it. On the one hand, the League of Nations was founded on both pluralistic and cosmopolitan ideals; but it came to be seen as weak and ineffectual, and thus carried its founding values down with it. On the other hand, the dominant ideal of the interwar period was Wilson's call for national self-determination and the breaking up of the multinational European empires—an antipluralist vision if ever there was one. But nationalism for both majorities and minorities in states would become intellectually disrespectable for decades after its association with Nazism and Fascism. This led some in Europe over to Voltaire's side, if you will, with the dream of constructing a postnational European cosmopolitan patriotism that would leave particularistic identities (and hatreds) behind. At the same time, in the first postwar decades, most Western social scientists and technocrats became convinced that ethnocultural identities would soon disappear in the institutionally complete nation-state; so they saw little future in designing federative arrangements to keep them on life support.

By the last decade of the twentieth century, however, it was clear that particularistic, minority-cultural identities were not going to disappear. Quite the reverse. Long-standing national minorities like the Scots, the Quebecois, the Kosovars, Aboriginal peoples, and so on, seemed more prepared than ever to assert their rights to some form of national self-determination, even if within the bounds of more pluralistic states. Most Western states also found themselves hosts to new and increasingly prominent communities of immigrant minority groups seeking both equal citizenship rights and special accommodations. Meeting these demands would require innovations in both pluralistic theories and institutions. Also noteworthy is that the last two decades or so have seen the near-realization of the dream of the postwar founders of the European Union, the most significant confederation of our time. But this realization came not because of the more monistic cosmopolitan vision of some of the founders, but by political actors, commentators, theorists, and citizens coming to grips with the enormous complexities of overlapping plural identities.

In sum, although recent work on federalism has been marked by a growing tendency to recognize the plurality of allegiances that must be accommodated in a viable multinational federation,[53] students of federalism should keep in mind that both political thought, in general, and much of the federal tradition of political thought, in particular, are still dominated by monistic conceptions of identity.[54] In the next section, we attempt to elaborate some basic principles for a pluralist theory of multinational federalism.

3. NATIONAL SELF-DETERMINATION WITHIN A MULTINATIONAL FEDERATION

In the world today there are some 5,000–8,000 ethnocultural groups. The vast majority of these groups are minorities within their states, and distinguish themselves from the majority or other minorities by language, dialect, religion, ethnicity, or race. Perhaps one-tenth of these groups can be said to have developed a *national* or *quasi-national* identity, which means they do not think of themselves merely as ethnically distinct, they feel that they constitute a nation or a people with a right to self-determination. Even taking this relatively conservative estimate, there are about three or four "nations" for every state in the world. Some states, like Russia or India, have dozens of these so-called stateless nations. It is almost inconceivable that all of these national communities could be given a state of their own, not least because most of these peoples are intertwined geographically, and even within families, the way the peoples of the former Yugoslavia were; and nobody wants to envisage a world in which that tragedy is played out on a global scale. The most reasonable alternative for groups of this sort—that is, groups with national or quasi-national identities, who are typically living in a historic homeland that has been incorporated into a larger state—is some sort of self-determination and autonomy within a federal system.

In this section we survey some of the ways in which federal arrangements can serve as part of the solution to the very special kind of pluralism that arises in states with territorially based national minorities. Federalism should not be conceived of as the *entire* solution to the problems of these groups (e.g., in addition to the rights to autonomy that federal subunits might enjoy, it is still important to protect the individual citizenship rights of the members of vulnerable groups). Nor is federalism likely to provide much hope at all for minority groups that are not territorially concentrated and are therefore unable to control a federal subunit.

The big question for a normative theory of multinational federalism is, how do we determine the just, or otherwise "appropriate," type and degree of self-determination for national minorities within a federal state? This very general question gives rise to numerous more specific queries. We can ask about whether multinational federations (like Canada or India) need different principles and arrangements than uninational federations (like Australia or Argentina). For example, do subunits controlled by national minority groups (like Quebec), have rights to special arrangements that subunits controlled by a national majority group (like Ontario) do not have? And in cases where a national minority group does enjoy special rights and arrangements within a particular federal system, does it follow that it would be unreasonable or illegitimate for it to demand complete self-determination in the form of secession?

Before considering what *special* arrangements for national minorities might be justified in a federal system, we must clarify what types of arrangements must be made in *any* federal constitution. First of all, federal constitutions have to take stands on all of the issues treated by the constitutions of unitary states: from the division of "branches" of government (legislative, executive, and judiciary) and the design of the electoral system, to the possible entrenchment of a bill of rights. But in addition every federal system will be largely defined by its stand on the following basic issues:

(a) *The "Division of Powers"*: How are legislative and administrative powers and jurisdictions divided between the central and subunit governments? Some powers will be handled exclusively by the central government (defence and immigration are typical); some are exclusively handled by the subunit governments (often social services); and many are shared between the two orders of government (often transportation and education).
(b) *Representation in Central Institutions*: How are the citizens, minority groups, and subunits represented in important institutions of the federal state such as the parliament, the executive, the supreme or constitutional court, the central bank, the civil service, the military, and so on? Often one chamber of a bicameral parliament will represent equal citizens of the state, and the other will represent the subunits or their governments.[55] In some cases, minorities have a constitutional guarantee of a certain minimum representation in certain institutions. In other cases there are long-standing conventions, or recent "affirmative action" programs, to assure the adequate representation of certain groups. (And of course, in many multinational federations national minorities are actually underrepresented in federal institutions.)
(c) *The Integration of Markets and Legal Systems*: A number of federations include subunits with distinct legal systems and traditions (e.g., Louisiana and Quebec both have French-based civil law, and some Indian states use Muslim family law), and these must be integrated into the larger system of courts and appeals. Subunit governments will typically have numerous powers to regulate commerce and trade, so federal governments are generally given powers to maintain a relatively free market across the country.
(d) *The Amending Formula and Provisions for Secession*: The question of the subunits' role in amending (or vetoing amendments to) the constitution goes to the heart of the very idea of federalism. Many would say that an arrangement is not truly federal if it can be legally altered without the consent of the subunits. Similarly, if the subunits (or member states) are able to alter the constitution without the consent of the central government, then this is probably a confederation and not a federation. Most federal constitutions are difficult to amend, because their amending formulas require all or most of the subunits to ratify any significant constitutional change, along with a majority or a supermajority of the federal

> parliament. Very few federations have an explicit secession procedure. The former Soviet Union had one, at least on paper. And more recently, the Supreme Court of Canada has issued an *Opinion* that derives some vague rules for a legal secession from other long-standing constitutional principles, including its interpretation of the principle of federalism.[56]

Federal principles, and normative theories of federation more generally, guide arguments for and against specific arrangements of these four types. Of course, we should expect every federation to have different arrangements to suit its particular situation and traditions, just as all states have differing parliamentary or presidential systems, health-care or education systems, and so on. A theory of pluralistic or multinational federation will attempt to justify principles that citizens from both minority and majority groups should use in debates for constitutional reform. So even if we expect each federation to have somewhat different arrangements, it is possible that we can identify some general principles that could be used by citizens engaged in political debates in a wide variety of countries.

Now whether a federation is uninational or multinational, debates about the original design or the reform of any one of these federal arrangements tend to be highly contentious. In multinational federations each of these four types of arrangements takes on special significance, since collectively they demarcate the realm of self-determination for the minority-national community or communities.

Consider, for example, the question of the division of powers, which might look at first glance like a technocratic issue about which level of government can most effectively handle which jurisdictions. For minority nationalists, however, the division of powers determines much of the level of autonomy for their group: over which aspects of their collective life they will have exclusive control, and over which aspects they will be subject to the control of "outsiders" in the central government. Roughly speaking, the greater the list of important powers that are left to the subunits, the more autonomy or "self-determination" for the subunits.

National minority groups who dominate one or more of the subunits in a federation will also have special concerns when it comes to the representation of subunits in the central or federal institutions. In order to assure that their voices are heard and respected at the federal level, minorities are often given enhanced representation in federal institutions. They may also, in certain circumstances, be granted rights to veto some kinds of majority decisions in the federal parliament. For a clear illustration of this kind of special representation, one could imagine a group that makes up 15 percent of the population of a federation but is guaranteed 25 percent of the seats in the second chamber of parliament (this would be the enhanced representation, and it is similar in some ways to the enhanced representation that small states get in the U.S. Senate). In addition, imagine that there is a requirement that all successful legislation receives not merely a majority vote in the parliament, but also a majority of the votes from the members of parliament of this minority or its subunit (this would be the veto). Part of the principled rationale for arrangements like this comes straight from democratic theory. Many democratic theorists have worried about problems of permanent minorities who might be "tyrannized" by permanent majorities. Such mechanisms help prevent this kind of abuse of democratic procedures. But, at least from the minorities' point of view, this is not the only normative justification for special representation in central decision-making. A strong role for the minority group in the centre is also part and parcel of the basic desire for self-determination: it diminishes the likelihood that the federal government will use its constitutionally sovereign powers to oppress or subjugate the national minority.

Similar motivations underpin the importance minorities place on the procedures for amending the constitution. If subunits controlled by minorities are given a veto over constitutional changes, or if all amendments must be ratified by a supermajority of the subunits, then it will be less likely that fundamental aspects of the constitution, such as the division of powers, can be changed against the will of the minorities or the subunits more generally. This enhances their sense of self-determination.

In the preceding examples we have illustrated the normative rationale for adopting special federal arrangements to accommodate national minorities in terms of either (a) the legitimate desire of these groups for self-determination, or (b) traditional democratic responses to the "tyranny of the majority." Other values and principles also come into play within the political cultures and constitutional traditions of different federations. In recent years, much emphasis has been placed on the importance of clear constitutional *recognition* of minority groups' status and equality within the federation. The form of recognition demanded by a group varies considerably across federations and across time, and may include any of the following: explicit recognition as a "founding people," "constituent nation," or "distinct society" in the constitution; inclusion of the minority nation's symbols within the symbols of the federal state (e.g., its flag, coat of arms, or name); a special status, or a status equal to that of the majority group, for the minority's language, alphabet, or religion; an official presence within certain international organizations to which the federation belongs (e.g., the United Nations, the Commonwealth, la Francophonie, NAFTA, the EU, FIFA, the IOC); a special arrangement for the division of powers, representation, the legal system, the constitutional amending formula, a secession clause, and so on, that is, an arrangement not shared by subunits controlled by the national majority. The term "asymmetrical federalism" is used to describe federal systems that incorporate some of these forms of recognition—particularly the last one, where a subunit controlled by a minority group is given a different division of powers, and so on. The theoretical defense or critique of asymmetrical federalism has been one of the major preoccupations of political theorists of federalism over the past two decades (see, e.g., the readings by Watts, Stepan, Kymlicka, and Requejo in this volume).

Finally, it is important to mention that a comprehensive theory of multinational federalism must do more than justify (or criticize) special accommodations for the self-determination of national minorities within a federal system. It must also justify (or criticize) the aspects of federal design or practice that aim to bind all of the federal partners (minorities, majorities, subunits, the central government, etc.) to the particular federal state. Again, basic decisions about the division of powers, representation, integrated legal systems and markets, and the constitutional amending formula and secession procedure (or lack thereof) come into play here. If a particular federal arrangement is not just to be a long and bitter waiting station for minority groups hoping eventually to achieve full independence, then it will be important for the system to nurture a healthy sense of identity and loyalty of all citizens to both their subunit and the federal state.

* * *

This book is divided into five parts. Although the readings are grouped chronologically, history has also determined that each of the periods presented different challenges to theorists, so each of the parts also has a basic theme with a certain amount of debate taking place between the authors. Each part starts with an introduction that provides the historical context, summarizes the main issues of debates, and briefly presents each selection.

Part I is devoted to the birth of federal theory. It offers selections from two pioneering theorists of federalism, Althusius and Pufendorf, who came to challenge the rise of centralized modern states in the seventeenth century. The Enlightenment debate over the normative potential of international federalism is covered in *Part II*, with extracts from Montesquieu, Rousseau, and Kant. *Part III* introduces the "American invention" of a new form of federal system in 1787–1789 as well as the nineteenth-century debates over rival types of federalism. It includes selections from the *Federalist*, Calhoun, Tocqueville, Mill, and Proudhon. *Part IV* goes through the mid-twentieth century debate between theorists who were either highly critical of, or highly enthusiastic about, federalism (with Harold Laski and Franz Neumann, in the former camp, and Altiero Spinelli, Robert Schuman, and Pierre Elliott Trudeau in the latter). Finally, in *Part V*, selections from Ronald Watts, Alfred Stepan, Ferran Requejo, Will Kymlicka, and Richard Bellamy and Dario Castiglione provide an overview of contemporary debates over federalism in the context of globalization and culturally diverse democracies.

NOTES

1. German Foreign Minister Joschka Fischer contributed significantly to such debates with his famous speech of May 12, 2000. See Joschka Fischer, "De la confédération à la fédération, réflexion sur la finalité de l'intégration européenne," in *Le nouveau débat sur l'Europe*, ed., Hartmut Marhold (Nice: Presses d'Europe, 2002), pp. 176–189. For a French response to Fischer, see Hubert Védrine, "Réponse à Joschka Fischer," in ibid., pp. 190–194. More generally, the opposition between a federal union and a union of nation-states has been a recurrent

theme in the recent talks about the enlargement of Europe and the drafting of a European constitution.

2. See Will Kymlicka and Wayne Norman, eds., *Citizenship in Diverse Societies* (Oxford: Oxford University Press, 2000).
3. Examples include Murray Forsyth, ed., *Federalism and Nationalism* (London: Leicester University Press, 1989); Bertus de Villiers, ed., *Evaluating Federal Systems* (Cape Town/Dordrecht: Juta/Martinus Nijhoff, 1994); Stephen J. Randall and Roger Gibbins, eds., *Federalism and the New World Order* (Calgary: University of Calgary Press, 1994); Graham Smith, ed., *Federalism: The Multiethnic Challenge* (London: Longman, 1995); Karen Knop, Sylvia Ostry, Richard Simeon, and Katherine Swinton, eds., *Rethinking Federalism: Citizens, Markets, and Governments in a Changing World* (Vancouver: UBC Press, 1995); Daniel Elazar, *Constitutionalizing Globalization: The Postmodern Revival of Confederal Arrangements* (Lanham, Md.: Rowan & Littlefield, 1998); Kalypso Nicolaidis and Robert Howse, eds., *The Federal Vision: Legitimacy and Levels of Governance in the United States and the European Union* (Oxford: Oxford University Press, 2001); and David McKay, *Designing Europe: Comparative Lessons from the Federal Experience* (Oxford: Oxford University Press, 2001).
4. Examples include Murray Forsyth, *Union of States: The Theory and Practice of Confederation* (London: Leicester University Press, 1981); Daniel J. Elazar, ed., *Federalism as Grand Design: Political Philosophers and the Federal Principle* (Lanham, Md.: University Press of America and Center for the Study of Federalism, 1987); Michael Burgess and Alain-G. Gagnon, eds., *Comparative Federalism and Federation: Competing Traditions and Future Directions* (Toronto: University of Toronto Press, 1993); Daniel J. Elazar, *Federalism and the Way to Peace* (Kingston, Ont.: Institute of Intergovernmental Relations, Queen's University, 1994); Michael Burgess, *The British Federal Tradition* (London: Leicester University Press, 1995); S. Rufus Davis, *Theory and Reality: Federal Ideas in Australia, England and Europe* (University of Queensland Press, 1995); Joachim Jens Hesse and Vincent Wright, eds., *Federalizing Europe? The Costs, Benefits, and Preconditions of Federal Political Systems* (Oxford: Oxford University Press, 1996); Samuel LaSelva, *The Moral Foundations of Canadian Federalism: Paradoxes, Achievements, and Tragedies of Nationhood* (Montreal & Kingston: McGill-Queen's University Press, 1996); Thomas Hueglin, *Early Modern Concepts for a Late Modern World: Althusius on Community and Federalism* (Waterloo, Ont.: Wilfrid Laurier University Press, 1999); Frederick K. Lister, *The Early Security Confederations: From the Ancient Greeks to the United Colonies of New England* (Westport, Conn.: Greenwood Press, 1999); and Anthony Pagden, ed., *The Idea of Europe: From Antiquity to the European Union* (Cambridge: Cambridge University Press, 2002).
5. A consequentialist argument is one that recommends a particular institutional arrangement not because of its intrinsic features (such as its fairness or its conformity to the demands of political equality) but because of the sorts of results or consequences it is likely to produce over the long run. For more on the structure of normative arguments for federal arrangements, see Wayne Norman, "Federalism and Confederalism," in *Routledge Encyclopedia of Philosophy,* ed., Edward Craig (London: Routledge, 1998), volume 3, pp. 572–574; and "Towards a Philosophy of Federalism," *in Group Rights*, ed., J. Baker (Toronto: University of Toronto Press, 1994), pp. 79–100.
6. Among the first and most well-known versions of this thesis is Daniel J. Elazar's in his *Exploring Federalism* (Tuscaloosa, Al.: University of Alabama Press, 1987).

7. K.C. Wheare, *Federal Government* (Oxford: Oxford University Press, 1964 [1946]), p. 1; Bernard Voyenne, *Histoire de l'idée fédéraliste*, volume I: *Les sources* (Paris: Presses d'Europe, 1976), p. 42; and Elazar, *Exploring Federalism*, p. 147.
8. Wheare, *Federal Government*, pp. 10–11; Stephen Schechter, "Federalism and Community in Historical Perspective," *Publius* (Spring 1975), p. 4, note 3; and Bernard Voyenne, *Histoire de l'idée fédéraliste*, volume I, p. 62.
9. Ronald Watts, "Models of Federal Power Sharing," *International Social Science Journal* No: 167 (March 2001), p. 25.
10. On the meaning of *foedus*, see Bernard Voyenne, *Histoire de l'idée fédéraliste*, volume I, p. 27 and Solomon Rufus Davis, *The Federal Principle: A Journey Through Time in Quest of a Meaning* (Berkeley: University of California Press, 1978), pp. 215–216.
11. Martin Diamond, "What the Framers Meant by Federalism," in *A Nation of States: Essays on the American Federal System*, ed., Robert A. Goldwin (Chicago: Rand McNally, 1961), p. 27.
12. *Dictionnaire de l'Académie française*, 5th edition (Paris: Brunet, 1798), volume I, p. 573.
13. *Dictionnaire de Trévoux* (Paris: Libraires associés, 1771), volume II, p. 787, and volume IV, p. 80. It is with such a conception in mind that the Jacobins equated federalism with the disintegration of France and went as far as executing people suspected of federalist ideas during the Terror.
14. See *Complément du dictionnaire de l'Académie française* (Paris: Firmin Didot Frères, 1844), pp. 470–471.
15. Noah Webster, *An American Dictionary of the English Language* (Springfield, Mass.: George and Charles Merriam, 1856), pp. 245 and 444.
16. By this expression, they basically meant what we mean by a unitary constitution.
17. Alexander Hamilton, John Jay, and James Madison, *The Federalist* (New York: The Colonial Press, 1901), paper XXXIX, p. 211.
18. Ibid., paper XXXIX, pp. 208–209.
19. Ibid., paper XXXIX, p. 209. In the same paper, the authors point out another area in which the proposed constitution is federal, and two areas in which it is partly federal and partly national.
20. Diamond, "What the Framers Meant by Federalism," pp. 28–29.
21. Adams cited in Daniel J. Boorstin, *The Americans: The National Experience* (New York: Random House, 1965), p. 413.
22. Alexis de Tocqueville, *Democracy in America* (London and New York: Longmans, Green, and Co., 1889), volume I, p. 156.
23. According to Diamond, in the case of Hamilton, Jay, and Madison, it is very likely that they did that "to allay the fears of the 'true federalists' " (Martin Diamond, "The Federalist's View of Federalism," in *Essays in Federalism*, ed., Georges C. S. Benson [Claremont: Claremont Men's College, 1961], p. 24).
24. In 1835, Tocqueville talked about the creation of a "new species of confederation" (Alexis de Tocqueville, *Democracy in America*, volume I, p. 157). According to him, "the human understanding more easily invents new things than new words, and we are thence constrained to employ a multitude of improper and inadequate expressions" (ibid., p. 156).
25. Thomas Hueglin, "Federalism at the Crossroads: Old Meanings, New Significance," *Canadian Journal of Political Science/Revue canadienne de science politique* 36:2 (June 2003), p. 276.

26. After all, as paper XXXIX of *The Federalist* clearly indicates, Hamilton, Jay, and Madison did not advocate a unitary state. It is obvious that the book had centralist sympathies, but it advocated a compound political system that could have evolved in a much less centralist way than it actually did.
27. Hueglin, "Federalism at the Crossroads: Old Meanings, New Significance," pp. 280–284.
28. See ibid. and Thomas Hueglin, *Early Modern Concepts for a Late Modern World.*
29. See ibid., chap. 12.
30. Pierre-Joseph Proudhon, *Oeuvres complètes de P.-J. Proudhon*, volume 14: *Du principe fédératif et oeuvres diverses sur les problèmes politiques européens* (Paris: Marcel Rivière, 1959), p. 335.
31. It is important to emphasize that the components of a federal identity are engaged in relations of *coordination* rather than in "competitive" relations of *domination/subordination*. In other words, they are coherently organized to reflect the *shared* and *coexistent* political allegiances of the self. They do not reflect abnormality, incoherence, or ambiguity, as it is often implied by proponents of monistic authenticity. They are the result of a complex history of intercommunal relations and political federalization that have led certain individuals to shared allegiances. The federal citizen makes sense—often unconsciously—of the duality or plurality of conversational communities that constitutes her identity. The federal citizen may feel more attached to one community of identification than another, but she does not wish to make a choice among her allegiances. She cares for all of them; they all have a categorical importance. Only particular circumstances may force a choice.
32. The eighteenth century was marked by the beginning of the fusion of the old language of republican patriotism with the new language of nationalism. For a critical overview of this process and a plea for "patriotism without nationalism," see Maurizio Viroli, *For Love of Country: An Essay on Patriotism and Nationalism* (Oxford: Oxford University Press, 1995).
33. Jean-Jacques Rousseau, "Discourse on Political Economy," in *Rousseau's Political Writings* (New York: W. W. Norton, 1988), p. 69.
34. Rousseau cited in Josep R. Llobera, *The God of Modernity: The Development of Nationalism in Western Europe* (Oxford: Berg, 1994), pp. 153–154.
35. Voltaire, *Dictionnaire philosophique* (Paris: Flammarion, 1964), p. 308 (our translation).
36. Llobera, *The God of Modernity*, p. 154.
37. We do not mean that plural political identities were impossible in early modern confederations. We mean that it became much more of an issue with the advent of the new federal model introduced by the United States. More generally, the growing secularization and democratization of late eighteenth century contributed to make the whole question of identity a more pressing one.
38. See Hamilton, Jay, and Madison, *The Federalist*, paper II, pp. 5–7; and Tocqueville, *Democracy in America*, volume I, p. 169.
39. Hamilton, Jay, and Madison, *The Federalist*, paper XVII, p. 86.
40. Ibid., paper XLVI, p. 258.
41. Tocqueville, *Democracy in America*, volume I, p. 392.
42. Some evidence suggests that Tocqueville did not believe in the possibility of viable multinational federations. For example, although he knew the Canadian case, Tocqueville did not prescribe, or even really consider, a federal solution in any other case than the United States and Switzerland. And even in these two

cases, he did not consider a federal system with Aboriginal peoples as an option in America, while he presented Switzerland as historical exception very unlikely to be reproduced (see Dimitrios Karmis, "Fédéralisme et relations intercommunautaires chez Tocqueville: entre prudence et négation des possibles," *Politique et sociétés* 17:3 [1998], pp. 59–91).

43. Of course, given the deeply political nature of *The Federalist*, it remains open for debate whether Publius's competitive conception of identity is the result of strategic calculations with the purpose of making the central government—and consequently the United States—the hegemonic pole of allegiance of the federation.
44. John C. Calhoun, "A Disquisition on Government," in *Union and Liberty: The Political Philosophy of John C. Calhoun* (Indianapolis: Liberty Fund, 1992), p. 11.
45. John C. Calhoun, "On the relation which the States and General Government bear to each other [The Fort Hill Address]," in *The Works of John Calhoun*, volume VI: *Reports and Public Letters of John Calhoun* (New York: D. Appleton and Company, 1855), pp. 63–64.
46. John Stuart Mill, *Utilitarianism, On Liberty, Considerations on Representative Government* (London: J. M. Dent, 1993), p. 392.
47. Ibid., p. 395.
48. Ibid., pp. 398–400.
49. Pierre-Joseph Proudhon, *Oeuvres complètes de P.-J. Proudhon*, volume 14, pp. 263 and 366.
50. Pierre-Joseph Proudhon, *La fédération et l'unité en Italie* (Paris: E. Dentu, 1863), p. 118 (our translation).
51. Pierre-Joseph Proudhon, *Oeuvres complètes de P.-J. Proudhon*, volume 14, pp. 211, 219–237, 507, 546; and Pierre-Joseph Proudhon, *La fédération et l'unité en Italie*, pp. 56–57.
52. Pierre-Joseph Proudhon, *Oeuvres complètes de P.-J. Proudhon*, volume 14, pp. 319–321.
53. See notably Samuel LaSelva, *The Moral Foundations of Canadian Federalism*, chap. 1; and Will Kymlicka, *Finding Our Way: Rethinking Ethnocultural Relations in Canada* (Toronto: Oxford University Press, 1998), chap. 13.
54. As part of the explanation for this domination, we might say that both nationalists and federalists have been prompt to offer oversimplified antagonistic accounts of the relationship between nationalism and federalism. Among the most influential of those accounts, the cosmopolitan antinationalist type and the Jacobin monistic nationalist type have been particularly recurrent. The former states that federalism is an integrative framework of transition that will gradually lead to the triumph of universalism—and to the disappearance of nationalism—through regional and world institutions. The latter states that federalism is rather a disintegrative framework that will be conducive to the triumph of particularism through the gradual dissolution of federations into parochial states.
55. This was roughly the original idea behind the division between the House of Representatives and the Senate in the U.S. Congress. The second chamber of the German Parliament is composed of members appointed by each of the subunit (*Länder*) governments.
56. See Supreme Court of Canada, *Reference re Secession of Quebec*, [1998] 2 S.C.R. 217, as well as commentary in Wayne Norman, "Domesticating Secession," in *Secession and Self-Determination*, eds., Stephen Macedo and Allen Buchanan, NOMOS XLV (New York: New York University Press, 2003), pp. 193–237.

I

The Birth of Federal Theory: An Alternative Political Language in the Early Era of Centralized States

2

Editors' Introduction

Two or more parties, be they individuals or communities, will often find cooperation mutually advantageous. It can be much better for all parties concerned, over the long run, than conflict and war. For this reason, there have been federative arrangements (broadly construed) throughout recorded history. Federal *theory*, however, is a much more recent human creation: there is little to speak of before the sixteenth century. The first real theories of federation were formulated in response to the rise of centralized modern states and to the theory of sovereignty that came to support them. The Holy Roman and Germanic Empires were weakening in Europe and power was being centralized in the hands of monarchs. As most students of the standard History of Ideas are well aware, the theory for these kinds of political entities—the precursors to modern "sovereign" nation-states—was first formulated by the Frenchman, Jean Bodin and the Englishman, Thomas Hobbes, in the sixteenth and early seventeenth centuries. What many standard histories of ideas leave out, however, is that these theories of absolute state sovereignty were soon joined by theories of "shared federative sovereignty," which took seriously the reality of ongoing political experiments like the Swiss and Dutch confederations. German jurist Johannes Althusius and German philosopher Samuel Pufendorf were among the pioneers of this alternative federalist approach.

The brief selection included here from Althusius's *Politica* (1603) shows a conception of politics as the art of *associating*; one that applies to associations between both interdependent individuals and interdependent groups. This and its accompanying conception of sovereignty are both a response to those of Bodin. While these conceptions were marginal in the seventeenth century, they have influenced theorists of federalism ever since the rediscovery of Althusius's political theory by Otto von Gierke in the 1870s. Indeed, to this day they are being adapted to help with the challenges posed by such apparently paradoxical trends as globalization, the revival of nationalism, and the multiplication of identity-based demands.

The selection from Pufendorf is taken from *The Law of Nature and Nations* (1672). Pufendorf was innovative and influential in three respects. First, he provided a precise definition for what is now generally known as a confederation. That definition accounted for "systems of states" that did not fit the model of the sovereign state—for example, the Swiss Confederation, the United Provinces, the Holy Roman Empire—and yet implied a closer integration than a mere alliance between sovereign states. Second, he offered a clear and explicit distinction between the "regular" forms of state and the "irregular" ones, the latter category including all types of "systems of states." Third, while he provided mostly pragmatic arguments for confederations, he also laid some of the groundwork for the development in eighteenth century of a much more *principled* debate over the role of federalism as a mechanism for international peace.

3

Politics as the Art of Associating

Johannes Althusius

Politics is the art of associating (*consociandi*) men for the purpose of establishing, cultivating, and conserving social life among them. Whence it is called "symbiotics." The subject matter of politics is therefore association (*consociatio*), in which the symbiotes[1] pledge themselves each to the other, by explicit or tacit agreement, to mutual communication of whatever is useful and necessary for the harmonious exercise of social life.

The end of political "symbiotic" man is holy, just, comfortable, and happy symbiosis,[2] a life lacking nothing either necessary or useful. Truly, in living this life no man is self-sufficient (αὐτάρκης), or adequately endowed by nature. For when he is born, destitute of all help, naked and defenceless, as if having lost all his goods in a shipwreck, he is cast forth into the hardships of this life, not able by his own efforts to reach a maternal breast, nor to endure the harshness of his condition, nor to move himself from the place where he was cast forth. By his weeping and tears, he can initiate nothing except the most miserable life, a very certain sign of pressing and immediate misfortune.[3] Bereft of all counsel and aid, for which nevertheless he is then in greatest need, he is unable to help himself without the intervention and assistance of another. Even if he is well nourished in body, he cannot show forth the light of reason. Nor in his adulthood is he able to obtain in and by himself those outward goods he needs for a comfortable and holy life, or to provide by his own energies all the requirements of life. The energies and industry of many men are expended to procure and supply these things. Therefore, as long as he remains isolated and does not mingle in the society of men, he cannot live at all comfortably and well while lacking so many necessary and useful things. As an aid and remedy for this state of affairs is offered him in symbiotic life, he is led, and almost impelled, to embrace it if he wants to live comfortably and well, even if he merely wants to live. Therein he is called upon to exercise and perform those virtues that are necessarily

[1] [*symbiotici*: those who live together.]

[2] [*symbiosis*: living together.]

[3] [This sentence and the previous one are taken without acknowledgment from Juan de Mariana, *The King and His Education*, I, 1.]

inactive except in this symbiosis. And so he begins to think by what means such symbiosis, from which he expects so many useful and enjoyable things, can be instituted, cultivated, and conserved. Concerning these matters we shall, by God's grace, speak in the following pages.

The word "polity" has three principal connotations, as noted by Plutarch.[4] First it indicates the communication of right (*jus*)[5] in the commonwealth, which the Apostle calls citizenship.[6] Then, it signifies the manner of administering and regulating the commonwealth. Finally, it notes the form and constitution of the commonwealth by which all actions of the citizens are guided. Aristotle understands by polity this last meaning.[7]

The symbiotes are co-workers who, by the bond of an associating and uniting agreement, communicate among themselves whatever is appropriate for a comfortable life of soul and body. In other words, they are participants or partners in a common life.

This mutual communication,[8] or common enterprise, involves (1) things, (2) services, and (3) common rights (*jura*) by which the numerous and various needs of each and every symbiote are supplied, the self-sufficiency and mutuality of life and human society are achieved, and social life is established and conserved. Whence Cicero said, "a political community is a gathering of men associated by a consensus as to the right and a sharing of what is useful."[9] By this communication, advantages and responsibilities are assumed and maintained according to the nature of each particular association. (1) The communication of things (*res*) is the bringing of useful and necessary goods to the social life by the symbiotes for the common advantage of the symbiotes individually and collectively. (2) The community of services (*operae*) is the contributing by the symbiotes of their labors and occupations

[4] "On Monarchy, Democracy, and Oligarchy," pars. 2 and 3. [Plutarch refers therein to polity as citizenship, as statecraft, and as forms of government.]

[5] [There is no precise English counterpart for the Latin word *jus* (pl. *jura*) as employed by Althusius. Often it means "right" (e.g., *jus coercendi*—right to coerce), sometimes "law" (e.g., *jus naturale*—natural law), and upon occasion even "authority," "responsibility," "power," "legal order," "structure," or "justice." It also functions in many instances as a Janus-headed word eluding the capacity of any single English term to express (e.g., *jura regni*—rights and laws of the realm). Notations in text and footnotes have therefore been made from time to time to assist the reader in observing its complex usage. The general rule employed throughout is to translate *jus* as "right" wherever possible, to indicate by notation all places where *jus* has been translated by some other term, and to insert occasional footnotes that provide variant translations in critical places where the full meaning of *jus* cannot be expressed by a single English word. In keeping with this rule, "right" will henceforth be the most frequent translation (usually without notation) of *jus*. (Unless noted, "law" will always be a translation of *lex*.) The reader should be on guard, however, not to attribute too readily to Althusius' understanding of "right" the connotation of a self-evident system of "public right" or the notion of "unalienable human rights."]

[6] Philippians 3:20.

[7] *Politics*, 1276^b 17–1277^b 4; 1293^a 35–1294^b 41.

[8] [*communicatio*: a sharing, a making common. Althusius sometimes uses communion (*communio*) and community (κοινωνία) interchangeably with communication.]

[9] *The Republic*, I, 25.

for the sake of social life. (3) The communion of right (*jus*) is the process by which the symbiotes live and are ruled by just laws in a common life among themselves.

This communion of right is called the law of association and symbiosis (*lex consociationis et symbiosis*), or the symbiotic right (*jus symbioticum*)[10], and consists especially of self-sufficiency (αὐταρκείᾳ), good order (εὐνομίᾳ), and proper discipline (εὐταξίᾳ). It includes two aspects, one functioning to direct and govern social life, the other prescribing a plan and manner for communicating things and services among the symbiotes.

The law of association in its first aspect is, in turn, either common or proper. Common law (*lex communis*), which is unchanging, indicates that in every association and type of symbiosis some persons are rulers (heads, overseers, prefects) or superiors, others are subjects or inferiors. For all government is held together by imperium and subjection; in fact, the human race started straightway from the beginning with imperium and subjection. God made Adam master and monarch of his wife, and of all creatures born or descendant from her.[11] Therefore all power and government is said to be from God.[12] And nothing, as Cicero affirms, "is as suited to the natural law (*jus naturae*)[13] and its requirements as imperium, without which neither household nor city nor nation nor the entire race of men can endure, nor the whole nature of things nor the world itself."[14] If the consensus and will of rulers and subjects is the same, how happy and blessed is their life! "Be subject to one another in fear of the Lord."[15]

The ruler, prefect, or chief directs and governs the functions of the social life for the utility of the subjects individually and collectively. He exercises his authority by administering, planning, appointing, teaching, forbidding, requiring, and diverting. Whence the ruler is called rector, director, governor, curator, and administrator. Petrus Gregorius says that just as the soul presides over the other members in the human body, directs and governs them according to the proper functions assigned to each member, and foresees and procures whatever useful and necessary things are due each member—some useful privately and at the same time to all or to the entire body, others useful publicly for the conservation of social life—so also it is necessary in civil society that one person rule the rest for the welfare and utility of both individuals and the whole group.[16] Therefore, as Augustine says,

[10] [the fundamental law of living together; the demand that social life makes upon human persons both by its nature and by their agreement. This demand has some elements common to all associations, and others proper to various species of association (family, collegium, city, province, and commonwealth). In this chapter it is usually called the law of association (*lex consociationis*), but in later chapters symbiotic right (*jus symbioticum*) is the more common expression.]

[11] Genesis 1:26 f.; 3:16; Ecclesiasticus 17.

[12] Romans 13.

[13] [Althusius employs *jus naturae* (or *naturale*) interchangeably with *lex naturae* (or *naturalis*). Both expressions are henceforth translated as "natural law".]

[14] *Laws*, III, 1.

[15] Ephesians 5:21.

[16] *De republica*, I, 1, 18 f. [I, 1, 8 and 10 in the 1609 edition].

to rule, to govern, to preside is nothing other than to serve and care for the utility of others, as parents rule their children, and a man his wife.[17] Or, as Thomas Aquinas says, "to govern is to lead what is governed to its appropriate end."[18] And so it pertains to the office of a governor not only to preserve something unharmed, but also to lead it to its end.[19] The rector and moderator so endeavors and proceeds that he leads the people by method, order, and discipline to that end in which all things are properly considered.

Government by superiors considers both the soul and the body of inferiors: the soul that it may be formed and imbued with doctrine and knowledge of things useful and necessary in human life, the body that it may be provided with nourishment and whatever else it needs. The first responsibility pertains to education, the second to sustentation and protection. Education centres on the instruction of inferiors in the true knowledge and worship of God, and in prescribed duties that ought to be performed towards one's neighbor; education also pertains to the correction of evil customs and errors. By the former, inferiors are imbued with a healthy knowledge of holy, just, and useful things; by the latter, they are held firm in duty. The responsibility for sustentation of the body is the process by which inferiors are carefully and diligently guided by superiors in matters pertaining to this life, and by which advantages for them are sought and disadvantages to them are avoided.[20] Protection is the legitimate defence against injuries and violence, the process by which the security of inferiors is maintained by superiors against any misfortune, violence, or injury directed against persons, reputations, or properties, and if already sustained, then avenged and compensated by lawful means.

The inferior, or subject, is one who carries on the business of the social life according to the will of his chief, or prefect, and arranges his life and actions submissively, provided his chief does not rule impiously or unjustly.

Proper laws (*leges propriae*)[21] are those enactments by which particular associations are ruled. They differ in each specie of association according as the nature of each requires.

The laws by which the communication of things, occupations, services, and actions is accomplished[22] are those that distribute and assign advantages and responsibilities among the symbiotes according to the nature and necessities of each association. At times the communication regulated by these laws is more extensive, at other times more restricted, according as the

[17] *The City of God*, XIX, 15 [XIX, 14 in the Modern Library edition]. *See also* Seneca, *Letters*, num. 91 [num. 90 in the Loeb edition]; Marius Salomonius, *De principatu*, II; Giovanni Botero, *The Greatness of Cities*, I, 1.

[18] *On Princely Government*, I, 13 and 14.

[19] Or, as Hieronymus Osorius says, to rule is to direct toward the right end. *De regis institutione*, I.

[20] "Whoever presides, let him preside with care." Romans 12:8. "If anyone does not take responsibility for his own, and especially those of his own household, he has denied the faith, and is worse than an infidel." I Timothy 5:8.

[21] [as contrasted with common law (*lex communis*), discussed in the last four paragraphs.]

[22] [the second aspect of the law of association.]

nature of each association is seen to require, or as may be agreed upon and established among the members.

* * *

On the basis of the foregoing considerations, I agree with Plutarch that a commonwealth is best and happiest when magistrates and citizens bring everything together for its welfare and advantage, and neither neglect nor despise anyone who can be helpful to the commonwealth.[23] The Apostle indeed advises us to seek and promote advantages for our neighbor, even to the point that we willingly give up our own right, by which we guard against misfortune, to obtain a great advantage for the other person.[24] For "we have not been born to ourselves, inasmuch as our country claims a share in our birth, and our friends a share."[25] The entire second table of the Decalogue pertains to this: "you shall love your neighbor as yourself"; "whatever you wish to be done to you do also to others," and conversely, "whatever you do not wish to be done to you do not do to others"; "live honorably, injure no one, and render to each his due."[26] Of what use to anyone is a hidden treasure, or a wise man who denies his services to the commonwealth?

In light of these several truths, the question of which life is to be preferred can be answered. Is it the contemplative or the active? Is it the theoretical and philosophical life or the practical and political life? Clearly, man by nature is a gregarious animal born for cultivating society with other men, not by nature living alone as wild beasts do, nor wandering about as birds. And so misanthropic and stateless hermits, living without fixed hearth or home, are useful neither to themselves nor to others, and separated from others are surely miserable. For how can they promote the advantage of their neighbor unless they find their way into human society?[27] How can they perform works of love when they live outside human fellowship? How can the church be built and the remaining duties of the first table of the Decalogue be performed? Whence Keckermann rightly says that politics leads the final end of all other disciplines to the highest point, and thus builds public from private happiness.[28]

For this reason God willed to train and teach men not by angels, but by men.[29] For the same reason God distributed his gifts unevenly among men. He did not give all things to one person, but some to one and some to others, so that you have need for my gifts, and I for yours. And so was born, as it were,

[23] "Sayings of Kings and Magistrates." [1st par.]

[24] Philippians 2:4–6; I Corinthians 10:24; 12:25 f.; Galatians 1:3, 5; 5:14; Romans 12:18, 20; 13:8, 10.

[25] Cicero, *Duties*, I, 7.

[26] Matthew 22:39; 7:12. [Shabbath 31a; Digest I, 1, 10, 1.]

[27] *See* Ecclesiastes 4:5–8 and the *Commentarius* thereon of Franciscus Junius, in which are indicated the benefits of social life.

[28] Bartholomaeus Keckermann, *Systema disciplinae politicae*.

[29] John Calvin, *Institutes of the Christian Religion*, IV, 3, 1.

the need for communicating necessary and useful things, which communication was not possible except in social and political life. God therefore willed that each need the service and aid of others in order that friendship would bind all together, and no one would consider another to be valueless. For if each did not need the aid of others, what would society be? What would reverence and order be? What would reason and humanity be? Everyone therefore needs the experience and contributions of others, and no one lives to himself alone.

Thus the needs of body and soul, and the seeds of virtue implanted in our souls, drew dispersed men together into one place. These causes have built villages, established cities, founded academic institutions, and united by civil unity and society a diversity of farmers, craftsmen, laborers, builders, soldiers, merchants, learned and unlearned men and so many members of the same body. Consequently, while some persons provided for others, and some received from others what they themselves lacked, all came together into a certain public body that we call the commonwealth, and by mutual aid devoted themselves to the general good and welfare of this body. And that this was the true origin first of villages, and then of larger commonwealths embracing wide areas, is taught by the most ancient records of history and confirmed by daily experience. Opposed to this judgment is the life and teaching of recluses, monks, and hermits, who defend their error and heresy by an erroneous appeal to Luke 1:80; 10:41; Hebrews 11:38; 1 kings 19:8. But scripture places this kind of life among its maledictions. Deuteronomy 28: 64, 65; Psalms 107 and 144; Code X, 32, 26. Note also that a wandering and vagabond life was imposed upon Cain in punishment for his fratricide. Genesis 4:14. Contrary examples of pious men embracing active political life are to be found throughout sacred scripture.

From what has been said, we further conclude that the efficient cause of political association is consent and agreement among the communicating citizens. The formal cause is indeed the association brought about by contributing and communicating one with the other, in which political men institute, cultivate, maintain, and conserve the fellowship of human life through decisions about those things useful and necessary to this social life. The final cause of politics is the enjoyment of a comfortable, useful, and happy life, and of the common welfare—that we may live with piety and honor a peaceful and quiet life, that while true piety toward God and justice among the citizens may prevail at home, defence against the enemy from abroad may be maintained, and that concord and peace may always and everywhere thrive. The final cause is also the conservation of a human society that aims at a life in which you can worship God quietly and without error. The material of politics is the aggregate of precepts for communicating those things, services, and right that we bring together, each fairly and properly according to his ability, for symbiosis and the common advantage of the social life.

Moreover, Aristotle teaches that man by his nature is brought to this social life and mutual sharing.[30] For man is a more political animal than the bee or

[30] *Politics*, 1252ᵃ 24–1253ᵃ 38.

any other gregarious creature, and therefore by nature far more of a social animal than bees, ants, cranes, and such kind as feed and defend themselves in flocks. Since God himself endowed each being with a natural capacity to maintain itself and to resist whatever is contrary to it, so far as necessary to its welfare, and since dispersed men are not able to exercise this capacity, the instinct for living together and establishing civil society was given to them. Thus brought together and united, some men could aid others, many together could provide the necessities of life more easily than each alone, and all could live more safely from attack by wild beasts and enemies. It follows that no man is able to live well and happily to himself. Necessity therefore induces association; and the want of things necessary for life, which are acquired and communicated by the help and aid of one's associates, conserves it. For this reason it is evident that the commonwealth, or civil society, exists by nature, and that man is by nature a civil animal who strives eagerly for association. If, however, anyone wishes not to live in society, or needs nothing because of his own abundance, he is not considered a part of the commonwealth. He is therefore either a beast or a god, as Aristotle asserts.[31]

[31] *Politics*, 1253ª 31.

4

Regular States vs. Systems of States

Samuel Pufendorf

2. It should also be observed that most writers who have discussed political science have concerned themselves with explaining the regular forms of commonwealths, while many have apparently not even thought of irregular forms, and only a few have touched upon them in a perfunctory manner. Hence it was that if there ever was found a civil body which did not square with one of those three forms which are commonly called simple, scarcely any other name was left for it than that of a mixed state. And yet, not to mention the fact that such a designation is imperfectly applicable to some commonwealths, it is naïve indeed to hold that, besides those three regular forms, there are no other irregular ones. For even were it true that the laws of architecture require some certain type of buildings, not all men have constructed their dwellings by those laws. We hold that the regularity of states lies in this: that each and every one of them appears to be directed by a single soul, as it were, or, in other words, that the supreme sovereignty, without division and opposition, is exercised by one will in all the parts of a state, and in all its undertakings. From this it is not difficult to gather what an irregular state is. Furthermore, there are also systems made up of several perfect states, which, in the eyes of those who are not versed in these matters, assume the false form of one state; and these also must have their place in our explanation of the forms of commonwealths.

3. There are but three forms of a regular state, based upon the subject proper of the supreme sovereignty, according as that subject is one simple person, or one council, composed of a few, or of all the citizens. For supreme sovereignty is committed either to one man or to one council composed of a number of men. This council, again, is composed either of all the citizens, or of a smaller but select part. Therefore, the first species is when the supreme sovereignty is vested in a council which is made up of all the citizens, and in which every citizen has the right to vote; and this is called a *democracy*. The second, when the supreme sovereignty is vested in a council made up of select citizens, is called an *aristocracy*. The third, when the supreme sovereignty is vested in one man, is called a *monarchy* or kingdom. In the first that which

holds the reins of government is called the *people*, in the second the *nobles*, in the third the *monarch*. Pindar, *Pythian Odes*, ii [87–8]: "[. . .] Whether at the tyrant's court, or where the boisterous host, or where the wise, have care of the State." (S.) [. . .]

13. A number of the more recent writers imagine many kinds of mixed states, and yet in such a way that they in general reject the most of them as unsuitable, but commend especially two kinds. One kind is when the parts of supreme sovereignty are dividedly and independently in the hands of different persons and bodies of the same commonwealth, in such a way that each of them holds that part which they possess in their own right and administer it according to their own judgement, but in respect to the other parts of sovereignty are like subjects. This is much the manner in which, we are told by Appian, *Bellum Libycum* [*Punic Wars*, xvi. 106 f.], the affairs of the kingdom of Numidia were arranged by Scipio after the death of Masinissa, whereby the three legitimate sons bore the title of king, but the eldest of them, Micipsa, held Cirta, the capital, the second, Gulussa, controlled questions of war and peace, while Manastabal presided over justice. The second is when the supreme sovereignty is without division in the hands of more than one, yet so that neither a large majority can pass any final action or exercise parts of sovereignty against a small minority, nor even all against one. And this may be of two kinds, when either all are equal, or one or another possesses some extraordinary rights, which he can exercise without the approval of the rest. Many ancient authorities are cited, in whose works frequent mention is to be found of mixed states. But on these we have already observed that most of what they say about such states has no connexion at all with the division of supreme sovereignty among different persons or with councils, but that it concerns either the proper fixing of the qualifications of the persons of whom the sovereign council is composed, or the best combination of the institutions of different commonwealths.

Furthermore, it would be my feeling that some examples of such mixtures may be easily explained by drawing a distinction between actual sovereignty and the manner of administration. So that those commonwealths may be said to have some mixture from others, when it appears that their manner of administration was sought from another form; if, for example, in a state where the sovereignty is in the hands of the people, most of the affairs of the state should be carried on by a principal officer or a senate; or if in an aristocracy one magistrate should enjoy unusual authority, or the people should be consulted on many matters, or if in a monarchy difficult matters should be referred to a senate, or to the people. But if this explanation does not square with some cases cited by ancient writers, what follows will clear the matter up.

We have shown before that the essentials of a perfect and regular state require that in it there be such a union as makes everything which works to its administration appear to come, as it were, from one soul. It is, therefore, perfectly clear that by the first mixed form of state there is constituted a body which is held together not by the bond of a single sovereignty but only by a pact, and that it must, therefore, be classed not among regular states but among irregular commonwealths, being weak and extremely open to internal disorders. Regarding the second mixed form of state I feel that we should consider whether those in whom is indivisibly vested the supreme sovereignty constitute a permanent senate, which is to govern the entire state as a single and permanent body. In this case it will be an aristocracy, but one very ill-adapted to transact business, in that one or but a few, by interposing their votes in opposition, can render void the will of all the rest. But if, on the other hand, there belong to those individual members, who enjoy in other respects entire equality, and to them alone entire parts of the commonwealth, yet no one of them can exercise the functions of supreme sovereignty without the unanimous concurrence of all the rest, it will be a system, in the proper sense of the word, yet such as will likewise be highly unsuited to transact business, because of its great and undue inflexibility. But when one man signally outranks all others in authority and in some matters of the sovereignty, it will be an irregular commonwealth, thrust in, as it were, somewhere between a monarchy struggling up out of a mass of nobles, and a system. And the irregularity will be all the greater when several overtop all the rest.

14. Now just as we envy no man who remains set in his determination to retain the term of mixed commonwealth his praise for constancy, so it appears to us more convenient and clear, and at the same time more suited to the explanation of some phenomena in certain states, if we choose to call those states irregular, in which no one of the three regular forms is observable, nor any mere shortcoming or *παρέκβασις*[1] [deviation], and which cannot with accuracy be referred to the form of systems. On these in general it should be observed that they vary from a regular state in that not everything appears to proceed from one soul and will, nor is each and every person to be controlled by virtue of sovereignty. And they differ from systems in that they are not, like these, composed of distinct and perfect states. They likewise are foreign to diseases and aberrations, in that a disease always betrays itself by some show of illegitimacy and shame, since it arises from the evil administration of some worthy form, or from ill-conceived laws and institutions. But the irregularity affects intrinsically not the very form alone, but also dares to show itself openly and without shame, as though publicly and, as it were, legitimately sanctioned. And for this reason a disease should have been absent from the intention of those who established the state, and always appears in it as something base, while an irregularity arose from or was confirmed by the will or approbation of those who go to make up a commonwealth. It is just as in one building, the plan of which, indeed, agrees with the rules of architecture but the material of which is faulty, or the tenants negligent, the roof comes apart, the walls threaten to fall, the beams creak, and the foundations settle, while in another the architect himself departs from the common rules and makes a form to suit his fancy, or remedies a threatening defect by some unusual device.

[1] [For *παρέχβασις* read *παρέκβασις*.—*Tr.*]

Moreover, some irregularities have appeared at the very formation of the state, while others have crept in with the passage of time and at unguarded moments. It was also possible that, at the time of founding, or when some great change was being made, those concerned with the initial or the second step were unable to introduce a regular form, either through their lack of skill, or because the state of affairs did not suffer consideration of a settled and orderly status. Add Hobbes, *Leviathan*, chap. xxix, a little way past the beginning. Sometimes also those who were the chief assistants and leaders in securing the kingdom, bargained for such jurisdictions and privileges for themselves, that they cannot be regarded as true subjects. Often also a state is seized with sickness because of the slothfulness of its governors, or for some other reason, and when this has struck such deep root that it cannot be torn up without entailing the ruin of the state, nothing is left but for that sickness to put off, as it were, its evil force by receiving public sanction, and for what was formerly nothing but usurpation, faction, or contumacy, to pass thereafter as right or privilege.

15. Now of the irregular forms of commonwealths no certain number can be tabulated or species set up, because of the great variety which either actually exists or can be imagined. Therefore, little remains to us but to observe more in detail the nature of irregularity in some famous examples. Such an instance we have endeavoured to set forth in the Roman Republic; another Severinus de Monzambano has undertaken in the case of the German Empire. At this time it may be enough to make some observations on the irregularity which some observe in the case of the ancient Roman Empire, in that at one time it appeared to have two or three bodies, when one of the Augusti held the East, the other the West, or even three Augusti held the Roman world in as many divisions. Sometimes again it appeared to have two or three heads, when two or three Augusti controlled it without division as colleagues.

Now, on the first case, it is to be observed that whenever two emperors held the empire, one the East, and the other the West, so that the state was divided, and each was independent of the other, then there were, as a matter of fact, two distinct kingdoms, which still retained the name "Roman Empire," because they had both sprung from it. There was, furthermore, a similarity in laws and customs, a relationship between rulers and between peoples, and a mutual league and exchange, which gave somewhat the appearance of union. But how that may be called a form of state, when two or three Augusti held the empire without division, is not so easy to decide. Certainly two rulers cannot constitute an aristocracy. For since they both are vested with equal power (as is understood), they must necessarily be bound to each other by a pact; and there is no way to transact business in case they fail to agree, when there is no one who can add his voice to one side or the other. And although the same inconvenience may appear to attend a college which consists of an equal number of members, yet it will not so often happen that, upon a division of opinion, the votes will be equal; while it is easy among a number for one to be drawn over to the other side. Or when that cannot be done, the next course will be for that opinion to prevail which favours no innovation but a continuation in the beaten path.

Furthermore, not even when three Augusti held the empire at the same time does it appear that we may properly say that an aristocracy was established. For not even that triumvirate, or three Augusti, organized into such a body or college that a decision could be reached on affairs of state by a majority vote, and the agreement of two could authoritatively require the third to abide by their decision. But if there is a college where the majority cannot carry with it the minority, it appears to be held together by the bond of a mere pact rather than by sovereignty. We will conclude, therefore, that the supreme command lay actually and fully in the hands only of him who took the second to him as a colleague, although in external trappings they appear to have been equal. Julius Capitolinus, *Life of Lucius Verus* [i], says of him that "he enjoyed not unrestricted power, but a sovereignty on like terms and equal dignity with Marcus." (M.) Nor was there any need to fear that a man would be so ungrateful as to oppose the will of the one by whom he had been raised to such an eminence. It is a further consideration that usually a son was taken as a partner by his parent, a son-in-law by his father-in-law, or a brother by a brother, so that the subordinate was restrained by the further bond of a relation in blood or marriage from misusing the power given him against the giver. Therefore, that selection of a colleague was not a division of the supreme power, but merely the designation of a general assistant, as it were, or representative as well as successor, who was thereby admitted by the other to a share of the cares of the state, and in association with him administered the affairs of the empire, being also adorned with the insignia of the ruler. The fickleness of the legions also had its influence on this device, since they often saluted their leaders as emperor. Themistius, *Orations*, xvi [vi, p. 76 B], says of Valentinian, who had associated with himself in the sovereignty his brother Valens: "He who had received the whole and then dispensed it, brother and father at the same time, the former by nature, the latter by his own act, made a gift of equal power. And yet he still holds supreme control, by reason of the obedience of his consort." Solinus, chap. viii [ii. 14], says of Aeneas: "Then for three years he ruled with Latinus, associating him in the supreme authority."

But if this explanation does not satisfy some persons, or cannot be applied to each instance, nothing remains for us but to say that there intervened in that empire at that time an irregularity, in that several men, who were joined either by a pact or a faction, held the throne undivided. And if there arose between them dissension or enmities, then suspicions, mutual plottings, and finally civil wars were unavoidable. Lucan, Bk. I [92 ff.]: "No faith is there in partners in rule, and all power will be impatient of a sharer." (R.) Statius, *Thebaid*, Bk. I [130]: "Such discord rises from divided sway." (L.) It was clearly such an irregularity at Rome when Romulus and Tatius were co-rulers. See Plutarch, *Romulus*. Add Erycius Puteanus, *Historia Insubrica*, Bk. II, on Pertharitus and Gundebertus who reigned together over the Lombards. Here belongs a passage in Procopius, *Gothic War*, Bk. I [i. 24 f.]:

> The Goths [. . .] and the followers of Odoacer [. . .] came to an agreement with each other [. . .] that both Theoderic and Odoacer should reside in Ravenna on

> terms of complete equality. And for some time they observed the agreement; but afterwards Theoderic caught Odoacer, as they say, plotting against him, and bidding him to a feast with treacherous intent, slew him. (D.)

Much the same is in Euripides, *Andromacha* [471 ff.]:

> Never land but hath borne a twofold yoke
> Of kings with wearier straining:
> There is burden on burden, and feud 'mid her folk. (W.)

Pliny, *Panegyric:* "How little difference there is between laying down and sharing the sovereignty! Unless the latter be more difficult." Add Herodian, Bk. IV, chaps. i ff.

In general such divided sovereignty is well described by the remark of Selim, who compared the German Empire to a harp, which after great labour finally is tuned into a harmony that does not endure for long. We do not feel that we need class under an irregularity what Francis Carron recounts of the Dayro in Japan, who was the lawful heir to the throne, but was granted by the actual holder of the sovereignty nothing more than the splendour of majesty and office. Thus, as we are informed by Alexander of Rhodes, *Divers Voyages*, Pt. II, chap. vi, in the kingdom of Tonquin there are two kings with the titles of Bua and Choua, but the former holds the title, while the latter has the actual sovereignty; save that the Bua confers the title of doctor and receives the oath of the citizens, which is renewed each year, spending all the rest of his time in an old palace with nothing to bother him.

16. We speak of systems of states when more than one are so held together by some special and strict bond that they appear to form one body, each of whose members, however, retains supreme sovereignty over its own affairs. From this it appears, first of all, that if some state is composed of several subordinate bodies, it must not for that reason be at once classed among systems, although Hobbes, *Leviathan*, chap. xxii, includes such under that term and compares its parts to the muscles of the physical body. Just as great states, which have taken on additional territories by absorbing other states, and reducing them into one body with themselves, are not for that reason systems. Such an increase we see taking place in two ways. By the first the victor state transfers the citizens of conquered states to its own territory, or gives them the same rights with its own citizens; by the second the conquered states are left their old boundaries, and the sovereignty which was first vested in them is lost, while their citizens become subjects of the conquering state. In both cases the conquered state exists no longer, but in the former case the conquered are given equal rights with their conquerors, while in the second they are usually required to live in a worse condition, and the state is reduced to the form of a province. Yet at times such subdued provinces are left some of their ancient privileges or laws, however much they differ from those of the conquering state. See Hobbes, *Leviathan*, chap. xxvi. For the unity of a state does not require that all its integral parts have the same positive laws,

or that all its citizens enjoy equal rights, but it is enough if all of them acknowledge a single sovereignty. And often it is one of the arts of a conqueror to make no change in the former customs of the conquered, and even to adjust himself to them for a time.

Now on this matter we should examine what is said on the administration of provinces by Hobbes, *Leviathan*, chap. xix:

> Whereas heretofore the Roman people governed the land of Judea, for example, by a president; yet was not Judea therefore a democracy; because they were not governed by any assembly into the which any of them had right to enter; nor an aristocracy; because they were not governed by any assembly, into the which any man could enter by their election: but they were governed by one person, which as to the people of Judea, which had no right at all of participating in the government, was a monarch. For though where the people are governed by an assembly, chosen by themselves out of their own number, the government is called a democracy or aristocracy; yet when they are governed by an assembly not of their own choosing, it is a monarchy; not of "one" man over another man; but of one people over another people.

So, then, Hobbes appears to regard as monarchies even such provinces as are under an aristocracy or democracy. Now although we readily admit that it is more common for provinces to be ruled by one man than by an assembly of all the citizens, as he himself shows at length (*loc. cit.* chap. xxii), it still appears idle to us to inquire into the form of government in any province. For provinces no longer exist as states and are become but the appendages of other states, having no sovereignty in themselves. And it has no bearing on the question of sovereignty itself whether such a province is ruled by a single governor or by a council, since the former as well as the latter enjoy only a delegated power. So that the sovereignty exercised over the provinces or appendages of states appears to be the same as that of the mistress state, and can only with impropriety be called that of a monarchy or aristocracy, since such distinctions in the forms of a state belong to states properly so called, such as possess in themselves sovereignty over themselves.

17. We apprehend[1] that there are two species of systems properly speaking: one where two or more states have one and the same king; the other where two or more states are joined by a pact into one body.

As to systems of the first kind, it should be observed that it is possible with moral bodies for several to have but one head, and so for one person to be the head of several distinct bodies, which in the case of natural bodies would result in a monstrosity. But since a union of such systems is based solely upon the person of the king, or upon his family, it follows that when this dies out there returns at once to each of the peoples the right to decide as it will on its form of government, nor do they need any longer to be under one head. Nay, even while that head lives, the individual states remain entirely distinct.

[1] [For *deprehpndimus* read *deprehendimus.—Tr.*]

Now such systems can arise for various reasons, of which the most common appear to be the marriage of princes and the right of inheritance. For there are states in which the supreme sovereignty falls also upon women of the ruling house, not only when there are no males in the family, but also when there is none of a closer or of the same degree of relationship. Therefore, should a woman, who is the ruler of a kingdom, marry one who is likewise a king, there would be a union of the two kingdoms in their offspring. For in such marriages there is no necessity for a wife subjecting herself along with her kingdom to the sovereignty of her husband. So in case it should happen that in an indivisible kingdom where the line of succession is fixed as simple or direct, one of the more distant heirs of the kingdom should in some way acquire for himself another kingship, and the law of succession, upon lack of nearer heirs, should call him to the throne, he will unite the newly acquired kingdom with that which was his own before. The same thing happens when a people select as their king one who already holds another throne, or whom another succession awaits. So also two or more kingdoms may enter into an agreement to select one ruler by their united suffrage, and yet to remain in other respects separate states, and not even to carry on their affairs of state in a common council. Finally, such a system also arises if a king, constituted by the free will of a people, subjects to himself in war another people, in his own name, at his own risk, and at his own expense, not involving at all the name or resources of the people over whom he reigns. That this can happen despite the remarks to the contrary of Hotoman, *Quaestiones Illustres*, qu. I, is sufficiently established by Grotius, Bk. I, chap. iii, § 12.

Such systems may be dissolved by the death of the king on whose sole person the union was based, or by the extinction of the royal line, in case the individual kingdoms belong to it by hereditary right. For in this case there returns to each kingdom the separate right to set up a new king over itself, or to introduce whatever form of commonwealth it desires without consulting the others, inasmuch as we assume that those kingdoms were held together by no further bond. Thus should it happen that a king holds one kingdom by hereditary right, but is put over another merely by free election, the consequent union of the kingdoms will be dissolved at the death of that king, nor will the second kingdom have to accept as its ruler the son of the deceased monarch.

But if the union in question depends upon a treaty between the two states, it is obvious that when that treaty has been violated, at least in its principal heads, the union can be broken off by the injured party. Yet here a careful distinction should be drawn between an obligation binding separate kingdoms to a ruler, and one which binds the states to one another. When a king has once been elected and received a pledge of good faith, it will not be possible to dethrone him for any depraved deeds or such as run contrary to his agreement, so long as he does not show himself an open enemy to his kingdom. Unless it be that a commissory clause was expressly added to the pact between a king and his subjects, to the effect that all their obedience depends upon the fulfilment of each and every section of the pact as a condition. But the mutual obligation which lies between united kingdoms can be broken off on the side of the one which has been injured by a violation of the laws of that union, even though the hurt may be of little consequence, provided the other kingdoms concurred in that injury, or it is undertaken for or turns to their advantage. Consequently, upon the death of a king the injured kingdom will be able to renounce the union, reserving the right of an action against the authors and abettors of the hurt, and a claim to property lost. But if several states are united by the marriages of their rulers, who are hereditary princes in each land, and yet they observe a different order of succession, the union will be dissolved if such a case arises as that the same person is not fitted by the public laws to succeed to the throne of each nation. Let us suppose that two kingdoms are united, in one of which the succession is in line of agnation, in the other of cognation. In this case, upon the death of their common king without a son but with only a daughter, the second kingdom will fall to the daughter, the first to the nearest male relative. But if a union, which was at first occasioned by marriage be later confirmed and ordered to be perpetual, each and every kingdom entering into a treaty with one another, or approving a decree to this effect of their common king, it is understood that some such act disposes of the difference in succession which previously obtained. Thereafter that order of succession will have to be followed which is expressly set forth in the treaty or decree, or which is known to have met the approval of the author of the union, or which is most highly agreeable to reason and the welfare of the kingdoms. But in case one kingdom becomes subject to another as a province, the union resulting from the treaty expires, and its place is taken by a closer coalition into the same state.

18. The other kind of a system is that which consists of several states bound to each by a perpetual treaty, and which is usually occasioned by the fact that the individual states wished to preserve their *αὐτονομία* [autonomy], and yet had not sufficient strength to repel their common enemies. In this treaty there is commonly an agreement that one or other part of the supreme sovereignty should be exercised at the consent of all. For a treaty that gives rise to a system seems to differ from those treaties which are otherwise most commonly drawn up between states, chiefly in this: That in the others each people of the league agrees to certain mutual performances, yet in such a way that they are on no account willing to make the exercise of that part of the sovereignty from which those performances flow dependent upon the consent of their associates, nor to limit in any degree their complete and unlimited power to conduct the affairs of their state. So also simple treaties have usually before their eyes only the particular advantage of the different states, as it happens to coincide, and do not produce any lasting union in matters which concern the chief object of states.

The case is entirely different with the treaties that appear in systems, the purpose of which is that distinct states may intertwine for all time the prime interests of their safety, and on that score make the exercise of certain parts of the supreme sovereignty depend upon the mutual consent of their associates.

For there is a great difference between "I will bring you aid in this war, and we will consider in concert how we shall attack the enemy," and "No one of us who have entered this society will exercise his right of peace and war, save with the common consent of all."

We have said that in treaties of this kind the exercise of only certain parts of the supreme sovereignty is made to depend upon the consent of the associated states. For it hardly seems likely that the affairs of several states could be so closely interwoven that it would be to the advantage of one and all of them that no part of the supreme sovereignty be exercised without the consent of all. Or if there were any such, it would have been more to their advantage to unite in one state than to be joined only by a treaty. Therefore, it is convenient that the individual states reserve for themselves liberty in the exercise of those parts of supreme sovereignty, the manner of conducting which is of little or no interest, at least directly, to the rest. The same is true as well of such business as is of daily occurrence, or will not suffer the delay consequent upon a discussion of it with others. But matters upon which the safety of the entire league depends may with entire fairness be considered in common council. Of these war occupies the first place, both defensive and offensive, and that wherewith it is drawn to a close, even peace. To which should be joined taxes, in so far as they minister to war, and treaties with foreign powers looking to the common safety. Here also belongs the consideration that, if any controversy arises between the allies themselves, the others who have no direct interest in it may at once interpose as mediators, and not allow it to come to open warfare. In Polybius, Bk. IV, chap. xxiv, Philip of Macedon says:

> In the case of injuries inflicted by the allies upon each other separately, his intervention ought to be confined to remonstrance by word of mouth or letter; but[1] that it was only injuries affecting the whole body of the allies which demanded joint intervention and redress. (S.)

The other matters which apparently do not demand so much exercise of common counsel, such as commercial treaties, taxes which are required for the needs of the individual states, the appointment of magistrates, laws, the right over citizens of life and death, matters of religion, and the like, can without difficulty be left in the province of the individual states. Although every state will so control them that they will in no way disturb the entire system. From this it is evident that one or another of the allies cannot be prevented by the rest from exercising at their own pleasure those parts of the supreme sovereignty on the conduct of which by common counsel there was no special agreement in the treaty.

Yet on the right of life and death some scruple can arise regarding the ruling in *Digest*, XLIX. xv. 7, § I [XLIX. xv. 7, § 2]: "But citizens of states allied to us are put on trial in our courts, and punished when found guilty."

[1] [For *atquae* read *at quae.—Tr.*]

Grotius, Bk. I, chap. iii, § 21, has gone to great trouble to explain this, and yet any one who has examined the passage with much care will readily admit that he makes no progress. For he certainly makes no answer to this question: How can that state maintain its liberty unimpaired whose citizens another state can rightfully call before its tribunal and there inquire into their conduct? Surely it was held that the liberty of the Achaeans had suffered the grossest affront when, by the treachery of Callicrates, the most eminent men of that people were accused of favouring the cause of Perseus against the Romans, and were haled to Rome to plead their cause, the Romans seizing as an occasion a statement of Xenon, who, fully confident in the consciousness of his innocence, had said that if any one wished to accuse him he was ready to stand trial in the common assembly of the Achaeans, or even before the Romans. On this incident we are fully informed by Pausanias, in his sketch of the history of Achaea [VII. x. 9], and it is mentioned also by Polybius in *Selections on Embassies*, cv [XXX. xxxii]. So also the Achaeans appear to have transgressed the laws of a regular state in demanding that those Spartans who had been responsible for the attack upon Las, a village in their territory, be handed over to them for punishment. Livy, Bk. XXXVIII, chap. xxxi. For the cause should first have been discussed in the common council, and after the guilt had been determined, notice should have been served on the Spartans, either to punish the offenders or else to surrender them.

In our opinion the clearest reply to the passage in the *Digest* appears to be that, since in the preceding sections it had been set forth what the nature of treaties allows, and what should be done, it was stated in those words what had actually occurred in later times, when the Romans, as their fortune gave them haughtiness, fell into the habit of treating their allies who had of their free will sought their friendship by treaties, in the same way as if they had been subjugated in war. Of this injustice Cicero himself complains in his *On Duties* [II. viii]. Add the example of Decius Magius being put in chains by Hannibal, as recorded by Livy, Bk. XXIII, chaps. vii and x, and how Scipio urges that the Romans should give no audience to informers against Hannibal. *Idem*, Bk. XXXIII, chap. xlvii.

19. Since in such systems certain matters expressed in the treaty should be made the business of all, and since this cannot be done so conveniently sending around letters, it is necessary that a set place and time be appointed for holding assemblies, and that one or more be designated who shall be empowered to summon the confederates, in case something unusual arises that will bear no delay. Although it would be far more convenient if some permanent council, composed of delegates from each of the states, sit in a designated place, with the power to transact affairs of daily occurrence, or of minor importance, in accordance with the nature of their commission, while if anything of serious consequence arise, it can refer this to the individual states and publish as well as prosecute what they have decided. Such a body may also receive reports from the common ministers of the confederates who represent them among other nations, and may also treat with the ambassadors of foreign states, and conclude negotiations with them in the common

name of all the confederates. But it may issue no decree exceeding the bounds of its commission, unless the matter has first been brought to the attention of all the states. How much power belongs to such a council of deputies will have to be discovered from the treaty itself, or the commissions of such bodies. Whatever such power may be, it is entirely from another source, and delegated from the confederates, and although the decrees which it issues may bear only its own name, all of their force and authority flows from the confederated states which appointed it. And so those deputies are no more than ministers of the allies, and can no more enjoin anything upon them with authority than an ambassador can give orders to his master.

20. But the question may still be raised as to whether all the allied states, or the majority of them, have power over one, or a small number of their members, in those matters for which the league was formed, and which it was expressly stated in the treaty should be conducted by common counsel, in so far as that a small minority is bound, whether it will or not, to abide by the decision of the majority. This, it seems to us, must be answered in the negative, if we are concerned with regular systems and those where every state reserves to itself its liberty unimpaired, although there is nothing to prevent such a rule obtaining in an irregular system, and one that approaches more closely to the nature of a state. For the liberty of a state, which is nothing other than the power to decide on its own judgement about matters pertaining to its self-preservation, is unintelligible in case it can be forced by another, acting with authority, to undertake something against its will. Nor is it any objection that it was agreed in the treaty to exercise certain parts of the supreme sovereignty only by common counsel. For it is one thing if I say, "I will not exercise my right unless you are willing," and another to say, "You will have the right to require me to exercise my right, even though I be unwilling." The first, but not the second, is contained in the treaty of union.

In order to understand this more thoroughly, it should be carefully noted that, when the wills of several men are required to combine into one, this is due either to a mere agreement, or to the fact that one man has submitted his will to the will of another. A union of wills based upon mere agreement does not at all destroy that liberty of which we just spoke. For whether any decision is made beforehand, by common agreement, about matters to be carried on in common, or if the decision must be reached afterwards, the individual members wish to be led to it not by authority but by reason[1] alone. Yet when I have submitted my will to that of another, and have thereby conferred upon him sovereignty over me, I can be obligated even to what perhaps displeases me.

Nor is it of any use for one to harp to us on the "right of the majority." See above, Bk. VII, chap. ii, § 15. For, in the first place, the majority draws to itself the minority only in constituted groups, not in those which must yet be constituted. Furthermore, it is an institution and convention of men, not a natural law, that in constituted groups the majority obligates all, though

[1] [For *rariones* read *rationes.—Tr.*]

natural reason urges it as a most convenient rule in large groups, and where varied and routine business must be transacted. And yet, in order that this be done, it is necessary for each individual to submit his will to the will of the entire body or of the majority, to the extent that even when they dissent, they must under all conditions follow what the latter determine. And this is unintelligible without postulating the authority of the majority over the minority. Nor, as a matter of fact, does there seem to be any need in the assemblies of confederates of that right of the majority, since they are not usually made up of many peoples, and are met for the prime purpose of the common advantage, which it is presumed no sane man will persistently oppose. Yet if any one, maintaining a perverse stubbornness which refuses to yield to reason, scorns to join with the salutary counsels of the rest, and sets about to betray in this fashion the common safety or advantage, it will be lawful to employ against him such means as those who live in natural liberty may use against the violators of pacts, unless it please them better entirely to exclude such an unreasonable person from the league.

Another consideration is that it would often involve great injustice in a system of confederates, for the vote of a majority to bind the rest, when there is a great difference in resources, and so one contributes more to the common safety than another. For despite the fact that those who contribute in proportion to their wealth appear to bear equal burdens, it may frequently happen that one man is readier to expose his own modest fortune to risk than another his, a large one. Thus supposing that one state of a system contributes more to the common defence than all the others together, it would be manifestly unjust for it to be possible for the rest to force such a state to undertake something that would devolve the chief burden upon it. See Grotius, *Apologeticus*, chap. i, towards the end. But yet for the votes of each state to weigh in proportion to its contribution to the society would grant such a powerful state sovereignty over the rest. See Diodorus Siculus, Bk. XV, chap. xxviii.

The conclusion from all this is, that whenever affairs are decided on the principle of a majority of votes, so that the opposition is also obligated, it constitutes a departure from the regular form of systems, and the establishment of an irregular body, or of a single state.

21. Such systems are dissolved when some of the confederates voluntarily leave the league and administer their states to themselves, which usually happens from the consideration that they hope for more advantage from separation than from union, and that they feel their allies to be more of a burden than an assistance. Add Livy, Bk. XXXVIII, chaps. xxxi–xxxii. Internal wars also break them up, unless the agreements of the covenant are again renewed in the peace. When a system has had the worse of a foreign war, it is sometimes one of the stratagems of the victor to dissolve the league, and to command each state to exercise αὐτονομίαν [autonomy] in the way that the Romans once did to the Achaeans. Compare Xenophon [*Greek History*], Bk. III, chap. v. [IV. viii. I4; V. i. 28], where he discusses the Peace of Antalcidas.

It should furthermore be observed, touching the dissolution of systems by external force, that when one or more of the confederated states has been seized by an enemy, he does not in this way secure any right over the rest, nor must he at once be received into the league by reason of the treaty which joined the rest of them to it. But an entirely new treaty is needed for another state to join a league in the place of a conquered state. Thus we are informed in Diodorus Siculus, Bk. XVI, chap. lxi, that by a decree of the Amphictyons Philip took over the seat in their council formerly held by Phocis. For although the treaty by which several states are united into a system seems to be a real one, and a state does not cease to exist because it has changed its form, yet such a treaty will be held to have expired when a state has been brought under the yoke by force, or been made an appendage to another's sovereignty. For since a league is entered into by states as such, what ceases to exist as a state drops from it. And even though every precaution be taken in the articles of confederation, that there be no withdrawal from the League[1] because of a change in the form of government, yet it is presumed that such a change be made in a legitimate way, by the voluntary consent of its people. And so there will be no place in the council of the league for either an unjust usurper or an external enemy.

But it is possible for such systems to combine into a finished state, if all the confederates voluntarily submit themselves to the supreme sovereignty of a single council or man, or if one people, excelling the others in strength, reduce them to the state of provinces. This last usually happens when the weaker ones offer some permanent preferment to a stronger and are confederated unequally. See Grotius, Bk. I, chap. iii, § 21, towards the end. Finally, such systems become perfect states if some one man seizes the sovereignty by the favour of the soldiers, or on a wave of popularity, or by the influence of a faction.

22. Lastly, it is customary in this connexion to discuss the comparative excellence of forms of states, and what form should be preferred to another by reason of the fact that it procures more easily and surely the safety of the state, or that the force of sovereignty is less open to abuse. Now on this point so much is patent: That no form of state can be so thoroughly buttressed with laws but that, from the very form of government which is established for the safety of the citizens, some inconveniences can befall them by reason of the slothfulness or the wickedness of the rulers. The reason for this is that, although supreme sovereignty is established to repel the evils which threaten men from their fellows, yet that sovereignty had to be conferred upon men who are themselves not immune to the vices by which men are incited to do each other harm. "There will be vices so long as there are men." [Tacitus, *Histories*, IV. lxxiv.] And so we sometimes experience from men the very thing against which they should have defended us. Hence, it also happens that "for every folly of their princes the Greeks feel the scourge." [Horace, *Epistles*, I. ii. I4.]

[1] [For *foepere* read *foedere.—Tr.*]

Therefore, as the condition of human affairs does not allow full perfection, so many disagree on what form of state allows one to fear the minimum of evils. Now looking at it in this light the majority record their vote for[2] a monarchy. See Isocrates, *Nicocles*; Herodotus, Bk. III, where the Persian princes after killing the Magi debate on the form of state to be introduced; Euripides, *Suppliants*, lines 405 ff.; Bodin, *On the Republic*, Bk. VI, chap. iv; Arnisaeus, *Relectiones Politicae*, Bk. II, chap. vii, § 2; and many others. On the other hand, nothing that can be said out of hatred or envy of monarchs seems to have been overlooked by the Dutch author of the *Bilanx Politica*, although many of his arguments can be turned against him by what Hobbes sets forth, *De Cive*, chap. x; *Leviathan*, xix.

It is not our purpose to discuss the various positions, but we may only observe that there is no such force in their arguments that conclusions drawn from them should necessarily hold everywhere and always. Nor should the deeds of one or more governors lay any necessity upon all others of their type to follow their example. But I should suggest that every good and loyal citizen should meditate upon the remark of Marcellus in Tacitus, *Histories*, Bk. IV [viii]: "He was not unmindful of the times on which he had fallen, of the form of government established by their ancestors: he admired the past, and accommodated himself to the present system, devoutly wishing for virtuous princes, but willing to acquiesce under any sort." (O.)

It may not be foreign to our purpose, in this connexion, to show briefly why the ancient Greeks were so hostile to those who had seized a monarchical power in democracies and aristocracies, and why these men undertook to maintain their position by such evil practices as are found described in Aristotle and other writers, which caused a lasting hatred to cling to the word "tyrant." Now the Greek states usually held themselves to the limits of a single city; and to such states the most agreeable form is a democracy, or a mildly administered aristocracy, or, finally, a kingdom such as Aristotle calls the "heroic" type, that is, a principate which relies not so much upon sovereignty as the authority of persuasion and a reputation for outstanding virtue. Furthermore, the Greeks as a whole, because of their proud and restless nature, especially loved that status in which every man could form a part of the commonwealth. Therefore, whoever in such a state had seized the monarchy, a thing hateful to the citizens, and done so against their will, was forced to overawe the city with a fortress, surround himself with a strong body of troops, and these of foreign extraction, since he could not trust his own citizens, or by transferring troops from different places coerce one province by means of another. Then the loyalty of such mercenaries was only to be purchased by high pay, and to meet this expense the citizens had to be reduced to straitened circumstances by taxation, while it was also necessary for them to be disarmed, and to be reduced to a state in which they were unable to carry on war, that "the heads of the poppies be cut off" [Livy, I,

[2] [For *per* read *pro.*—*Tr.*]

liv and lvi], that public meetings be forbidden, and that a secret service be maintained. And so those tyrants were not only unjust but also insane, who aimed at such power as had to be preserved by evil practices which could not make for permanence, and afforded them no opportunity to win the love of their citizens. And it is quite as absurd to establish a monarchy in a state which consists of but a single city as to establish a democracy in a nation that occupies a large territory. But since monarchies of wide extent have no need of such arts for their self-preservation, inasmuch as one province can be balanced off against another, those who suggest the exercise of the arts of tyrants to the monarchs of great states are guilty of no less heinous a sin than those who ceaselessly pour out the odium due those petty tyrants of Greece upon all monarchs.

It is patent also from these reflections that monarchs live far more securely in a large state, because refractory citizens have no such easy opportunity to communicate and join with each other, and by contact[1] to infect all other citizens, as they do in a state which consists of a single city, where a few can spread their fury to all in a moment's time, and before their prince is aware of it.

1 [For *contractu* read *contactu.—Tr.*]

II

The Enlightenment Debate over the Normative Potential of International Federalism

5

Editors' Introduction

The development of federal theory, and especially normative federal theory, owes a great debt to some famous Enlightenment political thinkers. These philosophers did not do much to enrich the terminology and definitions of federalism: indeed, they perpetuated the conventional practice of using terms such as confederation, federation, (con)federated state, and league interchangeably. They were also not particularly clear about the institutional design of their preferred type of federal arrangement; although they all seemed to have in mind something more integrated than a mere alliance of sovereign states. Their major contribution lies elsewhere: in an era dominated by perpetual wars between absolute monarchies, they initiated a debate over the normative potential of federal institutions to secure peace at the international level, particularly in Europe.

In part II, we include selections from three of the main contributors to that debate: Montesquieu, Rousseau, and Kant. All three of these thinkers, of course, hold a prominent place in the canon of the nation-state-focused history of ideas; but their contributions to federalist theory have been largely ignored.

Montesquieu was the most important political thinker in France in his day, and his *Spirit of the Laws* (1748), contains an original argument that has been as influential in the history of federalist thought as it has been neglected in "standard" summaries of his great work. This is the idea we presented in the introduction to this volume: that a confederation of small republics combines the internal advantages of democratic republican government with the external force of large monarchies; in other words, the best of small states with the best of large states, avoiding the disadvantages of both. It also offers insights into the question of the best institutional design of such a confederation. Montesquieu clearly had in mind the small democratic–republic model of the Antiquity. (Both Kant and the American authors of *The Federalist* were inspired by this argument even though they would propose to combine federalism with a more modern form of republicanism.)

At the dawn of the eighteenth century a new purpose for federalism emerged in theories that played up its role as a mechanism for international peace. The rather unlikely source of this intellectual movement was a French priest, the Abbé de Saint-Pierre, who published his utopian *Project for*

Settling an Everlasting Peace in Europe in 1712. This book was important because it prompted major authors to write on the normative potential of federalism as a mechanism for perpetual peace. Because Saint-Pierre's work is long, repetitive, and philosophically unsophisticated, we present Saint-Pierre's ideas through Rousseau's *Statement of St. Pierre's Project* (1761). We also provide the integral version of Rousseau's *Judgement on Saint-Pierre's Project* (1782). Rousseau is, of course, the most famous French (or Swiss) political philosopher of the eighteenth century, and these reflections on the Abbé's work are our principal source of his thoughts on federalism. (Some scholars believe that he wrote an entire book manuscript on federalism that was accidentally destroyed during the French Revolution.) Rousseau was charged by the Abbé's followers with the task of editing the Abbé's work to make it accessible to a wider public. He fulfilled this task with care, although he could not resist adding a substantial critique. With subtlety, Rousseau tends to downplay the potential of the Abbé's project of federalism as a way to peace on the grounds that "Things of public utility [. . .] are seldom brought in but by force, for the simple reason that private interests are almost always ranged against them." Then, he concludes that "No Federation could ever be established except by a revolution," and that such a cure "would perhaps do more harm in a moment than it would guard against for ages."

Finally, this section provides extracts from Immanuel Kant's *Toward Perpetual Peace* (1795), widely recognized as one of the most sophisticated texts of normative federal theory. Kant, who was unquestionably the most celebrated philosopher of his era, argued that a federation of republican states could bring perpetual peace, and that "the good moral education of a people is to be expected from a good state constitution."

6

Combining the Advantages of Small and Large States

Montesquieu

1. In what Manner Republics Provide for Their Safety

If a republic be small, it is destroyed by a foreign force; if it be large, it is ruined by an internal imperfection.

To this twofold inconvenience democracies and aristocracies are equally liable, whether they be good or bad. The evil is in the very thing itself, and no form can redress it.

It is, therefore, very probable that mankind would have been, at length, obliged to live constantly under the government of a single person, had they not contrived a kind of constitution that has all the internal advantages of a republican, together with the external force of a monarchical, government. I mean a confederate republic.

This form of government is a convention by which several small states agree to become members of a larger one, which they intend to establish. It is a kind of society of societies, that constitute a new one, capable of increasing by means of further associations, till they arrive at such a degree of power as to be able to provide for the security of the whole body.

It was these associations that so long contributed to the prosperity of Greece. By these the Romans attacked the whole globe, and by these alone the whole globe withstood them; for when Rome had arrived at her highest pitch of grandeur, it was the associations beyond the Danube and the Rhine—associations formed by the terror of her arms—that enabled the barbarians to resist her.

Hence it proceeds that Holland,[a] Germany, and the Swiss cantons are considered in Europe as perpetual republics.

The associations of cities were formerly more necessary than in our times. A weak, defenceless town was exposed to greater danger. By conquest it was

[a] It is composed of about fifty different republics all different from one another.— "State of the United Provinces," by M. Janisson. Voltaire notes upon this remark that Montesquieu has taken each of the independent cities as a republic.—Ed.

deprived not only of the executive and legislative power, as at present, but, moreover, of all human property.[b]

A republic of this kind, able to withstand an external force, may support itself without any internal corruption; the form of this society prevents all manner of inconveniences.

If a single member should attempt to usurp the supreme power, he could not be supposed to have an equal authority and credit in all the confederate states. Were he to have too great an influence over one, this would alarm the rest; were he to subdue a part, that which would still remain free might oppose him with forces independent of those which he had usurped, and overpower him before he could be settled in his usurpation.

Should a popular insurrection happen in one of the confederate states, the others are able to quell it. Should abuses creep into one part, they are reformed by those that remain sound. The state may be destroyed on one side, and not on the other; the confederacy may be dissolved, and the confederates preserve their sovereignty.

As this government is composed of small republics, it enjoys the internal happiness of each; and with regard to its external situation, by means of the association, it possesses all the advantages of large monarchies.

2. That a Confederate Government Ought to be Composed of States of the Same Nature, Especially of the Republican Kind

The Canaanites were destroyed by reason that they were small monarchies that had no union or confederacy for their common defence; and, indeed, a confederacy is not agreeable to the nature of small monarchies.

As the confederate republic of Germany consists of free cities, and of petty states subject to different princes, experience shows us that it is much more imperfect than that of Holland and Switzerland.

The spirit of monarchy is war and enlargement of dominion: peace and moderation are the spirit of a republic. These two kinds of government cannot naturally subsist in a confederate republic.

Thus we observe, in the Roman history, that when the Veientes had chosen a king, they were immediately abandoned by all the other small republics of Tuscany. Greece was undone as soon as the kings of Macedon obtained a seat among the Amphictyons.

The confederate republic of Germany, composed of princes and free towns, subsists by means of a chief, who is, in some respects, the magistrate of the union, in others the monarch.

[b] Civil liberty, goods, wives, children, temples, and even burying-places.

3. Other Requisites in a Confederate Republic

In the republic of Holland one province cannot conclude an alliance without the consent of the others. This law, which is an excellent one, and even necessary in a confederate republic, is wanting in the Germanic constitution, where it would prevent the misfortunes that may happen to the whole confederacy, through the imprudence, ambition, or avarice of a single member. A republic united by a political confederacy has given itself entirely up, and has nothing more to resign.

It is difficult for the united states to be all of equal power and extent. The Lycian[c] republic was an association of twenty-three towns; the large ones had three votes in the common council, the middling ones two, and the small towns one. The Dutch republic consists of seven provinces of different extent of territory, which have each one voice.

The cities of Lycia[d] contributed to the expenses of the state, according to the proportion of suffrages. The provinces of the United Netherlands cannot follow this proportion; they must be directed by that of their power.

In Lycia[e] the judges and town magistrates were elected by the common council, and according to the proportion already mentioned. In the republic of Holland they are not chosen by the common council, but each town names its magistrates. Were I to give a model of an excellent confederate republic, I should pitch upon that of Lycia.

[c] Strabo, lib. XIV.

[d] Ibid.

[e] Ibid.

7

A Lasting Peace through the Federation of Europe: Exposition and Critique of St. Pierre's Project

Jean-Jacques Rousseau

Statement of St. Pierre's Project

Never did the mind of man conceive a scheme nobler, more beautiful, or more useful than that of a lasting peace between all the peoples of Europe. Never did a writer better deserve a respectful hearing than he who suggests means for putting that scheme in practice. What man, if he has a spark of goodness, but must feel his heart glow within him at so fair a prospect? Who would not prefer the illusions of a generous spirit, which overleaps all obstacles, to that dry, repulsive reason whose indifference to the welfare of mankind is ever the chief obstacle to all schemes for its attainment?

I doubt not that many readers will forearm themselves with scepticism, as the best defence against the pleasure of yielding to conviction. I pity the melancholy mood which makes them take obstinacy for wisdom. On the other hand, I trust that every generous spirit will share the thrill of emotion with which I take up the pen on a subject which concerns mankind so closely. I see in my mind's eye all men joined in the bonds of love. I call before my thoughts a gentle and peaceful brotherhood, all living in unbroken harmony, all guided by the same principles, all finding their happiness in the happiness of all. And, as I dwell upon this touching picture, the idea of an imaginary happiness will cheat me for a few moments into the enjoyment of a real one.

In these opening words, I could not refrain from giving way to the feelings which filled my heart. Now let us do our best to reason coolly. Resolved as I am to assert nothing which I cannot prove, I have the right to ask the reader in his turn to deny nothing which he is unable to refute. It is not so much the reasoners I am afraid of as those who, without yielding to my proofs, steadily refuse to bring any arguments against them.

No man can have thought long upon the means of bringing any Government to perfection without realising a host of difficulties and obstacles which flow less from its inherent nature than from its relation to its neighbours. The result of this is that the care which ought to be given to its internal welfare has to be largely spent upon its outward security; and we are compelled to think more of providing for its defence against others than of making it as good as may be in itself. If the social order were really, as is pretended, the work not of passion but of reason, should we have been so slow to see that, in the shaping of it, either too much, or too little, has been done for our happiness? that, each one of us being in the civil state as regards our fellow citizens, but in the state of nature as regards the rest of the world, we have taken all kinds of precautions against private wars only to kindle national wars a thousand times more terrible? and that, in joining a particular group of men, we have really declared ourselves the enemies of the whole race?

If there is any way of reconciling these dangerous contradictions, it is to be found only in such a form of federal Government as shall unite nations by bonds similar to those which already unite their individual members, and place the one no less than the other under the authority of the Law. Even apart from this, such a form of Government seems to carry the day over all others; because it combines the advantages of the small and the large State, because it is powerful enough to hold its neighbours in awe, because it upholds the supremacy of the Law, because it is the only force capable of holding the subject, the ruler, the foreigner equally in check.

Such a form of Government is to some extent a novelty, and its principles have been fully understood only by the moderns. But it was not unknown among the ancients. The Greeks had their Amphictyons and the Etruscans their Lucumonies; the Latins had their *feriæ* and the Gauls their city-leagues; the Achæan League gave lustre to the death-struggles of Greece. But not one of these Federations was built up with half the wisdom which has gone to the making of the Germanic Body, of the Helvetic League, or of the States General. And if these Bodies are still so scarce and so far from the perfection which we feel they might attain, that is because the realisation of the good invariably falls short of the ideal; because, in politics as in morals, the more we enlarge our knowledge, the more we are forced to recognise the extent of our misery.

In addition to these formal Confederations, it is possible to frame others, less visible but none the less real, which are silently cemented by community of interest, by conformity of habits and customs, by the acceptance of common principles, by other ties which establish mutual relations between nations politically divided. Thus the Powers of Europe constitute a kind of whole, united by identity of religion, of moral standard, of international law; by letters, by commerce, and finally by a species of balance which is the inevitable result of all these ties and, however little any man may strive consciously to maintain it, is not to be destroyed so easily as many men imagine.

This concert of Europe has not always existed; and the special causes which produced it are still working to preserve it. The truth is that, before the conquests of the Romans, the nations of this continent, all sunk in barbarism and each utterly unknown to the others, had nothing in common beyond the character which belonged to them as men: a character which, degraded by the practice of slavery, differed little enough in their eyes from that which constitutes the brute. Accordingly the Greeks, vain and disputatious, divided mankind, it may almost be said, into two distinct races: the one—their own, of course—made to rule; the other—the entire rest of the world—created solely to be slaves. From this principle it followed that a Gaul or a Spaniard was no more to a Greek than a Kaffir or Red Indian; and the barbarians themselves were as deeply divided from each other as the Greeks from all of them.

But when these men, born to rule, had been conquered by their slaves the Romans, when half of the known universe had passed beneath the same yoke, a common bond of laws and government was established, and all found themselves members of the same empire. This bond was still further tightened by the recognised principle, either supremely wise or supremely foolish, of imparting to the conquered all the rights of the conqueror: above all, by the famous decree of Claudius, which placed all the subjects of Rome on the roll of her citizens.

Thus all members of the Empire were united in one body politic. They were further united by laws and civil institutions which reinforced the political bond by defining equitably, clearly and precisely, so far as this was possible in so vast an empire, the mutual rights and duties of the ruler and the subject, of one citizen as against another. The Code of Theodosius and the later legislation of Justinian constituted a new bond of justice and reason, which came in to replace the sovereign power at the very moment when it showed unmistakable signs of slackening. This did more than anything else to stave off the break-up of the Empire and to maintain its authority even over the barbarians who ravaged it.

A third and yet stronger bond was furnished by religion; and it cannot be denied that Europe, even now, is indebted more to Christianity than to any other influence for the union, however imperfect, which survives among her members. So true is this that the one nation which has refused to accept Christianity has always remained an alien among the rest. Christianity, so despised in its infancy, ended by serving as a sanctuary to its slanderers. And the Roman Empire, which had persecuted it for centuries with fruitless cruelty, drew from it a power which she could no longer find in her own strength. The missionaries did more for her than any victory; she despatched bishops to redeem the mistake of her generals and triumphed by the aid of the priest when her soldiers were defeated. It is thus that the Franks, the Goths, the Burgundians, the Lombards, the Avars and many others ended by recognising the authority of the Empire which they had mastered, by admitting, at least in appearance, not only the law of the Gospel, but also that of the Prince at whose command it had been preached to them.

Such was the respect which this august body inspired even in its death-throes that, to the very end, its conquerors felt themselves honoured by the acceptance of its titles. The very generals who had humbled the Empire became its ministers and officials; the proudest kings welcomed, nay even canvassed for, the patriciate, the prefecture, the consulate; and, like the lion who fawns upon the man he could easily devour, these terrible conquerors did homage to the imperial throne which they might at any moment have cast down.

Thus the priesthood and the Empire wove a bond between various nations which, without any real community of interests, of rights, or of mutual dependence, found a tie in common principles and beliefs, the influence of which still survives even after its foundation is withdrawn. The venerable phantom of the Roman Empire has never ceased to unite the nations which once formed part of it; and as, after the fall of the Empire, Rome still asserted her authority under another form,[1] Europe, the home of the temporal and spiritual Powers, still retains a sense of fellowship far closer than is to be found elsewhere. The nations of the other continents are too scattered for mutual intercourse; and they lack any other point of union such as Europe has enjoyed.

There are other, and more special, causes for this difference. Europe is more evenly populated, more uniformly fertile; it is easier to pass from one part of her to another. The interests of her princes are united by ties of blood, by commerce, arts and colonies. Communication is made easy by countless rivers winding from one country to another. An inbred love of change impels her inhabitants to constant travel, which frequently leads them to foreign lands. The invention of printing and the general love of letters has given them a basis of common knowledge and common intellectual pursuits. Finally, the number and smallness of her States, the cravings of luxury and the large diversity of climates which Europe offers for their satisfaction, make them all necessary to each other. All these causes combine to make of Europe not, like Asia and Africa, a purely imaginary assemblage of peoples with nothing in common save the name, but a real community with a religion and a moral code, with customs and even laws of its own, which none of the component nations can renounce without causing a shock to the whole frame.

Now look at the other side of the picture. Observe the perpetual quarrels, the robberies, the usurpations, the revolts, the wars, the murders, which bring daily desolation to this venerable home of philosophy, this brilliant sanctuary of art and science. Consider our fair speeches and our abominable acts, the boundless humanity of our maxims and the boundless cruelty of our deeds; our religion so merciful and our intolerance so ferocious; our policy so mild in our text-books and so harsh in our acts; our rulers so beneficent and our people so wretched; our Governments so temperate and our wars so

[1] Respect for the Roman Empire has so completely survived her power that many jurists have questioned whether the Emperor of Germany is not the natural sovereign of the world; and Bartholus carried this doctrine so far as to treat anyone who dared to deny it as a heretic. The writings of the canonists are full of the corresponding doctrine of the temporal supremacy of the Roman Church. [Rousseau's note.]

savage: and then tell me how to reconcile these glaring contradictions; tell me if this alleged brotherhood of the nations of Europe is anything more than a bitter irony to denote their mutual hatred.

But, in truth, what else was to be expected? Every community without laws and without rulers, every union formed and maintained by nothing better than chance, must inevitably fall into quarrels and dissensions at the first change that comes about. The historic union of the nations of Europe has entangled their rights and interests in a thousand complications; they touch each other at so many points that no one of them can move without giving a jar to all the rest; their variances are all the more deadly, as their ties are more closely woven; their frequent quarrels are almost savage as civil wars.

Let us admit then that the Powers of Europe stand to each other strictly in a state of war, and that all the separate treaties between them are in the nature rather of a temporary truce than a real peace: whether because such treaties are seldom guaranteed by any except the contracting parties; or because the respective rights of those parties are never thoroughly determined and are therefore bound—they, or the claims which pass for rights in the eyes of Powers who recognise no earthly superior—to give rise to fresh wars as soon as a change of circumstances shall have given fresh strength to the claimants.

More than this: the public Law of Europe has never been passed or sanctioned by common agreement; it is not based upon any general principles; it varies incessantly from time to time and from place to place; it is therefore a mass of contradictory rules which nothing but the right of the stronger can reduce to order: so that, in the absence of any sure clue to guide her, reason is bound, in every case of doubt, to obey the promptings of self-interest—which, in itself, would make war inevitable, even if all parties desired to be just. With the best intentions in the world, all that can be done is to appeal to arms, or put the question to rest for the moment by a treaty. But the old quarrel soon comes to life again, complicated by others which have arisen in the interval; all is confusion and bewilderment; the truth is obscured so hopelessly that usurpation passes for right and weakness for wrong. In this general welter, all bearings have been so utterly lost that, if we could get back to the solid ground of primitive right, few would be the sovereigns in Europe who would not have to surrender all that they possess.

Another source of war, less obvious but not less real, is that things often change their spirit without any corresponding change of form; that States, hereditary in fact, remain elective in appearance; that we find Parliaments or States General in Monarchies and hereditary rulers in Republics; that a Power, in fact dependent on another, often retains the semblance of autonomy; that all the provinces ruled by the same sovereign are not always governed by the same laws; that the laws of succession differ in different dominions of the same sovereign; finally, that the tendency of every Government to degenerate is a process which no human power can possibly arrest. Such are the causes, general and special, which unite us only to work our ruin. Such are the reasons which condemn us to write our high-sounding theories of fellowship with hands ever dyed afresh in blood.

The causes of the disease, once known, suffice to indicate the remedy, if indeed there is one to be found. Every one can see that what unites any form of society is community of interests, and what disintegrates is their conflict; that either tendency may be changed or modified by a thousand accidents; and therefore that, as soon as a society is founded, some coercive power must be provided to co-ordinate the actions of its members and give to their common interests and mutual obligations that firmness and consistency which they could never acquire of themselves.

It would, indeed, be a great mistake to suppose that the reign of violence, described above, could ever be remedied by the mere force of circumstances, or without the aid of human wisdom. The present balance of Europe is just firm enough to remain in perpetual oscillation without losing itself altogether; and, if our troubles cannot increase, still less can we put an end to them, seeing that any sweeping revolution is henceforth an impossibility.

In proof of this conclusion, let us begin by glancing at the present condition of Europe. The lie of the mountains, seas and rivers, which serve as frontiers for the various nations who people it, seems to have fixed for ever their number and their size. We may fairly say that the political order of the continent is, in some sense, the work of nature.

In truth, we must not suppose that this much vaunted balance is the work of any man, or that any man has deliberately done anything to maintain it. It is there; and men who do not feel themselves strong enough to break it conceal the selfishness of their designs under the pretext of preserving it. But, whether we are aware of it or no, the balance continues to support itself without the aid of any special intervention; if it were to break for a moment on one side, it would soon restore itself on another; so that, if the princes who are accused of aiming at universal monarchy were in reality guilty of any such project, they gave more proof of ambition than of genius. How could any man look such a project in the face without instantly perceiving its absurdity, without realising that there is not a single potentate in Europe so much stronger than the others as ever to have a chance of making himself their master? No conqueror has ever changed the face of the world unless, appearing suddenly with an army of unexpected strength, or with foreign troops hardened to war in other service, he fell upon nations who were either disarmed, or divided, or undisciplined. But where is a European prince to find an army of unexpected strength sufficient to crush all the others, when the most powerful of them has only a fraction of the strength belonging to the whole body and all the rest are watching so carefully to prevent him? Will he have a larger army than all of them put together? It is impossible; or he will only ruin himself the sooner; or his troops will be less good, just because they are more numerous. Will his troops be better trained? They will be proportionally fewer; not to mention that discipline is now everywhere the same, or will have become so before long. Will he have more money? Its sources are open to all, and no great conquest was ever made by money. Will he fall upon his enemies suddenly? Famine, or fortresses, will bar his way at every step. Will he strive to win his way inch by inch? Then he will give his enemies time to unite their forces to resist him; time, money and men will all be bound to fail him. Will he try to divide the other Powers and conquer them one by one? The traditional maxims of Europe make such a policy impossible; the very most stupid of princes would never fall into such a trap as that. In a word, as all the sources of power are equally open to them all, the resistance is in the long run as strong as the attack; and time soon repairs the sudden accidents of fortune, if not for each prince individually, at least for the general balance of the whole.

Now let us take the supposition that two or three potentates league themselves together to conquer all the rest. Those three potentates, take them where you please, will not together have behind them as much as half of Europe. The other half will, quite certainly, make common cause against them. They will therefore have to conquer an enemy stronger than themselves. I may add that their interests are too contradictory and their mutual jealousies too great to allow of such a project ever being formed. I may add further that, even if it were formed, even if it were put in act, even if it had some measure of success, that very success would sow the seeds of discord among our victorious allies. It is beyond the bounds of possibility that the prizes of victory should be so equally divided, that each will be equally satisfied with his share. The least fortunate will soon set himself to resist the further progress of his rivals, who in their turn, for the same reason, will speedily fall out with one another. I doubt whether, since the beginning of the world, there has been a single case in which three, or even two, Powers have joined forces for the conquest of others, without quarrelling over their contingents, or over the division of the spoil, and without, in consequence of this disagreement, promptly giving new strength to their common enemy. From all this it appears improbable that, under any supposition, either a king, or a league of kings, is in a position to bring about any serious or permanent change in the established order of Europe.

This does not mean that the Alps, the Rhine, the sea, and the Pyrenees are in themselves a barrier which no ambition can surmount; but that these barriers are supported by others which either block the path of the enemy, or serve to restore the old frontiers directly the first onslaught has spent its force. The real strength of the existing order is, in truth, to be found partly in the play of conflicting policies which, in nine cases out of ten, keep each other mutually in check. But there is another bulwark more formidable yet. This is the Germanic Body, which lies almost in the center of Europe and holds all the other parts in their place, serving still more perhaps for the protection of its neighbours than for that of its own members: a Body formidable to all by its size and by the number and valour of its component peoples; but of service to all by its constitution which, depriving it both of the means and the will to conquer, makes it the rock on which all schemes of conquest are doomed infallibly to break. In spite of all its defects, it is certain that, so long as that constitution endures, the balance of Europe will never be broken; that no potentate need fear to be cast from his throne by any of his rivals; and that the Treaty of Westphalia will perhaps for ever remain the foundation of our international system. Accordingly, the system of public Right, which the Germans study so diligently, is even more important than they suppose. It is the public Right not only of Germany, but even, in many ways, of Europe as a whole.

But the established order, if indestructible, is for that very reason the more liable to constant storms. Between the Powers of Europe there is a constant action and reaction which, without overthrowing them altogether, keeps them in continual agitation. Ineffectual as they are, these shocks perpetually renew themselves, like the waves which for ever trouble the surface of the sea without ever altering its level. The nations are incessantly ravaged, without any appreciable advantage to the sovereigns.

It would be easy for me to draw the same lesson from a study of the special interests of all the Courts of Europe; to show that those interests are so cunningly interwoven as to hold their respective forces mutually in check. But current theories of commerce and money have bred a political bigotry which works such rapid changes in the apparent interests of princes that it is impossible to arrive at any firm conclusion as to their real interest, seeing that everything now depends upon the economic systems, for the most part thoroughly crazy, which chance to flit through a minister's brain. For all that, commerce tends more and more to establish a balance between State and State; and by depriving certain Powers of the exclusive advantages they once drew from it, deprives them at the same time of one of the chief weapons they once employed for imposing their will upon the rest.[1]

If I have dwelt upon the equal distribution of forces which springs from the present constitution of Europe, it was in order to draw from it a conclusion of the highest importance to the project for establishing a general league among her peoples. For, if we are to form a solid and lasting Federation, we must have put all the members of it in a state of such mutual dependence that no one of them is singly in a position to overbear all the others, and that separate leagues, capable of thwarting the general League, shall meet with obstacles formidable enough to hinder their formation. Failing this, the general League will be nothing but an empty name; and under an appearance of subjection, every member of it will in reality be independent. But, if those obstacles are such as I have described at the present moment—a moment when all the Powers are entirely free to form separate leagues and offensive alliances—judge what they would become, if there were a general League, fully armed and ready at any moment to forestall those who should conceive the design of destroying or resisting it. That in itself is enough to show that such a Federation, so far from ending in mere vain discussions to

[1] There has been a great change since I wrote these words (1756); but my principle will always remain true. It is easy enough to foresee, for instance, that England, with all her glory, will be ruined within twenty years, and, moreover, will have lost what remains of her freedom. All the world asserts that agriculture flourishes in that island. I would wager anything that it is dying fast. London grows every day; therefore the Kingdom is being depleted. The English have set their minds on being conquerors; therefore they are hastening to be slaves. [Rousseau's note, 1761. For *what remains of her freedom*, he had originally written simply *her freedom*.]

be set at defiance with impunity, would on the contrary give birth to an effective Power, capable of forcing any ambitious ruler to observe the terms of the general League which he has joined with others to set up.

From the above survey three certain conclusions may be drawn: the first that, Turkey excepted, there already exists among the nations of Europe a bond, imperfect indeed but still closer than the loose and general ties which exist between man and man in the state of nature; the second, that the imperfections of this association make the state of those who belong to it worse than it would be if they formed no community at all; the third, that these rudimentary ties, which make such an association injurious, make it at the same time readily capable of improvement, that all its members might easily find their happiness in what actually makes their misery, that from the state of war which now reigns among them they might perfectly well draw an abiding peace.

Let us now consider the means by which this great work, begun by chance, may be completed by wisdom. Let us ask how the free and voluntary association which now unites the States of Europe may be converted, by taking to itself the strength and firmness of a genuine Body politic, into an authentic Federation. There is no doubt that such a Federation, by giving to the existing bond the completeness which it now lacks, will increase all its advantages and compel all the parts to unite for the benefit of the whole body. But, before this result can be brought about, the Federation must embrace all the important Powers in its membership; it must have a Legislative Body, with powers to pass laws and ordinances binding upon all its members; it must have a coercive force capable of compelling every State to obey its common resolves whether in the way of command or of prohibition; finally, it must be strong and firm enough to make it impossible for any member to withdraw at his own pleasure the moment he conceives his private interest to clash with that of the whole body. Those are the sure signs by which the world may satisfy itself of the wisdom, usefulness and solidity of our structure. It only remains now to carry our speculation a stage further: to discover by analysis what are the practical consequences which should flow from it, what the means best fitted to realise it, and whether there is any reasonable hope of putting it in execution.

From time to time there are convoked in Europe certain general assemblies called Congresses, to which deputies from every State repair solemnly, to return in the same way; where men assemble to say nothing; where all the affairs of Europe are overhauled in detail; where men lay their heads together to deliberate whether the table they sit at shall be square or round; whether the hall shall have six doors or five; whether one plenipotentiary shall sit with his face or his back to the window, whether another shall come two inches further, or less far, into the room on a visit of ceremony: in fine, on a thousand questions of equal importance which have been discussed without any settlement for the last three centuries and are assuredly very fit to engross the statesmen of our own.

It is possible that the members of one of these assemblies may, once in a way, be blessed with common sense. It is even not impossible that they may have a sincere desire for the general good. For reasons to be assigned shortly, it is further conceivable that, after smoothing away a thousand difficulties, they will receive orders from their sovereigns to sign the Constitution of the Federation of Europe, which I suppose to have been summarily drafted in the five following Articles.

By the first, the contracting sovereigns shall enter into a perpetual and irrevocable alliance, and shall appoint plenipotentiaries to hold, in a specified place, a permanent Diet or Congress, at which all questions at issue between the contracting parties shall be settled and terminated by way of arbitration or judicial pronouncement.

By the second shall be specified the number of the sovereigns whose plenipotentiaries shall have a vote in the Diet; those who shall be invited to accede to the Treaty; the order, date and method by which the presidency shall pass, at equal intervals, from one to another; finally the quota of their respective contributions and the method of raising them for the defrayal of the common expenses.

By the third, the Federation shall guarantee to each of its members the possession and government of all the dominions which he holds at the moment of the Treaty, as well as the manner of succession to them, elective or hereditary, as established by the fundamental laws of each Province. Further, with a view to suppressing at a single stroke and at the source those incessant disputes which arise between them, it shall be agreed to take as basis of the respective rights of the contracting Parties the possession of the moment, as settled in each case by the last treaty concluded, with a general renunciation on all sides of every anterior claim: exception being made for all disputed successions and other claims to fall due in the future, all which shall be determined by arbitration of the Diet, to the absolute exclusion of all attempts to settle the matter by force or to take arms against each other under any pretext whatsoever.

By the fourth shall be specified the conditions under which any Confederate who may break this Treaty shall be put to the ban of Europe and proscribed as a public enemy: namely, if he shall have refused to execute the decisions of the Grand Alliance, if he shall have made preparations for war, if he shall have made a treaty hostile to the ends of the Federation, if he shall have taken up arms to resist it or to attack any one of the Confederates.

By the same Article, it shall be agreed that all the Confederates shall arm and take the offensive, conjointly and at the common expense, against any State put to the ban of Europe, and that they shall not desist until the moment when he shall have laid down his arms, carried out the decisions and orders of the Diet, made amends for his offence, paid all the costs and atoned even for such warlike preparations as he may have made in defiance of the Treaty.

Finally, by the fifth Article, the plenipotentiaries of the Federation of Europe shall receive standing powers to frame—provisionally by a bare majority, definitively (after an interval of five years) by a majority of three quarters—those measures which, on the instruction of their Courts, they shall consider expedient with a view to the greatest possible advantage of the Commonwealth of Europe and of its members, all and single. In none of the above five Articles, however, shall any change ever be made except with the unanimous consent of the Confederates.

These five Articles, thus summarised and reduced to the most general form, are, I am aware, exposed to countless petty objections, several of which would call for lengthy explanations. But petty objections are easily removed in case of need; and, in an enterprise of this importance, they are beside the point. When the policy of the Congress comes to be considered, a thousand obstacles will present themselves and ten thousand ways of removing them. It is *our* business to ask whether, in the nature of the case, the enterprise is possible or no. We should lose ourselves in volumes of trifles, if we had to foresee all and find an answer to all. Confining ourselves, as we do, to incontestable principles, we have no call to satisfy every reader, nor to solve every objection, nor to say how every detail will be settled. It is enough to show that a settlement is possible.

In judging of this scheme, then, what are the questions that have to be considered? Two only; for I will not insult the reader by proving to him the general proposition that the state of peace is a better thing than the state of war.

The first question is whether the Federation suggested would be certain to answer its purpose and give a solid and abiding peace to Europe. The second, whether it is for the interest of the various sovereigns to establish such a Federation and to pay the price I have mentioned to obtain a lasting peace.

When we have thus proved our scheme to be for the advantage both of Europe as a whole and of all the States composing her, what obstacle is left, we ask, that can possibly prevent the execution of a design which, after all, depends solely upon the will of those concerned?

In discussing the first Article, for instance, let us apply what has been said above of the general order now established in Europe and of the common resolve which confines each Power practically within its traditional limits and does not allow it wholly to crush any of the others. In order to make my argument clear, I give here a list of the nineteen Powers here assumed to constitute the Commonwealth of Europe, to each of which I give an equal voice, making altogether nineteen votes, in the deliberations of the Diet:

The Emperor of the Romans,[1]
The Emperor of Russia,
The King of France,
The King of Spain,
The King of England,
The States General,[2]
The King of Denmark,

[1] i.e., the Potentate commonly, but incorrectly, called the Emperor of Germany.
[2] i.e., the Dutch Netherlands.

Sweden,
Poland,
The King of Portugal,
The Sovereign of Rome,[3]
The King of Prussia,
The Elector of Bavaria and his associates,
The Elector Palatine and his associates,
The Swiss and their associates,
The ecclesiastical Electors and their associates,
The Republic of Venice and her associates,
The King of Naples,
The King of Sardinia.

Several minor sovereigns—for instance, the Republic of Genoa, the dukes of Parma and Modena, and others—are omitted from the list. They will be associated with one or other of the less powerful States, with whom they will share a vote, after the fashion of the joint vote (*votum curiatum*) of the Counts of the Empire. It is useless to make the list more precise because, at any moment before the scheme is put in force, things may happen which, without affecting the principle of the measure, may call for alterations of detail.

A glance at the list will be enough to prove conclusively that it is impossible either for any single Power to resist the united action of all the others, or for any partial league to be formed capable of defying the Federation as a whole.

How, indeed, could such a league be formed? Between the more powerful of the Confederates? We have already proved that such a league could never last; and with the list before us, it is easy enough to see that it could never be reconciled with the traditional policy of any of the great Powers, or with the interests inherent in their respective positions. Between a large State and a number of small ones? Then the other large States, with the Federation behind them, will crush such a league in no time; and it is clear that the Grand Alliance, being perpetually armed and concerted for action, will find no difficulty in forestalling and crushing in advance any partial and seditious alliance, likely to trouble the peace and the public order of Europe. Look at the cohesion of the Germanic Body: and that, inspite of its defective discipline and the glaring inequality of its members. Is there a single prince, not even excepting the most powerful, who would dare to expose himself to the ban of the Empire by openly defying its laws, unless indeed he had good reason to suppose that the Empire would never have the courage to take action against the culprit in good earnest?

That is why I regard it as proved that the Diet of Europe, once established, will have no rebellion to fear and that no abuses which may creep in are ever likely to defeat the aims with which it was founded. It remains to ask whether those aims are really secured by the proposed Federation.

[3] i.e., the Pope.

With a view to answering this question, let us consider the motives by which princes are commonly led to take up arms. These motives are: either to make conquests, or to protect themselves from aggression, or to weaken a too powerful neighbour, or to maintain their rights against attack, or to settle a difference which has defied friendly negotiation, or, lastly, to fulfil some treaty obligation. There is no cause or pretext of war which cannot be brought under one or other of these six heads; and it is manifest that not one of the six is left standing under the new order which I propose.

As for the first, the thought of conquests will have to be given up from the absolute impossibility of making them. The aggressor is sure to find his way barred by forces stronger than his own; he is powerless to gain anything, and he risks the loss of all he has. At present, an ambitious prince, who wishes to extend his dominions in Europe, relies upon two weapons; he begins by securing strong allies, and then seeks to catch his enemy unawares. But, under the new conditions, no special alliance could stand for a moment before the General Alliance, which is stronger and subsists permanently; and as there is no longer any pretext for arming, no prince can do so without being at once detected, stopped and punished by the Federation always under arms.

Again, the very thing which destroys all hope of conquest relieves him at the same time from all fear of being attacked. And, under the guarantee of all Europe, not only are his territories as strongly assured to him as the possessions of any citizen in a well-ordered community, but they are even more so than they were when he was their sole and only defender; in exactly the same proportion as the whole of Europe is stronger than any one of her princes taken singly.

Thirdly, having no more reason to fear his neighbour, neither has he any more reason for desiring to weaken him; and having no hope of success in such an enterprise, he is under no temptation to attempt it.

As for the maintenance of his rights, I begin by remarking that a whole host of pettifogging claims and obscure pretensions will be swept away at one stroke by the third Article of Federation, which settles for ever all the conflicting rights of the allied princes, on the basis of what they actually hold. By the same Article, we have a clear principle for settling all claims and pretensions which may be raised in the future: each will be decided in the Diet, as it arises. It may be added that, if my rights are attacked, I am bound to defend them by the weapon used against me. They cannot be attacked by force of arms without bringing the ban of the Diet upon the assailant. It is not by arms then that I shall have to defend them. The same may be said of injuries, wrongs and claims for damage—in short, of all the unforeseen differences which may arise between two Sovereigns. The same Power which is bound to maintain their rights is bound also to redress their grievances.

As for the last head, the question settles itself. It is clear at a glance that, having no longer any assailant to fear, I have no longer any use for treaties of defence; and that, as no treaty can be so strong or so trustworthy as that guaranteed by the Grand Federation, any other treaty would be useless, illegitimate and consequently null and void.

For all these reasons it is impossible that the Federation, once established, can leave any seed of war between its members; impossible that our object, an abiding peace, should not be absolutely attained by the proposed system, if it were once set on foot.

It now remains to settle the other question: that relating to the interests of the several parties concerned. For everyone knows that the general interest is powerless to silence that of the individual. To prove that peace, as a general principle, is a better thing than war is to say nothing to the man who has private reasons for preferring war to peace; to show him the means for securing a lasting peace is only to encourage him to work against them.

In truth, we shall be told: "You are taking from Sovereigns the right of doing themselves justice; that is to say, the precious right of being unjust when they please. You are taking from them the power of making themselves great at the expense of their neighbours. You are forcing them to renounce those antiquated claims whose value depends on their obscurity and which grow with every fresh growth in power; that parade of might and terror with which they love to awe the world; that pride of conquest which is the chief source of their glory. In one word, you are forcing them to be equitable and peaceful. What amends do you propose to make them for all these cruel privations?"

I do not venture to answer, with the Abbé de Saint Pierre, that the true glory of princes lies in serving the good of the community and the happiness of their subjects, that their highest interest is to win a good name, and that such a name is awarded by the wise in exact proportion to the good which the ruler has done in the world; that the scheme of founding a lasting peace is the most lofty ever conceived and the most certain, if executed, to cover its author with undying glory; that such a scheme would not only do a greater service than any other to the people but also confer higher honour upon the Sovereign; that this is the only ideal not stained with blood, rapine, curses and tears; in a word, that the surest way for a Sovereign to raise himself above the common herd of kings is to labour for the good of the community. Let such language, which has covered the author and his projects with ridicule in all the council-chambers of Europe, be left to irresponsible declaimers. But let us never join in the cry against the arguments it embodies; and, whatever may be the truth as to the virtues of princes, let us confine ourselves to their interests.

All the Powers of Europe have rights, or claims, as against each other. These rights are, from the nature of the case, incapable of ever being finally adjusted, because there is no common and unvarying standard for judging of their merits and because they are often based upon facts which are either disputed or of doubtful interpretation. Nor are the quarrels which spring from them any more capable of being settled beyond appeal, whether in default of any recognised umpire, or because, when the chance offers, every prince goes back shamelessly upon the cessions which have been forcibly torn from him by a stronger Power through treaties, or after an unsuccessful war. It is therefore a mistake to think only of the claims we have on others, and to forget those they have on us, when in reality there is no more justice on one side than the other and both are equally capable of acquiring the means for enforcing their demands. Directly fortune is taken for arbiter, actual possession acquires a value which no wise man will stake against a possible gain in the future, even where chances are equal on both sides; and the rich man who, in the hope of doubling his fortune, ventures to risk it all upon one throw is blamed by the whole world. We have shown, however, that in schemes of self-aggrandisement the chances are never equal and that, even in the present order of things, the aggressor is always bound to find his enemy stronger than himself. The inevitable conclusion is that, the more powerful having no motive for staking his possessions and the weaker no hope of gaining on the throw, both will find their advantage in renouncing what they would like to win, in order to secure what they possess.

Think of the waste of men, of money, of strength in every form; think of the exhaustion in which any State is plunged by the most successful war; compare these ravages with the profit which results: and we shall find that we commonly lose where we suppose ourselves to gain; that the conqueror, always enfeebled by the war, can only console himself with the thought that the conquered is still more enfeebled than himself. And even this advantage is more in appearance than reality; for the strength which has been gained upon our opponent has been lost against the neutrals who, without changing themselves, are nevertheless stronger relatively to us by all the strength that we have lost.

If all kings have not yet thrown off the folly of conquests, it would seem that the wiser of them at any rate are beginning to realise that they sometimes cost more than they are worth. Without going into a thousand distinctions which would only distract us from our purpose, we may say broadly that a prince who, in extending his frontiers, loses as many of his old subjects as he gains new ones in the process only weakens himself by his aggrandisement; because, with a larger territory to defend, he has no more soldiers to defend it. Everyone knows, however, that, as war is waged nowadays, the smallest part of the resultant loss of life is due to losses in the field. Certainly, that is the loss which everyone sees and feels. But all the time there is taking place through the whole kingdom a loss far more serious and more irreparable than that of those who die: a loss due to those who are not born, to the increase of taxes, to the interruption of trade, to the desertion of the fields, to the neglect of their cultivation. This evil, which no one sees at first, makes itself felt cruelly in the end. And then the king is astonished to find himself so weak, as the result of making himself so strong.

There is another thing which makes conquests even less profitable than they used to be. It is that kings have at last learned the secret of doubling or trebling their power not only without enlarging their territory but even, it may be, by contracting it, after the wise example of Hadrian. The secret is that the strength of kings lies only in that of their subjects; and it follows from what I have just said that, given two States supporting an equal number of inhabitants, that which covers the smaller extent of territory is in reality the more powerful. It is then by good laws, by a wise discipline, by large views on economic policy that a sagacious sovereign is sure of increasing his power without incurring any hazard. It is in carrying out works more useful than his neighbours' that he makes conquests—the only true conquests—at their expense; and every subject born to him in excess of theirs is another enemy killed.

It may be objected that I prove too much and that, if the matter were as I put it, everyone being manifestly interested in avoiding war and the public interest combining with that of individuals for the preservation of peace, that peace ought to come of itself and of itself last for ever without any need of Federation. Given the present state of things, however, that would be to reason very ill. It is quite true that it would be much better for all men to remain always at peace. But so long as there is no security for this, everyone, having no guarantee that he can avoid war, is anxious to begin it at the moment which suits his own interest and so forestall a neighbour, who would not fail to forestall the attack in his turn at any moment favourable to himself, so that many wars, even offensive wars, are rather in the nature of unjust precautions for the protection of the assailant's own possessions than a device for seizing those of others. However salutary it may be in theory to obey the dictates of public spirit, it is certain that, politically and even morally, those dictates are liable to prove fatal to the man who persists in observing them with all the world when no one thinks of observing them towards him.

I have nothing to say on the question of military parade because, when supported by no solid foundation either of hope or fear, such parade is mere child's play, and kings have no business to keep dolls. I am equally silent as to the glory of conquest because, if there really were men who would break their hearts at the thought of having no one to massacre, our duty would be not to reason with such monsters but to deprive them of all means for putting their murderous frenzy into act. All solid grounds of war being swept away by the third Article, no king can have any motive for kindling its horrors against a rival which would not furnish that rival with equally strong grounds for kindling them against him. And it is a great gain to be delivered from a danger in which each finds himself alone against the world.

As for the dependence of all upon the Tribunal of Europe, it is abundantly clear by the same Article that the rights of sovereignty, so far from being weakened, will, on the contrary, be strengthened and confirmed. For that Article guarantees to each Sovereign not only that his dominions shall be protected against foreign invasion, but also that his authority shall be upheld against the rebellion of his subjects. The prince accordingly will be none the less absolute, and his crown will be more fully assured. By submitting to the decision of the Diet in all disputes with his equals, and by surrendering the perilous right of seizing other men's possessions, he is, in fact, doing nothing more than securing his real rights and renouncing those which are purely fictitious. Besides, there is all the difference in the world between dependence upon a rival and dependence upon a Body of which he is himself a member and of which each member in turn becomes the head. In the latter case, the pledges that are given him are really the security for his freedom: it would be forfeited, if lodged with a superior; it is confirmed, when lodged with equals. In support of this, I appeal to the example of the Germanic Body. It is quite true that the constitution of this is such as to trench in many ways upon the sovereignty of its members. It is quite true that their position is consequently less favourable than it would be in the Federation of Europe. But, in spite of those drawbacks, there is not one of them, however jealous he may be of his dignity, who would choose, even if he had the power, to win absolute independence at the cost of severance from the Empire.

Observe further that the head of the Germanic Body, being permanent, is bound to usurp ceaselessly upon the rights of the other members. In the Diet of Europe, where the presidency passes from one to another without any regard to disparities of power, no such danger is to be feared.

There is yet another consideration which is likely to weigh even more with men so greedy of money as princes always are. Not only will an unbroken peace give them, as well as their subjects, every means of amassing abundant riches; they will also be spared vast expenses by the reduction of their military budget, of those innumerable fortresses, of those enormous armies, which swallow up their revenue and become daily more and more of a burden to their subjects and themselves. I know that it will not suit all Sovereigns to suppress their army bodily and leave themselves with no force in hand to crush an unexpected revolt or repel a sudden invasion. I know also that they will have their contingent to furnish to the Federation with a view both to guarding the frontiers of Europe and to maintaining the federal army whose duty it will be, in case of need, to carry out the decrees of the Diet. But, when all these charges are met and, at the same time, the extraordinary expenses of war suppressed for ever, there will still be a saving of more than half the ordinary military budget; and that saving can be divided between the relief of the subject and the coffers of the prince. The result will be that the people will have to pay much less; that the prince, being much better off, will be in a position to encourage commerce, agriculture and the arts and to create useful foundations which will still further increase his subjects' riches and his own; and, over and above all this, that the State will enjoy a security far greater than it now draws from all its armies and from all that warlike parade which drains its strength in the very bosom of peace.

It will be said perhaps that the frontier countries of Europe will then be relatively worse off, since they will still have to face the chance of war either with the Turk, or the African Corsairs, or the Tartars.

The answer to this is (1) that those countries are under the same necessity at present, from which it follows that they will not be put to any positive disadvantage, but will only have an advantage the less; and this, in fact, is an inevitable consequence of their geographical position; (2) that, being freed from all anxiety on the side of Europe, they will be much more capable of resisting attacks from other quarters; (3) that the suppression of all fortresses in the inner parts of Europe and of all expenses needed for their maintenance would enable the Federation to build a large number on the eastern frontiers without bringing any fresh charge upon its members; (4) that these fortresses, built, maintained and garrisoned at the common charge, will mean so many fresh guarantees, and so much expense saved to the frontier Powers for whose benefit they are built; (5) that the troops of the Federation, posted on the frontiers of Europe, will stand permanently ready to drive back the invader; (6) and finally, that a Body so formidable as the Commonwealth of Europe will make the foreigner think twice before attacking any of its members: just as the Germanic Body, though infinitely less powerful, is still strong enough to command the respect of its neighbours and offer valuable protection to all the princes who compose it.

It may be further objected that, when the nations of Europe have ceased to war among themselves, the art of war will be gradually forgotten, that her armies will lose their courage and discipline, that there will be no more soldiers or generals, and that Europe will lie at the mercy of the first comer.

My answer is that one of two things will happen. Either the neighbours of Europe will attack her and wage war against her; or they will be afraid of the Federation and leave her in peace.

In the former case, there will be plenty of opportunities for training military genius and talent, for practising and hardening our troops. The armies of the Federation will, in this way, be the school of Europe. Men will go to the frontiers to learn war, while in the heart of Europe there will reign the blessings of peace. The advantages of war and peace will be combined. Does anyone believe that no nation can become warlike without perpetual civil war? And are the French the less brave because Anjou and Touraine are not constantly fighting with each other?

In the latter case, it is true that there can be no more hardening for war. But neither will there be any more need for it. Of what use would it be to train for war, when you have no intention of ever making it? And which is the better course—to cultivate a pernicious art, or to destroy the need of it for ever? If the secret of perpetual health were discovered, would there be any sense in rejecting it, on the ground that doctors must not be deprived of the chance of gaining experience? And in making this parallel we have still to ask which of the two arts is the more beneficent in itself and the more deserving of encouragement.

Let no one threaten us with a sudden invasion. It is perfectly obvious that Europe has no invader to fear, and that the "first comer" will never come. The day of those barbarian irruptions, which seemed to fall from the clouds, is gone for ever. Now that the whole surface of the earth lies bare to our scrutiny, no danger can reach us which we have not foreseen for years. There is no Power in the world now capable of threatening all Europe; and if one ever appears, Europe will either have time to make ready or, at the worst, will be much more capable of resisting him when she is united in one corporate body than she is now, when she would have to put a sudden end to all her quarrels and league herself in haste against the common invader.

We have thus seen that all the alleged evils of Federation, when duly weighed, come to nothing. I now ask whether anyone in the world would dare to say as much of those which flow from the recognised method of settling disputes between one prince and another—the appeal to the sword: a method inseparable from the state of anarchy and war, which necessarily springs from the absolute independence conceded to all sovereigns under the imperfect conditions now prevailing in Europe. In order to put the reader in a better position to estimate these evils, I will give a short summary of them and leave him to judge of their significance.

(1) The existence of no solid right, except that of the stronger. (2) The perpetual and inevitable shifting of the balance from nation to nation, which makes it impossible for any one of them to keep in its grasp the power it holds at any moment. (3) The absence of complete security for any nation, so long as its neighbours are not subdued or annihilated. (4) The impossibility of annihilating them, in view of the fact that, directly one is conquered, another springs up in its place. (5) The necessity of endless precautions and expenses to keep guard against possible enemies. (6) Weakness, and consequent exposure to attack, during minorities or revolts; for, when the State is divided, who can support one faction against the other? (7) The absence of any guarantee for international agreements. (8) The impossibility of obtaining justice from others without enormous cost and loss, which even so do not always obtain it, while the object in dispute is seldom worth the price. (9) The invariable risk of the prince's possessions, and sometimes of his life, in the quest of his rights. (10) The necessity of taking part against his will in the quarrels of his neighbours and of engaging in war at the moment when he would least have chosen it. (11) The stoppage of trade and revenue at the moment when they are most indispensable. (12) The perpetual dangers threatened by a powerful neighbour, if the prince is weak, and by an armed alliance, if he is strong. (13) Finally, the uselessness of prudence, when everything is left to change; the perpetual impoverishment of nations; the enfeeblement of the State alike in victory and defeat; and the total inability of the prince ever to establish good government, ever to count upon his own possessions, ever to secure happiness either for himself or for his subjects.

In the same way, let us sum up the advantages which the arbitration of Europe would confer upon the princes who agree to it.

1. Absolute certainty that all their disputes, present and future, will always be settled without war: a certainty incomparably more useful to princes than total immunity from lawsuits to the individual.
2. The abolition, either total or nearly so, of matters of dispute, thanks to the extinction of all existing claims—a boon which, in itself, will make up for all the prince renounces and secure what he possesses.
3. An absolute and indefeasible guarantee not only for the persons of the prince and his family, but also for his dominions and the law of succession recognised by the custom of each province: and this, not only against the ambition of unjust and grasping claimants, but also against the rebellion of his subjects.

4. Absolute security for the execution of all engagements between princes, under the guarantee of the Commonwealth of Europe.
5. Perfect freedom of trade for all time whether between State and State, or between any of them and the more distant regions of the earth.
6. The total suppression for all time of the extraordinary military expenses incurred by land and sea in time of war, and a considerable reduction of the corresponding ordinary expenses in time of peace.
7. A notable increase of population and agriculture, of the public wealth and the revenues of the prince.
8. An open door for all useful foundations, calculated to increase the power and glory of the Sovereign, the public wealth and the happiness of the subject.

As I have already said, I leave it to the reader to weigh all these points and to make his own comparison between the state of peace which results from Federation and the state of war which follows from the present anarchy of Europe.

If our reasoning has been sound in the exposition of this Project, it has been proved: firstly, that the establishment of a lasting peace depends solely upon the consent of the Sovereigns concerned and offers no obstacle except what may be expected from their opposition; secondly, that the establishment of such a peace would be profitable to them in all manner of ways and that, even from their point of view, there is no comparison between its drawbacks and advantages; thirdly, that it is reasonable to expect their decision in this matter will coincide with their plain interest; and lastly, that such a peace, once established on the proposed basis, will be solid and lasting and will completely fulfil the purpose with which it was concluded.

This is not, of course, to say that the Sovereigns will adopt this project—who can answer for the reason of another?—but only that they would adopt it, if they took counsel of their true interest. It must be observed that we have not assumed men such as they ought to be, good, generous, disinterested and devoted to the public good from motives of pure humanity; but such as they are, unjust, grasping and setting their own interest above all things. All that I do assume in them is understanding enough to see their own interest, and courage enough to act for their own happiness. If, in spite of all this, the project remains unrealised, that is not because it is utopian; it is because men are crazy, and because to be sane in a world of madmen is in itself a kind of madness.

Rousseau's Criticism of Saint Pierre's Project

The scheme of a lasting peace was of all others the most worthy to fascinate a man of high principle. Of all those which engaged the Abbé de Saint Pierre, it was therefore that over which he brooded the longest and followed up with the greatest obstinacy. It is indeed hard to give any other name to the missionary zeal which never failed him in this enterprise: and that, in spite of the manifest impossibility of success, the ridicule which he brought upon himself day by day and the rebuffs which he had continually to endure. It would seem that his well-balanced spirit, intent solely on the public good, led him to measure his devotion to a cause purely by its utility, never letting himself be daunted by difficulties, never thinking of his own personal interest.

If ever moral truth were demonstrated, I should say it is the utility, national no less than international, of this project. The advantages which its realisation would bring to each prince, to each nation, to the whole of Europe, are immense, manifest, incontestable; and nothing could be more solid or more precise than the arguments which the author employs to prove them. Realise his Commonwealth of Europe for a single day, and you may be sure it will last for ever; so fully would experience convince men that their own gain is to be found in the good of all. For all that, the very princes who would defend it with all their might, if it once existed, would resist with all their might any proposal for its creation; they will as infallibly throw obstacles in the way of its establishment as they would in the way of its abolition. Accordingly Saint Pierre's book on *A Lasting Peace* seems to be ineffectual for founding it and unnecessary for maintaining it. "It is then an empty dream," will be the verdict of the impatient reader. No: it is a work of solid judgment, and it is of the last importance for us to possess it.

Let us begin by examining the criticisms of those who judge of reasons not by reason, but by the event, and who have no objection to bring against the scheme except that it has never been put in practice. Well, such men will doubtless say, if its advantages are so certain, why is it that the Sovereigns of Europe have never adopted it? Why do they ignore their own interest, if that interest is demonstrated so clearly? Do we see them reject any other means of increasing their revenue and their power? And, if this means were as efficacious as you pretend, is it conceivable that they should be less eager to try it than any of the schemes they have pursued for all these centuries? that they should prefer a thousand delusive expedients to so evident an advantage?

Yes, without doubt, that is conceivable; unless it be assumed that their wisdom is equal to their ambition, and that the more keenly they desire their own interest, the more clearly do they see it. The truth is that the severest penalty of excessive self-love is that it always defeats itself, that the keener the passion the more certain it is to be cheated of its goal. Let us distinguish then, in politics as in morals, between real and apparent interest. The former would be secured by an abiding peace; that is demonstrated in the *Project*. The latter is to be found in the state of absolute independence which frees Sovereigns from the reign of Law only to put them under that of chance. They are, in fact, like a madcap pilot who, to show off his idle skill and his power over his sailors, would rather toss to and fro among the rocks in a storm than moor his vessel at anchor in safety.

The whole life of kings, or of those on whom they shuffle off their duties, is devoted solely to two objects: to extend their rule beyond their frontiers and to make it more absolute within them. Any other purpose they may have is either subservient to one of these aims, or merely a pretext for attaining them. Such pretexts are "the good of the community," "the happiness of their subjects," or "the glory of the nation": phrases for ever banished from the council chamber, and employed so clumsily in proclamations that they are always taken as warnings of coming misery and that the people groans with apprehension when its masters speak to it of their "fatherly solicitude."

From these two fundamental maxims we can easily judge of the spirit in which princes are likely to receive a proposal which runs directly counter to the one and is hardly more favourable to the other. Anyone can see that the establishment of the Diet of Europe will fix the constitution of each State as inexorably as its frontiers; that it is impossible to guarantee the prince against the rebellion of his subjects without at the same time securing the subjects against the tyranny of the prince; and that, without this, the Federation could not possibly endure. And I ask whether there is in the whole world a single Sovereign who, finding himself thus bridled for ever in his most cherished designs, would endure without indignation the very thought of seeing himself forced to be just not only with the foreigner, but even with his own subjects?

Again, anyone can understand that war and conquest without and the encroachments of despotism within give each other mutual support; that money and men are habitually taken at pleasure from a people of slaves, to bring others beneath the same yoke; and that conversely war furnishes a pretext for exactions of money and another, no less plausible, for keeping large armies constantly on foot, to hold the people in awe. In a word, anyone can see that aggressive princes wage war at least as much on their subjects as on their enemies, and that the conquering nation is left no better off than the conquered. "I have beaten the Romans," so Hannibal used to write to Carthage, "send me more troops. I have exacted an indemnity from Italy, send me more money." That is the real meaning of the *Te Deums*, the bonfires and rejoicings with which the people hail the triumphs of their masters.

As for disputes between prince and prince, is it reasonable to hope that we can force before a higher tribunal men who boast that they hold their power only by the sword, and who bring in the name of God solely because He "is in heaven"? Will Sovereigns ever submit their quarrels to legal arbitration, when all the rigour of the laws has never succeeded in forcing private individuals to admit the principle in theirs? A private gentleman with a grievance is too proud to carry his case before the Court of the Marshals of France; and you expect a king to carry his claims before the Diet of Europe? Not to mention that the former offends against the laws, so risking his life twice over, while the latter seldom risks anything but the life of his subjects; and that, in taking up arms, he avails himself of a right recognised by all the world—a right for the use of which he claims to be accountable to God alone.

A prince who stakes his cause on the hazards of war knows well enough that he is running risks. But he is less struck with the risks than with the gains on which he reckons, because he is much less afraid of fortune than he is confident in his own wisdom. If he is strong, he counts upon his armies; if weak, upon his allies. Sometimes he finds it useful to purge ill humours, to weaken restive subjects, even to sustain reverses; and the wily statesman knows how to draw profit even from his own defeats. I trust it will be remembered that it is not I who reason in this fashion, but the court sophist, who would rather have a large territory with few subjects, poor and submissive, than that unshaken rule over the hearts of a happy and prosperous people, which is the reward of a prince who observes justice and obeys the laws.

It is on the same principle that he meets in his own mind the argument drawn from the interruption of commerce, from the loss of life, from the financial confusion and the real loss which result from an unprofitable conquest. It is a great miscalculation always to estimate the losses and gains of princes in terms of money; the degree of power they aim at is not to be reckoned by the millions in their coffers. The prince always makes his schemes rotate: he seeks to command in order to enrich himself, and to enrich himself in order to command. He is ready by turns to sacrifice the one aim to the other, with a view to obtaining whichever of the two is most wanting at the moment. But it is only in the hope of winning them both in the long run that he pursues each of them apart. If he is to be master both of men and things, he must have empire and money at the same time.

Let us add finally that, though the advantages resulting to commerce from a general and lasting peace are in themselves certain and indisputable, still, being common to all States, they will be appreciated by none. For such advantages make themselves felt only by contrast, and he who wishes to increase his relative power is bound to seek only such gains as are exclusive.

So it is that, ceaselessly deluded by appearances, princes would have nothing to do with peace on these terms, even if they calculated their interests for themselves. How will it be, when the calculation is made for them by their ministers, whose interests are always opposed to those of the people and almost always to the prince's? Ministers are in perpetual need of war, as a means of making themselves indispensable to their master, of throwing him into difficulties from which he cannot escape without their aid, of ruining the State, if things come to the worst, as the price of keeping their own office. They are in need of it, as a means of oppressing the people on the plea of national necessity, of finding places for their creatures, of rigging the market and setting up a thousand odious monopolies. They are in need of it, as a means of gratifying their passions and driving their rivals out of favour. They are in need of it, as a means of controlling the prince and withdrawing him from court whenever a dangerous plot is formed against their power. With a lasting peace, all these resources would be gone. And the world still persists in asking why, if such a scheme is practicable, these men have not adopted it. Is it not obvious that there is nothing impracticable about it, except its adoption by these men? What then will they do to oppose it? What they have always done: they will turn it into ridicule.

Again, even given the good will that we shall never find either in princes or their ministers, we are not to assume, with the Abbé de Saint Pierre, that it would be easy to find the right moment for putting the project into act. For this, it would be essential that all the private interests concerned, taken together, should not be stronger than the general interest, and that everyone should believe himself to see in the good of all the highest good to which he can aspire for himself. But this requires a concurrence of wisdom in so many heads, a fortuitous concourse of so many interests, such as chance can hardly be expected ever to bring about. But, in default of such spontaneous agreement, the one thing left is force; and then the question is no longer to persuade but to compel, not to write books but to raise armies.

Accordingly, though the scheme in itself was wise enough, the means proposed for its execution betray the simplicity of the author. He fairly supposed that nothing was needed but to convoke a Congress and lay the Articles before it; that they would be signed directly and all be over on the spot. It must be admitted that, in all his projects, this good man saw clearly enough how things would work, when once set going, but that he judged like a child of the means for setting them in motion.

To prove that the project of the Christian Commonwealth is not utopian, I need do no more than name its original author. For no one will say that Henry IV was a madman, or Sully a dreamer. The Abbé de Saint Pierre took refuge behind these great names, to revive their policy. But what a difference in the time, the circumstances, the scheme itself, the manner of bringing it forward and, above all, in its author!

To judge of this, let us glance at the state of Europe as it was at the moment which Henry chose for the execution of his project.

The power of Charles V, who reigned over one half of the world and struck awe into the other, had led him to aspire to universal empire, with great chances of success and great talents for making use of them. His son, more rich and less powerful, never ceased to nurse a design which he was incapable of carrying out, and throughout his reign kept Europe in a state of perpetual alarm. In truth, the House of Austria had acquired such an ascendancy over the other Powers that no prince was safe upon his throne, unless he stood well with the Hapsburgs. Philip III, with even fewer talents, inherited all his father's pretensions. Europe was still held in awe by the power of Spain, which continued to dominate the others rather by long habit of commanding than from any power to make herself obeyed. In truth, the revolt of the Low Countries, the struggle against England, the long drain of the civil wars in France had exhausted the strength of Spain and the riches of the Indies. The House of Austria, now divided into two branches, had ceased to act with the same unity; and the Emperor, although he strained every nerve to maintain or recover the authority of Charles V, only succeeded in affronting the lesser princes and provoking conspiracies which speedily broke out and came near to costing him his throne. Such were the slow stages which prepared the fall of the House of Austria and the new birth of the liberties of Europe. No one, however, had the courage to be the first to risk throwing off the yoke and exposing himself alone to the dangers of war; the example of Henry himself, who had come so ill out of the enterprise, damped the courage of all the rest. Moreover, if we except the Duke of Savoy, who was too weak and too much under the curb to move a step, there was not among all the Sovereigns of the time a single one of ability enough to form and carry through such an enterprise; each one of them waited on time and circumstances for the moment to break his chains. Such, in rough outline, was the state of things at the time when Henry formed the plan of the Christian Commonwealth and prepared to put it in act. The project was vast indeed and, in itself, quite beyond praise. I have no wish to dim its glory. But, prompted as it was by the secret hope of humbling a formidable enemy, it took from this urgent motive an impulse which could hardly have come from humanity alone.

Let us now see what were the means employed by this great man to pave the way for so lofty an undertaking. In the front rank of these I should be disposed to put that he had clearly recognised all the difficulties of the task; so that, having formed the project in his youth, he brooded over it all his life and reserved its accomplishment for his old age. This proves in the first place that ardent and sustained passion by which alone great obstacles can be overcome; and secondly, that patient and considerate wisdom which smoothes the way in advance by forethought and calculation. For there is a great difference between an enforced undertaking, in which prudence itself counsels to leave something to chance, and one which is to be justified only by success; seeing that, being under no compulsion to engage in it, we ought never to have attempted it unless that success were beyond doubt. Again, the deep secrecy which he maintained all his life, until the very moment of action, was as essential as it was difficult in so vast an enterprise, where the concurrence of so many men was a necessity and which so many men were interested in thwarting. It would seem that, though he had drawn the greater part of Europe to his side and was in league with her chief potentates, there was only one man to whom he had confided the full extent of his design; and, by a boon granted by heaven only to the best of kings, that one man was an honest minister. But, though nothing was allowed to transpire of these high aims, everything was silently moving towards their execution. Twice over did Sully make the journey to London: James I was a party to the plan, and the King of Sweden had fallen in with it. A league was made with the Protestants of Germany; even the princes of Italy had been secured. All were ready to join in the great purpose, though none could say what it was; just as workmen are employed in making the separate parts of a new machine, of whose shape and use they know nothing. What was it then that set all these springs in motion? Was it the craving for a lasting peace, which was foreseen by no one and with which few would have troubled their heads? Was it the public interest, which is never the interest of anyone? The Abbé de Saint Pierre might have supposed so. But the truth is that each of them was working for his own private interest which Henry had been clever enough to display to all of them in the most attractive light. The King of England was glad to deliver himself from the perpetual conspiracies of his Catholic subjects, all of them fomented by Spain. He found a further advantage in the liberation of the United

Provinces, in whose support he was spending large sums, while every moment he was placed on the brink of a war which he dreaded, or in which he preferred to join once for all with the whole of Europe and then be quit of it for ever. The King of Sweden was anxious to make sure of Pomerania and so win a footing in Germany. The Elector Palatine, at that time a Protestant and head of the Lutheran Confession, had designs on Bohemia and shared all the plans of the King of England. The Princes of Germany aimed at checking the encroachments of the House of Austria. The Duke of Savoy was to receive Milan and the crown of Lombardy which he passionately coveted. The Pope himself, weary of the Spanish tyranny, was in the league, bribed by the promise of the Kingdom of Naples. The Dutch, better paid than all the rest, gained the assurance of their freedom. In a word, quite apart from the common interest of humbling a haughty Power which was striving to tyrannise over all of them, each State had a private interest all the more keenly felt because it was not countered by the fear of exchanging one tyrant for another. It was agreed that the conquests should be distributed among all the Allies to the exclusion of France and England, who were bound to keep nothing for themselves. This was enough to quiet the most suspicious as to the ambitions of Henry. But that wise prince was well aware that in keeping nothing for himself by this treaty, he gained more than all the rest. Without adding a yard to his own patrimony, it was enough to partition that of the only man who excelled him in power, and he became the most powerful himself. And it is perfectly clear that, in taking all the precautions which would assure the success of his enterprise, he in no wise neglected those which were sure to give him the first place in the Body he was creating.

More than that: he did not confine himself to forming formidable leagues beyond his frontiers, to making alliances with his own neighbours and the neighbours of his enemy. While engaging all these nations in the abasement of the first Power in Europe, he did not forget to put himself in the way of securing the coveted position for himself. He spent fifteen years of peace in preparations worthy of the enterprise he had in mind. He filled his coffers with money, his arsenals with artillery, arms and munitions. He amassed resources of all kinds against unforeseen demands. But he did more than all, we may be very sure, by governing his people wisely, by silently removing all seeds of division, by putting his finances in such order as to meet all possible needs without any vexation of his subjects. So it was that, at peace within and formidable abroad, he saw himself in a position to arm and maintain sixty thousand men and twenty vessels of war, to quit his kingdom without leaving behind him the smallest germ of disorder and to carry on war for six years without touching his ordinary revenue or laying on a penny of new taxes.

To all these preparations must be added the assurance that the enterprise would be carried out, both by his minister and himself, with the same energy and prudence that had conceived and framed it. And, finally, the knowledge that all the military operations would be directed by a captain of his skill, while the enemy had none left to put against him. From all this it may be judged if any element which could promise success was wanting to his prospects. Without having fathomed his designs, all Europe was watching his preparations with a kind of awe. The great revolution was about to be launched on a slight pretext. A war, destined to be the end of all wars, was about to usher in eternal peace, when a deed, the horror of which is only increased by its mystery, came to quench for ever the last hope of the world. The blow which cut short the days of this good king, also plunged Europe back into ceaseless wars, of which she can now never hope to see the end.

Such were the means prepared by Henry IV for founding the Federation which the Abbé de Saint Pierre proposed to set up by a book.

Let us not say, then, that, if his system has not been adopted, that is because it was not good. Let us rather say that it was too good to be adopted. Evils and abuses, by which so many men profit, come in of themselves. Things of public utility, on the other hand, are seldom brought in but by force, for the simple reason that private interests are almost always ranged against them. Beyond doubt, a lasting peace is, under present circumstances, a project ridiculous enough. But give us back Henry IV and Sully, and it will become once more a reasonable proposal. Or rather, while we admire so fair a project, let us console ourselves for its failure by the thought that it could only have been carried out by violent means from which humanity must needs shrink.

No Federation could ever be established except by a revolution. That being so, which of us would dare to say whether the League of Europe is a thing more to be desired or feared? It would perhaps do more harm in a moment than it would guard against for ages.

8

Toward Perpetual Peace

Immanuel Kant

A condition of peace among men living near one another is not a state of nature (*status naturalis*), which is much rather a condition of war, that is, it involves the constant threat of an outbreak of hostilities even if this does not always occur. A condition of peace must therefore be *established;* for suspension of hostilities is not yet assurance of peace, and unless such assurance is afforded one neighbor by another (as can happen only in a *lawful* condition), the former, who has called upon the latter for it, can treat him as an enemy.[1]

First Definitive Article for Perpetual Peace

The civil constitution in every state shall be republican.

A constitution established, first on principles of the *freedom* of the members of a society (as individuals), second on principles of the *dependence* of all upon a single common legislation (as subjects), and third on the law of their *equality* (*as citizens of a state*)—the sole constitution that issues from the idea of the original contract, on which all rightful legislation of a people must be based—is a *republican* constitution.[2] The republican constitution is thus, as far as right is concerned, in itself that which every kind of civil constitution has as its original basis; the question now is only whether it is also the sole constitution that can lead toward perpetual peace.

Now, in addition to the purity of its origin—its having arisen from the pure source of the concept of right—the republican constitution does offer the prospect of the result wished for, namely perpetual peace; the ground of this is as follows. When the consent of the citizens of a state is required in order to decide whether there shall be war or not (and it cannot be otherwise in this constitution), nothing is more natural than that they will be very hesitant to begin such a bad game, since they would have to decide to take upon themselves all the hardships of war (such as themselves doing the fighting and paying the costs of the war from their own belongings, painfully making good the devastation it leaves behind, and finally—to make the cup of troubles overflow—a burden of debt that embitters peace itself, and that can never be paid off because of new wars always impending); on the other hand, under a constitution in which subjects are not citizens of the state, which is therefore not republican [deciding upon war] is the easiest thing in the world; because the head of state is not a member of the state but its proprietor and gives up nothing at all of his feasts, hunts, pleasure palaces, court festivals, and so forth, he can decide upon war, as upon a kind of pleasure party, for insignificant cause, and can with indifference leave the justification of the war, for the sake of propriety, to the diplomatic corps, which is always ready to provide it.

* * *

So that a republican constitution will not be confused with a democratic constitution (as usually happens), the following must be noted. The forms of a state (*civitas*) can be divided either according to the different persons who have supreme power within a state or according to the *way* a people is *governed* by its head of state, whoever this may be; the first is called, strictly speaking, the form of *sovereignty (forma imperii)*, and only three such forms are possible: namely, either only *one*, or *some* in association, or *all* those together who constitute the civil society possess sovereign power (*autocracy, aristocracy*, and *democracy*, the power of a prince, the power of a nobility, and the power of a people). The second is the form of government (*forma regiminis*) and has to do with the way a state, on the basis of its civil constitution (the act of the general will by which a multitude becomes a people), makes use of its plenary power; and with regard to this, the form of a state is either *republican* or *despotic. Republicanism* is the political principle of separation of the executive power (the government) from the legislative power; despotism is that of the high-handed management of the state by laws the regent has himself given, inasmuch as he handles the public will as his private will. Of the three forms of state, that of *democracy* in the strict sense of the word is necessarily a *despotism* because it establishes an executive power in which all decide for and, if need be, against one (who thus does not agree), so that all, who are nevertheless not all, decide; and this is a contradiction of the general will with itself and with freedom.

This is to say that any form of government which is not *representative* is, strictly speaking, *without form*, because the legislator cannot be in one and the same person also executor of its will (any more than the universal of the major premise in a syllogism can also be the subsumption of the particular under it in the minor premise); and even if the other two state constitutions are always defective insofar as they leave room for this kind of government, in their case it is at least possible for them to adopt a kind of government in conformity with the *spirit* of a representative system, as Frederick II, for example, at least *said* that he was only the highest servant of the state,[3] whereas a democratic constitution makes this impossible because there everyone wants to be ruler. It can therefore be said that the smaller the number of persons exercising the power of a state (the number of rulers) and the greater their representation, so much the more does its constitution accord with the possibility of republicanism, and the constitution can hope by gradual reforms finally to raise itself to this. On this basis it is already harder in an aristocracy than in a monarchy to achieve this sole constitution that is perfectly rightful, but in a democracy it is impossible except by violent revolution. The kind of government, however, is of incomparably greater concern to the people than is the form of state (though a good deal also depends on how adequate the latter is to the former's end). But if the kind of government is to be in conformity with the concept of right, it must have a representative system, in which alone a republican kind of government is possible and without which the government is despotic and violent (whatever the constitution may be). None of the ancient republics, so called, knew this system, and because of this they simply had to disintegrate into despotism, which under the rule of a single individual is still the most bearable of all.

SECOND DEFINITIVE ARTICLE FOR PERPETUAL PEACE

The right of nations shall be based on a *federalism* of free states.

Nations, as states, can be appraised as individuals, who in their natural condition (that is, in their independence from external laws) already wrong one another by being near one another; and each of them, for the sake of its security, can and ought to require the others to enter with it into a constitution similar to a civil constitution, in which each can be assured of its right. This would be a *league of nations*, which, however, need not be a state of nations. That would be a contradiction, inasmuch as every state involves the relation of a *superior* (legislating) to an *inferior* (obeying, namely the people); but a number of nations within one state would constitute only one nation, and this contradicts the presupposition (since here we have to consider the right of *nations* in relation to one another insofar as they comprise different states and are not to be fused into a single state).

Just as we now regard with profound contempt, as barbarous, crude, and brutishly degrading to humanity, the attachment of savages to their lawless freedom, by which they would rather struggle unceasingly than subject themselves to a lawful coercion to be instituted by themselves, thus preferring a mad freedom to a rational freedom, so, one would think, civilized peoples (each united into a state) must hasten to leave such a depraved condition, the sooner the better; but instead each *state* puts its majesty (for the majesty of a people is an absurd expression) just in its not being subject to any external lawful coercion at all, and the splendor of its chief consists in his being able, without even having to put himself in danger, to command many thousands to sacrifice themselves for a matter that is of no concern to them;[4] and the difference between the European and the American savages consists mainly in this: that whereas many tribes of the latter have been eaten up by their enemies, the former know how to make better use of those they have defeated than to make a meal of them, and would rather increase the number of their subjects, and so too the multitude of their instruments for even more extensive wars, by means of them.

In view of the malevolence of human nature, which can be seen unconcealed in the free relations of nations (whereas in a condition under civil laws it is greatly veiled by the government's constraint), it is surprising that the word *right* could still not be altogether banished as pedantic from the politics of war and that no state has yet been bold enough to declare itself publicly in favor of this view; for Hugo Grotius, Pufendorf, Vattel, and the like (only sorry comforters)—although their code, couched philosophically or diplomatically, has not the slightest *lawful* force and cannot even have such force (since states as such are not subject to a common external constraint)—are always duly cited in *justification* of an offensive war, though there is no instance of a state ever having been moved to desist from its plan by arguments armed with the testimony of such important men. This homage that every state pays the concept of right (at least verbally) nevertheless proves that there is to be found in the human being a still greater, though at present dormant, moral predisposition to eventually become master of the evil principle within him (which he cannot deny) and also to hope for this from others; for otherwise the word *right* would never be spoken by states wanting to attack one another, unless merely to make fun of it, as a certain Gallic prince defined right: "It is the prerogative nature has given the stronger over the weaker, that the latter should obey him."

The way in which states pursue their right can never be legal proceedings before an external court but can only be war; but right cannot be decided by war and its favorable outcome, *victory*; and by a *peace pact* a current war can be brought to an end but not a condition of war, of always finding pretexts for a new war (and this cannot straightaway be declared wrong, since in this condition each is judge in his own case); however, what holds in accordance with natural right for human beings in a lawless condition, "they ought to leave this condition," cannot hold for states in accordance with the right of nations (since, as states, they already have a rightful constitution internally and hence have outgrown the constraint of others to bring them under a more extended law-governed constitution in accordance with their concepts of right); yet reason, from the throne of the highest morally legislative power, delivers an absolute condemnation of war as a procedure for determining rights and, on the contrary, makes a condition of peace, which cannot be instituted or assured without a pact of nations among themselves, a direct duty; so there must be a league of a special kind, which can be called a *pacific league (foedus pacificum)*, and what would distinguish it from a *peace pact (pactum pacis)* is that the latter seeks to end only *one* war whereas the former seeks to end *all war* forever. This league does not look to acquiring any power of a state but only to preserving and securing the *freedom* of a state itself and of other states in league with it, but without there being any need for them to subject themselves to public laws and coercion under them (as people in a state of nature must do). The practicability (objective reality) of this idea of a *federalism* that should gradually extend over all states and so lead to perpetual peace can be shown. For if good fortune should ordain that a powerful and enlightened people can form itself into a republic (which by its nature must be inclined to perpetual peace), this would provide a focal point of federative union for other states, to attach themselves to it and so to secure a condition of freedom of states conformably with the idea of the right of nations; and by further alliances of this kind, it would gradually extend further and further.

It is understandable for a people to say, "There shall be no war among us; for we want to form ourselves into a state, that is, to establish for ourselves a supreme legislative, executive, and judicial power, which settles our disputes peaceably." But if this state says, "There shall be no war between myself and other states, although I recognize no supreme legislative power which secures my right to me and to which I secure its right," it is not understandable on what I want to base my confidence in my right, unless it is the surrogate of the civil social union, namely the free federalism that reason must connect necessarily with the concept of the right of nations if this is to retain any meaning at all.

The concept of the right of nations as that of the right *to go to* war is, strictly speaking, unintelligible (since it is supposed to be a right to determine what is right not by universally valid external laws limiting the freedom of each but by unilateral maxims through force); one would have to mean by it that it is quite right if human beings so disposed destroy one another and thus find perpetual peace in the vast grave that covers all the horrors of violence along with their authors. In accordance with reason there is only one way that states in relation with one another can leave the lawless condition, which involves nothing but war; it is that, like individual human beings, they give up their savage (lawless) freedom, accommodate themselves to public coercive laws, and so form an (always growing) *state of nations (civitas gentium)* that would finally encompass all the nations of the earth. But, in accordance with their idea of the right of nations, they do not at all want this, thus rejecting *in hypothesi* what is correct *in thesi;* so (if all is not to be lost) in place of the positive idea *of a world republic* only the *negative* surrogate of a *league* that averts war, endures, and always expands can hold back the stream of hostile inclination that shies away from right, though with constant danger of its breaking out.[5] (*Furor impius intus—fremit horridus ore cruento.* Virgil.)[6][. . .]

Now we come to the question concerning what is essential to the purpose of perpetual peace: what nature does for this purpose with reference to the end that the human being's own reason makes a duty for him, hence to the favoring of his *moral purpose*, and how it affords the guarantee that what man *ought* to do in accordance with laws of freedom but does not do, it is assured he *will* do, without prejudice to this freedom, even by a constraint of nature, and this in terms of all three relations of public right: the *right of a state*, the *right of nations* and *cosmopolitan right.* When I say of nature, it *wills* that this or that happen, this does not mean, it lays upon us a *duty* to do it (for only practical reason, without coercion, can do that) but rather that nature itself *does* it, whether we will it or not (*fata volentem ducunt, nolentem trahunt*).[7]

1. Even if a people were not forced by internal discord to submit to the constraint of public laws, war would still force them from without to do so, inasmuch as by the natural arrangement discussed above each people would

find itself in the neighborhood of another people pressing upon it, against which it must form itself internally into a *state* in order to be armed as a *power* against it. Now the *republican* constitution is the only one that is completely compatible with the right of human beings, but it is also the most difficult one to establish and even more to maintain, so much so that many assert it would have to be a state of *angels* because human beings, with their self-seeking inclinations, would not be capable of such a sublime form of constitution. But now nature comes to the aid of the general will grounded in reason, revered but impotent in practice, and does so precisely through those self-seeking inclinations, so that it is a matter only of a good organization of a state (which is certainly within the capacity of human beings), of arranging those forces of nature in opposition to one another in such a way that one checks the destructive effect of the other or cancels it, so that the result for reason turns out as if neither of them existed at all and the human being is constrained to become a good citizen even if not a morally good human being. The problem of establishing a state, no matter how hard it may sound, is *soluble* even for a nation of devils (if only they have understanding) and goes like this: "Given a multitude of rational beings all of whom need universal laws for their preservation but each of whom is inclined covertly to exempt himself from them, so to order this multitude and establish their constitution that, although in their private dispositions they strive against one another, these yet so check one another that in their public conduct the result is the same as if they had no such evil dispositions." Such a problem must be soluble. For the problem is not the moral improvement of human beings but only the mechanism of nature, and what the task requires one to know is how this can be put to use in human beings in order so to arrange the conflict of their unpeaceable dispositions within a people that they themselves have to constrain one another to submit to coercive law and so bring about a condition of peace in which laws have force. It can be seen even in actually existing states, still very imperfectly organized, that they are already closely approaching in external conduct what the idea of right prescribes, though the cause of this is surely not inner morality (for it is not the case that a good state constitution is to be expected from inner morality; on the contrary, the good moral education of a people is to be expected from a good state constitution), and thus that reason can use the mechanism of nature, through self-seeking inclinations that naturally counteract one another externally as well, as a means to make room for its own end, the rule of right, and in so doing also to promote and secure peace within as well as without, so far as a state itself can do so. Here it is therefore said that nature *wills* irresistibly that right should eventually gain supremacy. What we here neglect to do eventually comes about of its own accord, though with great inconvenience. "If one bends the reed too hard it breaks; and he who wills too much wills nothing." Bouterwek.

2. The idea of the right of nations presupposes the *separation* of many neighboring states independent of one another; and though such a condition is of itself a condition of war (unless a federative union of them prevents the

outbreak of hostilities), this is nevertheless better, in accordance with the idea of reason, than the fusion of them by one power overgrowing the rest and passing into a universal monarchy, since as the range of government expands laws progressively lose their vigor, and a soulless despotism, after it has destroyed the seed of good, finally deteriorates into anarchy. Yet the craving of every state (or of its head) is to attain a lasting condition of peace in this way, by ruling the whole world where possible. But *nature wills* it otherwise. It makes use of two means to prevent peoples from intermingling and to separate them: differences of *language* and of *religion*,[8] which do bring with them the propensity to mutual hatred and pretexts for war but yet, with increasing culture and the gradual approach of human beings to greater agreement in principles, leads to understanding in a peace that is produced and secured, not as in such a despotism (in the graveyard of freedom), by means of a weakening of all forces, but by means of their equilibrium in liveliest competition.

Just as nature wisely separates states that the will of each state, and even on grounds of the right of nations, would like to unite under itself by cunning or force, so on the other hand it also unites nations that the concept of cosmopolitan right would not have secured against violence and war, and does so by means of their mutual self-interest. It is the *spirit of commerce*, which cannot coexist with war and which sooner or later takes hold of every nation. In other words, since the *power of money* may well be the most reliable of all the powers (means) subordinate to that of a state, states find themselves compelled (admittedly not through incentives of morality) to promote honorable peace and, whenever war threatens to break out anywhere in the world, to prevent it by mediation, just as if they were in a permanent league for this purpose; for, by the nature of things, great alliances for war can only rarely be formed and even more rarely succeed. In this way nature guarantees perpetual peace through the mechanism of human inclinations itself, with an assurance that is admittedly not adequate for *predicting* its future (theoretically) but that is still enough for practical purposes and makes it a duty to work toward this (not merely chimerical) end. [. . .]

From all these twistings and turnings by which an immoral doctrine of prudence tries to bring a condition of peace among human beings out of the warlike condition of a state of nature, at least this much is clear: people can no more get away from the concept of right in their private relations than in their public relations, and they dare not openly base politics merely on the machinations of prudence and so disown all allegiance to the concept of a public right (this is especially noticeable in the concept of the right of nations); instead they give it all the honor due it, even if they should think up a hundred pretexts and subterfuges to evade it in practice, and attribute to cunning force the authority of being the source and the bond of all right. In order to put an end to this sophistry (if not to the injustice glossed over by it) and to bring the false *representatives* of the powerful on earth to confess that they speak not on behalf of right but of force—the tone of which they adopt, as if it were for them to give orders—it will be well to expose the illusion with which they dupe themselves and others, to find the supreme principle from which the aim of perpetual peace issues, and to show that all the evil standing in its way arises from the fact that the political moralist begins where the moral politician correctly leaves off and, in thus subordinating principles to the end (i.e., putting the cart before the horse), frustrates his own purpose of bringing politics into agreement with morals.

In order to make practical philosophy consistent with itself, it is necessary first to decide the question, whether in problems of practical reason one must begin from its *material principle*, the *end* (as object of choice), or from its *formal* principle, that is, the principle (resting only on freedom in external relations) in accordance with which it is said: So act that you can will that your maxim should become a universal law (whatever the end may be).

The latter principle must undoubtedly take precedence; for, as a principle of right, it has unconditional necessity, whereas the former necessitates only if the empirical conditions of the proposed end, namely of its being realized, are presupposed; and even if this end (e.g., perpetual peace) were also a duty, it would still have to be derived from the formal principle of maxims for acting externally. Now the first principle, that of the *political moralist* (the problem of the right of a state, the right of nations, and cosmopolitan right), is a mere *technical problem (problema technicum)*, whereas the second, as the principle of the *moral politician*, for whom it is a *moral problem (problema morale)*, is far removed from the other in its procedure for leading to perpetual peace, which is now wished for not only as a natural good but also as a condition[9] arising from acknowledgment of duty.

For the solution of the first problem, namely that of political prudence, much knowledge of nature is required in order to make use of its mechanism for the end proposed, and yet all this is uncertain with respect to its result concerning perpetual peace, whichever of the three divisions of public right one takes. Whether a people can better be kept obedient and also prosperous for a long period of time by severity or by the bait of vanity, whether by the supreme power of one individual or by several leaders united, perhaps even by an aristocracy of merit only or by the power of the people within it, is uncertain. History provides examples of the opposite [resulting] from all kinds of government (with the single exception of the truly republican one, which, however, can occur only to a moral politician). Still more uncertain is a *right of nations* supposedly established on statutes according to ministerial plans, which right is in fact only an empty word and rests on pacts that contain in the very act of their being concluded the secret reservation that they may be violated. On the other hand, the solution of the second problem, namely *that of political wisdom*, urges itself upon us of its own accord, so to speak, is clear to everyone, and puts all artifices to shame; moreover, it leads straight to the end, but with the reminder of prudence not to draw toward it precipitately by force but to approach it steadily as favorable circumstances arise.

It can therefore be said, "Seek ye first the kingdom of pure practical reason and its *justice*, and your end (the blessing of perpetual peace) will come to you of itself." For morals has in it the peculiarity—and indeed with respect to its principles of public right (hence with reference to a politics cognizable a priori)—that the less it makes conduct dependent upon the proposed end, the intended advantage whether natural or moral, so much the more does it harmonize with it on the whole; and this happens because it is just the general will given a priori (within a nation or in the relation of various nations to one another) that alone determines what is laid down as right among human beings; but this union of the will of all, if only it is acted upon consistently in practice, can also, in accordance with the mechanism of nature, be the cause bringing about the effect aimed at and providing the concept of right with efficacy. Thus it is, for example, a principle of moral politics that a people is to unite itself into a state in accordance with freedom and equality as the sole concepts of right, and this principle is not based upon prudence but upon duty. On the other hand political moralists, however subtly they reason about how the natural mechanism of a multitude of human beings entering into society would invalidate those principles and thwart their purpose, and also try to prove their contention against them by examples of badly organized constitutions of ancient and modern times (e.g., of democracies without a representative system), do not deserve a hearing, especially since such a pernicious theory itself produces the trouble it predicts, throwing human beings into one class with other living machines, which need only be aware that they are not free in order to become, in their own judgment, the most miserable of all beings in the world.

The proposition that has become proverbial, *fiat iustitia, pereat mundus*,[10] or in German, "let justice reign even if all the rogues in the world perish because of it," sounds rather boastful but it is true; it is a sturdy principle of right, which bars all the devious paths marked out by cunning or force, provided it is not misinterpreted and taken, as it might be, as permission to make use of one's own right with utmost rigor (which would conflict with ethical duty) but is taken instead as the obligation of those in power not to deny anyone his right or to encroach upon it out of disfavor or sympathy for others; and for this there is required, above all, a constitution organized in accordance with pure principles of right within a state, and then too the union of this state with other neighboring or even distant states for a lawful settlement of their disputes (by analogy with a universal state). This proposition means nothing other than that political maxims must not issue from the welfare and happiness of each state that is to be expected from following them, and so not from the end that each of them makes its object—(from "I will")[11] as the supreme (though empirical) principle of political wisdom—but must issue from the pure concept of duty of right (from "I ought,"[12] the principle of which is given a priori by pure reason), whatever the natural consequences may be. The world will by no means perish by there coming to be fewer evil people. What is morally evil has the property, inseparable from its nature, of being at odds with itself in its aims and destructive of them (especially in relation to others similarly disposed), so that it clears the way for the (moral) principle of the good, even if progress is slow.

Thus there is *objectively* (in theory) no conflict at all between morals and politics. But *subjectively* (in the self-seeking propensity of human beings, which, however, because it is not based on maxims of reason, must still not be called practice), such conflict will remain; and it may always remain because it serves as the whetstone of virtue, whose true courage (according to the principle *tu ne cede malis, sed contra audientior ito*)[13] in the present case consists, not so much in resolutely standing up to the troubles and sacrifices one must thereby take upon oneself, but in looking straight in the face what is far more dangerous, the deceitful and treacherous but yet subtly reasoning principle in ourselves which pretends that the weakness of human nature justifies any transgression, and in overcoming its craftiness.

In fact the political moralist can say that regent and people or nation and nation do *each other* no wrong when they attack each other by force or fraud, though they do wrong generally in that they deny all respect to the concept of right, which alone could found peace in perpetuity. For since one of them transgresses his duty toward the other, who is just as wrongfully disposed toward him, when the two destroy themselves it *happens* to both of them quite rightly, though in such a way that there is always enough of this race left to keep this game going to the most distant times, so that posterity may some day take a warning example from them. Providence is thus justified in the course of the world; for the moral principle in the human being never dies out, and reason, which is capable pragmatically of carrying out rightful ideas in accordance with that principle, grows steadily with advancing culture, but so too does the guilt for those transgressions. It seems that creation alone, namely that such a race of corrupt beings should have been put on earth at all, cannot be justified by any theodicy (if we assume that the human race never will be or can be better off); but this standpoint for appraising matters is much too high for us, as if we could support for theoretical purposes our concepts (of the wisdom) of the supreme power inscrutable to us. To such desperate conclusions we are unavoidably driven if we do not assume that pure principles of right have objective reality, that is, that they can be carried out; and people within a state as well as states in their relations with one another must act in accordance with those principles, regardless of what objections empirical politics may bring against them. True politics can therefore not take a step without having already paid homage to morals, and although politics by itself is a difficult art, its union with morals is no art at all; for as soon as the two conflict with each other, morals cuts the knot that politics cannot untie. The right of human beings must be held sacred, however great a sacrifice this may cost the ruling power. One cannot compromise here and devise something intermediate, a pragmatically conditioned right (a cross between right and expediency); instead, all politics must bend its knee before right, but in return it can hope to reach, though slowly, the level where it will shine unfailingly. [. . .]

NOTES

1. It is usually assumed that one may not behave with hostility toward another unless he has actively *wronged* me; and that is also quite correct if both are in a condition of *being under civil laws*. For by having entered into such a condition one affords the other the requisite assurance (by means of a superior having power over both).—But a human being (or a nation) in a mere state of nature denies me this assurance and already wrongs me just by being near me in this condition, even if not actively (*facto*) yet by the lawlessness of his condition (*statu iniusto*), by which he constantly threatens me; and I can coerce him either to enter with me into a condition of being under civil laws or to leave my neighborhood. Hence the postulate on which all the following articles are based is that all men who can mutually affect one another must belong to some civil constitution.

   But any rightful constitution is, with regard to the persons within it,

   (1) one in accord with the *right of citizens of a state*, of individuals within a people (*ius civitatis*),
   (2) one in accord with the *right of nations*, of states in relation to one another (*ius gentium*),
   (3) one in accord with the *right of citizens of the world*, insofar as individuals and states, standing in the relation of externally affecting one another, are to be regarded as citizens of a universal state of mankind (*ius cosmopoliticum*). This division is not made at will [*willkürlich*] but is necessary with reference to the idea of perpetual peace. For if only one of these were in a relation of physically affecting another and were yet in a state of nature, the condition of war would be bound up with this, and the aim here is just to be freed from it.

2. *Rightful* (hence external) *freedom* cannot be defined, as it usually is, by the warrant to do whatever one wants provided one does wrong be anyone. For what does *warrant* mean? The possibility of an action insofar as one thereby does no wrong to anyone. So the definition would go as follows: freedom is the possibility of actions whereby one does no wrong to anyone. One does no wrong to anyone (one may do what one wants) provided one does no wrong to anyone; hence it is an empty tautology. My external (rightful) *freedom* is, instead, to be defined as follows: it is the warrant to obey no other external laws than those to which I could have given my consent. Similarly, external (rightful) *equality* within a state is that relation of its citizens in which no one can rightfully bind another to something without also being subject to a law by which he in turn *can* be bound in the same way by the other. (There is no need to define the principle of *rightful* dependence, since it is already present in the concept of a state constitution as such.) The validity of these innate and inalienable rights belonging necessarily to humanity is confirmed and enhanced by the principle of rightful relations of a human being even to higher beings (if he thinks of them), inasmuch as he represents himself, in accord with the very same principles, as also a citizen of a state in a supersensible world. For, as regards my freedom, I have no obligation even with respect to divine laws that I can cognize by reason alone except insofar as I could have given my consent to them (since it is by the law of freedom of my own reason that I first make for myself a concept of the divine will). As regards the principle of equality with respect to the most sublime being in the world, except for God, that I might happen to think of (a great *Aeon*): if I do my duty in my post as that Aeon does his

duty in his, there is no basis for mere obedience to duty belonging to me and the right to command to him. That this principle of *equality* is not (like the principle of freedom) also appropriate to our relation to God has its ground in this: that he is the only being to whom the concept of duty is inapplicable.

But as regards the right of equality of all citizens of a state as subjects, the answer to the question, whether a *hereditary nobility* is allowable, turns only on whether the *rank* granted by a state (of one subject being above another) would have to precede *merit*, or whether the latter would have to precede the former. Now it is obvious that if rank is connected with birth, it is quite uncertain whether merit (skill and fidelity in one's office) will follow; hence it will be just as if rank (being in command) were granted to a favorite without any merit, and the general will of a people in the original contract (which is yet the principle of all rights) will never decide upon this. For a nobleman is not necessarily a *noble* man. As for *nobility of office* (as the rank of a higher magistracy could be called, which must be acquired for oneself by merit), there rank adheres to a post, not as property to a person, and equality is not violated by it; for, when he retires from his office, he also lays down his rank and goes back among the people.

3. The exalted epithets often bestowed on a ruler ("the divinely anointed," "the administrator of the divine will on earth and its representative") have often been censured as gross and dizzying flattery, but, it seems to me, without grounds. Far from making the ruler of a country arrogant, they would rather have to humble him in his soul if he is intelligent (as must be assumed) and make him reflect that he has taken on an office too great for a human being—namely the most sacred office that God has on earth, that of trustee of *the right of human beings*—and that he must always be concerned about having in some way offended against this "apple of God's eye."
4. Thus a Bulgarian prince gave the following reply to the Greek emperor's benign offer to settle their dispute by a duel: "A smith who has tongs will not lift the glowing iron from the coals with his own hands."
5. At the end of a war, when peace is concluded, it would not be unfitting for a nation to proclaim, after the festival of thanksgiving, a day of atonement, calling upon heaven, in the name of the state, to forgive the great sin of which the human race continues to be guilty, that of being unwilling to acquiesce in any lawful constitution in relation to other nations but, proud of its independence, preferring instead to use the barbarous means of war (even though what is sought by war, namely the right of each state, is not decided by it). Festivals of thanksgiving during a war for a *victory* won, hymns that (in the style of the Israelites) are sung to the *Lord of Hosts*, stand in no less marked contrast with the moral idea of the father of human beings; for, beyond indifference to the way nations seek their mutual rights (which is regrettable enough), they bring in joy at having annihilated a great many human beings or their happiness.
6. Within, impious rage—shall roar savagely with bloody mouth. *Aeneid* I.294–6.
7. The Fates lead the willing, drive the unwilling. Seneca *Epist. Mor.* 18.4.
8. *Different religions:* an odd expression! just as if one could also speak of different *morals*. There can indeed be historically different *creeds* [to be found] not in religion but in the history of means used to promote it, which is the province of scholarship, and just as many different *religious books* (the Zendavesta, the Vedas, the Koran, and so forth), but there can be only one single *religion* holding for all human beings and in all times. Those can therefore contain nothing more than the

vehicle of religion, what is contingent and can differ according to differences of time and place.

9. *Zustand.*
10. Do justice though the world perish.
11. *vom Wollen.*
12. *vom Sollen.*
13. Do not yield to troubles, but press on more boldly. Virgil *Aeneid* 6.95.

III

The "American Invention" and Nineteenth-Century Debates Over Rival Types of Federalism

9

Editors' Introduction

The history of federal theory takes a radical turn with the American invention of a new type of federal system in late eighteenth century. With the transition from the Articles of Confederation of 1781 to the Constitution of 1787, the United States became the first example of what we now refer to as a federation, as distinguished from a confederation. For the first time in both practice and theory, the new Constitution proposed a union not just of political entities, like states, but also of all of the citizens of all of these entities. The new central or federal government would represent two kinds of members, states (in the Senate at that time), and individual citizens of the federation itself (in the House of Representatives and the presidency). We now refer to this model of governance as a "federation," and distinguish it from a "confederation," which is a union primarily of independent states (and not really of all of the citizens of all of these states). While this terminological distinction would not appear until the late nineteenth century—50 years later Tocqueville was using the terms "*new* and *ancient* species of confederation" to mark the difference between what we now call "federation" and "confederation"— the innovative features of the new American system did not take long to generate a major debate. In this third section, we have included selections from five central figures of this new debate: "Publius" (the pseudonym of the three authors of *The Federalist*, namely, James Madison, John Jay, and Alexander Hamilton); John Calhoun, an antebellum Southern political figure and scholar; Alexis de Tocqueville, an aristocratic observer of the young American republic a half-century after its founding; John Stuart Mill, the great English political philosopher of the Victorian era; and Pierre-Joseph Proudhon, the late-nineteenth-century French utopian–socialist theorist.

Written with obvious political purpose as a series of newspaper articles during the ratification debate of the Constitution of 1787, *The Federalist* (1787–1788) is nonetheless widely recognized as the first and most influential theoretical reflection on the new type of federal arrangement inaugurated in the United States. Our selection focuses on the following key theses of *The Federalist:* America is "one nation"; federalism may protect republics against domestic faction and insurrection; the authority of the Union must be extended to the persons of the citizens; the proposed Constitution is "neither a national nor a federal [i.e., *con*federal] Constitution, but a composition of both"; the State governments benefit from structural advantages and there is more risk of anarchy among them than there is of tyranny from the federal government.

In the first part of the nineteenth century, Calhoun provided the most influential critique of Publius's interpretation of the American model of federalism. His political speeches and more theoretical works contributed significantly to the pre–Civil War debates over the nature of the American federal system. We have included the first part of the Fort Hill Address (entitled "On the Relation which the States and General Government Bear to Each Other," 1831), an early application of Calhoun's political theory to the American case. Although it was written with prudence when the author was vice president of the United States, it provides a succinct summary of the conceptions of community interests, self-preservation rights, constitution, federal government, compact, concurrent majority and nullification expressed in his two principal works, *A Disquisition on Government* and *A Discourse on the Constitution and Government of the United States* (1851).

The selections from Tocqueville's *Democracy in America* (1835) and Mill's *Considerations on Representative Government* (1861) were both major contributions to the nineteenth-century debates. First, while Tocqueville and Mill were clearly sympathetic with Publius's characterization of the American federal system, they also clarified and refined "his" analysis and concepts (with the benefit of several decades of hindsight, of course). Second, they provided two pioneering and mostly complementary syntheses of the advantages, defects, and conditions of success of this new species of federal system. These syntheses are still of considerable interest for contemporary theorists of federalism.

Finally, we present extracts from Proudhon's *The Principle of Federation* (1863). Proudhon's conception of federalism broke with previous models in several ways, although it was institutionally much closer to the "ancient" species of (con)federal system. In the twentieth-century debate over the integration of Europe, his relatively numerous followers in Europe would call this conception "integral federalism," involving confederations of confederations in the economic as well as in the political sphere, and at both the national and the international level. Our selection here presents Proudhon's case for why integral federalism is the solution to the political problem of reconciling liberty and authority.

10

Federal Theory in *The Federalist*

Alexander Hamilton, John Jay, and James Madison

No. II

Concerning Dangers from Foreign Force and Influence

When the people of America reflect that they are now called upon to decide a question which in its consequences must prove one of the most important that ever engaged their attention, the propriety of their taking a very comprehensive, as well as a very serious, view of it will be evident.

Nothing is more certain than the indispensable necessity of government, and it is equally undeniable that, whenever and however it is instituted, the people must cede to it some of their natural rights, in order to vest it with requisite powers. It is well worthy of consideration, therefore, whether it would conduce more to the interest of the people of America, that they should to all general purposes, be one nation, under one federal government, or that they should divide themselves into separate confederacies, and give to the head of each the same kind of powers which they are advised to place in one national government.

It has until lately been a received and uncontradicted opinion that the prosperity of the people of America depended on their continuing firmly united, and the wishes, prayers, and efforts of our best and wisest citizens have been constantly directed to that object. But politicians now appear who insist that this opinion is erroneous, and that instead of looking for safety and happiness in union we ought to seek it in a division of the States into distinct confederacies or sovereignties. However extraordinary this new doctrine may appear, it, nevertheless, has its advocates; and certain characters who were much opposed to it formerly, are at present of the number. Whatever may be the arguments or inducements which have wrought this change in the sentiments and declarations of these gentlemen, it certainly would not be wise in the people at large to adopt these new political tenets without being fully convinced that they are founded in truth and sound policy.

It has often given me pleasure to observe that independent America was not composed of detached and distant territories, but that one connected, fertile, wide-spreading country was the portion of our Western sons of liberty. Providence has in a particular manner blessed it with a variety of soils and productions, and watered it with innumerable streams, for the delight and accommodation of its inhabitants. A succession of navigable waters forms a kind of chain round its borders, as if to bind it together; while the most noble rivers in the world, running at convenient distances, present them with highways for the easy communication of friendly aids, and the mutual transportation and exchange of their various commodities.

With equal pleasure I have as often taken notice that Providence has been pleased to give this one connected country, to one united people, a people descended from the same ancestors, speaking the same language, professing the same religion, attached to the same principles of government, very similar in their manners and customs, and who, by their joint counsels, arms, and efforts, fighting side by side throughout a long and bloody war, have nobly established their general liberty and independence.

This country and this people seem to have been made for each other, and it appears as if it was the design of Providence that an inheritance so proper and convenient for a band of brethren, united to each other by the strongest ties, should never be split into a number of unsocial, jealous, and alien sovereignties.

Similar sentiments have hitherto prevailed among all orders and denominations of men among us. To all general purposes we have uniformly been one people; each individual citizen everywhere enjoying the same national rights, privileges, and protection. As a nation we have made peace and war: as a nation we have vanquished our common enemies: as a nation we have formed alliances and made treaties, and entered into various compacts and conventions with foreign States.

A strong sense of the value and blessings of Union induced the people, at a very early period, to institute a federal government to preserve and perpetuate it. They formed it almost as soon as they had a political existence; nay, at a time when their habitations were in flames, when many of their citizens were bleeding, and when the progress of hostility and desolation left little room for those calm and mature inquiries and reflections which must ever precede the formation of a wise and well-balanced government for a free people. It is not to be wondered at that a government instituted in times so inauspicious should on experiment be found greatly deficient and inadequate to the purpose it was intended to answer.

This intelligent people perceived and regretted these defects. Still continuing no less attached to Union, than enamoured of liberty, they observed the danger, which immediately threatened the former and more remotely the latter; and being persuaded that ample security for both could only be found in a national government more wisely framed, they, as with one voice, convened the late Convention at Philadelphia, to take that important subject under consideration.

This Convention, composed of men who possessed the confidence of the people, and many of whom had become highly distinguished by their patriotism, virtue, and wisdom, in times which tried the minds and hearts of men, undertook the arduous task. In the mild season of peace, with minds unoccupied by other subjects, they passed many months in cool, uninterrupted, and daily consultations; and finally, without having been awed by power, or influenced by any passions except love for their country, they presented and recommended to the people the plan produced by their joint and very unanimous councils. [. . .] PUBLIUS

No. IX

Union a Safeguard Against Faction and Insurrection

A Firm Union will be of the utmost moment to the peace and liberty of the States, as a barrier against domestic faction and insurrection. It is impossible to read the history of the petty republics of Greece and Italy without feeling sensations of horror and disgust at the distractions with which they were continually agitated, and at the rapid succession of revolutions, by which they were kept in a state of perpetual vibration, between the extremes of tyranny and anarchy. If they exhibit occasional calms, these only serve as short-lived contrasts to the furious storms that are to succeed. If, now and then, intervals of felicity open themselves to view, we behold them with a mixture of regret, arising from the reflection that the pleasing scenes before us are soon to be overwhelmed by the tempestuous waves of sedition and party rage. If momentary rays of glory break forth from the gloom, while they dazzle us with a transient and fleeting brilliancy, they at the same time admonish us to lament that the vices of government should pervert the direction and tarnish the lustre of those bright talents and exalted endowments for which the favored soils that produced them have been so justly celebrated.

From the disorders that disfigure the annals of those republics the advocates of despotism have drawn arguments, not only against the forms of republican government, but against the very principles of civil liberty. They have decried all free government as inconsistent with the order of society, and have indulged themselves in malicious exultation over its friends and partisans. Happily for mankind, stupendous fabrics reared on the basis of liberty, which have flourished for ages, have, in a few glorious instances, refuted their gloomy sophisms. And, I trust, America will be the broad and solid foundation of other edifices, not less magnificent, which will be equally permanent monuments of their errors.

But it is not to be denied that the portraits they have sketched of republican government were too just copies of the originals from which they were taken. If it had been found impracticable to have devised models of a more perfect structure, the enlightened friends to liberty would have been obliged to abandon the cause of that species of government as indefensible. The science of politics, however, like most other sciences, has received great improvement. The efficacy of various principles is now well understood, which were either not known at all or imperfectly known to the ancients. The regular distribution of power into distinct departments; the introduction of legislative balances and checks; the institution of courts composed of judges holding their offices during good behavior; the representation of the people in the legislature, by deputies of their own election—these are either wholly new discoveries or have made their principal progress toward perfection in modern times. They are means, and powerful means, by which the excellences of republican government may be retained, and its imperfections lessened or avoided. To this catalogue of circumstances that tend to the amelioration of popular systems of civil government, I shall venture, however novel it may appear to some, to add one more, on a principle which has been made the foundation of an objection to the new Constitution; I mean the enlargement of the orbit within which such systems are to revolve, either in respect to the dimensions of a single State or to the consolidation of several smaller States into one great confederacy. The latter is that which immediately concerns the object under consideration. It will, however, be of use to examine the principle, in its application to a single State, which shall be attended to in another place.

The utility of a confederacy, as well to suppress faction, and to guard the internal tranquillity of States, as to increase their external force and security, is in reality not a new idea. It has been practised upon, in different countries and ages, and has received the sanction of the most approved writers on the subjects of politics. The opponents of the plan proposed, have, with great assiduity, cited and circulated the observations of Montesquieu on the necessity of a contracted territory for a republican government. But they seem not to have been apprised of the sentiments of that great man, expressed in another part of his work, nor to have adverted to the consequences of the principle, to which they subscribe with such ready acquiescence.

When Montesquieu recommends a small extent for republics, the standards he had in view were of dimensions far short of the limits of almost every one of these States. Neither Virginia, Massachusetts, Pennsylvania, New York, North Carolina, nor Georgia can by any means be compared with the models from which he reasoned, and to which the terms of his description apply. If we, therefore, take his ideas on this point as the criterion of truth, we shall be driven to the alternative either of taking refuge at once in the arms of monarchy or of splitting ourselves into an infinity of little, jealous, clashing, tumultuous commonwealths, the wretched nurseries of unceasing discord and the miserable objects of universal pity or contempt. Some of the writers, who have come forward on the other side of the question, seem to have been aware of the dilemma; and have even been bold enough to hint at the division of the larger States as a desirable thing. Such an infatuated policy, such a desperate expedient, might, by the multiplication of petty offices, answer the views of men who possess not qualifications to extend their influence beyond the narrow circles of personal intrigue; but it could never promote the greatness or happiness of the people of America.

Referring the examination of the principle itself to another place, as has been already mentioned, it will be sufficient to remark here that in the sense of the author who has been most emphatically quoted upon the occasion, it would only dictate a reduction of the size of the more considerable members of the Union; but would not militate against their being all comprehended in one confederate government. And this is the true question, in the discussion of which we are at present interested.

So far are the suggestions of Montesquieu from standing in opposition to a general Union of the States, that he explicitly treats of a confederate republic as the expedient for extending the sphere of popular government, and reconciling the advantages of monarchy with those of republicanism.

"It is very probable," says he,* "that mankind would have been obliged, at length, to live constantly under the Government of a single person, had they not contrived a kind of Constitution, that has all the internal advantages of a Republican, together with the external force of a Monarchical Government. I mean a Confederate Republic.

"This form of Government is a Convention by which several smaller States agree to become members of a larger one, which they intend to form. It is a kind of assemblage of societies, that constitute a new one, capable of increasing by means of new associations, till they arrive to such a degree of power, as to be able to provide for the security of the united body.

"A Republic of this kind, able to withstand an external force, may support itself without any internal corruptions. The form of this society prevents all manner of inconveniences.

"If a single member should attempt to usurp the supreme authority, he could not be supposed to have an equal authority and credit in all the Confederate States. Were he to have too great influence over one, this would alarm the rest. Were he to subdue a part, that which would still remain free might oppose him with forces, independent of those which he had usurped, and overpower him before he could be settled in his usurpation.

"Should a popular insurrection happen in one of the Confederate States, the others are able to quell it. Should abuses creep into one part, they are reformed by those that remain sound. The State may be destroyed on one side, and not on the other; the Confederacy may be dissolved, and the Confederates preserve their Sovereignty.

"As this Government is composed of small Republics, it enjoys the internal happiness of each; and with respect to its external situation, it is possessed, by means of the Association, of all the advantages of large Monarchies."

I have thought it proper to quote at length these interesting passages, because they contain a luminous abridgment of the principal arguments in favor of the Union, and must effectually remove the false impressions, which a misapplication of other parts of the work was calculated to make. They have, at the same time, an intimate connection with the more immediate

* "Spirit of Laws," Vol. I. bk. IX. Chap. I.

design of this paper which is, to illustrate the tendency of the Union to repress domestic faction and insurrection.

A distinction, more subtle than accurate, has been raised between a confederacy and a consolidation of the States. The essential characteristic of the first is said to be, the restriction of its authority to the members in their collective capacities, without reaching to the individuals of whom they are composed. It is contended that the national council ought to have no concern with any object of internal administration. An exact equality of suffrage between the members has also been insisted upon as a leading feature of a confederate government. These positions are, in the main, arbitrary; they are supported neither by principle nor precedent. It has, indeed, happened that governments of this kind have generally operated in the manner which the distinction, taken notice of, supposes to be inherent in their nature; but there have been in most of them extensive exceptions to the practice, which serve to prove, as far as example will go, that there is no absolute rule on the subject. And it will be clearly shown, in the course of this investigation, that as far as the principle contended for has prevailed, it has been the cause of incurable disorder and imbecility in the government.

The definition of a confederate republic seems simply to be, "an assemblage of societies," or an association of two or more States into one State. The extent, modifications, and objects of the federal authority are mere matters of discretion. So long as the separate organization of the members be not abolished; so long as it exists, by a constitutional necessity, for local purposes; though it should be in perfect subordination to the general authority of the Union, it would still be, in fact and in theory, an association of States, or a confederacy. The proposed Constitution, so far from implying an abolition of the State governments, makes them constituent parts of the national sovereignty, by allowing them a direct representation in the Senate, and leaves in their possession certain exclusive and very important portions of sovereign power. This fully corresponds, in every rational import of the terms, with the idea of a federal government.

In the Lycian Confederacy, which consisted of twenty-three "cities," or republics, the largest were entitled to three votes in the Common Council, those of the middle class to two, and the smallest to one. The Common Council had the appointment of all the judges and magistrates of the respective cities. This was certainly the most delicate species of interference in their internal administration; for if there be anything that seems exclusively appropriated to the local jurisdictions, it is the appointment of their own officers. Yet Montesquieu, speaking of this association, says, "Were I to give a model of an excellent confederate republic, it would be that of Lycia." Thus we perceive that the distinctions insisted upon were not within the contemplation of this enlightened civilian; and we shall be led to conclude that they are the novel refinements of an erroneous theory.

PUBLIUS

No. X

The Numerous Advantages of the Union

Among the numerous advantages promised by a well-constructed union, none deserves to be more accurately developed than its tendency to break and control the violence of faction. The friend of popular governments never finds himself so much alarmed for their character and fate as when he contemplates their propensity to this dangerous vice. He will not fail, therefore, to set a due value on any plan which, without violating the principles to which he is attached, provides a proper cure for it. The instability, injustice, and confusion introduced into the public councils have, in truth, been the mortal diseases under which popular governments have everywhere perished; as they continue to be the favorite and fruitful topics from which the adversaries to liberty derive their most specious declamations. The valuable improvements made by the American constitutions on the popular models, both ancient and modern, cannot certainly be too much admired; but it would be an unwarrantable partiality, to contend that they have as effectually obviated the danger on this side as was wished and expected. Complaints are everywhere heard from our most considerate and virtuous citizens, equally the friends of public and private faith and of public and personal liberty, that our governments are too unstable; that the public good is disregarded in the conflicts of rival parties; and that measures are too often decided, not according to the rules of justice, and the rights of the minor party, but by the superior force of an interested and overbearing majority. However anxiously we may wish that these complaints had no foundation, the evidence of known facts will not permit us to deny that they are in some degree true. It will be found, indeed, on a candid review of our situation, that some of the distresses under which we labor have been erroneously charged on the operation of our governments; but it will be found, at the same time, that other causes will not alone account for many of our heaviest misfortunes; and, particularly, for that prevailing and increasing distrust of public engagements, and alarm for private rights, which are echoed from one end of the continent to the other. These must be chiefly, if not wholly, effects of the unsteadiness and injustice with which a factious spirit has tainted our public administrations.

By a faction, I understand a number of citizens, whether amounting to a majority or minority of the whole, who are united and actuated by some common impulse of passion, or of interest, adverse to the rights of other citizens or to the permanent and aggregate interests of the community.

There are two methods of curing the mischiefs of faction: the one, by removing its causes; the other, by controlling its effects.

There are again two methods of removing the causes of faction: the one, by destroying the liberty which is essential to its existence; the other, by giving to every citizen the same opinions, the same passions, and the same interests.

It could never be more truly said than of the first remedy, that it was worse than the disease. Liberty is to faction what air is to fire, an ailment without which it instantly expires. But it could not be less folly to abolish liberty, which is essential to political life, because it nourishes faction, than it would be to wish the annihilation of air, which is essential to animal life, because it imparts to fire its destructive agency.

The second expedient is as impracticable as the first would be unwise. As long as the reason of man continues fallible, and he is at liberty to exercise it, different opinions will be formed. As long as the connection subsists between his reason and his self-love, his opinions and his passions will have a reciprocal influence on each other; and the former will be objects to which the latter will attach themselves. The diversity in the faculties of men, from which the rights of property originate, is not less an insuperable obstacle to a uniformity, of interests. The protection of these faculties is the first object of government. From the protection of different and unequal faculties of acquiring property, the possession of different degrees and kinds of property immediately results; and from the influence of these on the sentiments and views of the respective proprietors, ensues a division of the society into different interests and parties.

The latent causes of faction are thus sown in the nature of man; and we see them everywhere brought into different degrees of activity, according to the different circumstances of civil society. A zeal for different opinions concerning religion, concerning government and many other points, as well of speculation as of practice; an attachment to different leaders ambitiously contending for pre-eminence and power, or to persons of other descriptions whose fortunes have been interesting to the human passions, have, in turn, divided mankind into parties, inflamed them with mutual animosity, and rendered them much more disposed to vex and oppress each other, than to co-operate for their common good. So strong is this propensity of mankind to fall into mutual animosities, that where no substantial occasion presents itself, the most frivolous and fanciful distinctions have been sufficient to kindle their unfriendly passions and excite their most violent conflicts. But the most common and durable source of factions has been the various and unequal distribution of property. Those who hold and those who are without property have ever formed distinct interests in society. Those who are creditors and those who are debtors fall under a like discrimination. A landed interest, a manufacturing interest, a mercantile interest, a moneyed interest, with many lesser interests, grow up of necessity in civilized nations, and divide them into different classes, actuated by different sentiments and views. The regulation of these various and interfering interests forms the principal task of modern legislation, and involves the spirit of party and faction in the necessary and ordinary operations of the government.

No man is allowed to be a judge in his own cause; because his interest would certainly bias his judgment and, not improbably, corrupt his integrity. With equal, nay, with greater reason, a body of men are unfit to be both judges and parties at the same time; yet what are many of the most important acts of legislation, but so many judicial determinations, not indeed concerning the rights of single persons, but concerning the rights of large bodies of citizens? and what are the different classes of legislators, but advocates and parties to the causes which they determine? Is a law proposed concerning private debts?—it is a question to which the creditors are parties on one side, and the debtors on the other. Justice ought to hold the balance between them. Yet the parties are, and must be, themselves the judges; and the most numerous party, or, in other words, the most powerful faction, must be expected to prevail. Shall domestic manufactures be encouraged, and in what degree, by restrictions on foreign manufactures? are questions which would be differently decided by the landed and the manufacturing classes, and probably by neither with a sole regard to justice and the public good. The apportionment of taxes on the various descriptions of property is an act which seems to require the most exact impartiality; yet there is, perhaps, no legislative act in which greater opportunity and temptation are given to a predominant party, to trample on the rules of justice. Every shilling with which they overburden the inferior number is a shilling saved to their own pockets.

It is in vain to say that enlightened statesmen will be able to adjust these clashing interests and render them all subservient to the public good. Enlightened statesmen will not always be at the helm; nor, in many cases, can such an adjustment be made at all, without taking into view indirect and remote considerations, which will rarely prevail over the immediate interest which one party may find in disregarding the rights of another or the good of the whole.

The inference to which we are brought is that the causes of faction cannot be removed, and that relief is only to be sought in the means of controlling its effects.

If a faction consists of less than a majority, relief is supplied by the republican principle, which enables the majority to defeat its sinister views by regular vote. It may clog the administration, it may convulse the society; but it will be unable to execute and mask its violence under the forms of the Constitution. When a majority is included in a faction, the form of popular government, on the other hand, enables it to sacrifice to its ruling passion or interest both the public good and the rights of other citizens. To secure the public good, and private rights, against the danger of such a faction, and at the same time to preserve the spirit and the form of popular government, is then the great object to which our inquiries are directed. Let me add that it is the great *desideratum*, by which alone this form of government can be rescued from the opprobrium under which it has so long labored, and be recommended to the esteem and adoption of mankind.

By what means is this object attainable? Evidently by one of two only. Either the existence of the same passion or interest in a majority, at the same time, must be prevented; or the majority, having such coexistent passion or interest, must be rendered, by their number and local situation, unable to concert and carry into effect schemes of oppression. If the impulse and the opportunity be suffered to coincide, we well know that neither moral nor religious motives can be relied on as an adequate control. They are not found to be such on the injustice and violence of individuals, and lose their efficacy in proportion to the number combined together; that is, in proportion as their efficacy becomes needful.

From this view of the subject it may be concluded that a pure democracy, by which I mean a society consisting of a small number of citizens, who assemble and administer the government in person, can admit of no cure for the mischiefs of faction. A common passion or interest will, in almost every case, be felt by a majority of the whole; a communication and concert results from the form of government itself; and there is nothing to check the inducements to sacrifice the weaker party or an obnoxious individual. Hence it is that such democracies have ever been spectacles of turbulence and contention; have ever been found incompatible with personal security, or the rights of property, and have in general been as short in their lives as they have been violent in their deaths. Theoretic politicians, who have patronized this species of government, have erroneously supposed that by reducing mankind to a perfect equality in their political rights, they would at the same time be perfectly equalized and assimilated in their possessions, their opinions, and their passions.

A republic, by which I mean a government in which the scheme of representation takes place, opens a different prospect, and promises the cure for which we are seeking. Let us examine the points in which it varies from pure democracy, and we shall comprehend both the nature of the cure and the efficacy which it must derive from the union.

The two great points of difference between a democracy and a republic are: First, the delegation of the government, in the latter, to a small number of citizens elected by the rest; secondly, the greater number of citizens, and greater sphere of country, over which the latter may be extended.

The effect of the first difference is, on the one hand, to refine and enlarge the public views, by passing them through the medium of a chosen body of citizens, whose wisdom may best discern the true interest of their country, and whose patriotism and love of justice will be least likely to sacrifice it to temporary or partial considerations. Under such a regulation, it may well happen that the public voice, pronounced by the representatives of the people, will be more consonant to the public good than if pronounced by the people themselves, convened for the purpose. On the other hand, the effect may be inverted. Men of factious tempers, of local prejudices, or of sinister designs, may by intrigue, by corruption, or by other means, first obtain the suffrages, and then betray the interests of the people. The question resulting is, whether small or extensive republics are most favorable to the election of proper guardians of the public weal; and it is clearly decided in favor of the latter by two obvious considerations.

In the first place, it is to be remarked that, however small the republic may be, the representatives must be raised to a certain number, in order to guard against the cabals of a few; and that, however large it may be, they must be limited to a certain number, in order to guard against the confusion of a multitude. Hence, the number of representatives in the two cases not being in proportion to that of the constituents, and being proportionally greatest in the small republic, it follows that if the proportion of fit characters be not less in the large than in the small republic, the former will present a greater option, and consequently a greater probability of a fit choice.

In the next place, as each representative will be chosen by a greater number of citizens in the large than in the small republic, it will be more difficult for unworthy candidates to practise with success the vicious arts, by which elections are too often carried; and the suffrages of the people, being more free, will be more likely to centre in men who possess the most attractive merit and the most diffusive and established characters.

It must be confessed that in this as in most other cases, there is a mean, on both sides of which inconveniences will be found to lie. By enlarging too much the number of electors, you render the representative too little acquainted with all their local circumstances and lesser interests; as by reducing it too much, you render him unduly attached to these, and too little fit to comprehend and pursue great and national objects. The federal Constitution forms a happy combination in this respect; the great and aggregate interests being referred to the national, the local and particular to the State, legislatures.

The other point of difference is, the greater number of citizens and extent of territory which may be brought within the compass of republican than of democratic government; and it is this circumstance principally which renders factious combinations less to be dreaded in the former, than in the latter. The smaller the society, the fewer probably will be the distinct parties and interests composing it; the fewer the distinct parties and interests, the more frequently will a majority be found of the same party; and the smaller the number of individuals composing a majority, and the smaller the compass within which they are placed, the more easily will they concert and execute their plans of oppression. Extend the sphere, and you take in a greater variety of parties and interests; you make it less probable that a majority of the whole will have a common motive to invade the rights of other citizens ; or if such a common motive exists, it will be more difficult for all who feel it to discover their own strength, and to act in unison with each other. Besides other impediments, it may be remarked that where there is a consciousness of unjust or dishonorable purposes, communication is always checked by distrust, in proportion to the number whose concurrence is necessary.

Hence it clearly appears that the same advantage which a republic has over a democracy, in controlling the effects of faction, is enjoyed by a large over a small republic—is enjoyed by the Union over the States composing it. Does the advantage consist in the substitution of representatives, whose enlightened views and virtuous sentiments render them superior to local prejudices, and to schemes of injustice? It will not be denied that the representation of the Union will be most likely to possess these requisite endowments. Does it consist in the greater security afforded by a greater variety of parties, against the event of any one party being able to outnumber and oppress the rest?

In an equal degree does the increased variety of parties, comprised within the Union, increase this security. Does it, in fine, consist in the greater obstacles opposed to the concert and accomplishment of the secret wishes of an unjust and interested majority? Here, again, the extent of the Union gives it the most palpable advantage.

The influence of factious leaders may kindle a flame within their particular States, but will be unable to spread a general conflagration through the other States. A religious sect may degenerate into a political faction in a part of the confederacy; but the variety of sects dispersed over the entire face of it must secure the national councils against any danger from that source. A rage for paper money, for an abolition of debts, for an equal division of property, or for any other improper or wicked project will be less apt to pervade the whole body of the Union than a particular member of it; in the same proportion as such a malady is more likely to taint a particular county or district than an entire State.

In the extent and proper structure of the Union, therefore, we behold a republican remedy for the diseases most incident to republican government. And according to the degree of pleasure and pride we feel in being republicans, ought to be our zeal in cherishing the spirit and supporting the character of federalists.

PUBLIUS

No. XV

Legislative Defects of the Confederation

In the course of the preceding papers I have endeavored, my fellow-citizens, to place before you, in a clear and convincing light, the importance of Union to your political safety and happiness. I have unfolded to you a complication of dangers to which you would be exposed, should you permit that sacred knot which binds the people of America together to be severed or dissolved by ambition or by avarice, by jealousy or by misrepresentation. In the sequel of the inquiry through which I propose to accompany you, the truths intended to be inculcated will receive further confirmation from facts and arguments hitherto unnoticed. If the road, over which you will still have to pass, should in some places appear to you tedious or irksome, you will recollect that you are in quest of information on a subject the most momentous which can engage the attention of a free people; that the field through which you have to travel is in itself spacious, and that the difficulties of the journey have been unnecessarily increased by the mazes with which sophistry has beset the way. It will be my aim to remove the obstacles to your progress, in as compendious a manner as it can be done, without sacrificing utility to despatch.

In pursuance of the plan which I have laid down, for the discussion of the subject, the point next in order to be examined is the "insufficiency of the present confederation to the preservation of the Union." It may perhaps be asked, what need there is of reasoning or proof to illustrate a position which is not either controverted or doubted; to which the understandings and feelings of all classes of men assent, and which in substance is admitted by the opponents as well as by the friends of the new Constitution? It must in truth be acknowledged that, however these may differ in other respects, they in general appear to harmonize in this sentiment, at least, that there are material imperfections in our national system, and that something is necessary to be done to rescue us from impending anarchy. The facts that support this opinion are no longer objects of speculation. They have forced themselves upon the sensibility of the people at large, and have at length extorted from those, whose mistaken policy has had the principal share in precipitating the extremity at which we are arrived, a reluctant confession of the reality of those defects in the scheme of our federal government which have been long pointed out and regretted by the intelligent friends of the Union.

We may, indeed, with propriety, be said to have reached almost the last stage of national humiliation. There is scarcely anything that can wound the pride, or degrade the character of an independent nation, which we do not experience. Are there engagements, to the performance of which we are held by every tie respectable among men? These are the subjects of constant and unblushing violation. Do we owe debts to foreigners and to our own citizens, contracted in a time of imminent peril, for the preservation of our political existence? These remain without any proper or satisfactory provision for their discharge. Have we valuable territories and important posts in the possession of a foreign power, which, by express stipulations, ought long since to have been surrendered? These are still retained, to the prejudice of our interests not less than of our rights. Are we in a condition to resent or to repel the aggression? We have neither troops, nor treasury, nor government.* Are we even in a condition to remonstrate with dignity? The just imputations on our own faith, in respect to the same treaty, ought first to be removed. Are we entitled by nature and compact to a free participation in the navigation of the Mississippi? Spain excludes us from it. Is public credit an indispensable resource in time of public danger? We seem to have abandoned its cause as desperate and irretrievable. Is commerce of importance to national wealth? Ours is at the lowest point of declension. Is respectability in the eyes of foreign powers a safeguard against foreign encroachments? The imbecility of our government even forbids them to treat with us. Our ambassadors abroad are the mere pageants of mimic sovereignty. Is a violent and unnatural decrease in the value of land a symptom of national distress? The price of improved land in most parts of the country is much lower than can be accounted for by the quantity of waste land at market, and can only be fully explained by that want of private and public confidence which is so alarmingly prevalent among all ranks, and which have a direct tendency to depreciate property of every kind. Is private credit the friend and patron of industry? That most useful kind which relates to borrowing and lending is

* I mean for the Union.

reduced within the narrowest limits, and this still more from an opinion of insecurity than from the scarcity of money. To shorten an enumeration of particulars which can afford neither pleasure nor instruction, it may in general be demanded what indication is there of national disorder, poverty, and insignificance that could befall a community so peculiarly blessed with natural advantages as we are, which does not form a part of the dark catalogue of our public misfortunes?

This is the melancholy situation, to which we have been brought by those very maxims and councils, which would now deter us from adopting the proposed Constitution; and which, not content with having conducted us to the brink of a precipice, seem resolved to plunge us into the abyss that awaits us below. Here, my countrymen, impelled by every motive that ought to influence an enlightened people, let us make a firm stand for our safety, our tranquillity, our dignity, our reputation. Let us at last break the fatal charm which has too long seduced us from the paths of felicity and prosperity.

It is true, as has been before observed, that facts, too stubborn to be resisted, have produced a species of general assent to the abstract proposition that there exist material defects in our national system; but the usefulness of the concession, on the part of the old adversaries of federal measures, is destroyed by a strenuous opposition to a remedy, upon the only principles that can give it a chance of success. While they admit that the government of the United States is destitute of energy, they contend against conferring upon it those powers which are requisite to supply that energy: They seem still to aim at things repugnant and irreconcilable; at an augmentation of federal authority, without a diminution of State authority; at sovereignty in the Union, and complete independence in the members. They still, in fine, seem to cherish with blind devotion the political monster of an *imperium in imperio.* This renders a full display of the principal defects of the confederation necessary, in order to show, that the evils we experience do not proceed from minute or partial imperfections, but from fundamental errors in the structure of the building, which cannot be amended, otherwise than by an alteration in the first principles and main pillars of the fabric.

The great and radical vice in the construction of the existing confederation is in the principle of legislation for States or governments, in their corporate or collective capacities, and as contradistinguished from the individuals of which they consist. Though this principle does not run through all the powers delegated to the Union, yet it pervades and governs those on which the efficacy of the rest depends. Except as to the rule of apportionment, the United States have an indefinite discretion to make requisitions for men and money; but they have no authority to raise either, by regulations extending to the individual citizens of America. The consequence of this is that, though in theory their resolutions concerning those objects are laws, constitutionally binding on the members of the Union, yet in practice they are mere recommendations, which the States observe or disregard at their option.

It is a singular instance of the capriciousness of the human mind that after all the admonitions we have had from experience on this head, there should still be found men who object to the new Constitution, for deviating from a principle which has been found the bane of the old, and which is, in itself, evidently incompatible with the idea of government; a principle, in short, which, if it is to be executed at all, must substitute the violent and sanguinary agency of the sword to the mild influence of the magistracy.

There is nothing absurd or impracticable in the idea of a league or alliance between independent nations for certain defined purposes precisely stated in a treaty regulating all the details of time, place, circumstance, and quantity, leaving nothing to future discretion, and depending for its execution on the good faith of the parties. Compacts of this kind exist among all civilized nations, subject to the usual vicissitudes of peace and war, of observance and non-observance, as the interests or passions of the contracting powers dictate. In the early part of the present century there was an epidemical rage in Europe for this species of compacts; from which the politicians of the times fondly hoped for benefits which were never realized. With a view to establishing the equilibrium of power and the peace of that part of the world, all the resources of negotiation were exhausted, and triple and quadruple alliances were formed; but they were scarcely formed before they were broken, giving an instructive but afflicting lesson to mankind, how little dependence is to be placed on treaties which have no other sanction than the obligations of good faith; and which oppose general considerations of peace and justice to the impulse of any immediate interest or passion.

If the particular States in this country are disposed to stand in a similar relation to each other, and to drop the project of a general discretionary superintendence, the scheme would indeed be pernicious, and would entail upon us all the mischiefs which have been enumerated under the first head; but it would have the merit of being, at least, consistent and practicable. Abandoning all views toward a confederate government, this would bring us to a simple alliance offensive and defensive, and would place us in a situation to be alternately friends and enemies of each other, as our mutual jealousies and rivalships, nourished by the intrigues of foreign nations, should prescribe to us.

But if we are unwilling to be placed in this perilous situation; if we still adhere to the design of a national government, or, which is the same thing, of a superintending power, under the direction of a common council, we must resolve to incorporate into our plan those ingredients which may be considered as forming the characteristic difference between a league and a government; we must extend the authority of the Union to the persons of the citizens—the only proper objects of government.

Government implies the power of making laws. It is essential to the idea of a law that it be attended with a sanction, or, in other words, a penalty or punishment for disobedience. If there be no penalty annexed to disobedience, the resolutions or commands which pretend to be laws will, in fact, amount to nothing more than advice or recommendation. This penalty, whatever it may be, can only be inflicted in two ways—by the agency of the courts and ministers of justice or by military force; by the coercion of the magistracy or by the coercion of arms. The first kind can evidently apply only to men; the last kind must, of necessity, be employed against bodies politic or communities or States. It is evident that there is no process of a court by which the observance of the laws can, in the last resort, be enforced. Sentences may be denounced against them for violations of their duty; but these sentences can only be carried into execution by the sword. In an association where the general authority is confined to the collective bodies of the communities that compose it, every breach of the laws must involve a state of war; and military execution must become the only instrument of civil obedience. Such a state of things can certainly not deserve the name of government, nor would any prudent man choose to commit his happiness to it.

There was a time when we were told that breaches, by the States, of the regulations of the federal authority were not to be expected; that a sense of common interest would preside over the conduct of the respective members, and would beget a full compliance with all the constitutional requisitions of the Union. This language, at the present day, would appear as wild as a great part of what we now hear from the same quarter will be thought, when we shall have received further lessons from that best oracle of wisdom, experience. It at all times betrayed an ignorance of the true springs by which human conduct is actuated, and belied the original inducements to the establishment of civil power. Why has government been instituted at all? Because the passions of men will not conform to the dictates of reason and justice, without constraint. Has it been found that bodies of men act with more rectitude or greater disinterestedness than individuals? The contrary of this has been inferred by all accurate observers of the conduct of mankind; and the inference is founded upon obvious reasons. Regard to reputation has a less active influence, when the infamy of a bad action is to be divided among a number, than when it is to fall singly upon one. A spirit of faction, which is apt to mingle its poison in the deliberations of all bodies of men, will often hurry the persons of whom they are composed into improprieties and excesses, for which they would blush in a private capacity.

In addition to all this, there is in the nature of sovereign power an impatience of control that disposes those who are invested with the exercise of it to look with an evil eye upon all external attempts to restrain or direct its operations. From this spirit it happens that in every political association which is formed upon the principle of uniting in a common interest a number of lesser sovereignties, there will be found a kind of eccentric tendency in the subordinate or inferior orbs, by the operation of which there will be a perpetual effort in each to fly off from the common centre. This tendency is not difficult to be accounted for. It has its origin in the love of power. Power controlled or abridged is almost always the rival and enemy of that power by which it is controlled or abridged. This simple proposition will teach us how little reason there is to expect that the persons intrusted with the administration of the affairs of the particular members of a confederacy will at all times be ready, with perfect good-humor, and an unbiased regard to the public weal, to execute the resolutions or decrees of the general authority. The reverse of this results from the constitution of human nature.

If, therefore, the measures of the confederacy cannot be executed without the intervention of the particular administrations, there will be little prospect of their being executed at all. The rulers of the respective members, whether they have a constitutional right to do it or not, will undertake to judge of the propriety of the measures, themselves. They will consider the conformity of the thing proposed or required to their immediate interests or aims; the momentary conveniences or inconveniences that would attend its adoption. All this will be done, and in a spirit of interested and suspicious scrutiny, without that knowledge of national circumstances and reasons of state which is essential to a right judgment, and with that strong predilection in favor of local objects which can hardly fail to mislead the decision. The same process must be repeated in every member of which the body is constituted; and the execution of the plans, framed by the councils of the whole, will always fluctuate on the discretion of the ill-informed and prejudiced opinion of every part. Those who have been conversant in the proceedings of popular assemblies; who have seen how difficult it often is, when there is no exterior pressure of circumstances, to bring them to harmonious resolutions on important points, will readily conceive how impossible it must be to induce a number of such assemblies, deliberating at a distance from each other, at different times, and under different impressions, long to co-operate in the same views and pursuits.

In our case, the concurrence of thirteen distinct sovereign wills is requisite, under the confederation, to the complete execution of every important measure that proceeds from the Union. It has happened as was to have been foreseen. The measures of the Union have not been executed; the delinquencies of the States have, step by step, matured themselves to an extreme which has at length arrested all the wheels of the national government and brought them to an awful stand. Congress at this time scarcely possess the means of keeping up the forms of administration, till the States can have time to agree upon a more substantial substitute for the present shadow of a federal government. Things did not come to this desperate extremity at once. The causes which have been specified produced at first only unequal and disproportionate degrees of compliance with the requisitions of the Union. The greater deficiencies of some States furnished the pretext of example and the temptation of interest to the complying or to the least delinquent States. Why should we do more in proportion than those who are embarked with us in the same political voyage? Why should we consent to bear more than our proper share of the common burden? These were suggestions which human selfishness could not withstand, and which even speculative men, who looked forward to remote consequences, could not, without hesitation, combat. Each State, yielding to the persuasive voice of immediate interest or convenience, has successively withdrawn its support, till the frail and tottering edifice seems ready to fall upon our heads, and to crush us beneath its ruins. PUBLIUS

No. XVII

As to the Tendency of Federal Governments

An objection, of a nature different from that which has been stated and answered in my last address, may perhaps be likewise urged against the principle of legislation for the individual citizens of America. It may be said that it would tend to render the government of the Union too powerful, and to enable it to absorb those residuary authorities which it might be judged proper to leave with the States for local purposes. Allowing the utmost latitude to the love of power which any reasonable man can require, I confess I am at a loss to discover what temptation the persons intrusted with the administration of the general government could ever feel to divest the States of the authorities of that description. The regulation of the mere domestic police of a State appears to me to hold out slender allurements to ambition. Commerce, finance, negotiation, and war seem to comprehend all the objects which have charms for minds governed by that passion; and all the powers necessary to those objects ought, in the first instance, to be lodged in the national depositary. The administration of private justice between the citizens of the same State, the supervision of agriculture and of other concerns of a similar nature, all those things, in short, which are proper to be provided for by local legislation, can never be desirable cares of a general jurisdiction. It is therefore improbable that there should exist a disposition in the federal councils to usurp the powers with which they are connected; because the attempt to exercise those powers would be as troublesome as it would be nugatory; and the possession of them, for that reason, would contribute nothing to the dignity, to the importance, or to the splendor of the national government.

But let it be admitted, for argument's sake, that mere wantonness and lust of domination would be sufficient to beget that disposition; still it may be safely affirmed that the sense of the constituent body of the national representatives, or, in other words, of the people of the several States, would control the indulgence of so extravagant an appetite. It will always be far more easy for the State governments to encroach upon the national authorities than for the national government to encroach upon the State authorities. The proof of this proposition turns upon the greater degree of influence which the State governments, if they administer their affairs with uprightness and prudence, will generally possess over the people; a circumstance which at the same time teaches us that there is an inherent and intrinsic weakness in all federal constitutions; and that too much pains cannot be taken in their organization, to give them all the force which is compatible with the principles of liberty.

The superiority of influence in favor of the particular governments would result partly from the diffusive construction of the national government, but chiefly from the nature of the objects to which the attention of the State administrations would be directed.

It is a known fact in human nature that its affections are commonly weak in proportion to the distance or diffusiveness of the object. Upon the same principle that a man is more attached to his family than to his neighborhood, to his neighborhood than to the community at large, the people of each State would be apt to feel a stronger bias toward their local governments than toward the Government of the Union; unless the force of that principle should be destroyed by a much better administration of the latter.

This strong propensity of the human heart would find powerful auxiliaries in the objects of State regulation.

The variety of more minute interests, which will necessarily fall under the superintendence of the local administrations, and which will form so many rivulets of influence, running through every part of the society, cannot be particularized, without involving a detail too tedious and uninteresting to compensate for the instruction it might afford.

There is one transcendent advantage belonging to the province of the State governments, which alone suffices to place the matter in a clear and satisfactory light; I mean the ordinary administration of criminal and civil justice. This, of all others, is the most powerful, most universal, and most attractive source of popular obedience and attachment. It is that which, being the immediate and visible guardian of life and property; having its benefits and its terrors in constant activity before the public eye; regulating all those personal interests, and familiar concerns, to which the sensibility of individuals is more immediately awake—contributes, more than any other circumstance, to impressing upon the minds of the people affection, esteem, and reverence toward the government. This great cement of society, which will diffuse itself almost wholly through the channels of the particular governments, independent of all other causes of influence, would insure them so decided an empire over their respective citizens as to render them at all times a complete counterpoise, and not unfrequently dangerous rivals to the power of the Union.

The operations of the national government, on the other hand, falling less immediately under the observation of the mass of the citizens, the benefits derived from it will chiefly be perceived and attended to by speculative men. Relating to more general interests, they will be less apt to come home to the feelings of the people; and, in proportion, less likely to inspire a habitual sense of obligation and an active sentiment of attachment.

The reasoning on this head has been abundantly exemplified by the experience of all federal constitutions with which we are acquainted, and of all others which have borne the least analogy to them.

Though the ancient feudal systems were not, strictly speaking, confederacies, yet they partook of the nature of that species of association. There was a common head, chieftain, or sovereign, whose authority extended over the whole nation; and a number of subordinate vassals, or feudatories, who had large portions of land allotted to them, and numerous trains of inferior vassals or retainers, who occupied and cultivated that land upon the tenure of fealty or obedience to the persons of whom they held it. Each principal vassal was a kind of sovereign within his particular demesnes. The consequences of this situation were a continual opposition to the authority of the sovereign, and frequent wars between the great barons or chief feudatories themselves. The power of the head of the nation was commonly too weak either to preserve the public peace or to protect the people against the oppressions of their immediate lords. This period of European affairs is emphatically styled by historians the times of feudal anarchy.

When the sovereign happened to be a man of vigorous and warlike temper and of superior abilities he would acquire a personal weight and influence which answered for the time the purposes of a more regular authority. But in general the power of the barons triumphed over that of the prince; and in many instances his dominion was entirely thrown off, and the great fiefs were erected into independent principalities or States. In those instances in which the monarch finally prevailed over his vassals, his success was chiefly owing to the tyranny of those vassals over their dependents. The barons or nobles, equally the enemies of the sovereign and the oppressors of the common people, were dreaded and detested by both, till mutual danger and mutual interest effected a union between them fatal to the power of the aristocracy. Had the nobles, by a conduct of clemency and justice, preserved the fidelity and devotion of their retainers and followers, the contests between them and the prince must almost always have ended in their favor and in the abridgment or subversion of the royal authority.

This is not an assertion founded merely in speculation or conjecture. Among other illustrations of its truth which might be cited, Scotland will furnish a cogent example. The spirit of clanship which was, at an early day, introduced into that kingdom, uniting the nobles and their dependents by ties equivalent to those of kindred, rendered the aristocracy a constant overmatch for the power of the monarch, till the incorporation with England subdued its fierce and ungovernable spirit, and reduced it within those rules of subordination, which a more rational and more energetic system of civil polity had previously established in the latter kingdom.

The separate governments in a confederacy may aptly be compared with the feudal baronies; with this advantage in their favor, that from the reasons already explained, they will generally possess the confidence and good-will of the people, and, with so important a support, will be able effectually to oppose all encroachments of the national government. It will be well, if they are not able to counteract its legitimate and necessary authority. The points of similitude consist in the rivalship of power, applicable to both, and in the concentration of large portions of the strength of the community into particular deposits, in one case at the disposal of individuals, in the other case at the disposal of political bodies.

A concise review of the events that have attended confederate governments will further illustrate this important doctrine; an inattention to which has been the great source of our political mistakes, and has given our jealousy a direction to the wrong side. This review shall form the subject of some ensuing papers.

PUBLIUS

No. XXXIX

The Plan of the Convention Republican in Principle

The last paper having concluded the observations which were meant to introduce a candid survey of the plan of government reported by the Convention, we now proceed to the execution of that part of our undertaking.

The first question that offers itself is whether the general form and aspect of the government be strictly republican. It is evident that no other form would be reconcilable with the genius of the people of America; with the fundamental principles of the Revolution; or with that honorable determination which animates every votary of freedom, to rest all our political experiments on the capacity of mankind for self-government. If the plan of the Convention, therefore, be found to depart from the republican character, its advocates must abandon it as no longer defensible.

What, then, are the distinctive characters of the republican form? Were an answer to this question to be sought, not by recurring to principles, but in the application of the term by political writers, to the constitutions of different States, no satisfactory one would ever be found. Holland, in which no particle of the supreme authority is derived from the people, has passed almost universally under the denomination of a republic. The same title has been bestowed on Venice, where absolute power over the great body of the people is exercised, in the most absolute manner, by a small body of hereditary nobles. Poland, which is a mixture of aristocracy and of monarchy in their worst forms, has been dignified with the same appellation. The government of England, which has one republican branch only, combined with an hereditary aristocracy and monarchy, has, with equal impropriety, been frequently placed on the list of republics. These examples, which are nearly as dissimilar to each other as to a genuine republic, show the extreme inaccuracy with which the term has been used in political disquisitions.

If we resort, for a criterion, to the different principles on which different forms of government are established, we may define a republic to be, or at least may bestow that name on a government which derives all its powers directly or indirectly from the great body of the people, and is administered by persons holding their offices during pleasure, for a limited period, or during good behavior. It is essential to such a government that it be derived from the great body of the society, not from an inconsiderable proportion or a favored class of it; otherwise a handful of tyrannical nobles, exercising their oppressions by a delegation of their powers, might aspire to the rank of republicans and claim for their government the honorable title of "republic." It is sufficient for such a government that the persons administering it be appointed, either directly or indirectly, by the people, and that they hold their appointments by either of the tenures just specified; otherwise every government in the United States, as well as every other popular government that has been or can be well organized or well executed, would be degraded from the republican character. According to the constitution of every State in the Union, some or other of the officers of government are appointed indirectly only by the people. According to most of them, the chief magistrate himself is so appointed. And according to one, this mode of appointment is extended to one of the co-ordinate branches of the legislature. According to all the constitutions, also, the tenure of the highest offices is extended to a definite period, and in many instances, both within the legislative and executive departments, to a period of years. According to the provisions of most of the constitutions, as well as according to the most respectable and received opinions on the subject, the members of the judiciary department are to retain their offices by the firm tenure of good behavior.

On comparing the Constitution planned by the Convention with the standard here fixed, we perceive at once that it is, in the most rigid sense, conformable to it. The House of Representatives, like that of one branch at least of all the State legislatures, is elected immediately by the great body of the people. The Senate, like the present Congress and the Senate of Maryland, derives its appointment indirectly from the people. The President is indirectly derived from the choice of the people, according to the example in most of the States. Even the judges, with all other officers of the Union, will, as in the several States, be the choice, though a remote choice, of the people themselves. The duration of the appointments is equally conformable to the republican standard, and to the model of the State constitutions. The House of Representatives is periodically elective, as in all the States, and for the period of two years, as in the State of South Carolina. The Senate is elective, for the period of six years, which is but one year more than the period of the Senate of Maryland, and but two more than that of the Senates of New York and Virginia. The President is to continue in office for the period of four years; as in New York and Delaware the chief magistrate is elected for three years, and in South Carolina for two years. In the other States the election is annual. In several of the States, however, no constitutional provision is made for the impeachment of the chief magistrate. And in Delaware and Virginia, he is not impeachable till out of office. The President of the United States is impeachable at any time during his continuance in office. The tenure by which the judges are to hold their places is, as it unquestionably ought to be, that of good behavior. The tenure of the ministerial offices generally will be a subject of legal regulation, conformably to the reason of the case and the example of the State constitutions.

Could any further proof be required of the republican complexion of this system, the most decisive one might be found in its absolute prohibition of titles of nobility, both under the federal and the State governments, and in its express guaranty of the republican form to each of the latter.

"But it was not sufficient," say the adversaries of the proposed Constitution, "for the Convention to adhere to the republican form. They ought, with equal care, to have preserved the federal form, which regards the Union as a confederacy of sovereign States; instead of which, they have framed a national government, which regards the Union as a consolidation of the States." And it is asked by what authority this bold and radical innovation was undertaken? The handle which has been made of this objection requires that it should be examined with some precision.

Without inquiring into the accuracy of the distinction on which the objection is founded, it will be necessary to a just estimate of its force, first, to ascertain the real character of the government in question; secondly, to inquire how far the Convention were authorized to propose such a government; and thirdly, how far the duty they owed to their country could supply any defect of regular authority.

First. In order to ascertain the real character of the government it may be considered in relation to the foundation on which it is to be established; to the sources from which its ordinary powers are to be drawn; to the operation of those powers; to the extent of them; and to the authority by which future changes in the government are to be introduced.

On examining the first relation, it appears, on one hand, that the Constitution is to be founded on the assent and ratification of the people of America, given by deputies elected for the special purpose; but, on the other, that this assent and ratification is to be given by the people, not as individuals composing one entire nation, but as composing the distinct and independent States to which they respectively belong. It is to be the assent and ratification of the several States, derived from the supreme authority in each State—the authority of the people themselves. The act, therefore, establishing the Constitution will not be a national, but a federal act.

That it will be a federal, and not a national act, as these terms are understood by the objectors, the act of the people, as forming so many independent States, not as forming one aggregate nation, is obvious from this single consideration, that it is to result neither from the decision of a majority of the people of the Union, nor from that of a majority of the States. It must result from the unanimous assent of the several States that are parties to it, differing no otherwise from their ordinary assent than in its being expressed, not by the legislative authority, but by that of the people themselves. Were the people regarded in this transaction as forming one nation, the will of the majority of the whole people of the United States would bind the minority, in the same manner as the majority in each State must bind the minority; and the will of the majority must be determined either by a comparison of the individual votes or by considering the will of the majority of the States as evidence of the will of a majority of the people of the United States. Neither of these rules has been adopted. Each State, in ratifying the Constitution, is considered as a sovereign body, independent of all others, and only to be bound by its own voluntary act. In this relation, then, the new Constitution will, if established, be a federal, and not a national Constitution.

The next relation is to the sources from which the ordinary powers of government are to be derived. The House of Representatives will derive its powers from the people of America; and the people will be represented in the same proportion, and on the same principle, as they are in the legislature of a particular State. So far the government is national, not federal. The Senate, on the other hand, will derive its powers from the States, as political and coequal societies; and these will be represented on the principle of equality in the Senate, as they now are in the existing Congress. So far the government is federal, not national. The executive power will be derived from a very compound source. The immediate election of the President is to be made by the States in their political characters. The votes allotted to them are in a compound ratio, which considers them partly as distinct and coequal societies, partly as unequal members of the same society. The eventual election, again, is to be made by that branch of the legislature which consists of the national representatives; but in this particular act, they are to be thrown into the form of individual delegations, from so many distinct and coequal bodies politic. From this aspect of the government, it appears to be of a mixed character, presenting at least as many federal as national features.

The difference between a federal and national government, as it relates to the operation of the government, is supposed to consist in this, that in the former the powers operate on the political bodies composing the confederacy, in their political capacities; in the latter, on the individual citizens composing the nation, in their individual capacities. On trying the Constitution by this criterion, it falls under the national, not the federal character, though, perhaps, not so completely as has been understood. In several cases, and particularly in the trial of controversies to which States may be parties, they must be viewed and proceeded against in their collective political capacities only. So far the national countenance of the government on this side seems to be disfigured by a few federal features. But this blemish is, perhaps, unavoidable in any plan; and the operation of the government on the people, in their individual capacities, in its ordinary and most essential proceedings, may, on the whole, designate it in this relation a national government.

But if the government be national with regard to the operation of its powers, it changes its aspect again when we contemplate it in relation to the extent of its powers. The idea of a national government involves in it, not only an authority over the individual citizens, but an indefinite supremacy over all persons and things, so far as they are objects of lawful government. Among a people consolidated into one nation, this supremacy is completely vested in the national legislature. Among communities united for particular purposes it is vested partly in the general and partly in the municipal legislatures. In the former case all local authorities are subordinate to the supreme, and may be controlled, directed, or abolished by it at pleasure. In the latter the local or municipal authorities form distinct and independent portions of the supremacy, no more subject within their respective spheres to the general authority than the general authority is subject to them within its own sphere. In this relation, then, the proposed government cannot be deemed a national one; since its jurisdiction extends to certain enumerated objects only, and leaves to the several States a residuary and inviolable sovereignty over all other objects. It is true that in controversies relating to the boundary between the two jurisdictions the tribunal which is ultimately to decide is to be established under the general government. But this does not change the principle of the case. The decision is to be impartially made, according to the rules of the Constitution; and all the usual and most effectual precautions are taken to secure this impartiality. Some such tribunal is clearly essential to prevent an appeal to the sword and a dissolution of the compact; and that it ought to be established under the general, rather than under the local governments, or, to speak more properly, that it could be safely established under the first alone, is a position not likely to be combated.

If we try the Constitution by its last relation, to the authority by which amendments are to be made, we find it neither wholly national nor wholly federal. Were it wholly national, the supreme and ultimate authority would reside in the majority of the people of the Union; and this authority would be competent at all times, like that of a majority of every national society, to alter or abolish its established government. Were it wholly federal, on the other hand, the concurrence of each State in the Union would be essential to every alteration that would be binding on all. The mode provided by the plan of the Convention is not founded on either of these principles. In requiring more than a majority, and particularly, in computing the proportion by States, not by citizens, it departs from the national, and advances toward the federal character: in rendering the concurrence of less than the whole number of States sufficient, it loses, again, the federal, and partakes of the national character.

The proposed Constitution, therefore, is, in strictness, neither a national nor a federal Constitution, but a composition of both. In its foundation it is federal, not national; in the sources from which the ordinary powers of the government are drawn, it is partly federal and partly national; in the operation of these powers, it is national, not federal; in the extent of them, again, it is federal, not national; and, finally, in the authoritative mode of introducing amendments it is neither wholly federal nor wholly national. PUBLIUS

NO. LI

ON MAINTAINING A JUST PARTITION OF POWER AMONG THE NECESSARY DEPARTMENTS

To what expedient, then, shall we finally resort, for maintaining in practice the necessary partition of power among the several departments, as laid down in the Constitution? The only answer that can be given is that as all these exterior provisions are found to be inadequate, the defect must be supplied, by so contriving the interior structure of the government as that its several constituent parts may, by their mutual relations, be the means of keeping each other in their proper places. Without presuming to undertake a full development of this important idea, I will hazard a few general observations, which may, perhaps, place it in a clearer light, and enable us to form a more correct judgment of the principles and structure of the government planned by the Convention.

In order to lay a due foundation for that separate and distinct exercise of the different powers of government which to a certain extent is admitted on all hands to be essential to the preservation of liberty, it is evident that each department should have a will of its own, and consequently should be so constituted that the members of each should have as little agency as possible in the appointment of the members of the others. Were this principle rigorously adhered to, it would require that all the appointments for the supreme executive, legislative, and judiciary magistracies should be drawn from the same fountain of authority, the people, through channels having no communication whatever with one another. Perhaps such a plan of constructing the several departments would be less difficult in practice than it may in contemplation appear. Some difficulties, however, and some additional expense would attend the execution of it. Some deviations, therefore, from the principle must be admitted. In the constitution of the judiciary department, in particular, it might be inexpedient to insist rigorously on the principle: First, because peculiar qualifications being essential in the members, the primary consideration ought to be to select that mode of choice which best secures these qualifications; secondly, because the permanent tenure by which the appointments are held in that department must soon destroy all sense of dependence on the authority conferring them.

It is equally evident that the members of each department should be as little dependent as possible on those of the others, for the emoluments annexed to their offices. Were the executive magistrate, or the judges not independent of the Legislature in this particular, their independence in every other would be merely nominal.

But the great security against a gradual concentration of the several powers in the same department consists in giving to those who administer each department the necessary constitutional means and personal motives to resist encroachments of the others. The provision for defence must in this, as in all other cases, be made commensurate to the danger of attack. Ambition must be made to counteract ambition. The interest of the man must be connected with the constitutional rights of the place. It may be a reflection on human nature that such devices should be necessary to control the abuses of government. But what is government itself, but the greatest of all reflections on human nature? If men were angels, no government would be necessary. If angels were to govern men, neither external nor internal controls on government would be necessary. In framing a government which is to be administered by men over men, the great difficulty lies in this: you must first enable the government to control the governed; and in the next place oblige it to control itself. A dependence on the people is, no doubt, the primary control on the government; but experience has taught mankind the necessity of auxiliary precautions.

This policy of supplying, by opposite and rival interests, the defect of better motives, might be traced through the whole system of human affairs, private as well as public. We see it particularly displayed in all the subordinate distributions of power, where the constant aim is to divide and arrange the several offices in such a manner as that each may be a check on the other; that the private interest of every individual may be a sentinel over the public rights. These inventions of prudence cannot be less requisite in the distribution of the supreme powers of the State.

But it is not possible to give to each department an equal power of self-defence. In republican government, the legislative authority necessarily predominates. The remedy for this inconveniency is to divide the legislature into different branches; and to render them, by different modes of election and different principles of action, as little connected with each other as the nature of their common functions and their common dependence on the society will admit. It may even be necessary to guard against dangerous encroachments by still further precautions. As the weight of the legislative authority requires that it should be thus divided, the weakness of the executive may require, on the other hand, that it should be fortified. An absolute negative on the legislature appears at first view to be the natural defence with which the executive magistrate should be armed. But perhaps it would be neither altogether safe nor alone sufficient. On ordinary occasions it might not be exerted with the requisite firmness, and on extraordinary occasions it might be perfidiously abused. May not this defect of an absolute negative be supplied by some qualified connection between this weaker department and the weaker branch of the stronger department, by which the latter may be led to support the constitutional rights of the former, without being too much detached from the rights of its own department?

If the principles on which these observations are founded be just, as I persuade myself they are, and they be applied as a criterion to the several State constitutions, and to the federal Constitution, it will be found that, if the latter does not perfectly correspond with them, the former are infinitely less able to bear such a test.

There are, moreover, two considerations particularly applicable to the federal system of America, which place that system in a very interesting point of view:

First. In a single republic all the power surrendered by the people is submitted to the administration of a single government, and the usurpations are guarded against by a division of the government into distinct and separate departments. In the compound republic of America, the power surrendered by the people is first divided between two distinct governments, and then the portion allotted to each subdivided among distinct and separate departments. Hence a double security arises to the rights of the people. The different governments will control each other, at the same time that each will be controlled by itself.

Second. It is of great importance in a republic not only to guard the society against the oppression of its rulers, but to guard one part of the society against the injustice of the other part. Different interests necessarily exist in different classes of citizens. If a majority be united by a common interest, the rights of the minority will be insecure. There are but two methods of providing against this evil; the one by creating a will in the community independent of the majority, that is, of the society itself; the other by comprehending in the society so many separate descriptions of citizens as will render an unjust combination of a majority of the whole very improbable, if not impracticable. The first method prevails in all governments possessing a hereditary or self-appointed authority. This at best is but a precarious security; because a power independent of the society may as well espouse the unjust views of the major as the rightful interests of the minor party, and may possibly be turned against both parties. The second method will be exemplified in the federal republic of the United States. While all authority in it will be derived from and dependent on the society, the society itself will be broken into so many parts, interests, and classes of citizens that the rights of individuals or of the minority will be in little danger from interested combinations of the majority. In a free government the security for civil rights must be the same as that for religious rights. It consists in the one case in the multiplicity of interests, and in the other in the multiplicity of sects. The degree of security in both cases will depend on the number of interests and sects; and this may be presumed to depend on the extent of country and number of people comprehended under the same government. This view of the subject must particularly recommend a proper federal system to all the sincere and considerate friends of republican government; since it shows that in exact proportion as the territory of the Union may be formed into more circumscribed confederacies, or States, oppressive combinations of a majority will be facilitated; the best security under republican forms, for the rights of every class of citizens, will be diminished; and, consequently, the stability and independence of some member of the government, the only other security, must be proportionally increased. Justice is the end of government. It is the end of civil society. It ever has been and ever will be pursued until it be obtained or until liberty be lost in the pursuit. In a society, under the forms of which the stronger faction can readily unite and oppress the weaker, anarchy may as truly be said to reign, as in a state of nature, where the weaker individual is not secured against the violence of the stronger; and as in the latter state even the stronger individuals are prompted by the uncertainty of their condition to submit to a government which may protect the weak as well as themselves, so in the former state will the more powerful factions or parties be gradually induced by a like motive to wish for a government which will protect all parties, the weaker as well as the more powerful. It can be little doubted that if the State of Rhode Island was separated from the confederacy, and left to itself, the insecurity of rights under the popular form of government within such narrow limits would be displayed by such reiterated oppressions of factious majorities that some power altogether independent of the people would soon be called for by the voice of the very factions whose misrule had proved the necessity of it. In the extended republic of the United States, and among the great variety of interests, parties, and sects which it embraces, a coalition of a majority of the whole society could seldom take place on any other principles than those of justice and the general good; while there being thus less danger to a minor from the will of a major party, there must be less pretext, also, to provide for the security of the former, by introducing into the government a will not dependent on the latter; or, in other words, a will independent of the society itself. It is no less certain than it is important, notwithstanding the contrary opinions which have been entertained, that the larger the society, provided it lie within a practical sphere, the more duly capable it will be of self-government. And happily for the republican cause, the practicable sphere may be carried to a very great extent, by a judicious modification and mixture of the federal principle. PUBLIUS

11

On the Relation which the States and General Government Bear to Each Other (The Fort Hill Address)

John C. Calhoun

The question of the relation which the States and General Government bear to each other is not one of recent origin. From the commencement of our system, it has divided public sentiment. Even in the Convention, while the Constitution was struggling into existence, there were two parties as to what this relation should be, whose different sentiments constituted no small impediment in forming that instrument. After the General Government went into operation, experience soon proved that the question had not terminated with the labors of the Convention. The great struggle that preceded the political revolution of 1801, which brought Mr. Jefferson into power, turned essentially on it, and the doctrines and arguments on both sides were embodied and ably sustained;—on the one, in the Virginia and Kentucky Resolutions, and the Report to the Virginia Legislature;—and on the other, in the replies of the Legislature of Massachusetts and some of the other States. These Resolutions and this Report, with the decision of the Supreme Court of Pennsylvania about the same time (particularly in the case of Cobbett, delivered by Chief Justice M'Kean, and concurred in by the whole bench), contain what I believe to be the true doctrine on this important subject. I refer to them in order to avoid the necessity of presenting my views, with the reasons in support of them, in detail.

As my object is simply to state my opinions, I might pause with this reference to documents that so fully and ably state all the points immediately connected with this deeply-important subject; but as there are many who may not have the opportunity or leisure to refer to them, and as it is possible, however clear they may be, that different persons may place different interpretations on their meaning, I will, in order that my sentiments may be fully known, and to avoid all ambiguity, proceed to state, summarily, the doctrines which I conceive they embrace.

The great and leading principle is, that the General Government emanated from the people of the several States, forming distinct political communities, and acting in their separate and sovereign capacity, and not from all of the people forming one aggregate political community; that the Constitution of the United States is, in fact, a compact, to which each State is a party, in the character already described; and that the several States, or parties, have a right to judge of its infractions; and in case of a deliberate, palpable, and dangerous exercise of power not delegated, they have the right, in the last resort, to use the language of the Virginia Resolutions, "*to interpose for arresting the progress of the evil, and for maintaining, within their respective limits, the authorities, rights, and liberties appertaining to them.*" This right of interposition, thus solemnly asserted by the State of Virginia, be it called what it may,—State-right, veto, nullification, or by any other name,—I conceive to be the fundamental principle of our system, resting on facts historically as certain as our revolution itself, and deductions as simple and demonstrative as that of any political or moral truth whatever; and I firmly believe that on its recognition depend the stability and safety of our political institutions.

I am not ignorant that those opposed to the doctrine have always, now and formerly, regarded it in a very different light, as anarchical and revolutionary. Could I believe such, in fact, to be its tendency, to me it would be no recommendation. I yield to none, I trust, in a deep and sincere attachment to our political institutions and the union of these States. I never breathed an opposite sentiment; but, on the contrary, I have ever considered them the great instruments of preserving our liberty, and promoting the happiness of ourselves and our posterity; and next to these I have ever held them most dear. Nearly half my life has been passed in the service of the Union, and whatever public reputation I have acquired is indissolubly identified with it. To be too national has, indeed, been considered by many, even of my friends, my greatest political fault. With these strong feelings of attachment, I have examined, with the utmost care, the bearing of the doctrine in question; and, so far from anarchical or revolutionary, I solemnly believe it to be the only solid foundation of our system, and of the Union itself; and that the opposite doctrine, which denies to the States the right of protecting their reserved powers, and which would vest in the General Government (it matters not through what department) the right of determining, exclusively and finally, the powers delegated to it, is incompatible with the sovereignty of the States, and of the Constitution itself, considered as the basis of a Federal Union. As strong as this language is, it is not stronger than that used by the illustrious Jefferson, who said, to give to the General Government the final and exclusive right to judge of its powers, is to make "*its discretion,* and *not the Constitution, the measure of its powers*"; and that, "*in all cases of compact between parties having no common judge, each party has an equal right to judge for itself, as well of the infraction as of the mode and measure of redress.*" Language cannot be more explicit, nor can higher authority be adduced.

That different opinions are entertained on this subject, I consider but as an additional evidence of the great diversity of the human intellect. Had not able, experienced, and patriotic individuals, for whom I have the highest respect, taken different views, I would have thought the right too clear to admit of doubt; but I am taught by this, as well as by many similar instances, to treat with deference opinions differing from my own. The error may, possibly, be with me; but if so, I can only say that, after the most mature and conscientious examination, I have not been able to detect it. But, with all proper deference, I must think that theirs is the error who deny what seems to be an essential attribute of the conceded sovereignty of the States, and who attribute to the General Government a right utterly incompatible with what all acknowledge to be its limited and restricted character: an error originating principally, as I must think, in not duly reflecting on the nature of our institutions, and on what constitutes the only rational object of all political constitutions.

It has been well said by one of the most sagacious men of antiquity, that the object of a constitution is, to *restrain the government, as that of laws* is to restrain *individuals*. The remark is correct; nor is it less true where the government is vested in a majority, than where it is in a single or a few individuals—in a republic, than a monarchy or aristocracy. No one can have a higher respect for the maxim that the majority ought to govern than I have, taken in its proper sense, subject to the restrictions imposed by the Constitution, and confined to objects in which every portion of the community have similar interests; but it is a great error to suppose, as many do, that the right of a majority to govern is a natural and not a conventional right, and therefore absolute and unlimited. By nature, every individual has the right to govern himself; and governments, whether founded on majorities or minorities, must derive their right from the assent, expressed or implied, of the governed, and be subject to such limitations as they may impose. Where the interests are the same, that is, where the laws that may benefit one will benefit all, or the reverse, it is just and proper to place them under the control of the majority; but where they are dissimilar, so that the law that may benefit one portion may be ruinous to another, it would be, on the contrary, unjust and absurd to subject them to its will; and such I conceive to be the theory on which our Constitution rests.

That such dissimilarity of interests may exist, it is impossible to doubt. They are to be found in every community, in a greater or less degree, however small or homogeneous; and they constitute every where the great difficulty of forming and preserving free institutions. To guard against the unequal action of the laws, when applied to dissimilar and opposing interests, is, in fact, what mainly renders a constitution indispensable; to overlook which, in reasoning on our Constitution, would be to omit the principal element by which to determine its character. Were there no contrariety of interests, nothing would be more simple and easy than to form and preserve free institutions. The right of suffrage alone would be a sufficient guarantee. It is the conflict of opposing interests which renders it the most difficult work of man.

Where the diversity of interests exists in separate and distinct classes of the community, as is the case in England, and was formerly the case in Sparta,

Rome, and most of the free States of antiquity, the rational constitutional provision is, that each should be represented in the government, as a separate estate, with a distinct voice, and a negative on the acts of its co-estates, in order to check their encroachments. In England, the Constitution has assumed expressly this form, while in the governments of Sparta and Rome, the same thing was effected under different, but not much less efficacious forms. The perfection of their organization, in this particular, was that which gave to the constitutions of these renowned States all their celebrity, which secured their liberty for so many centuries, and raised them to so great a height of power and prosperity. Indeed, a constitutional provision giving to the great and separate interests of the community the right of self-protection, must appear, to those who will duly reflect on the subject, not less essential to the preservation of liberty than the right of suffrage itself. They, in fact, have a common object, to effect which the one is as necessary as the other to secure *responsibility*; that is, *that those who make and execute the laws should be accountable to those on whom the laws in reality operate—the only solid and durable foundation of liberty.* If, without the right of suffrage, our rulers would oppress us, so, without the right of self-protection, the major would equally oppress the minor interests of the community. The absence of the former would make the governed the slaves of the rulers; and of the latter, the feebler interests, the victim of the stronger.

Happily for us, we have no artificial and separate classes of society. We have wisely exploded all such distinctions; but we are not, on that account, exempt from all contrariety of interests, as the present distracted and dangerous condition of our country, unfortunately, but too clearly proves. With us they are almost exclusively geographical, resulting mainly from difference of climate, soil, situation, industry, and production; but are not, therefore, less necessary to be protected by an adequate constitutional provision, than where the distinct interests exist in separate classes. The necessity is, in truth, greater, as such separate and dissimilar geographical interests are more liable to come into conflict, and more dangerous, when in that state, than those of any other description: so much so, that *ours is the first instance on record where they have not formed, in an extensive territory, separate and independent* communities, *or subjected the whole to despotic sway.* That such may not be our unhappy fate also, must be the sincere prayer of every lover of his country.

So numerous and diversified are the interests of our country, that they could not be fairly represented in a single government, organized so as to give to each great and leading interest a separate and distinct voice, as in governments to which I have referred. A plan was adopted better suited to our situation, but perfectly novel in its character. The powers of government were divided, not, as heretofore, in reference to classes, but geographically. One General Government was formed for the whole, to which were delegated all the powers supposed to be necessary to regulate the interests common to all the States, leaving others subject to the separate control of the States, being, from their local and peculiar character, such that they could not be subject to the will of a majority of the whole Union, without the certain hazard of injustice and oppression. It was thus that the interests of the whole were subjected, as they ought to be, to the will of the whole, while the peculiar and local interests were left under the control of the States separately, to whose custody only they could be safely confided. This distribution of power, settled solemnly by a constitutional compact, to which all the States are parties, constitutes the peculiar character and excellence of our political system. It is truly and emphatically *American, without example or parallel.*

To realize its perfection, we must view the General Government and those of the States as a whole, each in its proper sphere independent; each perfectly adapted to its respective objects; the States acting separately, representing and protecting the local and peculiar interests; and acting jointly through one General Government, with the weight respectively assigned to each by the Constitution, representing and protecting the interest of the whole; and thus perfecting, by an admirable but simple arrangement, the great principle of representation and responsibility, without which no government can be free or just. To preserve this sacred distribution as originally settled, by coercing each to move in its prescribed orbit, is the great and difficult problem, on the solution of which the duration of our Constitution, of our Union, and, in all probability, our liberty depends. How is this to be effected?

The question is new, when applied to our peculiar political organization, where the separate and conflicting interests of society are represented by distinct but connected governments; but it is, in reality, an old question under a new form, long since perfectly solved. Whenever separate and dissimilar interests have been separately represented in any government; whenever the sovereign power has been divided in its exercise, the experience and wisdom of ages have devised but one mode by which such political organization can be preserved,—the mode adopted in England, and by all governments, ancient and modern, blessed with constitutions deserving to be called free,—to give to each co-estate the right to judge of its powers, with a negative or veto on the acts of the others, in order to protect against encroachments the interests it particularly represents: a principle which all of our constitutions recognize in the distribution of power among their respective departments, as essential to maintain the independence of each; but which, to all who will duly reflect on the subject, must appear far more essential, for the same object, in that great and fundamental distribution of powers between the General and State Governments. So essential is the principle, that, to withhold the right from either, where the sovereign power is divided, is, in fact, *to annual the division* itself, and to *consolidate*, in the one left in the exclusive possession of the right, *all* powers of government; for it is not possible to distinguish, practically, between a government having all power, and one having the right to take what powers it pleases. Nor does it in the least vary the principle, whether the distribution of power be between co-estates, as in England, or between distinctly organized but connected governments, as with us. The reason is the same in both cases, while the necessity is greater in our case, as the danger of conflict is greater where the interests of a society are divided geographically than in any other, as has already been shown.

These truths do seem to me to be incontrovertible; and I am at a loss to understand how any one, who has maturely reflected on the nature of our institutions, or who has read history or studied the principles of free government to any purpose, can call them in question. The explanation must, it appears to me, be sought in the fact that, in every free State there are those who look more to the necessity of maintaining power than guarding against its abuses. I do not intend reproach, but simply to state a fact apparently necessary to explain the contrariety of opinions among the intelligent, where the abstract consideration of the subject would seem scarcely to admit of doubt. If such be the true cause, I must think the fear of weakening the government too much, in this case, to be in a great measure unfounded, or, at least, that the danger is much less from that than the opposite side. I do not deny that a power of so high a nature may be abused by a State; but when I reflect that the States unanimously called the General Government into existence with all its powers, which they freely delegated on their part, under the conviction that their common peace, safety, and prosperity required it; that they are bound together by a common origin, and the recollection of common suffering and common triumph in the great and splendid achievement of their independence; and that the strongest feelings of our nature, and among them the love of national power and distinction, are on the side of the Union, it does seem to me that the fear which would strip the States of their sovereignty, and degrade them, in fact, to mere dependent corporations, lest they should abuse a right indispensable to the peaceable protection of those interests which they reserved under their own peculiar guardianship when they created the General Government, is unnatural and unreasonable. If those who voluntarily created the system cannot be trusted to preserve it, who can?

So far from extreme danger, I hold that there never was a free State in which this great conservative principle, indispensable to all, was ever so safely lodged. In others, when the co-estates representing the dissimilar and conflicting interests of the community came into contact, the only alternative was compromise, submission, or force. Not so in ours. Should the General Government and a State come into conflict, we have a higher remedy: the power which called the General Government into existence, which gave it all its authority, and can enlarge, contract, or abolish its powers at its pleasure, may be invoked. The States themselves may be appealed to,—three fourths of which, in fact, form a power, whose decrees are the Constitution itself, and whose voice can silence all discontent. The utmost extent, then, of the power is, that a State, acting in its sovereign capacity as one of the parties to the constitutional compact, may compel the Government, created by that compact, to submit a question touching its infraction, to the parties who created it; to avoid the supposed dangers of which, it is proposed to resort to the novel, the hazardous, and, I must add, fatal project of giving to the General Government the sole and final right of interpreting the Constitution;—thereby reversing the whole system, making that instrument the creature of its will, instead of a rule of action impressed on it at its creation, and annihilating, in fact, the authority which imposed it, and from which the Government itself derives its existence.

That such would be the result, were the right in question vested in the Legislative or Executive branch of the Government, is conceded by all. No one has been so hardy as to assert that Congress or the President ought to have the right, or deny that, if vested finally and exclusively in either, the consequences which I have stated would necessarily follow; but its advocates have been reconciled to the doctrine, on the supposition that there is one department of the General Government which, from its peculiar organization, affords an independent tribunal, through which the Government may exercise the high authority which is the subject of consideration, with perfect safety to all.

I yield, I trust, to few in my attachment to the Judiciary Department. I am fully sensible of its importance, and would maintain it, to the fullest extent, in its constitutional powers and independence; but it is impossible for me to believe it was ever intended by the Constitution that it should exercise the power in question, or that it is competent to do so; and, if it were, that it would be a safe depository of the power.

Its powers are judicial, and not political; and are expressly confined by the Constitution "to all *cases* in law and equity arising under this Constitution, the laws of the United States, and the treaties made, or which shall be made, under its authority"; and which I have high authority in asserting excludes political questions, and comprehends those only where there are parties amenable to the process of the court.* Nor is its incompetency less clear than its want of constitutional authority. There may be many, and the most dangerous infractions on the part of Congress, of which, it is conceded by all, the court, as a judicial tribunal, cannot, from its nature, take cognizance. The Tariff itself is a strong case in point; and the reason applies equally *to all others where Congress perverts a power from an object intended, to one not intended, the most insidious and dangerous of all infractions; and which may be extended to all of its powers, more especially to the taxing and appropriating.* But, supposing it competent to take cognizance of all infractions of every description,

* I refer to the authority of Chief Justice Marshall, in the case of Jonathan Robbins. I have not been able to refer to the speech, and speak from memory.

The following are the remarks referred to by Mr. Calhoun:

"By extending the judicial power to all cases in law and equity, the Constitution *had never been understood* to confer on that department any *political power whatever.* To come within this description, a question must assume a *legal* form, for forensic litigation and judicial decision. There must be parties to come into court, who can be reached by its process, and bound by its power; whose rights admit of ultimate decision by a tribunal, to which they are bound to submit. A 'case in Law and Equity,' proper for judicial decision, may arise under a treaty, where the *rights of individuals,* acquired or secured by a treaty, are to be asserted or defended in court;—as under the fourth and sixth articles of the treaty of peace with Great Britain; or under those articles of our late treaties with France, Prussia, and other nations, which secure to *the subjects* of these nations *their property* within the United States; but the *judicial power cannot extend to political compacts.*" Speech in the House of Representatives, in the case of Thomas Nash, *alias* Jonathan Robbins, Sept. 1797.—*Editor.*

the insuperable objection still remains, that it would not be a safe tribunal to exercise the power in question.

It is a universal and fundamental political principle, that the power to protect can safely be confided only to those interested in protecting, or their responsible agents,—a maxim not less true in private than in public affairs. The danger in our system is, that the General Government, which represents the interests of the whole, may encroach on the States, which represent the peculiar and local interests, or that the latter may encroach on the former.

In examining this point, we ought not to forget that the Government, through all its departments, judicial as well as others, is administered by delegated and responsible agents; and that the *power which really controls, ultimately, all the movements, is not in the agents, but those who elect or appoint them.* To understand, then, its real character, and what would be the action of the system in any supposable case, we must raise our view from the mere agents to this high controlling power, which finally impels every movement of the machine. By doing so, we shall find all under the control of the will of a majority, compounded of the majority of the States, taken as political bodies, and the majority of the people of the States, estimated in federal numbers. These, united, constitute the real and final power which impels and directs the movements of the General Government. The majority of the States elect the majority of the Senate; of the people of the States, that of the House of Representatives; the two united, the President; and the President and a majority of the Senate appoint the judges: a majority of whom, and a majority of the Senate and House, with the President, really exercise all the powers of the Government, with the exception of the cases where the Constitution requires a greater number than a majority. The judges are, in fact, as truly the judicial representatives of this united majority, as the majority of Congress itself, or the President, is its legislative or executive representative; and to confide the power to the Judiciary to determine finally and conclusively what powers are delegated and what reserved, would be, in reality, to confide it to the majority, whose agents they are, and by whom they can be controlled in various ways; and, of course, to subject (against the fundamental principle of our system and all sound political reasoning) the reserved powers of the States, with all the local and peculiar interests they were intended to protect, to the will of the very majority against which the protection was intended. Nor will the tenure by which the judges hold their office, however valuable the provision in many other respects, materially vary the case. Its highest possible effect would be to *retard*, and not *finally* to *resist*, the will of a dominant majority.

But it is useless to multiply arguments. Were it possible that reason could settle a question where the passions and interests of men are concerned, this point would have been long since settled for ever by the State of Virginia. The report of her Legislature, to which I have already referred, has really, in my opinion, placed it beyond controversy. Speaking in reference to this subject, it says: "It has been objected" (to the right of a State to interpose for the protection of her reserved rights) "that the judicial authority is to be regarded as the sole expositor of the Constitution. On this objection it might be observed, first, that there may be instances of usurped powers which the forms of the Constitution could never draw within the control of the Judicial Department; secondly, that, if the decision of the judiciary be raised above the sovereign parties to the Constitution, the decisions of the other departments, not carried by the forms of the Constitution before the Judiciary, must be equally authoritative and final with the decision of that department. But the proper answer to the objection is, that the resolution of the General Assembly relates to those great and extraordinary cases, in which all the forms of the Constitution may prove ineffectual against infractions dangerous to the essential rights of the parties to it. The resolution supposes that dangerous powers, not delegated, may not only be usurped and executed by the other departments, but that the Judicial Department may also exercise or sanction dangerous powers, beyond the grant of the Constitution, and, consequently, that the ultimate right of the parties to the Constitution to judge whether the compact has been dangerously violated, must extend to violations by one delegated authority, as well as by another,—by the judiciary, as well as by the executive or legislative."

Against these conclusive arguments, as they seem to me, it is objected that, if one of the parties has the right to judge of infractions of the Constitution, so has the other; and that, consequently, in cases of contested powers between a State and the General Government, each would have a right to maintain its opinion, as is the case when sovereign powers differ in the construction of treaties or compacts; and that, of course, it would come to be a mere question of force. The error is in the assumption that the General Government is a party to the constitutional compact. The States, as has been shown, formed the compact, acting as sovereign and independent communities. The General Government is but its creature; and though, in reality, a government, with all the rights and authority which belong to any other government, within the orbit of its powers, it is, nevertheless, a government emanating from a compact between sovereigns, and partaking, in its nature and object, of the character of a joint commission, appointed to superintend and administer the interests in which all are jointly concerned; but having, beyond its proper sphere, no more power than if it did not exist. To deny this would be to deny the most incontestable facts and the clearest conclusions; while to acknowledge its truth is, to destroy utterly the objection that the appeal would be to force, in the case supposed. For, if each party has a right to judge, then, under our system of government, the final cognizance of a question of contested power would be in the States, and not in the General Government. It would be the duty of the latter, as in all similar cases of a contest between one or more of the principals and a joint commission or agency, to refer the contest to the principals themselves. Such are the plain dictates of both reason and analogy. On no sound principle can the agents have a right to final cognizance, as against the principals, much less to use force against them to maintain their construction of their powers. Such a right would be monstrous, and has never, heretofore, been claimed in similar cases.

That the doctrine is applicable to the case of a contested power between the States and the General Government, we have the authority, not only of reason and analogy, but of the distinguished statesman already referred to. Mr. Jefferson, at a late period of his life, after long experience and mature reflection, says, "With respect to our State and Federal Governments, I do not think their relations are correctly understood by foreigners. They suppose the former are subordinate to the latter. This is not the case. They are co-ordinate departments of one simple and integral whole. But you may ask, If the two departments should claim each the same subject of power, where is the umpire to decide between them? In cases of little urgency or importance, the prudence of both parties will keep them aloof from the questionable ground; but, if it can neither be avoided nor compromised, a convention of the States must be called to ascribe the doubtful power to that department which they may think best."

It is thus that our Constitution, by authorizing amendments, and by prescribing the authority and mode of making them, has, by a simple contrivance, with its characteristic wisdom, provided a power which, in the last resort, supersedes effectually the necessity, and even the pretext for force: a power to which none can fairly object; with which the interests of all are safe; which can definitively close all controversies in the only effectual mode, by freeing the compact of every defect and uncertainty, by an amendment of the instrument itself. It is impossible for human wisdom, in a system like ours, to devise another mode which shall be safe and effectual, and, at the same time, consistent with what are the relations and acknowledged powers of the two great departments of our Government. It gives a beauty and security peculiar to our system, which, if duly appreciated, will transmit its blessings to the remotest generations; but, if not, our splendid anticipations of the future will prove but an empty dream. Stripped of all its covering, the naked question is, whether ours is a federal or a consolidated government, a constitutional or absolute one; a government resting ultimately on the solid basis of the sovereignty of the States or on the unrestrained will of a majority; a form of government, as in all other unlimited ones, in which injustice, and violence, and force must finally prevail. *Let it never be forgotten that, where the majority rules without restriction, the minority is the subject*; and that, if we should absurdly attribute to the former the exclusive right of construing the Constitution, there would be, in fact, between the sovereign and subject, under such a government, no Constitution, or, at least, nothing deserving the name, or serving the legitimate object of so sacred an instrument.

How the States are to exercise this high power of interposition, which constitutes so essential a portion of their reserved rights that it *cannot be delegated without an entire surrender of their sovereignty*, and converting our system from a *federal* into a *consolidated* Government, is a question that the States only are competent to determine. The arguments which prove that they possess the power, equally prove that they are, in the language of Jefferson, "*the rightful judges of the mode and measure of redress.*" But the spirit of forbearance, as well as the nature of the right itself, forbids a recourse to it, except in cases of dangerous infractions of the Constitution; and then only in the last resort, when all reasonable hope of relief from the ordinary action of the Government has failed; when, if the right to interpose did not exist, the alternative would be submission and oppression on one side, or resistance by force on the other. That our system should afford, in such extreme cases, an intermediate point between these dire alternatives, by which the Government may be brought to a pause, and thereby an interval obtained to compromise differences, or, if impracticable, be compelled to submit the question to a constitutional adjustment, through an appeal to the States themselves, is an evidence of its high wisdom: an element not, as is supposed by some, of weakness, but of strength; not of anarchy or revolution, but of peace and safety. *Its general recognition would of itself, in a great measure, if not altogether, supersede the necessity of its exercise, by impressing on the movements of the Government that moderation and justice so essential to harmony and peace, in a country of such vast extent and diversity of interests as ours;* and would, if controversy should come, turn the resentment of the aggrieved from the system to those who had abused its powers (a point all-important), and cause them to seek redress, *not in revolution or overthrow, but in reformation.* It is, in fact, properly understood, *a substitute,—where the alternative would be force,—tending to prevent, and, if that fails, to correct peaceably the aberrations to which all systems are liable, and which, if permitted to accumulate without correction, must finally end in a general catastrophe.* [. . .]

12

Federal Theory in *Democracy in America*

Alexis de Tocqueville

In What Respects the Federal Constitution is Superior to that of the States

In what respects the Constitution of the Union can be compared to that of the States—Superiority of the Constitution of the Union attributable to the wisdom of the Federal legislators—Legislature of the Union less dependent on the people than that of the States—Executive power more independent in its sphere—Judicial power less subjected to the inclinations of the majority—Practical consequence of these facts—The dangers inherent in a democratic government eluded by the Federal legislators, and increased by the legislators of the States.

The Federal Constitution differs essentially from that of the States in the ends which it is intended to accomplish, but in the means by which these ends are promoted a greater analogy exists between them. The objects of the Governments are different, but their forms are the same; and in this special point of view there is some advantage in comparing them together.

I am of opinion that the Federal Constitution is superior to all the Constitutions of the States, for several reasons.

The present Constitution of the Union was formed at a later period than those of the majority of the States, and it may have derived some ameliorations from past experience. But we shall be led to acknowledge that this is only a secondary cause of its superiority, when we recollect that eleven new States have been added to the American Confederation since the promulgation of the Federal Constitution, and that these new republics have always rather exaggerated than avoided the defects which existed in the former Constitutions.

The chief cause of the superiority of the Federal Constitution lay in the character of the legislators who composed it. At the time when it was formed the dangers of the Confederation were imminent, and its ruin seemed inevitable. In this extremity the people chose the men who most deserved the esteem, rather than those who had gained the affections, of the country. I have already observed that distinguished as almost all the legislators of the

Union were for their intelligence, they were still more so for their patriotism. They had all been nurtured at a time when the spirit of liberty was braced by a continual struggle against a powerful and predominant authority. When the contest was terminated, whilst the excited passions of the populace persisted in warring with dangers which had ceased to threaten them, these men stopped short in their career; they cast a calmer and more penetrating look upon the country which was now their own; they perceived that the war of independence was definitely ended, and that the only dangers which America had to fear were those which might result from the abuse of the freedom she had won. They had the courage to say what they believed to be true, because they were animated by a warm and sincere love of liberty; and they ventured to propose restrictions, because they were resolutely opposed to destruction.[1]

The greater number of the Constitutions of the States assign one year for the duration of the House of Representatives, and two years for that of the Senate; so that members of the legislative body are constantly and narrowly tied down by the slightest desires of their constituents. The legislators of the Union were of opinion that this excessive dependence of the Legislature tended to alter the nature of the main consequences of the representative system, since it vested the source, not only of authority, but of government, in the people. They increased the length of the time for which the representatives were returned, in order to give them freer scope for the exercise of their own judgment.

The Federal Constitution, as well as the Constitutions of the different States, divided the legislative body into two branches. But in the States these two branches were composed of the same elements, and elected in the same

[1] At this time Alexander Hamilton, who was one of the principal founders of the Constitution, ventured to express the following sentiments in *The Federalist*, no. 71:—

"There are some who would be inclined to regard the servile pliancy of the Executive to a prevailing current, either in the community or in the Legislature, as its best recommendation. But such men entertain very crude notions, as well of the purposes for which government was instituted as of the true means by which the public happiness may be promoted. The Republican principle demands that the deliberative sense of the community should govern the conduct of those to whom they entrust the management of their affairs; but it does not require an unqualified complaisance to every sudden breeze of passion, or to every transient impulse which the people may receive from the arts of men who flatter their prejudices to betray their interests. It is a just observation, that the people commonly *intend the public good*. This often applies to their very errors. But their good sense would despise the adulator who should pretend that they always *reason right* about the *means* of promoting it. They know from experience that they sometimes err; and the wonder is that they so seldom err as they do, beset, as they continually are, by the wiles of parasites and sycophants; by the snares of the ambitious, the avaricious, the desperate; by the artifices of men who possess their confidence more than they deserve it, and of those who seek to possess rather than to deserve it. When occasions present themselves in which the interests of the people are at variance with their inclinations, it is the duty of persons whom they have appointed to be the guardians of those interests to withstand the temporary delusion, in order to give them time and opportunity for more cool and sedate reflection. Instances might be cited in which a conduct of this kind has saved the people from very fatal consequences of their own mistakes, and has procured lasting monuments of their gratitude to the men who had courage and magnanimity enough to serve them at the peril of their displeasure."

manner. The consequence was that the passions and inclinations of the populace were as rapidly and as energetically represented in one chamber as in the other, and that laws were made with all the characteristics of violence and precipitation. By the Federal Constitution the two houses originate in like manner in the choice of the people; but the conditions of eligibility and the mode of election were changed, to the end that, if, as is the case in certain nations, one branch of the Legislature represents the same interests as the other, it may at least represent a superior degree of intelligence and discretion. A mature age was made one of the conditions of the senatorial dignity, and the Upper House was chosen by an elected assembly of a limited number of members.

To concentrate the whole social force in the hands of the legislative body is the natural tendency of democracies; for as this is the power which emanates the most directly from the people, it is made to participate most fully in the preponderating authority of the multitude, and it is naturally led to monopolize every species of influence. This concentration is at once prejudicial to a well-conducted administration, and favourable to the despotism of the majority. The legislators of the States frequently yielded to these democratic propensities, which were invariably and courageously resisted by the founders of the Union.

In the States the executive power is vested in the hands of a magistrate, who is apparently placed upon a level with the legislature, but who is in reality nothing more than the blind agent and the passive instrument of its decisions. He can derive no influence from the duration of his functions, which terminate with the revolving year, or from the exercise of prerogatives which can scarcely be said to exist. The Legislature can condemn him to inaction by entrusting the execution of the laws to special committees of its own members, and can annul his temporary dignity by depriving him of his salary. The Federal Constitution vests all the privileges and all the responsibility of the executive power in a single individual. The duration of the Presidency is fixed at four years; the salary of the individual who fills that office cannot be altered during the term of his functions; he is protected by a body of official dependents, and armed with a suspensive veto. In short, every effort was made to confer a strong and independent position upon the executive authority within the limits which had been prescribed to it.

In the Constitutions of all the States the judicial power is that which remains the most independent of the legislative authority; nevertheless, in all the States the legislature has reserved to itself the right of regulating the emoluments of the judges, a practice which necessarily subjects these magistrates to its immediate influence. In some States the judges are only temporarily appointed, which deprives them of a great portion of their power and their freedom. In others the legislative and judicial powers are entirely confounded; thus the Senate of New York, for instance, constitutes in certain cases the superior court of the State. The Federal Constitution, on the other hand, carefully separates the judicial authority from all external influences; and it provides for the independence of the judges, by declaring that their salary shall not be altered, and that their functions shall be inalienable.

The practical consequences of these different systems may easily be perceived. An attentive observer will soon remark that the business of the Union is incomparably better conducted than that of any individual State. The conduct of the Federal Government is more fair and more temperate than that of the States, its designs are more fraught with wisdom, its projects are more durable and more skilfully combined, its measures are put into execution with more vigour and consistency.

I recapitulate the substance of this chapter in a few words: The existence of democracies is threatened by two dangers, viz., the complete subjection of the legislative body to the caprices of the electoral body, and the concentration of all the powers of the Government in the legislative authority. The growth of these evils has been encouraged by the policy of the legislators of the States, but it has been resisted by the legislators of the Union by every means which lay within their control.

Characteristics which Distinguish The Federal Constitution of the United States of America from all other Federal Constitutions

American Union appears to resemble all other confederations—Nevertheless its effects are different—Reason of this—Distinctions between the Union and all other confederations—The American Government not a federal but an imperfect national Government.

The United States of America do not afford either the first or the only instance of confederate States, several of which have existed in modern Europe, without adverting to those of antiquity. Switzerland, the Germanic Empire, and the Republic of the United Provinces either have been or still are confederations. In studying the constitutions of these different countries, the politician is surprised to observe that the powers with which they invested the Federal Government are nearly identical with the privileges awarded by the American Constitution to the Government of the United States. They confer upon the central power the same rights of making peace and war of raising money and troops, and of providing for the general exigencies and the common interests of the nation. Nevertheless the Federal Government of these different peoples has always been as remarkable for its weakness and inefficiency as that of the Union is for its vigorous and enterprising spirit. Again, the first American Confederation perished through the excessive weakness of its Government; and this weak Government was, notwithstanding, in possession of rights even more extensive than those of the Federal Government of the present day. But the more recent Constitution of the United States contains certain principles which exercise a most important influence, although they do not at once strike the observer.

This Constitution, which may at first sight be confounded with the federal constitutions which preceded it, rests upon a novel theory, which may be considered as a great invention in modern political science. In all the confederations which had been formed before the American Constitution of 1789 the allied States agreed to obey the injunctions of a Federal Government; but they reserved to themselves the right of ordaining and enforcing the execution of the laws of the Union. The American States which combined in 1789 agreed that the Federal Government should not only dictate the laws, but that it should execute it own enactments. In both cases the right is the same, but the exercise of the right is different; and this alteration produced the most momentous consequences.

In all the confederations which had been formed before the American Union the Federal Government demanded its supplies at the hands of the separate Governments; and if the measure it prescribed was onerous to any one of those bodies means were found to evade its claims: if the State was powerful, it had recourse to arms; if it was weak, it connived at the resistance which the law of the Union, its sovereign, met with, and resorted to inaction under the plea of inability. Under these circumstances one of the two alternatives has invariably occurred; either the most preponderant of the allied peoples has assumed the privileges of the Federal authority and ruled all the States in its name,[1] or the Federal Government has been abandoned by its natural supporters, anarchy has arisen between the confederates, and the Union has lost all powers of action.[2]

In America the subjects of the Union are not States, but private citizens: the national Government levies a tax, not upon the State of Massachusetts, but upon each inhabitant of Massachusetts. All former confederate governments presided over communities, but that of the Union rules individuals; its force is not borrowed, but self-derived; and it is served by its own civil and military officers, by its own army, and its own courts of justice. It cannot be doubted that the spirit of the nation, the passions of the multitude, and the provincial prejudices of each State tend singularly to diminish the authority of a Federal authority thus constituted, and to facilitate the means of resistance to its mandates; but the comparative weakness of a resticted sovereignty is an evil inherent in the Federal system. In America, each State has fewer opportunities of resistance and fewer temptations to non-compliance; nor can such a design be put in execution (if indeed it be entertained) without an open violation of the laws of the Union, a direct interruption of the ordinary course of justice, and a bold declaration of revolt; in a word, without taking a decisive step which men hesitate to adopt.

[1] This was the case in Greece, when Philip undertook to excute the decree of the Amphictyons; in the Low Countries, where the province of Holland always gave the law; and, in our own time, in the Germanic Confederation, in which Austria and Prussia assume a great degree of influence over the whole country, in the name of the Diet.

[2] Such has always been the situation of the Swiss Confederation, which would have perished ages ago but for the mutual jealousies of its neighbors.

In all former confederations the privileges of the Union furnished more elements of discord than of power, since they multiplied the claims of the nation without augmenting the means of enforcing them: and in accordance with this fact it may be remarked that the real weakness of federal governments has almost always been in the exact ratio of their nominal power. Such is not the case in the American Union, in which, as in ordinary governments, the Federal Government has the means of enforcing all it is empowered to demand.

The human understanding more easily invents new things than new words, and we are thence constrained to employ a multitude of improper and inadequate expressions. When several nations form a permanent league and establish a supreme authority, which, although it has not the same influence over the members of the community as a national government, acts upon each of the confederate States in a body, this government, which is so essentially different from all others, is denominated a Federal one. Another form of society is afterwards discovered, in which several peoples are fused into one and the same nation with regard to certain common interests, although they remain distinct, or at least only confederate, with regard to all their other concerns. In this case the central power acts directly upon those whom it governs, whom it rules, and whom it judges, in the same manner as, but in a more limited circle than, a national government. Here the term Federal government is clearly no longer applicable to a state of things which must be styled an incomplete national government: a form of government has been found out which is neither exactly national nor federal; but no further progress has been made, and the new word which will one day designate this novel invention does not yet exist.

The absence of this new species of confederation has been the cause which has brought all Unions to civil war, to subjection, or to a stagnant apathy; and the peoples which formed these leagues have been either too dull to discern, or too pusillanimous to apply, this great remedy. The American Confederation perished by the same defects.

But the confederate States of America had been long accustomed to form a portion of one empire before they had won their independence; they had not contracted the habit of governing themselves, and their national prejudices had not taken deep root in their minds. Superior to the rest of the world in political knowledge, and sharing that knowledge equally amongst themselves, they were little agitated by the passions which generally oppose the extension of federal authority in a nation, and those passions were checked by the wisdom of the chief citizens. The Americans applied the remedy with prudent firmness as soon as they were conscious of the evil; they amended their laws, and they saved their country.

Advantages of the Federal System in General, and its Special Utility in America

Happiness and freedom of small nations—Power of great nations—Great empires favourable to the growth of civilization—Strength often the first element of national prosperity—Aim of the Federal system to unite the twofold advantages resulting from a small and from a large territory—Advantages derived by the United States from this system—The law adapts itself to the exigencies of the population; population does not conform to the exigencies of the law—Activity, amelioration, love and enjoyment of freedom in the American communities—Public spirit of the Union the abstract of provincial patriotism—Principles and things circulate freely over the territory of the United States—The Union is happy and free as a little nation, and respected as a great empire.

In small nations the scrutiny of society penetrates into every part, and the spirit of improvement enters into the most trifling details; as the ambition of the people is necessarily checked by its weakness, all the efforts and resources of the citizens are turned to the internal benefit of the community, and are not likely to evaporate in the fleeting breath of glory. The desires of every individual are limited, because extraordinary faculties are rarely to be met with. The gifts of an equal fortune render the various conditions of life uniform, and the manners of the inhabitants are orderly and simple. Thus, if one estimate the gradations of popular morality and enlightenment, we shall generally find that in small nations there are more persons in easy circumstances, a more numerous population, and a more tranquil state of society, than in great empires.

When tyranny is established in the bosom of a small nation, it is more galling than elsewhere, because, as it acts within a narrow circle, every point of that circle is subject to its direct influence. It supplies the place of those great designs which it cannot entertain by a violent or an exasperating interference in a multitude of minute details; and it leaves the political world, to which it properly belongs, to meddle with the arrangements of domestic life. Tastes as well as actions are to be regulated at its pleasure; and the families of the citizens as well as the affairs of the State are to be governed by its decisions. This invasion of rights occurs, however, but seldom, and freedom is in truth the natural state of small communities. The temptations which the Government offers to ambition are too weak, and the resources of private individuals are too slender, for the sovereign power easily to fall within the grasp of a single citizen; and should such an event have occurred, the subjects of the State can without difficulty overthrow the tyrant and his oppression by a simultaneous effort.

Small nations have therefore ever been the cradle of political liberty; and the fact that many of them have lost their immunities by extending their dominion shows that the freedom, they enjoyed was more a consequence of the inferior size than of the character of the people.

The history of the world affords no instance of a great nation retaining the form of republican government for a long series of years,[1] and this has led to the conclusion that such a state of things is impracticable. For my own part, I cannot but censure the imprudence of attempting to limit the possible and

[1] I do not speak of a confederation of small republics, but of a great consolidated Republic.

to judge the future on the part of a being who is hourly deceived by the most palpable realities of life, and who is constantly taken by surprise in the circumstances with which he is most familiar. But it may be advanced with confidence that the existence of a great republic will always be exposed to far greater perils than that of a small one.

All the passions which are most fatal to republican institutions spread with an increasing territory, whilst the virtues which maintain their dignity do not augment in the same proportion. The ambition of the citizens increases with the power of the State; the strength of parties with the importance of the ends they have in view; but that devotion to the common weal which is the surest check on destructive passions is not stronger in a large than in a small republic. It might, indeed, be proved without difficulty that it is less powerful and less sincere. The arrogance of wealth and the dejection of wretchedness, capital cities of unwonted extent, a lax morality, a vulgar egotism, and a great confusion of interests, are the dangers which almost invariably arise from the magnitude of States. But several of these evils are scarcely prejudicial to a monarchy, and some of them contribute to maintain its existence. In monarchical States the strength of the government is its own; it may use, but it does not depend on, the community, and the authority of the prince is proportioned to the prosperity of the nation; but the only security which a republican government possesses against these evils lies in the support of the majority. This support is not, however, proportionably greater in a large republic that it is in a small one; and thus, whilst the means of attack perpetually increase both in number and in influence, the power of resistance remains the same, or it may rather be said to diminish, since the propensities and interests of the people are diversified by the increase of the population, and the difficulty of forming a compact majority is constantly augmented. It has been observed, moreover, that the intensity of human passions is heightened, not only by the importance of the end which they propose to attain, but by the multitude of individuals who are animated by them at the same time. Every one has had occasion to remark that his emotions in the midst of a sympathising crowd are far greater than those which he would have felt in solitude. In great republics the impetus of political passion is irresistible, not only because it aims at gigantic purposes, but because it is felt and shared by millions of men at the same time.

It may therefore be asserted as a general proposition that nothing is more opposed to the well-being and the freedom of man than vast empires. Nevertheless it is important to acknowledge the peculiar advantages of great States. For the very reason which renders the desire of power more intense in these communities than amongst ordinary men, the love of glory is also more prominent in the hearts of a class of citizens, who regard the applause of a great people as a reward worthy of their exertions, and an elevating encouragement to man. If we would learn why is it that great nations contribute more powerfully to the spread of human improvement than small States, we shall discover an adequate cause in the rapid and energetic circulation of ideas, and in those great cities which are the intellectual centres where all the rays of human genius are reflected and combined. To this it may be added that most important discoveries demand a display of national power which the Government of a small State is unable to make; in great nations the Government entertains a greater number of general notions, and is more completely disengaged from the routine of precedent and the egotism of local prejudice; its designs are conceived with more talent, and executed with more boldness.

In time of peace the well-being of small nations is undoubtedly more general and more complete, but they are apt to suffer more acutely from the calamities of war than those great empires whose distant frontiers may for ages avert the presence of the danger from the mass of the people, which is therefore more frequently afflicted than ruined by the evil.

But in this matter, as in many others, the argument derived from the necessity of the case predominates over all others. If none but small nations existed, I do not doubt that mankind would be more happy and more free; but the existence of great nations is unavoidable.

This consideration introduces the element of physical strength as a condition of national prosperity. It profits a people but little to be affluent and free if it is perpetually exposed to be pillaged or subjugated; the number of its manufactures and the extent of its commerce are of small advantage if another nation has the empire of the seas and gives the law in all the markets of the globe. Small nations are often impoverished, not because they are small, but because they are weak; the great empires prosper less because they are great than because they are strong. Physical strength is therefore one of the first conditions of the happiness and even of the existence of nations. Hence it occurs that, unless very peculiar circumstances intervene, small nations are always united to large empires in the end, either by force or by their own consent: yet I am unacquainted with a more deplorable spectacle than that of a people unable either to defend or to maintain its independence.

The Federal system was created with the intention of combining the different advantages which result from the greater and the lesser extent of nations; and a single glance over the United States of America suffices to discover the advantages which they have derived from its adoption.

In great centralized nations the legislator is obliged to impart a character of uniformity to the laws which does not always suit the diversity of customs and of districts; as he takes no cognizance of special cases, he can only proceed upon general principles; and the population is obliged to conform to the exigencies of the legislation, since the legislation cannot adapt itself to the exigencies and the customs of the population, which is the cause of endless trouble and misery. This advantage does not exist in confederations. Congress regulates the principal measures of the national Government, and all the details of the administration are reserved to the provincial legislatures. It is impossible to imagine how much this division of sovereignty contributes to the well-being of each of the States which compose the Union. In these small communities, which are never agitated by the desire of aggrandisement or the cares of selfdefence, all public authority and private energy is employed in internal amelioration. The central government of each State, which is in immediate juxtaposition to the citizens, is daily apprised of the wants which arise in society; and new projects are proposed every year, which are discussed either at town meetings or by the legislature of the State, and which are transmitted by the press to stimulate the zeal and to excite the interest of the citizens. This spirit of amelioration is constantly alive in the American republics, without compromising their tranquillity; the ambition of power yields to the less refined and less dangerous love of comfort. It is generally believed in America that the existence and the permanence of the republican form of government in the New World depend upon the existence and the permanence of the Federal system; and it is not unusual to attribute a large share of the misfortunes which have befallen the new States of South America to the injudicious erection of great republics, instead of a divided and confederate sovereignty.

It is incontestably true that the love and the habits of republican government in the United States were engendered in the townships and in the provincial assemblies. In a small State, like that of Connecticut for instance, where cutting a canal or laying down a road is a momentous political question, where the State has no army to pay and no wars to carry on, and where much wealth and much honour cannot be bestowed upon the chief citizens, no form of government can be more natural or more appropriate than that of a republic. But it is this same republican spirit, it is these manners and customs of a free people, which are engendered and nurtured in the different States, to be afterwards applied to the country at large. The public spirit of the Union is, so to speak, nothing more than an abstract of the patriotic zeal of the provinces. Every citizen of the United States transfuses his attachment to his little republic in the common store of American patriotism. In defending the Union he defends the increasing prosperity of his own district, the right of conducting its affairs, and the hope of causing measures of improvement to be adopted which may be favourable to his own interests; and these are motives which are wont to stir men more readily than the general interests of the country and the glory of the nation.

On the other hand, if the temper and the manners of the inhabitants especially fitted them to promote the welfare of a great republic, the Federal system smoothed the obstacles which they might have encountered. The confederation of all the American States presents none of the ordinary disadvantages resulting from great agglomerations of men. The Union is a great republic in extent, but the paucity of objects for which its Government provides assimilates it to a small State. Its acts are important, but they are rare. As the sovereignty of the Union is limited and incomplete, its exercise is not incompatible with liberty; for it does not excite those insatiable desires of fame and power which have proved so fatal to great republics. As there is no common centre to the country, vast capital cities, colossal wealth, abject poverty, and sudden revolutions are alike unknown; and political passion, instead of spreading over the land like a torrent of desolation, spends its strength against the interests and the individual passions of every State.

Nevertheless, all commodities and ideas circulate throughout the Union as freely as in a country inhabited by one people. Nothing checks the spirit of enterprise. Government avails itself of the assistance of all who have talents or knowledge to serve it. Within the frontiers of the Union the profoundest peace prevails, as within the heart of some great empire; abroad, it ranks with the most powerful nations of the earth; two thousand miles of coast are open to the commerce of the world; and as it possesses the keys of the globe, its flag is respected in the most remote seas. The Union is as happy and as free as a small people, and as glorious and as strong as a great nation.

WHY THE FEDERAL SYSTEM IS NOT ADAPTED TO ALL PEOPLES, AND HOW THE ANGLO-AMERICANS WERE ENABLED TO ADOPT IT

Every Federal system contains defects which baffle the efforts of the legislator—The Federal system is complex—It demands a daily exercise of discretion on the part of the citizens—Practical knowledge of government common amongst the Americans—Relative weakness of the Government of the Union, another defect inherent in the Federal system—The Americans have diminished without remedying it—The sovereignty of the separate States apparently weaker, but really stronger, than that of the Union—Why?—Natural causes of union must exist between confederate peoples beside the laws—What these causes are amongst the Anglo-Americans—Maine and Georgia, separated by a distance of a thousand miles, more naturally united than Normandy and Brittany—War, the main peril of confederations—This proved even by the example of the United States—The Union has no great wars to fear—Why?—Dangers to which Europeans would be exposed if they adopted the Federal system of the Americans.

When a legislator succeeds, after persevering efforts, in exercising an indirect influence upon the destiny of nations, his genius is lauded by mankind, whilst, in point of fact, the geographical position of the country which he is unable to change, a social condition which arose without his co-operation, manners and opinions which he cannot trace to their source, and an origin with which he is unacquainted, exercise so irresistible an influence over the courses of society that he is himself borne away by the current, after an ineffectual resistance. Like the navigator, he may direct the vessel which bears him along, but he can neither change its structure, nor raise the winds, nor lull the waters which swell beneath him.

I have shown the advantages which the Americans derive from their Federal system; it remains for me to point out the circumstances which rendered that system practicable, as its benefits are not to be enjoyed by all nations. The incidental defects of the Federal system which originate in the laws may be corrected by the skill of the legislator, but there are further evils inherent in the system which cannot be counteracted by the peoples which adopt it. These nations must therefore find the strength necessary to support the natural imperfections of their Government.

The most prominent evil of all Federal systems is the very complex nature of the means they employ. Two sovereignties are necessarily in presence of each other. The legislator may simplify and equalize the action of these two sovereignties, by limiting each of them to a sphere of authority accurately defined; but he cannot combine them into one, or prevent them from coming into collision at certain points. The Federal system therefore rests upon a theory which is necessarily complicated, and which demands the daily exercise of a considerable share of discretion on the part of those it governs.

A proposition must be plain to be adopted by the understanding of a people. A false notion which is clear and precise will always meet with a greater number of adherents in the world than a true principle which is obscure or involved. Hence it arises that parties, which are like small communities in the heart of the nation, invariably adopt some principle or some name as a symbol, which very inadequately represents the end they have in view and the means which are at their disposal, but without which they could neither act nor subsist. The Governments which are founded upon a single principle or a single feeling which is easily defined are perhaps not the best, but they are unquestionably the strongest and the most durable in the world.

In examining the Constitution of the United States, which is the most perfect Federal Constitution that ever existed, one is startled, on the other hand, at the variety of information and the excellence of discretion which it presupposes in the people whom it is meant to govern. The Government of the Union depends entirely upon legal fictions; the Union is an ideal nation which only exists in the mind, and whose limits and extent can only be discerned by the understanding.

When once the general theory is comprehended, numberless difficulties remain to be solved in its application; for the sovereignty of the Union is so involved in that of the States that it is impossible to distinguish its boundaries at the first glance. The whole structure of the Government is artificial and conventional; and it would be ill adapted to a people which has not been long accustomed to conduct its own affairs, or to one in which the science of politics has not descended to the humblest classes of society. I have never been more struck by the good sense and the practical judgment of the Americans than in the ingenious devices by which they elude the numberless difficulties resulting from their Federal Constitution. I scarcely ever met with a plain American citizen who could not distinguish, with surprising facility, the obligations created by the laws of Congress from those created by the laws of his own State; and who, after having discriminated between the matters which come under the cognizance of the Union and those which the local legislature is competent to regulate, could not point out the exact limit of the several jurisdictions of the Federal Courts and the tribunals of the State.

The Constitution of the United States is like those exquisite productions of human industry which ensure wealth and renown to their inventors, but which are profitless in any other hands. This truth is exemplified by the condition of Mexico at the present time. The Mexicans were desirous of establishing a Federal system, and they took the Federal Constitution of their neighbours the Anglo-Americans as their model, and copied it with considerable accuracy.[1] But although they had borrowed the letter of the law, they were unable to create or to introduce the spirit and the sense which give it life. They were involved in ceaseless embarrassments between the mechanism of their double Government; the sovereignty of the States and that of the Union perpetually exceeded their respective privileges, and entered into collision; and to the present day Mexico is alternately the victim of anarchy and the slave of military despotism.

The second and the most fatal of all the defects I have alluded to, and that which I believe to be inherent in the Federal system, is the relative weakness of the Government of the Union. The principle upon which all confederations rest is that of a divided sovereignty. The legislator may render this partition less perceptible, he may even conceal it for a time from the public eye, but he cannot prevent it from existing, and a divided sovereignty must always be less powerful than an entire supremacy. The reader has seen in the remarks I have made on the Constitution of the United States that the Americans have displayed singular ingenuity in combining the restriction of the power of the Union within the narrow limits of a Federal Government with the semblance and, to a certain extent, with the force of a national Government. By this means the legislators of the Union have succeeded in diminishing, though not in counteracting, the natural danger of confederations.

It has been remarked that the American Government does not apply itself to the States, but that it immediately transmits its injunctions to the citizens, and compels them as isolated individuals to comply with its demands. But if the Federal law were to clash with the interests and the prejudices of a State, it might be feared that all the citizens of that State would conceive themselves to be interested in the cause of a single individual who should refuse to obey. If all the citizens of the State were aggrieved at the same time and in the same manner by the authority of the Union, the Federal Government would vainly attempt to subdue them individually; they would instinctively unite in a common defence, and they would derive a ready-prepared organization from the share of sovereignty which the institution of their State allows them to enjoy. Fiction would give way to reality, and an organized portion of the territory might then contest the central authority. The same observation holds good with regard to the Federal jurisdiction. If the courts of the Union violated an important law of a State in a private case, the real, if not the apparent, contest would arise between the aggrieved State represented by a citizen and the Union represented by its courts of justice.[2]

[1] See the Mexican Constitution of 1824.

[2] For instance, the Union possesses by the Constitution the right of selling unoccupied lands for its own profit. Supposing that the State of Ohio should claim the same right in behalf of certain territories lying within its boundaries, upon the plea that the Constitution refers to those lands alone which do not belong to the jurisdiction of any particular State, and consequently should choose to dispose of them itself, the litigation would be carried on in the names of the purchasers from the State of Ohio and the purchasers from the Union, and not in the names of Ohio and the Union. But what would become of this legal fiction if the Federal purchaser was confirmed in his right by the courts of the Union, whilst the other competitor was ordered to retain possession by the tribunals of the State of Ohio?

He would have but a partial knowledge of the world who should imagine that it is possible, by the aid of legal fictions, to prevent men from finding out and employing those means of gratifying their passions which have been left open to them; and it may be doubted whether the American legislators, when they rendered a collision between the two sovereigns less probable, destroyed the cause of such a misfortune. But it may even be affirmed that they were unable to ensure the preponderance of the Federal element in a case of this kind. The Union is possessed of money and of troops, but the affections and the prejudices of the people are in the bosom of the States. The sovereignty of the Union is an abstract being, which is connected with but few external objects; the sovereignty of the States is hourly perceptible, easily understood, constantly active; and if the former is of recent creation, the latter is coeval with the people itself. The sovereignty of the Union is factitious, that of the States is natural, and derives its existence from its own simple influence, like the authority of a parent. The supreme power of the nation only affects a few of the chief interests of society; it represents an immense but remote country, and claims a feeling of patriotism which is vague and ill defined; but the authority of the States controls every individual citizen at every hour and in all circumstances; it protects his property, his freedom, and his life; and when we recollect the traditions, the customs, the prejudices of local and familiar attachment with which it is connected, we cannot doubt of the superiority of a power which is interwoven with every circumstance that renders the love of one's native country instinctive in the human heart.

Since legislators are unable to obviate such dangerous collisions as occur between the two sovereignties which coexist in the Federal system, their first object must be, not only to dissuade the confederate States from warfare, but to encourage such institutions as may promote the maintenance of peace. Hence it results that the Federal compact cannot be lasting unless there exists in the communities which are leagued together a certain number of inducements to union which render their common dependence agreeable, and the task of the Government light, and that system cannot succeed without the presence of favourable circumstances added to the influence of good laws. All the peoples which have ever formed a confederation have been held together by a certain number of common interests, which served as the intellectual ties of association.

But the sentiments and the principles of man must be taken into consideration as well as his immediate interests. A certain uniformity of civilization is not less necessary to the durability of a confederation than a uniformity of interests in the States which compose it. In Switzerland the difference which exists between the Canton of Uri and the Canton of Vaud is equal to that between the fifteenth and the nineteenth centuries; and, properly speaking, Switzerland has never possessed a Federal Government. The union between these two cantons only subsists upon the map, and their discrepancies would soon be perceived if an attempt were made by a central authority to prescribe the same laws to the whole territory.

One of the circumstances which most powerfully contribute to support the Federal Government in America is that the States have not only similar interests, a common origin, and a common tongue, but that they are also arrived at the same stage of civilization; which almost always renders a union feasible. I do not know of any European nation, how small soever it may be, which does not present less uniformity in its different provinces than the American people, which occupies a territory as extensive as one-half of Europe. The distance from the State of Maine to that of Georgia is reckoned at about one thousand miles; but the difference between the civilization of Maine and that of Georgia is slighter than the difference between the habits of Normandy and those of Brittany. Maine and Georgia, which are placed at the opposite extremities of a great empire, are consequently in the natural possession of more real inducements to form a confederation than Normandy and Brittany, which are only separated by a bridge.

The geographical position of the country contributed to increase the facilities which the American legislators derived from the manners and customs of the inhabitants; and it is to this circumstance that the adoption and the maintenance of the Federal system are mainly attributable.

The most important occurrence which can mark the annals of a people is the breaking out of a war. In war a people struggles with the energy of a single man against foreign nations in the defence of its very existence. The skill of a Government, the good sense of the community, and the natural fondness which men entertain for their country, may suffice to maintain peace in the interior of a district, and to favour its internal prosperity; but a nation can only carry on a great war at the cost of more numerous and more painful sacrifices; and to suppose that a great number of men will of their own accord comply with these exigencies of the State is to betray an ignorance of mankind. All the peoples which have been obliged to sustain a long and serious warfare have consequently been led to augment the power of their Government. Those which have not succeeded in this attempt have been subjugated. A long war almost always places nations in the wretched alternative of being abandoned to ruin by defeat or to despotism by success. War therefore renders the symptoms of the weakness of a Government most palpable and most alarming; and I have shown that the inherent defect of Federal Governments is that of being weak.

The Federal system is not only deficient in every kind of centralized administration, but the central Government itself is imperfectly organized, which is invariably an influential cause of inferiority when the nation is opposed to other countries which are themselves governed by a single authority. In the Federal Constitution of the United States, by which the central Government possesses more real force, this evil is still extremely sensible. An example will illustrate the case to the reader.

The Constitution confers upon Congress the right of "calling forth militia to execute the laws of the Union, suppress insurrections, and repel invasions"; and another article declares that the President of the United States is the commander-in-chief of the militia. In the war of 1812 the President ordered the militia of the Northern States to march to the frontiers; but Connecticut and Massachusetts, whose interests were impaired by the war, refused to obey the command. They argued that the Constitution authorizes the Federal Government to call forth the militia in cases of insurrection or invasion, but that in the present instance there was neither invasion nor insurrection. They added, that the same Constitution which conferred upon the Union the right of calling forth the militia reserved to the States that of naming the officers; and that consequently (as they understood the clause) no officer of the Union had any right to command the militia, even during war, except the President in person; and in this case they were ordered to join an army commanded by another individual. These absurd and pernicious doctrines received the sanction not only of the Governors and the Legislative bodies, but also of the courts of justice in both States; and the Federal Government was constrained to raise elsewhere the troops which it required.[1]

The only safeguard which the American Union, with all the relative perfection of its laws, possesses against the dissolution which would be produced by a great war, lies in its probable exemption from that calamity. Placed in the centre of an immense continent, which offers a boundless field for human industry, the Union is almost as much insulated from the world as if its frontiers were girt by the ocean. Canada contains only a million of inhabitants, and its population is divided into two inimical nations. The rigour of the climate limits the extension of its territory, and shuts up its ports during the six months of winter. From Canada to the Gulf of Mexico a few savage tribes are to be met with, which retire, perishing in their retreat, before six thousand soldiers. To the South, the Union has a point of contact with the empire of Mexico; and it is thence that serious hostilities may one day be expected to arise. But for a long while to come the uncivilized state of the Mexican community, the depravity of its morals, and its extreme poverty, will prevent that country from ranking high amongst nations. As for the Powers of Europe, they are too distant to be formidable.

The great advantage of the United States does not, then, consist in a Federal Constitution which allows them to carry on great wars, but in a geographical position which renders such enterprises extremely improbable.

No one can be more inclined than I am myself to appreciate the advantages of the Federal system, which I hold to be one of the combinations most favourable to the prosperity and freedom of man. I envy the lot of those nations which have been enabled to adopt it; but I cannot believe that any confederate peoples could maintain a long or an equal contest with a nation

[1] "Kent's Commentaries," vol. i. p. 244. I have selected an example which relates to a time posterior to the promulgation of the present Constitution. If I had gone back to the days of the Confederation, I might have given still more striking instances. The whole nation was at that time in a state of enthusiastic excitement; the Revolution was represented by a man who was the idol of the people; but at that very period Congress had, to say the truth, no resources at all at its disposal. Troops and supplies were perpetually wanting. The best-devised projects failed in the execution, and the Union, which was constantly on the verge of destruction, was saved by the weakness of its enemies far more than by its own strength.

of similar strength in which the Government should be centralized. A people which should divide its sovereignty into fractional powers, in the presence of the great military monarchies of Europe, would, in my opinion, by that very act, abdicate its power, and perhaps its existence and its name. But such is the admirable position of the New World that man has no other enemy than himself; and that, in order to be happy and to be free, it suffices to seek the gifts of prosperity and the knowledge of freedom.

13

Of Federal Representative Governments

John Stuart Mill

Portions of mankind who are not fitted or not disposed to live under the same internal government may often, with advantage, be federally united as to their relations with foreigners both to prevent wars among themselves, and for the sake of more effectual protection against the aggression of powerful States.

To render a federation advisable several conditions are necessary. The first is that there should be a sufficient amount of mutual sympathy among the populations. The federation binds them always to fight on the same side; and if they have such feelings toward one another, or such diversity of feeling toward their neighbors that they would generally prefer to fight on opposite sides, the federal tie is neither likely to be of long duration, not to be well observed while it subsists. The sympathies available for the purpose are those of race, language, religion, and, above all, of political institutions, as conducing most to a feeling of identity of political interest. When a few free states, separately insufficient for their own defense, are hemmed in on all sides by military or feudal monarchs, who hate and despise freedom even in a neighbor, those states have no chance for preserving liberty and its blessings but by a federal union. The common interest arising from this cause has in Switzerland, for several centuries, been found adequate to maintain efficiently the federal bond, in spite not only of difference of religion when religion was the grand source of irreconcilable political enmity throughout Europe, but also in spite of great weakness in the constitution of the federation itself. In America, where all the conditions for the maintenance of union exist at the highest point, with the sole drawback of difference of institutions in the single but most important article of slavery, this one difference goes so far in alienating from each other's sympathies the two divisions of the Union as to be now actually effecting the disruption of a tie of so much value to them both.

The second condition of the stability of a federal government is that the separate states be not so powerful as to be able to rely for protection against foreign encroachment on their individual strength. If they are, they will be apt to think that they do not gain, by union with others, the equivalent of what they sacrifice in their own liberty of action; and consequently, whenever the policy of the confederation, in things reserved to its cognizance, is different from that which any one of its members would separately pursue, the internal and sectional breach will, through absence of sufficient anxiety to preserve the Union, be in danger of going so far as to dissolve it.

A third condition, not less important than the two others, is that there be not a very marked inequality of strength among the several contracting states. They can not, indeed, be exactly equal in resources; in all federations there will be a gradation of power among the members; some will be more populous, rich, and civilized than others. There is a wide difference in wealth and population between New York and Rhode Island; between Berne, and Zug or Glaris. The essential is, that there should not be any one State so much more powerful than the rest as to be capable of vying in strength with many of them combined. If there be such a one, and only one, it will insist on being master of the joint deliberations; if there be two, they will be irresistible when they agree; and whenever they differ, everything will be decided by a struggle for ascendancy between the rivals. This cause is alone enough to reduce the German Bund to almost a nullity, independently of its wretched internal constitution. It effects none of the real purposes of a confederation. It has never bestowed on Germany a uniform system of customs, nor so much as a uniform coinage, and has served only to give Austria and Prussia a legal right of pouring in their troops to assist the local sovereigns in keeping their subjects obedient to despotism, while, in regard to external concerns, the Bund would make all Germany a dependency of Prussia if there were no Austria, and of Austria if there were no Prussia; and, in the meantime, each petty prince has little choice but to be a partisan of one or the other, or to intrigue with foreign governments against both.

There are two different modes of organizing a federal union. The federal authorities may represent the Governments solely, and their acts may be obligatory only on the Governments as such, or they may have the power of enacting laws and issuing orders which are binding directly on individual citizens. The former is the plan of the German so-called Confederation, and of the Swiss Constitution previous to 1847. It was tried in America for a few years immediately following the War of Independence. The other principle is that of the existing Constitution of the United States, and has been adopted within the last dozen years by the Swiss Confederacy. The Federal Congress of the American Union is a substantive part of the government of every individual state. Within the limits of its attributions, it makes laws which are obeyed by every citizen individually, executes them through its own officers, and enforces them by its own tribunals. This is the only principle which has been found, or which is ever likely to produce an effective federal government. A union between the governments only is a mere alliance, and subject to all the contingencies which render alliances precarious. If the acts of the President and of Congress were binding solely on the Governments of New York, Virginia, or Pennsylvania, and could only be carried into effect through orders issued by those governments to officers appointed by them, under responsibility to their own courts of justice, no mandates of the federal government which were disagreeable to a local majority would ever be executed. Requisitions issued to a government have no other sanction, or means of enforcement than war, and a federal army would have to be always in readiness to enforce the decrees of the federation against any recalcitrant state; subject to the probability that other states, sympathizing with the recusant, and perhaps sharing its sentiments on the particular point in dispute, would withhold their contingents, if not send them to fight in the ranks of the disobedient state. Such a federation is more likely to be a cause than a preventive of internal wars; and if such was not its effect in Switzerland until the events of the years immediately preceding 1847, it was only because the federal government felt its weakness so strongly that it hardly ever attempted to exercise any real authority. In America, the experiment of a federation on this principle broke down in the first few years of its existence, happily while the men of enlarged knowledge and acquired ascendancy who founded the independence of the republic, were still alive to guide it through the difficult transition. *The Federalist*, a collection of papers by three of these eminent men, written in explanation and defense of the new federal Constitution while still awaiting the national acceptance, is even now the most instructive treatise we possess on federal government.[1] In Germany, the more imperfect kind of federation, as all know, has not even answered the purpose of maintaining an alliance. It has never, in any European war, prevented single members of the confederation from allying themselves with foreign powers against the rest. Yet this is the only federation which seems possible among monarchical states. A king, who holds his power by inheritance, not by delegation, and who can not be deprived of it, nor made responsible to any one for its use, is not likely to renounce having a separate army, or to brook the exercise of sovereign authority over his own subjects, not through him, but directly by another power. To enable two or more countries under kingly government to be joined together in an effectual confederation, it seems necessary that they should all be under the same king. England and Scotland were a federation of this description during the interval of about a century between the union of the crowns and that of the Parliaments. Even this was effective, not through federal institutions, for none existed, but because the regal power in both Constitutions was during the greater part of that time so nearly absolute as to enable the foreign policy of both to be shaped according to a single will.

Under the more perfect mode of federation, where every citizen of each particular state owes obedience to two governments, that of his own state and that of the federation, it is evidently necessary not only that the constitutional limits of the authority of each should be precisely and clearly defined, but that the power to decide between them in any case of dispute should not reside in either of the governments, or in any functionary subject to it, but in an umpire independent of both. There must be a Supreme Court of Justice, and a system of subordinate courts in every state of the Union, before whom such questions shall be carried, and whose judgment on them, in the last stage of appeal, shall be final. Every state of the Union, and the federal government itself, as well as every functionary of each, must be liable to be sued in those courts for exceeding their powers, or for non-performance of their federal duties, and must in general be obliged to employ those courts as the instrument for enforcing their federal rights. This involves the remarkable consequence, actually realized in the United States, that a court of justice, the highest federal tribunal, is supreme over the various governments, both state and federal, having the right to declare that any law made, or act done by them, exceeds the powers assigned to them by the federal Constitution, and, in consequence, has no legal validity. It was natural to feel strong doubts, before trial had been made, how such a provision would work; whether the tribunal would have the courage to exercise its constitutional power; if it did, whether it would exercise it wisely and whether the Governments would consent to submit peaceably to its decision. The discussions on the American Constitution, before its final adoption, give evidence that these natural apprehensions were strongly felt; but they are now entirely quieted, since, during the two generations and more which have subsequently elapsed, nothing has occurred to verify them, though there have at times been disputes of considerable acrimony, and which became the badges of parties, respecting the limits of the authority of the federal and state governments. The eminently beneficial working of so singular a provision is probably, as M. de Tocqueville remarks, in a great measure attributable to the peculiarity inherent in a court of justice acting as such—namely, that it does not declare the law *eo nomine* and in the abstract, but waits until a case between man and man is brought before it judicially, involving the point in dispute; from which arises the happy effect that its declarations are not made in a very early stage of the controversy; that much popular discussion usually precedes them; that the court decides after hearing the point fully argued on both sides by lawyers of reputation; decides only as much of the question at a time as is required by the case before it, and its decision, instead of being volunteered for political purposes, is drawn from it by the duty which it cannot refuse to fulfill, of dispensing justice impartially between adverse litigants. Even these grounds of confidence would not have sufficed to produce the respectful submission with which all authorities have yielded to the decisions of the Supreme Court on the interpretation of the Constitution, were it not that complete reliance has been felt, not only on the intellectual pre-eminence of the judges composing that exalted tribunal, but on their entire superiority over either private or sectional partialities. This reliance has been in the main justified; but there is nothing which more vitally imports the American people than to guard with the most watchful solicitude against everything which has the remotest tendency to produce deterioration in the quality of this great national institution. The confidence on which depends the stability of federal institutions was for the first time impaired by the judgment declaring slavery to be of common right, and consequently lawful in the Territories while not yet constituted as states, even against the will of a majority of their inhabitants. The main pillar of the American Constitution is scarcely strong enough to bear many more such shocks.

The tribunals which act as umpires between the federal and the state governments naturally also decide all disputes between two states, or between a citizen of one state and the government of another. The usual remedies between nations, war and diplomacy, being precluded by the federal union, it is necessary that a judicial remedy should supply their place. The Supreme Court of the federation dispenses international law, and is the first great example of what is now one of the most prominent wants of civilized society, a real international tribunal.

The powers of a federal government naturally extend not only to peace and war, and all questions which arise between the country and foreign governments, but to making any other arrangements which are, in the opinion of the states, necessary to their enjoyment of the full benefits of union. For example, it is a great advantage to them that their mutual commerce should be free, without the impediment of frontier duties and custom-houses. But this internal freedom can not exist if each state has the power of fixing the duties on interchange of commodities between itself and foreign countries, since every foreign product let in by one state would be let into all the rest; and hence all custom duties and trade regulations in the United States are made or repealed by the federal government exclusively. Again, it is a great convenience to the states to have but one coinage, and but one system of weights and measures; which can only be ensured if the regulation of these matters is entrusted to the federal government. The certainty and celerity of post-office communication is impeded, and its expense increased, if a letter has to pass through half a dozen sets of public officers, subject to different supreme authorities: it is convenient, therefore, that all post-offices should be under the federal government; but on such questions the feelings of different communities are liable to be different. One of the American states, under the guidance of a man who has displayed powers as a speculative political thinker superior to any who has appeared in American politics since the authors of *The Federalist*,[2] claimed a veto for each State on the custom laws of the federal congress; and that statesman, in a posthumous work of great ability, which has been printed and widely circulated by the legislature of South Carolina, vindicated this pretension on the general principle of limiting the tyranny of the majority, and protecting minorities by admitting them to a substantial participation in political power. One of the most disputed topics in American politics during the early part of this century was whether the power of the federal government ought to extend, and whether by the Constitution it did extend, to making roads and canals at the cost of the Union. It is only in transactions with foreign powers that the authority of the federal government is of necessity complete. On every other subject the question depends on how closely the people in general wish to draw the federal tie; what portion of their local freedom of action they are willing to surrender, in order to enjoy more fully the benefit of being one nation.

Respecting the fitting constitution of a federal government within itself, much needs not be said. It of course consists of a legislative branch and an executive, and the constitution of each is amenable to the same principles as that of representative governments generally. As regards the mode of adapting these general principles to a federal government, the provision of the American Constitution seems exceedingly judicious, that Congress should consist of two houses, and that while one of them is constituted according to population, each state being entitled to representatives in the ratio of the number of its inhabitants, the other should represent not the citizens, but the state governments, and every state, whether large or small, should be represented in it by the same number of members. This provision precludes any undue power from being exercised by the more powerful states over the rest, and guarantees the reserved rights of the state governments by making it impossible, as far as the mode of representation can prevent, that any measure should pass Congress unless approved not only by a majority of the citizens, but by a majority of the states. I have before adverted to the further incidental advantage obtained of raising the standard of qualifications in one of the houses. Being nominated by select bodies, the Legislatures of the various states, whose choice, for reasons already indicated, is more likely to fall on eminent men than any popular election—who have not only the power of electing such, but a strong motive to do so, because the influence of their state in the general deliberations must be materially affected by the personal weight and abilities of its representatives—the Senate of the United States, thus chosen, has always contained nearly all the political men of established and high reputation in the Union; while the Lower House of Congress has, in the opinion of competent observers, been generally as remarkable for the absence of conspicuous personal merit, as the Upper House for its presence.

When the conditions exist for the formation of efficient and durable federal unions, the multiplication of such is always a benefit to the world. It has the same salutary effect as any other extension of the practice of co-operation, through which the weak, by uniting, can meet on equal terms with the strong. By diminishing the number of those petty states which are not equal to their own defense, it weakens the temptations to an aggressive policy, whether working directly by arms, or through the *prestige* of superior power. It of course puts an end to war and diplomatic quarrels, and usually also to restrictions on commerce, between the states composing the Union; while, in reference to neighboring nations, the increased military strength conferred by it is of a kind to be almost exclusively available for defensive, scarcely at all for aggressive purposes. A federal government has not a sufficiently concentrated authority to conduct with much efficiency any war but one of self-defense, in which it can rely on the voluntary co-operation of every citizen; nor is there anything very flattering to national vanity or ambition in acquiring, by a successful war, not subjects, nor even fellow-citizens, but only new, and perhaps troublesome independent members of the confederation. The warlike proceedings of the Americans in Mexico was purely exceptional, having been carried on principally by volunteers, under the influence of the migratory propensity which prompts individual Americans to possess themselves of unoccupied land, and stimulated, if by any public motive, not by that of national aggrandizement, but by the purely sectional purpose of extending slavery. There are few signs in the proceedings of Americans, nationally or individually, that the desire of territorial acquisition for their country as such has any considerable power over them. Their hankering after Cuba is, in the same manner, merely sectional, and the Northern States, those opposed to slavery, have never in any way favored it.

The question may present itself (as in Italy at its present uprising) whether a country which is determined to be united should form a complete or a merely federal union. The point is sometimes necessarily decided by the mere territorial magnitude of the united whole. There is a limit to the extent of country which can advantageously be governed, or even whose government can be conveniently superintended from a single centre. There are vast countries so governed; but they, or at least their distant provinces, are in general deplorably ill administered, and it is only when the inhabitants are almost savages that they could not manage their affairs better separately. This obstacle does not exist in the case of Italy, the size of which does not come up to that of several very efficiently governed single states in past and present times. The question then is, whether the different parts of the nation require to be governed in a way so essentially different that it is not probable the same Legislature, and the same ministry or administrative body, will give satisfaction to them all. Unless this be the case, which is a question of fact, it is better for them to be completely united. That a totally different system of laws and very different administrative institutions may exist in two portions of a country without being any obstacle to legislative unity, is proved by the case of England and Scotland. Perhaps, however, this undisturbed coexistence of two legal systems under one united Legislature, making different laws for the two sections of the country in adaptation to the previous differences, might not be so well preserved, or the same confidence might not be felt in its preservation, in a country whose legislators were more possessed (as is apt to be the case on the Continent) with the mania for uniformity. A people having that unbounded toleration which is characteristic of this country for every description of anomaly, so long as those whose interests it concerns do not feel aggrieved by it, afforded an exceptionally advantageous field for trying this difficult experiment. In most countries, if it was an object to retain different systems of law, it might probably be necessary to retain distinct Legislatures as guardians of them, which is perfectly compatible with a national Parliament and King, or a national Parliament without a King, supreme over the external relations of all the members of the body.

Whenever it is not deemed necessary to maintain permanently, in the different provinces, different systems of jurisprudence, and fundamental institutions grounded on different principles, it is always practicable to reconcile minor diversities with the maintenance of unity of government. All that is needful is to give a sufficiently large sphere of action to the local authorities. Under one and the same central government there may be local governors, and provincial assemblies for local purposes. It may happen, for instance, that the people of different provinces may have preferences in favor of different modes of taxation. If the general Legislature could not be depended on for being guided by the members for each province in modifying the general system of taxation to suit that province, the Constitution might provide that as many of the expenses of the government as could by any possibility be made local should be defrayed by local rates imposed by the provincial assemblies, and that those which must of necessity be general, such as the support of an army and navy, should, in the estimates for the year, be apportioned among the different provinces according to some general estimate of their resources, the amount assigned to each being levied by the local assembly on the principles most acceptable to the locality, and paid *en bloc* into the national treasury. A practice approaching to this existed even in the old French monarchy, so far as regarded the *pays d'états*, each of which, having consented or been required to furnish a fixed sum, was left to assess it upon the inhabitants by its own officers, thus escaping the grinding despotism of the royal *intendants* and *subdélégués*; and this privilege is always mentioned as one of the advantages which mainly contributed to render them, as they were, the most flourishing provinces of France.

Identity of central government is compatible with many different degrees of centralization, not only administrative, but even legislative. A people may have the desire and the capacity for a closer union than one merely federal, while yet their local peculiarities and antecedents render considerable diversities desirable in the details of their government. But if there is a real desire on all hands to make the experiment successful, there needs seldom be any difficulty in not only preserving these diversities, but giving them the guarantee of a constitutional provision against any attempt at assimilation except by the voluntary act of those who would be affected by the change.

Notes

1. Mr. Freeman's *History of Federal Governments*, of which only the first volume has yet appeared, is already an accession to the literature of the subject, equally valuable by its enlightened principles and its mastery of historical details.
2. Mr. Calhoun.

14

The Principle of Federation

Pierre-Joseph Proudhon

1. Political Dualism—Authority and Liberty: Opposition and Interconnection of the Two Ideas

Before saying what is meant by *federation*, it is as well to devote a few pages to the origin and context of the idea. The theory of the federal system is quite new; I think I may even say that no one has ever presented it before. But it is intimately bound up with the theory of government in general—to speak more precisely, it is its necessary conclusion.

Among the many constitutions proposed by philosophy and put to the test by history, one alone reconciles the demands of justice, order, liberty, and stability, without which neither society nor the individual can live. Truth, like nature, is one. It would be strange if it were otherwise for the mind and for its grandest work, society. All writers have recognized the unity of human legislation; and, without denying the diversity in application dictated by time and place and the special character of each nation, or neglecting the scope of discretion in every political system, all have been obliged to accommodate their doctrines to it. I shall undertake to show that this one constitution, which it will be the greatest triumph of human reason to have grasped, is nothing other than the federal system. Every form of government which departs from it must be considered an empirical creation, a preliminary sketch, more or less useful, under which society finds shelter for a moment, and which, like the Arab's tent, is folded up the morning after it has been erected. Rigorous analysis is therefore essential here, and the first truth which this account should impress upon the reader is that politics, though infinitely flexible as an applied art, is an exact science in its regulative principles, no more or less so than geometry or algebra.

Political order rests fundamentally on two contrary principles; *authority* and *liberty*. The one initiates, the other concludes; the one goes hand-in-hand with obedient faith, the other with free reason.

I doubt that a single voice will be raised against this first proposition. Authority and liberty are as old as the human race; they are born with us, and live on in each of us. Let us note but one thing, which few readers would notice otherwise: these two principles form a couple, so to speak, whose two terms, though indissolubly linked together, are nevertheless irreducible one to the other, and remain, despite all our efforts, perpetually at odds. Authority necessarily presupposes a liberty which recognizes or denies it; in turn liberty, in its political sense, likewise presupposes an authority which confronts it, repressing or tolerating it. Suppress one of the two, and the other has no sense: authority, without a Liberty to examine it, to resist or submit to it, is an empty word; liberty, without an authority as counterweight, is meaningless.

The principle of authority, familial, patriarchal, magisterial, monarchical, theocratic, tending to hierarchy, centralization, absorption, is given by nature, and is thus essentially predestined, divine, as you will. Its scope, resisted and impeded by the opposing principle, may expand or contract indefinitely, but can never be extinguished.

The principle of liberty, personal, individualist, critical, the instrument of dividing, choosing, arranging, is supplied by the mind. Essentially a principle of judgment, then, it is superior to the nature which it makes use of, and to the necessity which it masters. Its aspirations are unbounded; it is, like its contrary, subject to extension or restriction, but it likewise cannot be exhausted as it grows, nor can it be nullified by constraint.

It follows that in every society, even the most authoritarian, liberty necessarily plays some part; likewise in every society, even the most liberal, some portion is reserved for authority. This requirement is absolute; no political arrangement is exempt. Despite the efforts of the understanding to resolve diversity into unity, the two principles persist, always in opposition to each other. Political development arises from their inescapable logic and their mutual interaction.

All this, I confess, may contain little that is really new, and some readers will ask me if that is all I have to offer them. No one denies nature or mind, whatever the obscurity that may surround them; not one writer rejects either authority or liberty, even though their reconciliation, separation, or elimination seem equally impossible. What, then, is my purpose in reciting this commonplace?

What I have to say is this: that all political constitutions, all systems of government, including federations, fall within the scope of one formula, *the balancing of authority by liberty*, and vice versa; that in consequence the categories adopted by the great majority of writers, since Aristotle's time, in order to classify governments, differentiate states, and distinguish among the nations, *monarchy, aristocracy, democracy*, etc.—the federation excepted here—are reduced to hypothetical, empirical constructs, in which reason and justice find only imperfect satisfaction; that all established orders, founded upon these incomplete ideas, differ only from the standpoint of interest, prejudice, and habit, and are at bottom similar and equivalent; that were it not for the harm done by these false systems, in which ruffled passions, affronted interests, and vain self-deceptions are at odds with one another, we would be very close to agreement on fundamentals; that, finally, all those partisan divisions which we imagine to be so profound, all those conflicts of opinion which seem insoluble to us, all those random hostilities for which there appears to be no remedy, will instantly find a definitive solution in the theory of federal government.

Is there so much, you will ask, in a semantic opposition, *authority-liberty*? Indeed, yes! I have observed that the ordinary mind, even the child, can better grasp the truth cast in an abstract formula than when it is inflated with a mass of explanations and facts. I wished both to condense this study for those who cannot read books, and to make it more compelling by appealing to simple ideas. *Authority* and *liberty*: two concepts opposed to another, destined to live in struggle or to perish together; here, indeed, is something not very hard to grasp. Have the patience to continue, dear reader, and if you have understood this first and very short chapter, you will tell me your opinion afterwards. [. . .]

7. Isolation of the Idea of Federation

Since in theory and in history authority and liberty succeed one another in a polar movement; since the former declines imperceptibly and withdraws, while the latter expands and becomes prominent; since this dual movement leads to a subordination such that authority becomes progressively the instrument of liberty; since, in other words, the liberal or contractual system gains the upper hand day by day over the authoritarian system, it is the idea of contract that we must take to be the principal idea in politics.

What is meant, first of all, by *contract*?

> A contract [Civil Code, article 1101] is an agreement by which one or more persons oblige themselves to one or more others to perform or to refrain from some action.
>
> Article 1102: It is *synallagmatic* or *bilateral* when the contracting parties undertake reciprocal obligations.
>
> Article 1103: It is *unilateral*, when one or more persons have an obligation to one or more others, without the latter having any obligation.
>
> Article 1104: It is *commutative* when each of the parties undertakes to give something which is regarded as equal in value to what the other party gives or does in return. When the benefits consist in an opportunity for each party to gain, or to lose, the outcome being uncertain, the contract is *aleatory*.
>
> Article 1105: A contract of *goodwill* is that in which one of the parties provides the other with a purely gratuitous benefit.
>
> Article 1106: An *onerous* contract is one which obliges both parties to give or to do something.
>
> Article 1371: *Quasi-contracts* are those voluntary acts of men which give rise to an obligation to a third party, and sometimes to reciprocal obligations between two parties.

To these distinctions and definitions in the Code, which bear upon the forms and conditions of contracts, I shall add a further distinction regarding their objects: according to the nature of the things which are bargained for or to the object which one has in view, contracts are *domestic*, *civil*, *commercial*, or *political*. It is with the last of these, political contracts, that we shall be concerned.

The idea of contract is not entirely unknown in monarchies, or in families. But in terms of what we have said about the principles of authority and liberty and their role in the formation of governments, it will be clear that these principles relate in different ways to the political contract; the obligation uniting the monarch to his subjects, which is spontaneous and unwritten, arising from family feeling and personal qualities, is a *unilateral* obligation, for by virtue of the principle of obedience the subject is obliged to do more for his prince than the prince for him. The theory of divine right states expressly that the monarch is responsible only to God. It may even happen that the prince's contract with the subject degenerates into a contract of pure *good will*, when his subjects' incapacity or their idolatry leads the prince to treat his people, unable to govern or to defend themselves, as a shepherd treats his sheep. It is even worse when the hereditary principle is adopted. A conspirator like the Duke of Orleans, later Louis XII, a parricide like Louis XI, and an adulteress like Mary Stuart maintain their right to the throne despite their crimes. Birth renders them inviolable, and one may say that a *quasi-contract* exists between them and the loyal subjects of the prince whom they succeed. In a word, simply because authority is preponderant in the monarchical system, the contract is not equal.

The political contract does not attain its full dignity and morality except where (1) it is *synallagmatic* and *commutative*, (2) it is confined, in its object, within definite limits—two conditions which are held to exist in the democratic system, but which, even there, are generally only a fiction. Can one say that in a representative and centralized democracy, or in a constitutional monarchy with restricted franchise, or even more in a communist republic such as Plato's the political contract binding the citizen to the state can be equal and reciprocal? Can one say that these contracts, which remove from the citizens a half or two-thirds of their sovereignty and a quarter of their product, are confined within just limits? It would be closer to the truth to say that, as experience shows only too often, contracts in such systems are excessive, *onerous*, for they provide no compensation for a good many of those who are parties to them; and *aleatory*, for the promised advantage, inadequate as it is, is not even guaranteed.

In order for the political contract to become synallagmatic and commutative as the idea of democracy requires, in order for it to remain within reasonable limits and to become profitable and convenient for all, the citizen who enters the association must (1) have as much to gain from the state as he sacrifices to it, (2) retain all his liberty, sovereignty, and initiative, except that which he must abandon in order to attain that special object for which the contract is made, and which the state must guarantee. So confined and understood, the political contract is what I shall call a *federation*.

Federation, from the Latin *foedus*, genitive *foederis*, which means pact, contract, treaty, agreement, alliance, and so on, is an agreement by which one or more heads of family, one or more towns, one or more groups of towns or states, assume reciprocal and equal commitments to perform one or more specific tasks, the responsibility for which rests exclusively with the officers of the federation.*

Let us consider this definition more closely. What is essential to and characteristic of the federal contract, and what I most wish the reader to notice, is that in this system the contracting parties, whether heads of family, towns, cantons, provinces, or states, not only undertake bilateral and commutative obligations, but in making the pact reserve for themselves more rights, more liberty, more authority, more property than they abandon.

It is not so, for example, in the society of common property, or communism, authorized under the Civil Code, the replica in miniature of all absolute states. He who enters into such an association, especially if it is a permanent one, is loaded with chains and subjected to burdens which quite overwhelm his personal freedom. It is this that makes such contracts so rare, and monastic life always so intolerable. Any obligation, even a bilateral and commutative one, which requires those whom it binds to contribute all their efforts, to give up their independence, and to devote themselves totally to an association is an excessive obligation unworthy of man or citizen.

According to these principles the contract of federation has the purpose, in general terms, of guaranteeing to the federated states their sovereignty, their territory, the liberty of their subjects; of settling their disputes; of providing by common means for all matters of security and mutual prosperity; thus, despite the scale of the interests involved, it is essentially limited. The authority responsible for its execution can never overwhelm the constituent members; that is, the federal powers can never exceed in number and significance those of local or provincial authorities, just as the latter can never outweigh the rights and prerogatives of man and citizen. If it were otherwise, the community would become communistic; the federation would revert to centralized monarchy; the federal authority, instead of being a mere delegate and subordinate function as it should be, will be seen as dominant; instead of being confined to a specific task, it will tend to absorb all activity and all initiative; the confederated states will be reduced to administrative districts, branches, or local offices. Thus transformed, the body politic may be termed republican, democratic, or what you will; it will no longer be a state constituted by a plenitude of autonomies, it will no longer

* In J.-J. Rousseau's theory, which was also that of Robespierre and the Jacobins, the social contract is a legal *fiction*, imagined as an alternative to divine right, paternal authority, or social necessity, in explaining the origins of the state and the relations between government and individual. This theory, borrowed for the Calvinists, represented a step forward in 1764, for its purpose was to explain by a law of reason what had formerly been seen as belonging to the law of nature and to religion. In the federal system, the social contract is more than a fiction; it is a positive and effective compact, which has actually been proposed, discussed, voted upon, and adopted, and which can properly be amended at the contracting parties' will. Between the federal contract and that of Rousseau and 1793 there is all the difference between a reality and a hypothesis.

be a confederation. The same will hold, with even greater force, if for reasons of false economy, as a result of deference, or for any other reason the federated towns, cantons or states charge one among their number with the administration and government of the rest. The republic will become unitary, not federal, and will be on the road to despotism.*

In summary, the federal system is the contrary of hierarchy or administrative and governmental centralization which characterizes, to an equal extent, democratic empires, constitutional monarchies, and unitary republics. Its basic and essential law is this: in a federation, the powers of central authority are specialized and limited and diminish in number, in directness, and in what I may call intensity as the confederation grows by the adhesion of new states. In centralized governments, on the contrary, the powers of the supreme authority multiply, extend, and become more direct, bringing the business of provinces, towns, corporations, and individuals under the jurisdiction of the prince, as a direct function of territorial scale and the size of the population. Hence arises that suppression of all liberties, communal and provincial, and even individual and national.

One result of this, to conclude this chapter, is that since the unitary system is the contrary of the federal system, a confederation of great monarchies, or even more of democratic empires, is impossible. States such as France,

* The Helvetian Confederation consists of twenty-five sovereign states (nineteen cantons and six half-cantons), containing a population of two million, four hundred thousand inhabitants. It is therefore governed by twenty-five constitutions, comparable to our charters or constitutions of 1791, 1793, 1795, 1799, 1814, 1830, 1848, 1852, together with a federal constitution to which of course there is no parallel in France. The spirit of this constitution, which conforms to the principles outlined above, is contained in the following articles:
"Article 2. The purpose of confederation is to secure the independence of the nation against foreign powers, to maintain internal peace and order, to protect the rights and liberties of its members, and to increase their common prosperity."

"Article 3. The cantons are sovereign within the limits of federal sovereignty, and as such they exercise all rights which have not been delegated to the federal power."

"Article 5. The confederation guarantees to the cantons their territory, their sovereignty within the limits established by Article 3, their constitutions, the liberty and rights of their inhabitants, the constitutional rights of their citizens, as well as the rights and powers which the people have conferred upon the authorities."

Thus a confederation is not exactly a state; it is a group of sovereign and independent states, associated by a pact of mutual guarantees. Nor is a federal constitution the same as what is understood in France by a charter or constitution, an abridged statement of public law; the pact contains the conditions of association, that is, the rights and reciprocal obligations of the states. What is called federal authority, finally, is no longer a government; it is an agency created by the states for the joint execution of certain functions which the states abandon, and which thus become federal powers.

In Switzerland the federal authority resides in a deliberative assembly elected by the citizens of the twenty-five cantons, and an executive council composed of seven members appointed by the assembly. The members of the assembly and the federal council are elected for three-year terms; since the federal constitution can be revised at any time, the powers of office, no less than its occupants, may be altered. Thus the federal power is in the full sense of the word an agent, under the strict control of his principals, whose power varies at their pleasure.

Austria, England, Russia, or Prussia may make treaties of alliance or trade among themselves; but they resist federalization because their principles are contrary to it and will set them against any federal compact, and because they would have to abandon some part of their sovereignty and recognize an arbiter set above them, at least for certain matters. Their nature is to command, not to compromise or to obey. The princes who in 1813, supported by mass uprisings, fought for the freedom of Europe against Napoleon and later formed the Holy Alliance did not form a federation; their absolutism prevented them from accepting such a title. They formed, as in 1792, a *coalition*; history gives them no other name. It is otherwise with the German confederation, currently on the road to reform, and whose characteristics of freedom and nationality promise eventually to destroy the dynasties who impede it.*

* The public law of federation raises several difficult questions. For example, can a state containing slaves join a confederation? It seems that it cannot, any more than an absolute state can; the enslavement of part of a nation denies the federal principle itself. In this respect, the Southern states of the United States have an even better right to demand secession in that they do not follow the Northerners in proposing to extend political rights to freed slaves, at present at least. But Washington, Madison, and the other founders of the Union did not take this view; they admitted slave-owning states to the federal pact. This unnatural pact, moreover, is now crumbling before our eyes, as the Southern states, to preserve their economy, lean towards a unitary constitution, while those of the North, in order to maintain the Union, decree the deportation of slaves.

The Swiss federal constitution, as reformed in 1848, comes down on the side of equality; according to Article 4, "All Swiss are equal before the law. In Switzerland there are neither subjects nor privileges of place, birth, person, or family." The adoption of this article, which purges Switzerland of any trace of aristocracy, inaugurates a truly federal constitution.

If a conflict of interests arises, can a federal majority faced by a separatist minority claim that the pact is irrevocable? In 1846 the *Sonderbund*, opposed by a majority of cantons, claimed that it could not; the same is maintained by the Confederacy of the American South in opposition to the Northern Unionists. As for me, I believe that separation is fully legitimate, on a matter of cantonal sovereignty not embraced by the federal pact. Thus it is not clear to me that the Swiss majority derived its right against the *Sonderbund* from the pact; the proof is that in 1848 the federal constitution was amended precisely in order to settle the problem that had led to the formation of the *Sonderbund*. But it may happen that, in terms of utility, minority claims conflict with majority needs, that divisiveness imperils the liberty of the states. In such a case the question is resolved by the right of war, which means that the larger party, whose ruin would involve the greater loss, must triumph over the weaker. This is what took place in Switzerland and could also occur in the United States, if what was in question was simply a matter of the interpretation or better application of the principles of the pact, such as improving the lot of the blacks to the level enjoyed by the whites. Unfortunately, Mr Lincoln's message leaves no room for doubt: the North does not have in mind true emancipation any more than the South, which makes the problem insoluble even by means of war, and threatens to dissolve confederation.

In a monarchy all justice is the king's; in a confederation it arises in each state exclusively from its own citizens. Establishing a supreme federal court would in principle be a violation of the compact. The same goes for a court of appeal, for, each state being sovereign and legislating for itself, laws will not be uniform. However, as there are federal interests and federal business, and as offences and crimes may be committed against the federation, there are federal courts and federal justice bearing upon such specific cases.

8. A PROGRESSIVE CONSTITUTION

History and analysis, theory and observation have led us through the struggles of liberty and power to the idea of a political contract.

In at once applying this idea and trying to come to terms with it we have seen that the social contract *par excellence* is a federal contract, which we define as follows: a bilateral and commutative contract concerning one or more specific objects, having as its necessary condition that the contracting parties retain more sovereignty and a greater scope of action than they give up.

This is just the opposite of what takes place in the old monarchical, democratic, or constitutional systems, where, thanks to the logic of situation and principle, individuals and groups are held to have given up all their sovereignty to an imposed or elected authority, the rights which they gain and the security and independence which they retain being outweighed by their new burdens and duties.

This definition of the contract of federation is an immense step forward and will give us the solution which we have sought for so long.

As we said in chapter 1, the political problem, reduced to its simplest expression, is that of finding an equilibrium between two contrary elements, authority and liberty. Any error in balancing the two leads at once to the disorder and ruin of the state and the oppression and distress of the people. In other words the anomalies and disturbances of society arise from contradictions between its principles and will vanish when its principles are harmonized in such a manner that they can damage one another no longer.

To balance two forces is to submit them to a *law* which, obliging each to respect the other brings them into agreement. What will supply us with this new element, superior to both authority and liberty, and acquiring pre-eminence with the consent of both?—the contract, whose terms establish *right*, and bear equally upon two contending forces.*

But in a concrete and living reality such as society, right cannot be only an abstract notion, a nebulous aspiration, something which would plunge us into fiction and myth. To found a society requires not merely an idea but a

* There are three ways of conceiving of law, depending upon the point of view adopted by a moral being and the capacity which he assumes: *believer, philosopher,* or *citizen.*

Law is a *command* transmitted to man in God's name by a competent authority: this is the definition of theology and divine right.

Law is an *expression of the relations* of things: this is the philosopher's definition, supplied by Montesquieu.

Law is a *statute of arbitration* willed by man (see *De la Justice dans la Révolution et dans l'Eglise*, 8th study): this is the theory of contract and of federation.

Since truth is one, though its aspect varies, these three definitions converge with one another and must be regarded as at bottom identical. But the social orders which they generate are not the same; in the first, man declares himself the subject of the law and of its author or representative; in the second he regards himself as an integral part of a great organism; in the third, he makes law his own and frees himself from all authority, from fate and domination. The first is that of the religious man, the second that of the pantheist, the third that of the republican. The last of these alone is compatible with liberty.

juridical act, the making of a real contract. The men of 1789 grasped this, in undertaking to give France a constitution, and all the regimes which have succeeded them have taken the same view. Unfortunately, though the intention was good, their understanding was inadequate; until now, there has been no notary to witness the contract. We know what the spirit of the contract must be; let us now examine the letter of it in detail.

All the articles of a contract may be reduced to one, that which concerns the role and jurisdiction of that great functionary called the state. Our national assemblies have vied with one another in distinguishing and separating powers or the state's faculties of action; as for the jurisdiction of the state as such, its scope, its object, no one seems to have worried much about the matter. Men have dreamed of *sharing*, as a minister naively said in 1848; as for the thing to be shared, the bigger, it seems, the better. And yet the limitation of the role of the state is a question of life and death for liberty, whether collective or individual.

The contract of federation, whose essence is always to reserve more powers for the citizen than for the state, and for municipal and provincial authorities than for the central power, is the only thing that can set us on the right path.

In a free society, the role of the state or government is essentially that of legislating, instituting, creating, beginning, establishing; as little as possible should it be executive. In this respect, the term *executive power*, which is used to designate one of the aspects of sovereignty, has made a notable contribution to error. The state is not an entrepreneur in the public sector, to be confused with the contractors who perform public works. Whether it commands, acts, or supervises, the state is the initiator and ultimate director of change; if from time to time it involves itself in tasks directly, it does so by way of demonstration, to make a start and to set an example. Once a beginning has been made, the machinery established, the state withdraws, leaving the execution of the new task to local authorities and citizens.

The state establishes weights and measures, prescribes the units, value, and divisions of currency. Once the model has been provided, the first issue completed, the manufacture of gold and silver and copper coins ceases to be a public function, a task of the state, a ministerial power; it is an industry left to the towns, and there is nothing that requires it to be any less free than the manufacture of scales, weighing-machines, barrels, or bottles. That it should be done cheaply is all that matters. What is required, in France, for gold and silver currency to maintain its standing? Simply that coins should contain no more that one-tenth alloy. That there should be an inspector to supervise its manufacture, I admit; but the role of the state extends no further than that.

What I have said of currency I would repeat of a whole host of services which have quite wrongly been placed in the hands of government: roads, canals, tobacco licensing, the postal service, telegraphs, railways, and so on. I understand, I admit, I insist that the state must intervene in all such major public utilities; but I cannot see any need to leave them in the hands of the state once they have been initiated. Such a concentration, as far as I can see, amounts to truly excessive power. In 1848 I called for the state to intervene in establishing national banks, credit, savings, and insurance institutions, as it had done in the case of railways. It never entered my head that once the state had completed its task of creation it would stay in the banking, insurance, and transportation business. True, the organization of public education calls for a major effort by central authority, but nevertheless I believe in the cause of freedom in education, as of all freedoms.* I wish the school to be no less strictly separated from the state than the church. That there should be an accounting office, even a bureau of statistics, to assemble, check, and classify the financial data of the whole republic, all well and good. But why should all expenses and revenues pass through the hands of a treasurer, a single collector and paymaster, a minister of the state, when by the nature of its function the state should have little or no service to perform, therefore little or no expense?**

Is it really necessary, furthermore, that the courts should be subordinate to central authority? Administering justice has been since the beginning of time the highest power of the prince, indeed; but this power is a vestige of divine right and cannot be claimed by a constitutional monarch, still less by an emperor elected by universal suffrage. Thus from the moment that the idea of right becomes human once more and acquires pre-eminence in the political order, the independence of the judiciary will necessarily be implied. Justice will no longer be seen as a power of central or federal authority; it can be no more than a delegation by the citizens to municipal authority, or provincial at most. Justice is a human power which no reason of state can cancel. Nor do I except even military service from this argument; militias, armouries, and forts pass into the hands of federal authorities only in time of war, and only for the purposes of war; otherwise, soldiers and arms remain under the control of local authorities.†

In a properly organized society, everything must be in continuous growth—science, industry, work, wealth, public health; liberty and morality must follow the same path. Their movement, their life, does not cease for a moment. As the principal organ of this movement, the state is always active; for new needs to be satisfied, new problems to solve, never cease to emerge. If its function as prime mover and general director is continuous, its work, however, is not repetitive. It is the highest expression of progress. What happens if, as is almost everywhere the case, the state continues to provide the services it has created and succumbs to the temptations of monopoly? It

* According to the Swiss federal constitution of 1848, *the Confederation has the right to found a University of Switzerland.* This idea was vigorously opposed as an affront to the sovereignty of cantons, which seems to me to have been a good policy. I do not know what finally become of the project.

** In Switzerland there is a federal budget, administered by the federal council; but it provides only for the expenses of the Confederation and is quite separate from the budgets of cantons and towns.

† Article 13 of the federal constitution of Switzerland: "The Confederation does not have the right to maintain a standing army." Our unitary republicans might reflect upon this article.

exchanges the founder's role for that of a mechanic; it is no longer the spirit of the community, giving it life, directing and enriching it, without impeding it; it becomes a vast limited company, with six hundred thousand employees and six hundred thousand soldiers, ready for every task, and instead of coming to the nation's aid, instead of serving its citizens and communities, it expropriates and crushes them. Soon corruption, embezzlement, and laxness enter into the system; absorbed in maintaining itself, extending its prerogatives, multiplying its tasks, and swelling its budget, power loses sight of its true role and collapses into autocracy and immobility; society is the victim, and the nation, contrary to its historic law, begins to decline.

Have we not seen, in chapter 6, that authority and liberty follow in logical and temporal succession in the evolution of states; that, moreover, the first is in continuous decline, the second in the ascendant; that government, the organ of authority, is imperceptibly subordinated to the representatives or organs of liberty—that is, the central power to the representatives of departments or provinces, provincial authority to the delegates of townships, and municipal authority to its inhabitants; that liberty thus aspires to make itself paramount, authority to make itself the servant of liberty, and that the contractual principle tends to substitute itself everywhere for the authoritarian principle in public affairs?

If this is true, the consequence cannot be in doubt. Since, according to the nature of things and the play of principles, authority retreats and liberty advances, in such a way that conflict between them is avoided, society's constitution is essentially progressive, or increasingly liberal, and its goal cannot be realized except in a society whose governing hierarchy is no longer imposed from the top down but rests securely on its base—that is, a federal system.

The whole science of constitutions is here. I shall summarize it in three propositions.

(1) Form groups of a modest size, individually sovereign, and unite them by a federal pact.

(2) Within each federated state organize government on the principle of organic separation; that is, separate all powers that can be separated, define everything that can be defined, distribute what has been separated and defined among distinct organs and functionaries; leave nothing undivided; subject public administration to all the constraints of publicity and control.

(3) Instead of absorbing the federated states and provincial and municipal authorities within a central authority, reduce the role of the centre to that of general initiation, of providing guarantees and supervising, and make the execution of its orders subject to the approval of the federated governments and their responsible agents—just as, in a constitutional monarchy, every order by the king must be countersigned by a minister in order to become effective.

Certainly, the separation of powers as practised under the 1830 Charter was a fine and very significant institution, but it is childish to confine the principle to the members of a cabinet. The government of a nation is not to be shared among seven or eight elected officials drawn from a parliamentary majority and criticized by the opposition, but among the provinces and townships; otherwise political life abandons the periphery for the centre, and collapse overcomes a hydrocephalous nation.

The federal system is applicable to all nations and all ages, for humanity is progressive in each of its generations and peoples; the policy of federation, essentially the policy of progress, consists in ruling every people, at any given moment, by decreasing the sway of authority and central power to the point permitted by the level of consciousness and morality.

9. What has Delayed Federation; Factors Hindering the Idea

The idea of federation appears to be as ancient as the ideas of monarchy and democracy, as old as authority and liberty themselves. How could it be otherwise? Everything produced in society over time by the law of progress has its roots in nature itself. Civilization advances enveloped by its principles, its ideas in procession before and after, and encircling it ceaselessly. Founded upon contract, the solemn expression of liberty, federation could never fail to appeal to man. More than twelve centuries before Christ, it appeared among the Hebrew tribes, separate from one another in their own valleys, but, like the tribes of Ishmael, united by a sort of contract of kinship. Only a little later it emerged in the Amphictyonic league, which, it is true, was powerless to suppress internal discord or to stave off conquest, or, eventually, imperial absorption but was all the same vivid testimony to the future right of men and to universal liberty. We remember still the great leagues of the Slav and German peoples, continued in modern times by the federal constitutions of Switzerland and Germany, and even by the Austrian Empire, formed of nations which are so heterogeneous and yet, despite all efforts, inseparable. It is the federal contract which will become step by step the basis of true government, will everywhere put an end to the contradictions of empiricism, eliminate arbitrariness, and establish justice and peace upon an unshakeable equilibrium.

For centuries, the idea of federation seems to have been hidden and held in reserve; the reason for this eclipse is to be found in the initial incapacity of nations and the need to form them by means of stern discipline. Such is the role which seems to have been assigned, by a sort of sovereign design, to the unitary system.

It was necessary to tame and settle the fickle, rough, undisciplined multitude; to form isolated and hostile cities into groups; to found by authority, step by step, a common law, and to promulgate the general laws of humanity in the form of imperial decrees. This alone must have been the significance of those vast political structures of antiquity, succeeded, in this role, by the Greek, Roman, and Frankish empires, the Christian church, Luther's rebellion, and finally the French Revolution.

Federation cannot fulfil this initial educational mission because it is liberty; because it excludes the idea of constraint, resting upon the notion of bilateral, commutative, and limited contracts; and because its object is to guarantee the sovereignty and autonomy of the peoples whom it unites, peoples who must suffer domination until they become capable of governing themselves by reason. Since civilization is, in a word, progressive, it would be contradictory to suppose that a federal government could have arisen at the beginning.

Another reason for the temporary eclipse of the federal principle is supplied by the weak expansive tendency of states gathered under federal constitutions.

The natural limits of federal states. We have seen in chapter 2 that monarchy, by its own nature and that of its principle, knows no limits to its own expansion, and that the same goes for democracy. This expansive power has been transmitted from the simple a priori governments to the mixed or *de facto* types, such as democracies and aristocracies, democratic empires and constitutional monarchies, which have all remained faithful in this respect to their ideal. From this arise messianic visions and many attempts to form universal monarchies or republics.

In these systems there is no end to the process of assimilation; one may say that here the idea of a *natural frontier* is a fiction, or, better, a political fraud; rivers, mountains, and seas are no longer considered as territorial limits but as obstacles which the liberty of king and nation must overcome. The logic of their principles, moreover, requires this; the power to possess, accumulate, command, and exploit is indefinite, it knows no bounds but the universe. The most noted example of the assimilation of regions and peoples, despite the mountains, rivers, forests, seas, and deserts, is that of the Roman Empire, with its centre and capital in a peninsula surrounded by a large sea, and its provinces as far-flung as its armies and tax-collectors could reach.

Every state is annexationist by nature. Nothing stops its aggressive march, unless it confronts another state, likewise an aggressor and capable of defending itself. The most ardent apostles of nationality fall into contradictions when the interest or, even more, the security of their country so dictates: who, among the French democrats, would have dared denounce the union of Savoy and Nice? It is not even unknown that annexations should be favoured by those who are annexed, who barter away their independence and autonomy.

It is otherwise in the federal system. Though capable indeed of defending themselves when attacked, the Swiss have shown several times that a confederation is incapable of conquest. Apart from the very rare case of a neighboring state requesting admission to the pact, one may say that the very existence of federations forbids all expansion. By virtue of the principle which limits the federal pact to the provision of mutual defence and certain purposes of common benefit, *guarantees* to each state its territory, its sovereignty, its constitution, and the liberty of its citizens, and reserves to each party more authority, independence, and power than it abandons, the confederation restrains its own growth all the more surely to the extent that the regions which form it are distant from one another; and thus one soon arrives at a point at which the pact loses its purpose. Let us suppose that one among the confederated states proposes a certain conquest, the annexation of a neighboring town or nearby province, or that it wishes to meddle in the affairs of another state. Not only will it not be able to count upon the support of the confederation, which will object that the pact was formed exclusively for the defence of the whole, not the aggrandizement of one part; it would find itself actually constrained by the solidarity of the others, who would not wish that all should go to war for the advantage of one. In this way the confederation provides a guarantee to its neighbours as well as to its own members.

Contrary to what takes place in other systems, then, the idea of a universal confederation is contradictory. Here once more we see the moral superiority of the federal over the unitary system, which is subject to all the shortcomings and vices of the undefined, the unlimited, the absolute, the ideal. Even Europe would be too large to form a single confederation; it could form only a confederation of confederations. That is why, in my last book, I laid down as the first step towards the reform of public law in Europe the restoration of the confederations of Italy, Greece, the Netherlands, Scandinavia, and the Danube, as a prelude to the decentralization of the large states and hence to general disarmament. Thus each nationality would recover its liberty, and a European balance of power would be achieved—an idea foreseen by all the political theorists and statesmen, but impossible to realize among great powers with unitary constitutions.* [. . .]

11. ECONOMIC SANCTIONS: THE AGRO-INDUSTRIAL FEDERATION

But there is more to be said. However impeccable in its logic the federal constitution may be, and whatever practical guarantees it may supply, it will not survive if economic factors tend persistently to dissolve it. In other words, political right requires to be buttressed by economic right. If the production and distribution of wealth are given over to chance; if the federal order serves merely to preserve the anarchy of capital and commerce; if, as a result of this misguided anarchy, society comes to be divided into two classes—one of landlords, capitalists, and entrepreneurs, the other of wage-earning proletarians, one rich, the other poor—then the political order will still be unstable. The working class, the most numerous and poorest of the classes, will eventually regard it as nothing but a trick; the workers will unite against the

* Among French democrats there has been much talk of a European confederation, or a *United States of Europe.* By this they seem to understand nothing but an alliance of all the states which presently exist in Europe, great and small, presided over by a permanent congress. It is taken for granted that each state will retain the form of government that suits it best. Now since each state will have votes in the congress in proportion to its population and territory, the small states in this so-called confederation will soon be incorporated into the large ones; moreover, if this new Holy Alliance could have such a thing as a collective development, one would soon see it collapse, after internal strife, into a single power or great European monarchy. Such a federation would thus be a trap or else devoid of meaning.

bourgeois, who in turn will unite against the workers; and federation will degenerate into unitary democracy, if the people are stronger, or, if the bourgeoisie is victorious, into a constitutional monarchy. [. . .]

The reader may expect me to present a scheme of economic science as applied to federations, and to show in detail all that has to be done from this perspective. I shall simply say that after reforming the political order the federal government must necessarily proceed to a series of reforms in the economic realm. Here, in a few words, is what these reforms must be.

Just as, in a political context, two or more independent states may federate in order to guarantee mutually their territorial integrity or to protect their liberty, so too, in an economic context, confederation may be intended to provide reciprocal security in commerce and industry, or a *customs union;* or the object may be to construct and maintain means of transportation, such as roads, canals, and railways, or to organize credit, insurance, and so on. The purpose of such specific federal arrangements is to protect the citizens of the federated states from capitalist and financial exploitation, both within them and from the outside; in their aggregate they form, as opposed to the financial feudalism in the ascendant today, what I will call an *agro-industrial federation.*

I shall not go into this topic in any depth. Those of my readers who have followed my work to any extent for the last fifteen years will understand well enough what I mean. The purpose of industrial and financial feudalism is to confirm, by means of the monopoly of public services, educational privilege, the division of labour, interest on capital, inequitable taxation, and so on, the political neutralization of the masses, wagelabour or economic servitude, in short inequality of condition and wealth. The agro-industrial federation, on the other hand, will tend to foster increasing equality, by organizing all public services in an economical fashion and in hands other than the state's, through mutualism in credit and insurance, the equalization of the tax burden, guaranteeing the right to work and to education, and an organization of work which allows each labourer to become a skilled worker and an artist, each wage-earner to become his own master.

Such a revolution, it is clear, cannot be the work of a bourgeois monarchy or a unitary democracy; it will be accomplished by federation. It does not spring from the *unilateral* contract or the contract of *goodwill*, nor from the institutions of *charity*, but from bilateral and commutative contract.*

* A simple calculation makes this clear. The average period of schooling for both sexes, in a free society, cannot be less than ten or twelve years; hence almost one fifth of the population will be of school age—in France, seven and a half million individuals, boys and girls, out of a total population of thirty-eight million. In countries such as America, where families are larger, the proportion would be even higher. There are then *seven and a half million* individuals of both sexes who must be given a fair measure, certainly with nothing aristocratic about it, of literary, scientific, moral, and vocational education. How many people attend secondary and higher schools in France? One hundred and twenty-seven thousand, four hundred and seventy-four, according to M.Guillard's figures. The rest, seven million, three hundred and seventy thousand, five hundred and twenty-five of them, are condemned never to go beyond

Considered in itself, the idea of an industrial federation which serves to complement and support political federation is most strikingly justified by the principles of economics. It is the application on the largest possible scale of the principles of mutualism, division of labour, and economic solidarity, principles which the will of the people will have transformed into positive laws.

---

primary school. But they must all be educated: every year admissions committees report an increasing number of *illiterates*. What would our government do, I wonder, if they were obliged to resolve the problem of giving a modest education to seven million, three hundred and seventy thousand, five hundred and twenty-five individuals, on top of the one hundred and twenty-seven thousand, four hundred and seventy-four currently enrolled in the schools? Of what use here are the unilateral contract of bourgeois monarchy, the contract of goodwill of the paternalist empire, the charitable foundations of the church, Malthusian policies, and the promises of free trade? Even Committees of Public Safety, for all their revolutionary energy, would fail in the task. Such a goal can be achieved only by a combination of apprenticeship and schooling which will make each pupil into a worker—which presupposes a universal federation. I know of no consideration more devastating to the old policies than that.

IV

The Mid-Twentieth-Century Debate: Federalism between Obsolescence and Panacea

15

Editors' Introduction

The period from the American Civil War to the Second World War was a quiet one in the history of normative federal theory. Writers such as Otto von Gierke, Louis Le Fur, A.V. Dicey, and James Bryce developed an institutional and comparative approach to the study of federalism. Their focus was mainly on the formal aspects of federalism. Whatever their ideological perspective, most of the writers in this period considered federalism to be a conservative legalistic framework, a perception well encapsulated in Harold Laski's critical essay on the "obsolescence of federalism" (1939).

Things changed significantly during and after the Second World War. First, the consensus that nationalism (and nation-statism) had caused the war, and that the League of Nations had been powerless to prevent it, prompted many Resistance thinkers and their post-1945 followers to see federalism as an urgent panacea to Europe's chronic ills. And second, an occasion for rethinking the virtues of federalism was presented by the creation of dozens of new multiethnic states in the 1950s and 1960s as the European colonial powers retreated from Africa, Asia, and elsewhere (with Indian federation being the most spectacular and enduring example). Third, the postwar decades saw the emergence or reemergence of debates about intercommunity justice and autonomy in a number of multilingual states like Canada, Switzerland, Belgium, and Spain. All of these developments reinvigorated normative debates about whether federal systems were inherently conservative or progressive, and about how federal arrangements might best deal with problems of multiple and overlapping identities within a state or superstate. These debates remain active to this day.

In part IV, we include writings from five participants to these pre- and postwar debates: Harold Laski, a British socialist intellectual; Altiero Spinelli, one of the intellectual and political founders of the Italian and European federalist movements in the 1940s; Robert Schuman, the postwar French foreign minister following the advice of the intellectual and technocratic "father of the European Union," Jean Monnet; Franz Neumann; and Pierre Elliott Trudeau, in the years before he became the Canadian prime minister. Laski's article is important because he was an influential professor (at the London School of Economics) and political figure (within the British Labour Party) whose provocative assertions on the "obsolete" and "conservative" character of federalism came explicitly under attack from many postwar proponents of federalism. Furthermore, it provides insights into the intellectual background of the debate.

Written in collaboration with Ernesto Rossi in 1941 (and revised in 1944) when they were both interned on the island of Ventotene, Spinelli's manifesto develops several arguments that were influential at the time. The extracts we present in this volume feature three key arguments of the manifesto. First, the manifesto argues that the dominant system of nation-states is largely responsible for totalitarianism and war. Second, it emphasizes that the top priority of progressive forces in Europe must be to replace the nation-states system by a European federation, since this is the only possible way out of the crisis. Third, socialist reforms are also required, but they must occur in the institutional and political context of a federal Europe. In other words, federalization must precede social and economic reforms. While Spinelli would pragmatically support the Schuman Plan and the first steps of European integration in the 1950s, he soon became critical of the Schuman–Monnet approach, convinced that it was too "intergovernmental" and too slow to lead to the complete realization of a European federation. Nevertheless, he spent much of the rest of his life writing about and working within the institutions of the future European Union.

Along with his visionary technocrat, Jean Monnet, Robert Schuman is widely recognized as one of the inventors of the so-called European Communities formula and a leading figure of the very pragmatic "functionalist" approach to the integration of Europe. Our extract from a press conference of May 9, 1950 provides a good summary of his motivations and approach for supporting and implementing the precursor to today's European Union, the European Coal and Steel Community.

The case of Neumann's "Federalism and Freedom: A Critique" (1955) is very different. Against Montesquieu and most of the federal tradition, Neumann was the first author to clearly argue that federalism has no inherent values. Finally, the short selection from Trudeau's *Federalism and the French Canadians* (1968) was first presented in a 1964 conference, before Trudeau had entered electoral politics, and four years before he would become prime minister of Canada. It addresses the theoretical and empirical relationships between federalism and nationalism (especially the nationalism of minority nations) in a way typical of the federalism-as-a-panacea view: it contrasts emotion, nationalism, nation-state, and particularism, on the reactionary side; with reason, federalism, federation, and universalism, on the progressive side. Trudeau hoped "that in advanced societies, the glue of nationalism will become as obsolete as the divine right of kings." After he entered politics, many commentators would argue that he gave up that hope and spent most of his political career trying to build, at the federal level, a Canadian nationalism that could weaken and eventually supercede Quebec nationalism.

16

The Obsolescence of Federalism

Harold Laski

No one can travel the length and breadth of the United States without the conviction of its inexpugnable variety. East and West, South and North, its regions are real and different, and each has problems real and different too. The temptation is profound to insist that here, if ever, is the classic place for a federal experiment. Union without unity—except in the Soviet Union and China, has variety ever so fully invited the implications of the famous definition? Geography, climate, culture, all of them seem to have joined their forces to insist that, wherever centralization is appropriate, here, at least, it has no meaning. Tradition demands its absence; history has prohibited its coming. The large unit, as in Lamennais' phrase, would result in apoplexy at the center and anemia at the extremities. Imposed solutions from a distant Washington, blind, as it must be blind, to the subtle minutiae of local realities, cannot solve the ultimate problems that are in dispute. A creative America must be a federal America. The wider the powers exercised from Washington, the more ineffective will be the capacity for creative administration. Regional wisdom is the clue to the American future. The power to govern must go where that regional wisdom resides. So restrained, men learn by the exercise of responsibility the art of progress. They convince themselves by experiment from below. To fasten a uniformity that is not in nature upon an America destined to variety is to destroy the prospect of an ultimate salvation.

This kind of argument is familiar in a hundred forms. I believe that, more than any other philosophic pattern, it is responsible for the malaise of American democracy. My plea here is for the recognition that the federal form of state is unsuitable to the stage of economic and social development that America has reached. I infer from this postulate two conclusions: first, that the present division of powers, however liberal be the Supreme Court in its technique of interpretation, is inadequate to the needs America confronts; and, second, that any revision of those powers is one which must place in Washington, and Washington only, the power to amend that revision as circumstances change. I infer, in a word, that the epoch of federalism is over, and that only a centralized system can effectively confront the problems of a new time.

To continue with the old pattern, in the age of giant capitalism, is to strike into impotence that volume of governmental power which is necessary to deal with the issues giant capitalism has raised. Federalism, I suggest, is the appropriate governmental technique for an expanding capitalism, in which the price of local habit—which means, also, local delay—admits of compensation in the total outcome. But a contracting capitalism cannot afford the luxury of federalism. It is insufficiently positive in character; it does not provide for sufficient rapidity of action; it inhibits the emergence of necessary standards of uniformity; it relies upon compacts and compromises which take insufficient account of the urgent category of time; it leaves the backward areas a restraint, at once parasitic and poisonous, on those which seek to move forward; not least, its psychological results, especially in an age of crisis, are depressing to a democracy that needs the drama of positive achievement to retain its faith.

Before I turn to the case for this view, it is worthwhile to dwell for a moment upon the lessons of non-American experience. It is not, I think, accident that the heavy weather encountered by the federal system in the United States has been experienced also by the three major experiments elsewhere—by Germany, by Canada and by Australia. In the first, significantly, both federalism and democracy have gone. In the others the need for constitutional revision, the sense that the historic division of powers hampers the need for social and economic reconstruction at every turn, is one of the major themes of debate. Commissions seek to discover desirable terms of effective revision in both of them. Their literature speaks of "breakdown" and "collapse." In each, also, the federal government lacks, by its bondage to a past shaped in the faith of unlimited expansion, the power effectively to cope with its outstanding problems. In each, too, the older political parties are geared psychologically to that past; and their inability to escape from the framework in which it has imprisoned them, leads to the emergence of new political orientations which threaten alike their unity and their democratic foundation. Proportionately, I suspect, their problems are less susceptible of direct solution than those of the United States. But it is, I think, an expression, not of local circumstance, but of world-historical causes, which has made federalism everywhere in the world today a handicap and not a help to governmental progress.

Giant capitalism has, in effect, concentrated the control of economic power in a small proportion of the American people. It has built a growing contrast between the distribution of that economic power and the capacity of the political democracy effectively to control the results of its exercise. It has transcended the political boundaries of the units in the American federation so as to make them largely ineffective as areas of independent government. Whether we take the conditions of labor, the level of taxation, the standards of education, public health, or the supply of amenities like housing and recreation, it has become clear that the true source of decision is no longer at the circumference, but at the center, of the state. For forty-eight separate units to seek to compete with the integrated power of giant capitalism is to invite defeat in every element of social life where approximate uniformity of condition is the test of the good life.

The poor state is parasitic on the body politic. It offers privileges to giant capitalism to obtain its taxable capacity, offers escape from the impositions of rich states, in order to wrest from the wealthy some poor meed of compensation for its backwardness. It dare not risk offending the great industrial empires—cotton, coal, iron and steel, tobacco—lest it lose the benefits of their patronage. Their vested interests thus begin to define the limits within which the units of the federation may venture to move. And since the division of powers limits, in its turn, the authority of the federal government to intervene—the latter being a government of limited powers—it follows that the great industrial empires can, in fact, prevent the legislation necessary to implement the purposes of a democratic society. The situation may, briefly, be summarized by saying that the Constitution inhibits the federal government from exercising the authority inherent in the idea of a democracy; while the risk to a state government of attack upon the conditions exacted by those industrial empires for their patronage is too great to permit the states to jeopardize, what they have by issuing challenge. Whether, therefore, it be the hours of labor, the standards of health and housing, the effective organization of the trade unions, at every point the formal powers of the states are rarely commensurate with the actual authority they may venture to exercise. And it is the common citizen of the United States who pays the price of that margin between formal and effective power.

Political systems live by the results they can obtain for the great mass of their citizens. A democracy is not likely to survive on formal grounds merely; it will survive as it is able to convince its citizens that it adequately protects their powers to satisfy the expectations they deem their experience to warrant. In the present phase of American capitalist democracy, the central government largely lacks the power to implement the ends it is essential it should serve if its democratic context is to be maintained. It cannot obtain adequate standards of government in many of the major fields it seeks to enter. It is hamstrung, partly by the division of powers from which it derives its authority; partly because the Constitution has not enabled it to develop the instrumentalities essential to the purposes it must seek to fulfill. Its effort to obtain the proper recognition of collective bargaining may be stricken into impotence by a state law against picketing. Its effort to produce proper control of public utilities may be rendered vain by local franchises granted in a period when the recognition of the need for uniformity in this field had not dawned upon the public consciousness. So, also, with conservation; with the provision of adequate educational opportunity; with the effective prohibition (a commonplace of any well-ordered state) of child labor; with the coordination of relief for unemployment; with public works, especially in the utilization of the possible sources of electric power; with public-health legislation, not least in the field of maternity and child hygiene; with a proper policy of public roads—witness the breakdown of federal-state cooperation in Arkansas in 1923, in Kansas in 1926 and Maine in 1929; with a proper policy in housing.

I take examples only. The central point of my argument is the simple one that in every major field of social regulation, the authority of which the federal government can dispose is utterly inadequate to the issues it is expected to solve.

I do not think this argument is invalidated by the rise of cooperation between the federal government and the states, or between groups of states. That use has been carefully investigated in detail by Professor Jane Clark in an admirable and exhaustive monograph (Jane Perry Clark, *The Rise of a New Federalism: Federal-State Cooperation in the United States* (New York: Columbia University Press, 1938)). When all is made that can be made of the pattern she there reveals, I think it is true to say that, compared to the dimension of the problem, it amounts to very little. And set in the background of the urgent problems of time, it is, I think, clear from her account that in no fundamental matters will the pressure of political interests (behind which can be seen at every turn the hand of giant capitalism) permit the necessary uniformities to be attained by consent within the next fifty years. Not even the resiliency of American democracy can afford to wait so long. Professor Clark demonstrates admirably the inescapable interest of the federal government in a hundred subjects at every turn of which it encounters the power of the states; but she also demonstrates that the problems of dual occupancy of the same ground hinders at every turn the creative solution of the problems involved unless we conceive of those solutions in terms of geological time.

I am not arguing that the administration of government services ought to be centralized in Washington. It is true, as Professor Clark says, that "there is a line beyond which centralized administration cannot go without falling because of its own weight." My argument is the very different one: that (a) there are certain objects of administrative control now left to the states for which they are no longer suitable units of regulation. Economic centralization makes necessary at least minimum standards of uniform performance in these objects, for example, health, education, unemployment relief; and in others, for example, labor conditions, railroad rates, electric power, complete federal control without interference by the states; and (b) that the proper objects of federal supervision cannot any longer be dependent upon state consent. Where this dependency exists, state consent will be, in its turn, largely controlled by giant capitalism. That is why Delaware is merely a pseudonym of the du Ponts, and Montana little more than a symbol of the Anaconda Copper Corporation. That is why the people of the state of Washington, who ought long ago to have been permitted to have the advantage of the municipal electric-power plant of Seattle, still suffer from the division of its potential benefits through the survival of the Puget Sound Light and Power Company.

Nor would the problem be met if, instead of the states, America were divided, as writers like Professor Howard Odum suggest, into regions more correspondent with the economic realities of the situation. If America were to consist of seven or nine regions, instead of forty-eight states, that would still leave unsolved the main issues if they operated upon the basis of the present division of powers, and if their consent were necessary to any fundamental change in that division. Once again, it must be emphasized that the unity which giant capitalism postulates in the economic sphere postulates a corresponding unity in the conference of political powers upon the federal government. There is no other way, up to a required minimum, in which the questions of taxation, labor relations and conditions, conservation, public utilities (in the widest sense), to take examples only, can be met.

At this point, of course, the relation of a federal system to the power of judicial review becomes fundamental. No one now believes Marshall's famous assertion that "courts are the mere instruments of the law, and can will nothing"; it has been obvious, above all since the Civil War, that the Supreme Court is the effective master of federal legislation. And it is clear, further, that this mastery is exercised in the main not on objective tests of constitutionality (which do not exist), but upon the accident of a temporary majority's view of what it is "reasonable" for the federal government to undertake. The Court has become a non-elective third chamber of the government which may, as in the income-tax cases, defeat for many years purposes of which its members do not happen to approve. In an epoch of rapid change, it is a grave danger to any society that the will of a federal legislature should be subject to judicial control, and more especially when, as Marshall said, the amending process is "cumbrous and unwieldy." In a phase of liberal construction the difficulties of judicial review are obscured from the public. But the years before the controversy over the President's Court plan should be a sufficient reminder of the immense dangers lurking within it.

The view here urged, of course, looks toward a fundamental reconstruction of traditional American institutions. It is not impressed by the view, associated with the great name of Mr. Justice Brandeis, that the "curse of bigness" will descend upon any serious departure from the historic contours of federalism. The small unit of government is impotent against the big unit of giant capitalism. It may be that the very power of giant capitalism is no longer of itself compatible with the maintenance of a democratic political structure in society; there is much evidence to support this view. What, at least, is certain is this: that a government the powers of which are not commensurate with its problems will not be able to cope with them. Either, therefore, it must obtain those powers, or it must yield to a form of state more able to satisfy the demands that it encounters. That is the supreme issue before the United States today; and the more closely it is scrutinized the more obviously does its resolution seem to be bound up with the obsolescence of the federal system.

For that system presents the spectacle of forty-nine governments seeking to deal with issues for many of which they are inappropriate as instrumentalities whether in the area they cover or in the authority they may invoke. They are checked and balanced upon a theory of the state completely outmoded in the traditional ends upon which its postulates are based. Giant industry requires a positive state; federalism, in its American form, is geared to vital negations which contradict the implications of positivism. Giant industry requires uniformities in the field of its major influence; American federalism is the inherent foe, both in time and space, of those necessary uniformities. Giant industry, not least, requires the opposition of a unified public will to counteract its tendency to undemocratic procedure through the abuse of power; a federal system of the American kind dissipates the unity of public opinion in those fields where it is most urgently required. And, above all, it is urgent to note that giant industry, in an age of economic contraction, is able to exploit the diversities of a federal scheme, through the delays they permit in the attainment of uniformity, to reactionary ends. Thereby, they discredit the democratic process at a time when it is least able to afford that discredit. For, thereby, the confidence of the citizen body in its power to work out democratic solutions of its problems is gravely undermined.

Men who are deprived of faith by inability to attain results they greatly desire do not long remain content with the institutions under which they live. The price of democracy is the power to satisfy living demands. American federalism, in its traditional form, cannot keep pace with the tempo of the life giant capitalism has evolved. To judge it in terms of its historic success is to misconceive the criteria by which it becomes valid for the present and the future. No political system has the privilege of immortality; and there is no moment so fitting for the consideration of its remaking as that which permits of reconstruction with the prospect of a new era of creative achievement.

17

The 1944 Ventotene Manifesto: Towards a Free and United Europe

Altiero Spinelli and Ernesto Rossi

1. The Crisis of Modern Civilization

[. . .] the nation is no longer viewed as the historical product of co-existence between men who, as the result of a lengthy historical process, have acquired greater unity in their customs and aspirations and who see their State as being the most effective means of organizing collective life within the context of all human society. Rather the nation has become a divine entity, an organism which must only consider its own existence, its own development, without the least regard for the damage that others may suffer from this. The absolute sovereignty of national States has led to the desire of each of them to dominate, since each feels threatened by the strength of the others, and considers that its "living space" should include increasingly vast territories that give it the right to free movement and provide self-sustenance without needing to rely on others. This desire to dominate cannot be placated except by the hegemony of the strongest State over all the others.

As a consequence of this, from being the guardian of citizens' freedom, the State has been turned into a master of vassals bound into servitude, and has all the powers it needs to achieve the maximum war-efficiency. [. . .] Schools, science, production, administrative bodies are mainly directed towards increasing military strength. Women are considered merely as producers of soldiers and are rewarded with the same criteria as prolific cattle. [. . .]

Totalitarian States are precisely those which have unified all their forces in the most coherent way, by implementing the greatest possible degree of centralization and autarky. They have thus shown themselves to be the bodies most suited to the current international environment. It only needs one nation to take one step towards more accentuated totalitarianism for the others to follow suit, dragged down the same groove by their will to survive. [. . .]

2. Post-War Tasks: European Unity

Germany's defeat would not automatically lead to the reorganization of Europe in accordance with our ideal of civilization. In the brief, intense period of general crisis (when the States will lie broken, when the masses will be anxiously waiting for a new message, like molten matter, burning, and easily shaped into new moulds capable of accommodating the guidance of serious internationalist minded men), the most privileged classes in the old national systems will attempt, by underhand or violent methods, to dampen the wave of internationalist feelings and passions and will ostentatiously begin to reconstruct the old State institutions. [. . .]

The question which must be resolved first, failing which progress is no more than mere appearance, is the definitive abolition of the division of Europe into national, sovereign States. The collapse of the majority of the States on the continent under the German steam-roller has already given the people of Europe a common destiny: either they will all submit to Hitler's dominion, or, after his fall, they will all enter a revolutionary crisis and will not find themselves separated by, and entrenched in, solid State structures. Feelings today are already far more disposed than they were in the past to accept a federal reorganization of Europe. The harsh experience of recent decades has opened the eyes even of those who refused to see, and has matured many circumstances favourable to our ideal.

All reasonable men recognize that it is impossible to maintain a balance of power among European States with militarist Germany enjoying equal conditions with other countries, nor can Germany be broken up into pieces or held on a chain once it is conquered. We have seen a demonstration that no country within Europe can stay on the sidelines while the others battle: declarations of neutrality and non-aggression pacts come to nought. The uselessness, even harmfulness, of organizations like the League of Nations has been demonstrated: they claimed to guarantee international law without a military force capable of imposing its decisions and respecting the absolute sovereignty of the member States. The principle of non intervention turned out to be absurd: every population was supposed to be left free to choose the despotic government it thought best, in other words virtually assuming that the constitution of each individual State was not a question of vital interest for all the other European nations. The multiple problems which poison international life on the continent have proved to be insoluble: tracing boundaries through areas inhabited by mixed populations, defence of alien minorities, seaports for landlocked countries, the Balkan Question, the Irish problem, and so on. All matters which would find easy solutions in the European Federation, just as corresponding problems, suffered by the small States which became part of a vaster national unity, lost their harshness as they were turned into problems of relationships between various provinces. [. . .]

To all of this must be added the disappearance of some of the most important dynasties, and the fragility of the basis which sustains the ones that survive. It must be taken into account that these dynasties [. . .] represented a serious obstacle to the rational organization of the United States of Europe, which can only be based on the republican constitution of federated countries. And, once the horizon of the old Continent is superseded, and all the peoples who make up humanity are included in a single design, it will have to be recognized that the European Federation is the only conceivable guarantee ensuring that relationships with American and Asiatic peoples will work on the basis of peaceful co-operation, writing for a more distant future when the political unity of the entire world will become possible.

Therefore, the dividing line between progressive and reactionary parties no longer coincides with the formal lines of more or less democracy, or the pursuit of more or less socialism, but the division falls along a very new and substantial line: those who conceive the essential purpose and goal of struggle as being the ancient one, the conquest of national political power, and who, although involuntarily, play into the hands of reactionary forces, letting the incandescent lava of popular passions set in the old moulds, and thus allowing old absurdities to arise once again, and those who see the main purpose as the creation of a solid international State, who will direct popular forces towards this goal, and who, even if they were to win national power, would use it first and foremost as an instrument for achieving international unity.

With propaganda and action, seeking to establish in every possible way the agreements and links among the individual movements which are certainly in the process of being formed in the various countries, the foundation must be built now for a movement that knows how to mobilize all forces for the birth of the new organism which will be the grandest creation, and the newest, that has occurred in Europe for centuries; in order to constitute a steady federal State, that will have at its disposal a European armed service instead of national armies; that will break decisively economic autarkies, the backbone of totalitarian regimes; that will have sufficient means to see that its deliberations for the maintenance of common order are executed in the individual federal states, while each State will retain the autonomy it needs for a plastic articulation and development of political life according to the particular characteristics of the various peoples.

If a sufficient number of men in the main European countries understand this, then victory will soon fall into their hands, since both circumstances and opinion will be favourable to their efforts. They will have before them parties and factions that have already been disqualified by the disastrous experience of the last twenty years. Since it will be the moment for new action, it will also be the moment for new men: the MOVEMENT FOR A FREE AND UNITED EUROPE.

3. Postwar Duties: Reform of Society

A free and united Europe is the necessary premise to the strengthening of modern civilization as regards which the totalitarian era is only a temporary setback. As soon as this era ends the historical process of struggle against social inequalities and privileges will be restored in full. All the old conservative institutions that have hindered this process will either have collapsed or will be teetering on the verge of collapse. The crisis in these institutions must be boldly and decisively exploited.

In order to respond to our needs, the European revolution must be socialist, that is its goal must be the emancipation of the working classes and the creation of more humane conditions for them. The guiding light in determining what steps need to be taken, however, cannot simply be the utterly doctrinaire principle whereby private ownership of the material means of production must in principle be abolished and only temporarily tolerated when dispensing with it entirely. Wholesale nationalization of the economy under State control was the first, utopian form taken by the working classes' concept of their freedom from the yoke of capitalism. But when this State control is achieved, it does not produce the desired results but leads to a regime where the entire population is subservient to a restricted class of bureaucrats who run the economy.

The truly fundamental principle of socialism, vis-à-vis which general collectivization was no more than a hurried and erroneous inference, is the principle which states that, far from dominating man, economic forces, like the forces of nature, should be subject to man, guided and controlled by him in the most rational way, so that the broadest strata of the population will not become their victims. The huge forces of progress that spring from individual interests, must not be extinguished by the grey dullness of routine. [. . .]

Private property must be abolished, limited, corrected, or extended according to the circumstances and not according to any dogmatic principle. This guiding principle is a natural feature in the process of forming a European economic life freed from the nightmares of militarism or national bureaucratism. Rational solutions must replace irrational ones, even in the working class consciousness. With a view to indicating the content of this principle in greater detail, we emphasize the following points while stressing the need to assess the appropriateness of every point in the programme and means of achieving them in relationship to the indispensable premise of European unity. [. . .]

18

Declaration of 9 May 1950: The Schuman Plan for European Integration

Robert Schuman

World peace cannot be safeguarded without the making of creative efforts proportionate to the dangers which threaten it.

The contribution which an organized and living Europe can bring to civilization is indispensable to the maintenance of peaceful relations. In taking upon herself for more than 20 years the role of champion of a united Europe, France has always had as her essential aim the service of peace. A united Europe was not achieved and we had war.

Europe will not be made all at once, or according to a single plan. It will be built through concrete achievements which first create a de facto solidarity. The coming together of the nations of Europe requires the elimination of the age-old opposition of France and Germany. Any action taken must in the first place concern these two countries.

With this aim in view, the French Government proposes that action be taken immediately on one limited but decisive point:

It proposes that Franco-German production of coal and steel as a whole be placed under a common High Authority, within the framework of an organization open to the participation of the other countries of Europe. The pooling of coal and steel production should immediately provide for the setting up of common foundations for economic development as a first step in the federation of Europe, and will change the destinies of those regions which have long been devoted to the manufacture of munitions of war, of which they have been the most constant victims.

The solidarity in production thus established will make it plain that any war between France and Germany becomes not merely unthinkable, but materially impossible. The setting up of this powerful productive unit, open to all countries willing to take part and bound ultimately to provide all the member countries with the basic elements of industrial production on the same terms, will lay a true foundation for their economic unification.

This production will be offered to the world as a whole without distinction or exception, with the aim of contributing to raising living standards and to promoting peaceful achievements. In this way, there will be realized simply and speedily that fusion of interest which is indispensable to the establishment of a common economic system; it may be the leaven from which may grow a wider and deeper community between countries long opposed to one another by sanguinary divisions.

By pooling basic production and by instituting a new High Authority, whose decisions will bind France, Germany and other member countries, this proposal will lead to the realization of the first concrete foundation of a European federation indispensable to the preservation of peace.

To promote the realization of the objectives defined, the French Government is ready to open negotiations on the following bases:

The task with which this common High Authority will be charged will be that of securing in the shortest possible time the modernization of production and the improvement of its quality; the supply of coal and steel on identical terms to the French and German markets, as well as to the markets of other member countries; the development in common of exports to other countries; the equalization and improvement of the living conditions of workers in these industries.

To achieve these objectives, starting from the very different conditions in which the production of member countries is at present situated, it is proposed that certain transitional measures should be instituted, such as the application of a production and investment plan, the establishment of compensating machinery for equating prices, and the creation of a restructuring fund to facilitate the rationalization of production. The movement of coal and steel between member countries will immediately be freed from all customs duty, and will not be affected by differential transport rates. Conditions will gradually be created which will spontaneously provide for the more national distribution of production at the highest level of productivity.

In contrast to international cartels, which tend to impose restrictive practices on distribution and the exploitation of national markets, and to maintain high profits, the organization will ensure the fusion of markets and the expansion of production.

The essential principles and undertakings defined above will be the subject of a treaty signed between the States and submitted for the ratification of their parliaments. The negotiations required to settle details of applications will be undertaken with the help of an arbitrator appointed by common agreement. He will be entrusted with the task of seeing that the agreements reached conform with the principles laid down, and, in the event of a deadlock, he will decide what solution is to be adopted. The common High Authority entrusted with the management of the scheme will be composed of independent persons appointed by the governments, giving equal representation. A chairman will be chosen by common agreement between the governments. The Authority's decisions will be enforceable in France, Germany and other member countries. Appropriate measures will be provided for means of appeal against the decisions of the Authority.

A representative of the United Nations will be accredited to the Authority, and will be instructed to make a public report to the United Nations twice yearly, giving an account of the working of the new organization, particularly as concerns the safeguarding of its objectives.

The institution of the High Authority will in no way prejudge the methods of ownership of enterprises. In the exercise of its functions, the common High Authority will take into account the powers conferred upon the International Ruhr Authority and the obligations of all kinds imposed upon Germany, so long as these remain in force.

19

Federalism and Freedom: A Critique

Franz L. Neumann

It will be necessary to define, as briefly as possible, the meaning of the term "federalism" before we can answer the two fundamental questions:

1. Is there a value which inheres in federalism as such?
2. Are there goals that can be attained only through federalism?

I

Have the terms "federalism," "federal government," or "federal state" definable meanings? Even a most superficial study of the various kinds of federal government—those of the United States, Canada, Australia, Switzerland, Imperial Germany, the Austro-Hungarian Dual Monarchy, Weimar and Bonn Germany, the Central African Federation, India, and the USSR, to mention some modern federal states—fails to show any element common to all, except a juristic one. The common element is this: in each, the citizen of the federal state is subject to two jurisdictions: that of the federal government and that of the states.[1] Usually connected to this is a separation of the legislative, administrative, and judicial functions in order to insure the orderly operation of government. The lawyer—and the lawyer alone—is thus capable (and obligated) to make statements concerning federalism that can claim general validity.

Not so the political and social scientist. He will accept a legal definition of federalism, but he must go beyond it. The legal definition of federalism—like all legal definitions—is a negative one. It tells us that we cannot regard a mere treaty system or a confederation of states as a federal system. But it can tell us nothing about the political and social function of the federal system. If we wish to know this, we must ask the two questions: whether federalism as such has a value; and whether certain goals are attainable only through this governmental arrangement.

Posing the questions in such a manner creates extraordinary difficulties. How can one determine whether a certain value inheres in federalism? The federal arrangement operates always within a specific political, social, and cultural setting and the isolation of the federal element from this setting is obviously extremely difficult, perhaps even impossible. Even if we confine the analysis to democratic systems of government, the political and constitutional factors that tend to change the function of federalism are these:

1. presidential or parliamentary democracy
2. separation of powers (checks and balances)
3. the party system;

and the social and economic factors are these:

1. the extent of the pluralistic structure of society
2. the urban–rural ratio
3. the degree of concentration of economic power.

It seems obviously inadmissible to attribute to federalism values which form, in reality, a syndrome consisting of a specific constitutional arrangement within a specific socio-economic structure. What our statements amount to, therefore, is that the value of federalism (as against a unitary state on the one hand, and a looser form of cooperation on the other) can be determined solely through an empirical analysis of a given political system. The need for such an analysis will, moreover, become clearer if we analyze the claims made for the federal, as against the unitary, system.

II

The theoretical argument for federalism revolves around the potential of political power for evil. Federalism is seen as one of the devices to curb the evil use of power by dividing power among a number of competing power-units.

The underlying sentiment—the corruptive influence of power—is often not clearly formulated and the consequences thus not clearly seen.

1. In its most radical form, this sentiment appears in the various anarchist schemes. It has been popular in the anarcho-syndicalist theories and practices of the Latin-speaking countries and with the IWW of the United States. We may find in Proudhon the most precise expression of that trend and a most radical advocacy of "federalism." But one must, of course, not tear the federalist conception of Proudhon from the context of his social and political philosophy. His theory of federalism has nothing in common with that of the federal state; it is rather the very negation of it.

Proudhon indicts capitalism because he finds in it a basic injustice,[2] the exchange of non-equivalents. This injustice comes from two institutions: private property and the state. The property owner is able to draw advantages from the exchange process by selling commodities at prices that are above value, thus imposing a tax upon the social product. It is this exchange relationship which creates the two social classes: the new feudality of owners living on interests, rents, and dividends, and the workers who own no capital except their labor. The state—no matter what its form—is that agency which maintains the exchange of non-equivalents, protects the new feudality, and prevents the uprising of the majority against the minority. This is the sole role of the state which can never, under any circumstances and in any form, change the system, reform it, or create social justice—even when the state is a democracy. Justice can thus be obtained only against the state, against political power, only through a contractual industrial organization[3] of small-scale units.

One may, if one so desires, call this a "federalist" theory, but it is obvious that it cannot help us in our problem of determining whether the federal state, by lessening the corruptive effect of power and thereby increasing political freedom, becomes, on that account, preferable to the unitary state.

2. It is Lord Acton's statement on the corruptive effect of political power which appears to have today the greatest influence. Three statements of his on political power are:

> *a.* ". . . power tends to expand indefinitely, and will transcend all barriers, abroad and at home, until met by superior forces."
> *b.* "History is not a web woven with innocent hands. Among all the causes which degrade and demoralize men, power is the most constant and the most active."
> *c.* To Creighton: "I cannot accept your canon that we are to judge Pope and King unlike other men, with a favorable presumption that they did no wrong. If there is any presumption it is the other way against holders of power, increasing as the power increases. Historic responsibility has to make up for the want of legal responsibility. Power tends to corrupt and absolute power corrupts absolutely. Great men are almost always bad men, even when they exercise influence and not authority: still more when you superadd the tendency or the certainty of corruption by authority. There is no worse heresy than that the office sanctifies the holder of it."[4]

These statements have two aspects. The first one is, indeed, unobjectionable and, of course, not very original. Thucydides said much the same:[5]

> *Melians*—You may be sure that we are as well aware as you of the difficulty of contending against your power and fortune, unless the terms be equal. But we trust that the gods may grant us fortune as good as yours, since we are just men fighting against unjust, and that what we want in power will be made up by the alliance of the Lacedaemonians, who are bound, if only for very shame, to come to the aid of their kindred. Our confidence, therefore, after all is not so utterly irrational.
>
> *Athenians*—When you speak of the favour of the gods, we may as fairly hope for that as yourselves; neither our pretensions nor our conduct being in any way contrary to what men believe of the gods, or practise among themselves. *Of the gods we believe, and of men we know, that by a necessary law of their nature they rule wherever they can.* And it is not as if we were the first to make this law, or to act upon it when made: we found it existing before us, and shall leave it to exist for ever after us; all we do is to make use of it, knowing that you and everybody else, having the same power as we have, would do the same as we do. (emphasis supplied)

And Montesquieu[6] said this even more clearly. According to him[7] power could be checked only by power—a statement that few would be willing to quarrel with. Not ideologies and beliefs but only a counter-power can check power. In this he applies Cartesian principles and stands in the tradition of Spinoza who saw no way of limiting the state's absoluteness (which was logical consequence of his assumptions and of his geometric method) except by a counter-power.

The Montesquieu generalization is, of course, designed to give his doctrine of the separation of powers an adequate theoretical base. But as little as the theory of separate powers follows from his sociological observation, as little does that of the preferability of the federal state. Bentham[8] rejected the separation of powers not only as incompatible with democracy but also because it could not really maximize freedom if the three organs of government were controlled by the same social group. A quite similar argument can be raised against federalism as a guarantee for liberty. Those who assert that the federal state through the diffusion of *constitutional* powers actually diffuses *political* power often overlook the fact that the real cause for the existence of liberty is the pluralist structure of society and the multi-party (or two-party) system.[9] Federalism is not identical with social pluralism; and neither the two-party nor the multi-party system is the product of the federal state or the condition for its functioning.

3. Whether the federal state does indeed increase freedom[10] cannot be abstractly determined. We have some evidence that the federal state as such (i.e., regardless of the form of government) has not fulfilled this role. The German Imperial Constitution certainly created a federal state but there is little doubt that politically it had a dual purpose: to be a dynastic alliance against the forces of liberalism and democracy,[11] and to secure the hegemony of Prussia.[12] One may argue that a unitary state may even have been worse than the federal solution: that is quite possible. Nevertheless one may say, with reason, that the archaic Prussian three-class franchise could not possibly have been introduced as the system for a unitary German state. Thus a unitary German state in all likelihood would have been more progressive than the Bismarckian system. The Austro-Hungarian Dual Monarchy, after the *Ausgleich* of 1867, was an attempt to ensure the rule of the Germans and Magyars over all other nationalities.[13] The Dual Monarchy most certainly did not maximize freedom except for the oligarchies in its two constituent states.

Perhaps more striking are the respective roles of federalism and centralism in the coming to power of National Socialism. Some believe, indeed, that the centralization under the Weimar Republic is wholly or at least partly responsible for the rise of National Socialism. But there is no evidence for this statement—nor indeed for the opposite one. It is certain that Bavaria, with the strongest states' rights tradition, gave shelter to the National Socialist movement and it is equally certain that the federal character of the Weimar Republic did not, after Hitler's appointment, delay the process of synchronization (*Gleichschaltung*) of the various state governments. Nor is there any definable relation between democratic conviction and federalist (or unitary) sympathies. The National Socialists were both centralists and reactionary, as were the Nationalists. Democrats and Social Democrats were antifederalists and committed to the preservation of political freedom. The Catholic center was not whole-heartedly committed to any position, and the Communists were, in theory, for the unitary state but did not hesitate, during the revolution of 1918, to advocate the secession of Brunswick which they believed they had in their pocket.

4. But perhaps what is meant by saying that federalism maximizes freedom is that only in a democracy does the division of constitutional power among various autonomous territorial units effect a maximum of political liberty; in other words, that democracy and the federal state go together, even that federalism is necessary for democracy. Literally taken, this statement is most certainly untrue. The United Kingdom is a proof against it. Weimar Germany cannot be cited either for or against it. Bavaria—the most states' rights-conscious *land*—was certainly the most reactionary; Prussia, the most democratic. Insofar as the United States is concerned, it seems almost impossible to make any statement because of the extreme difficulty of attributing to the federal system—in isolation from other elements—any specific function. There are, perhaps, some tests like the protection of civil liberties. For a criminal, the federal system has obvious advantages in that it increases his margin of safety from prosecution. The need for extradition may, in isolated cases, permit a criminal to escape punishment. It is doubtful, however, that this can be taken as a compliment to federalism. Of real importance would be a study designed to prove or disprove that the federal nature of American government has strengthened civil liberties. The criminal syndicalism legislation of the post–World War I period[14] does not permit us to pass a final judgment. The "red hysteria" of that period "practically assured . . . passage (of this type of legislation) with only slight examination."[15] The bills were passed with "breathtaking swiftness and little debate, or with a great outburst of oratory characterized more by passion, prejudice, and misinformation than by a reasoned effort to get at the facts."[16] There seemed to be a race among the various states for the most drastic legislation, and vested interests, their influence enhanced by the makeup of the state legislatures, pushed through the bills.[17] Simultaneously, efforts to enact a federal bill failed from 1917 to 1920.[18] On the other hand, however, it is possible that without state laws a federal bill may have been enacted, and it is also true that in a few states[19] no legislation was enacted. On the whole, one may perhaps say that the federal system may have speeded up inroads into the civil liberties rather than have protected them.

The same, perhaps, may be said of the present situation.[20] The evidence is certainly too slight to be of great value in determining whether the federal system is preferable to the unitary state as an instrument to preserve or enhance civil liberties. Nor is it likely that convincing evidence can be obtained, since other factors—the plurality of the social structure, the functioning of a truly competitive party system, the strength of a favorable tradition, the intellectual level of the population, the attitude of the courts—do far more easily permit the formation of a counter power against forces hostile to civil liberties than does the federal structure of the government.

5. Lord Acton's statements, however, are also concerned with a second aspect: namely, the corruptive influence of power. This brilliant formula—that power tends to corrupt and absolute power corrupts absolutely—has attained the position of a classical remark; but, inevitably, it has also become a cliché of which neither the meaning nor the validity is ever questioned. The content of the statement is certainly not very original. While Plato's discussion of the same problem[21] shows a much deeper insight, Lord Acton's has the undoubted merits of brevity and of quotability.

Lord Acton asserts that the character of the man who has power is corrupted by the exercise of power, or as the German adage has it: Politics corrupts the character. This is probably a valid generalization—but what is its significance for politics, in general, and for our problem, in particular? A morally evil ruler does not necessarily make a bad ruler—he may accumulate riches, indulge in all kinds of vices—and yet his rule may be beneficial; while the paragon of virtue may lead his country to destruction. But if we turn from monarchy or tyranny to representative government, the applicability of the formula to politics is quite certainly small.

However, we may well redefine the formula to mean that too much power concentrated in any organ of government has evil consequences for the people and that federalism, by dividing power among independent territorial units, checks these evil potentialities.

Thus redefined, the statement is no longer defensible because the opposite may equally be true. It is, indeed, also true: Too little power tends to corrupt and absolute lack of power corrupts absolutely; or, as Edmund Burke put it: "Nothing turns out to be so oppressive and unjust as a feeble government."[22] One can accept Burke's assertion as absolute truth as little as one can Lord Acton's. Both are partially true generalizations, Burke's being, perhaps, a more realistic description of marginal situations than Lord Acton's. If one shares Burke's hatred of revolution, one may keep in mind that modern revolutions such as the French of 1789, the two Russian ones of 1917, and the German of 1918, had their immediate cause in the lack of power of the central governments and not in the excessive use or abuse of power.

6. It thus seems impossible to attribute to federalism, as such, a value; or to assert that the federal state—as contrasted to the unitary state—enhances political and civil freedom by dividing power among autonomous territorial subdivisions.

III

1. The argument for federalism may, however, have a quite different meaning. It may, in reality, express the theory of "grass-roots" democracy, the view that small-scale units alone permit the practice of democracy and that, consequently, the value of small units must be preserved even in large states so that mass participation in politics will remain a political practice.

The most precise formulation of this theory is found in Montesquieu who, through his analysis of the collapse of the Roman Empire,[23] came to the conclusion that democracy, being incompatible with a large empire, can be effectively practiced only by a small territorial entity.[24] Rousseau accepted this view and made it popular.

> In any case, the moment a people allows itself to be represented, it is no longer free: it no longer exists. All things considered, I do not see that it is possible henceforth for the Sovereign to preserve among us the exercise of its rights, unless the city is very small.[25]

But Montesquieu, Rousseau, and *The Federalist*[26] clearly recognized the dilemma of democracy. As Montesquieu put it, "If a Republic is small, it is destroyed by a foreign power; if it be large, it is ruined by internal imperfection."[27] Rousseau virtually copied this question from Montesquieu by continuing the above quotation: "But if it is very small, it will be conquered? No. I will show later on how the external strength of a great people may be combined with a convenient polity and good order of a small state." Both writers, and *The Federalist*, following Montesquieu, suggest federation as a device to attain both external security and internal democracy. It is well to realize that Jefferson, while omitting to copy the chapter on the separation of powers, carefully abstracted this view of Montesquieu.[28]

The Montesquieu-Rousseau theory raises a quite difficult problem: the relation of territorial size to the political structure. This problem has not been adequately discussed since the work of Ratzel.[29] Rousseau's adaptation of Montesquieu's statement raises a second difficulty, namely, the identification of democracy with direct democracy. Rousseau's quotation appears in the chapter entitled "Deputies or Representatives" and is concerned with the demonstration that democracy, being a complete identity of rulers and ruled, cannot be representative government. Yet our theory of democracy (although political scientists quite frequently long for "mass participation in politics") is a theory of representative government, of a form of government which is characterized by the electoral process and by the political responsibility of the representative organs to the electorate. The two doctrines have nothing in common with each other, although the instrumentalities of direct democracy, like initiative, referendum, plebiscite, and recall, may or may not serve as correctives to representative government.[30]

If, therefore, one does not accept the Rousseauist model or agree with Montesquieu's analysis of the cause of the collapse of the Roman Republic, then it is difficult to accept the consequence that a unitary system covering a large territory cannot be a democratic system.

2. Indeed, neither Madison nor John Stuart Mill, to name two, shared this view and yet both were quite deeply attached to the principle of political liberty. Madison wrote:

> Was, then, the American Revolution effected, was the American Confederacy formed, was the precious blood of thousands spilt, and the hardearned

> substance of millions lavished, not that the people of America should enjoy peace, liberty, and safety, but that the government of the individual States, that particular municipal establishments, might enjoy a certain extent of power, and be arrayed with certain dignities and attributes of power? . . . It is too early for politicians to presume on our forgetting that the public good, the real welfare of the great body of the people, is the supreme object to be pursued; and that no form of government whatever has any other value than as it may be fitted for the attainment of this object. Were the plan of the convention adverse to the public happiness, my voice would be, Reject the plan. Were the Union itself inconsistent with the public happiness, it would be, Abolish the Union. In like manner, as far as the sovereignty of the States cannot be reconciled to the happiness of the people, the voice of every good citizen must be, Let the former be sacrificed to the latter.[31]

The quotation exhibits a view quite at variance with the Montesquieu-Rousseau theory. It is the power of the central government which appears as the guarantor of political freedom—against the states. And John Stuart Mill, the great defender of diversity and individuality, when discussing Italy's future constitutional structure, reasoned in quite the same terms:

> The question may present itself (as in Italy at its present uprising) whether a country, which is determined to be united, should form a complete or a merely federal union. The point is sometimes necessarily decided by mere territorial magnitude of the united whole . . . This obstacle does not exist in the case of Italy, the size of which does not come to that of several very efficiently governed single states in past and present times. The question then is, whether the different parts of the nation require to be governed in a way so essentially different that it is not probable the same Legislature, and the same ministry or administrative body, will give satisfaction to them all. Unless this be the case, which is question of fact, it is better for them to be completely united . . . .
>
> Whenever it is not deemed necessary to maintain permanently in the different provinces, different systems of jurisprudence, and fundamental institutions grounded on different principles, it is always practicable to reconcile minor diversities with the maintenance of unity of government. All that is needful is to give a sufficiently large sphere of action to the local authorities.[32]

3. Yet there is one element of truth in the theory of Montesquieu and Rousseau: the smallest territorial unit—the municipality—is potentially the most responsive to the will and interests of the people and, consequently, local self-government must be considered the indispensable cornerstone of a modern large-scale democracy.

But is it possible to assert that the federal structure maximizes local self-government and that, in a unitary state, we therefore find a shrinkage of local powers? At the outset it must be made clear that the federal state, as such, does not mean strong local government[33] and that, therefore, it is not possible to answer the question abstractly, but that rather empirical investigations are necessary. In Weimar Germany the states (*Laender*) were steadily encroaching upon the powers of the municipalities and transformed, on a large scale, municipal into state police power, while the financial resources of the municipalities proved totally inadequate to finance the new and ever-growing tasks of the welfare state.

This may well be a universal phenomenon or it may vary considerably from state to state, or even within each state, according to the size of the municipalities.

4. While we have attempted to demonstrate that there is no necessary connection between democracy and federalism, one may go even beyond it and say that many of the major advocates of federalism are critics, doubters, and even enemies of democracy.[34]

De Tocqueville saw this connection clearly:

> I have already pointed out the distinction between a centralized government and centralized administration. The former exists in America, but the latter is nearly unknown there. If the directing power of the American communities had both these instruments of government at its disposal and united the habit of executing its commands to the right of commanding; if, after having established the general principles of government, it descended to the details of their application; and if, having regulated the great interests of the country, it would descend to the circle of individual interests, freedom would soon be banished from the New World.
>
> But in the United States the majority, which so frequently displays the tastes and the propensities of a despot, is still destitute of the most perfect instruments of tyranny.
>
> . . . when the central government which represents that majority has issued a decree, it must entrust the execution of its will to agents over whom it frequently has no control and whom it cannot perpetually direct. The townships, municipal bodies, and counties form so many concealed backwaters, which check or part the tide of popular determination.[35]

Madison—in the above quotation—implied it. Calhoun in the United States and Konstantin Frantz in Germany are the two best-known theorists of federalism per se, where the connection between federalism and anti-democracy is obvious.[36]

6. We must, therefore, answer our first question as follows: While it is asserted that federalism maximizes political freedom because

a. it establishes an effective counter-power to the power of the central government;
b. it curbs the potentialities for evil inherent in power;
c. it maximizes local government and thus promotes grass-roots democracy; it has been found that none of the statements can be accepted. It must rather concretely be demonstrated that a federal system is superior to a unitary system in maintaining freedom; that this is attributable to the federal structure and not to the governmental institutions (checks and balances, attitude of the courts, character and orientation of the federal administrative services); or to the nature of the party system (shaped, it is true, by the federal structure); or to the pluralistic and mobile structure of society; or to simply accidental historical circumstances; or to a combination of all or some of these factors.

IV

If federalism, as such, has nothing in it that automatically guarantees the preservation of political freedom, American federalism may have features that have hindered the solution of pressing economic problems.[37] It is not simply that early New Deal legislation was voided by the Supreme Court in the name of the Tenth Amendment. The impact of the American federal system, of the division of powers, on the condition of this country in the thirties was not reassuring.

George C.S. Benson, in his book *The New Centralization*,[38] tried to show how federalism worked in the setting of the Great Depression.

First, he found federalism as an "obstruction of social legislation." The states hesitated to enact this legislation not only for fear of placing their manufacturers at a competitive disadvantage with manufacturers of states that did not regulate wages and hours and provide benefits, but also for fear of driving larger industries into these latter states.[39]

Secondly, there was great disparity among the states' financial resources. Not only were most states incapable of financing serious efforts at reform, but "Complete decentralization—complete local responsibility for governmental services—may then result in a 'spread' between the standards of different districts which would shock even the uncritical believer in a national 'American' standard."[40]

Thirdly, Benson found little evidence that the states were really the "experimental laboratories" they were pictured to be.[41]

Fourthly, the ability of the states to put programs into action in an efficient way was seriously questioned. "With the exception of such cases as those noted on page 13 (auditing systems of Massachusetts, New York, Maryland, Virginia, and New Jersey), state governments are inferior administratively to the federal government. Two thirds of the states lack genuine merit systems for selection of personnel, and only three or four have salary levels sufficiently high to attract competent administrative or professional staffs."[42]

Fifthly, Benson found the functioning of many of the state legislatures faulty because of a lack of time or money for suitable research. "Proponents of states' rights might pause to consider whether the increase of federal activity is not so much a result of superior federal legislative procedure as of superior federal resources."[43]

Lastly, the nature of the economic system is such that its workings were and are obviously not confined to the territory of any given city or state. "As our great business concerns grow more specialized and conduct larger-scale operations in an age of complicated machinery, government cannot be expected to remain simple and pastoral."[44]

In sum, as Professor Key has written, "A characteristic of the federal system seems to be that entrenched interests in the long run can better protect themselves in dealing with state legislatures than with Congress or with federal administrators."[45]

V

The second question, however, still begs an answer: are there goals that can be attained only through federalism? Obviously the answer must be yes, but it requires a careful formulation of the problem.

When the Founding Fathers wrestled with the problem, they did not ask whether they desired a federal state. They rather, and correctly, asked whether there should be a union and how far this union should go. Once the first question had been answered affirmatively, and once it was clear that the existing territorial units could not be extinguished, the necessary result was, indeed, a federal state.[46]

If we apply this to present-day Europe, it seems obvious that one should not ask whether the Western European states should unite into a federal state but rather whether they should cooperate on a permanent basis—politically, as well as economically and militarily. If this is answered affirmatively (and I for one shall not answer a question which is a European responsibility) one must decide what constitutional form this cooperation should take. There exist, obviously, the following alternatives: (1) a tighter treaty system combined with more specialized agencies; (2) a confederation; (3) a federal state; (4) a unitary state with a substantial amount of decentralization; and (5) a unitary state with a centralized administration. The decision what constitutional solution is to be adopted should not be dictated by a doctrinaire preference for a federal state because of its alleged advantages but rather by political considerations such as the need to secure a maximum of popular support, the efficiency of the new constitutional form, etc.

If one simply poses the alternative between a federal state and a continuation of the present system of cooperation, one may wreck the chances for closer integration because those who prefer an expansion of the treaty system and more specialized agencies as well as the advocates of a confederation or a unitary state may be driven into the arms of those who desire no change or are even actively opposed to any form of closer cooperation.

VI

This chapter has tried to show the futility of any discussion of the merits of federalism as an arrangement considered abstractly. There are no values that inhere in federalism as such, and federalism cannot be defended successfully on the grounds that the inevitable tendency of a unitary state is toward political repression. The testimony of history will not support this assertion, nor will it support the assertion that a division of constitutional power is the best guarantee of political freedom. When to these considerations is joined that of the financial inadequacy or political unwillingness of the smaller units to respond satisfactorily to serious economic troubles, then unrestrained adulation of federalism seems all the more unwarranted.[47]

NOTES

1. See K.C. Wheare, *Federal Government*, New York, Oxford University Press, 1947, p. 15.
2. Based upon C. Bouglé, *La sociologie de Proudhon*, Paris, A. Colin, 1911; H. Bourgin, *Proudhon*, Paris, G. Bellais, 1901.
3. For details see Alexander Gray, *The Socialist Tradition, Moses to Lenin*, London, Longmans, Green, 1947, pp. 230–256; and G.D.H. Cole, *Socialist Thought, The Forerunners, 1789–1850*, London, Macmillan, 1953, pp. 201–218.
4. Quotations taken from G. Himmelfarb, *Lord Acton, A Study in Conscience and Politics*, Chicago, University of Chicago Press, 1952; a, p. 220; b, p. 139; c, p. 161.
5. Thucydides, *The Peloponnesian War*, Book V.
6. My edition of the *Spirit of the Laws*, New York, Hafner Library of Classics, 1949, XI, 4.
7. See my Introduction, *ibid.*, pp. lvii–lviii.
8. Bowring, ed., Vol. IX, pp. 41 *et seq.*; and Elie Halévy, *The Growth of Philosophic Radicalism*, trans. by Mary Morris, New York, Macmillan, 1928, pp. 458–459.
9. See my Montesquieu Introduction, pp. lviii and lxiv.
10. Cf. Carl J. Friedrich, *Constitutional Government and Democracy*, Boston, Ginn & Co., 1946, pp. 216–217.
11. Rudolf Schlesinger, *Federalism in Central and Eastern Europe*, New York, Oxford University Press, 1945, p. 71.
12. K.C. Wheare, *op. cit.*, p. 29.
13. For details see Oscar Jászi, *The Dissolution of the Hapsburg Monarchy*, Chicago, University of Chicago Press, 1929, pp. 271 *et seq.*; R. Schlesinger, *op. cit.*, pp. 184 *et seq.*
14. See Eldridge Foster Dowell, *A History of Criminal Syndicalism Legislation in the United States*, Baltimore, The Johns Hopkins Press, 1939.
15. Ibid., p. 47.
16. Ibid., p. 55.
17. Ibid., *passim.*
18. Ibid., p. 109.
19. Ibid., pp. 147 *et seq.*
20. For the dismal record of the states in preserving civil liberties, see Walter Gellhorn, ed., *The States and Subversion*, Ithaca, Cornell University Press, 1952.
21. Plato, *Laws*, III, 691:

    "Athenian stranger—Nothing can be clearer than the observation which I am about to make.
    Megillus—What is it?
    Athenian Stranger—That if any one gives too great a power to anything, too large a sail to a vessel, too much food to the body, too much authority to the mind, and does not observe the mean, everything is overthrown, and, in the wantonness of excess runs in the one case to disorders, and in the other to injustice, which is the child of excess. I mean to say, my dear friends, that there is no soul of man, young and irresponsible, who will be able to sustain the temptation of arbitrary power—no one who will not, under such circumstances, become filled with folly, that worst of diseases, and be hated by his nearest and dearest friends . . ."

22. Edmund Burke, *Reflections on the French Revolution* (Everyman's Library), p. 226.

23. *Considerations on the Causes of the Grandeur and Decadence of the Romans*, trans. by Jehu Baker, New York, D. Appleton, 1882.
24. *The Spirit of the Laws*, VIII, 16, and my Introduction, p. xliii.
25. *The Social Contract*, III, xv; transl. by G.D.H. Cole, Everyman Library ed.
26. Hamilton, No. IX.
27. Montesquieu, *The Spirit of the Laws*, IX, i.
28. Gilbert Chinard, ed., *Jefferson's Commonplace Book*, Baltimore, The Johns Hopkins Press, 1926, p. 267.
29. See Friedrich Ratzel, *Politische Geographie*, 3d ed., Munich and Berlin, R. Oldenbourg, 1923.
30. Carl J. Friedrich, *Constitutional Government and Democracy*, Revised edition, Boston, Ginn & Co., 1950, pp. 546–570.
31. *The Federalist*, No. XLV.
32. *Representative Government* (Everyman ed.), pp. 374–375.
33. Roscoe Pound, "Law and Federal Government," in *Federalism as a Democratic Process*. Essays by Roscoe Pound, Charles H. McIlwain, and Roy F. Nichols, New Brunswick, Rutgers University Press, 1942.

    Pound equates, or confuses, localism and federalism: "Even if the lines cannot be drawn at any one time absolutely—and in law and politics which deal with life none can be so drawn—the national and the local are distinct at the core, and the experience of English-speaking peoples has shown that local matters are best dealt with in the locality instead of by postulated *ex officio* supermen at a distance" (p. 21).
34. A.V. Dicey, *Introduction to the Study of the Law of the Constitution*, Ninth Edition, ed. by E.C.S. Wade, London, Macmillan, 1950.

    "Our survey from a legal point of view of the characteristics common to all federal government forcibly suggests conclusions of more than merely legal interest, as to the comparative merits of federal government, and the system of Parliamentary sovereignty.

    "Federal government means weak government.

    ". . . no more curious instance can be found of the inconsistent currents of popular opinion which may at the same time pervade a nation or a generation than the coincidence in England of a vague admiration for federalism alongside with a far more decided feeling against the doctrines of so-called *laissez faire*. A system meant to maintain the *status quo* in politics is incompatible with schemes for wide social innovation.

    "Federalism tends to produce conservatism.

    ". . . The difficulty of altering the constitution produces conservative sentiment, and national conservatism doubles the difficulty of altering the constitution . . . To this one must add that a federal constitution always lays down general principles which, from being placed in the constitution, gradually come to command a superstitious reverence, and thus are in fact, though not in theory, protected from change or criticism . . .

    "Federalism, lastly, means legalism—the predominance of the judiciary in the constitution—the prevalence of a spirit of legality among the people.

    ". . . Federalism substitutes litigation for legislation, and none but a law-fearing people will be inclined to regard the decision of a suit as equivalent to the enactment of a law" (pp. 171–179).
35. Alexis de Tocqueville, *Democracy in America*, New York, Knopf, 1945, Vol. I, pp. 271–272.

36. John C. Calhoun, *A Discourse on the Constitution and Government of the United States*, in *The Works*, Vol. I, New York, D. Appleton, 1854, pp. 168–169, 233–234, 241, 268, 383–386, 392; Konstantin Frantz, *Der Foederalismus als das leitende Princip fuer die sociale, staatliche und internationale Organisation . . .*, Mainz, Kirchheim, 1879.
37. For a discussion of this situation in Australia, see A.P. Canaway, *The Failure of Federalism in Australia*, London, Oxford University Press, 1930.
38. New York, Farrar and Rinehart, 1941. On this problem see, in addition, Harold Laski, "The Obsolescence of Federalism," *The New Republic*, Vol. 98 (May 3, 1939), pp. 367–369.
39. Benson, *op. cit.*, pp. 23–24.
40. Ibid., p. 30.
41. Ibid., p. 38.
42. Ibid., p. 40.
43. Ibid., p. 42.
44. Ibid., p. 42.
45. V.O. Key, Jr., *Politics, Parties, and Pressure Groups*, Third Edition, New York, Crowell, 1952, p. 102.
46. See Hamilton in *The Federalist*, IX, XV, and the above Madison quotation from *The Federalist.*
47. In preparing this chapter the author had the valued assistance of George A. Kateb.

20

Nationalism and Federalism

Pierre Elliott Trudeau

Many of the nations which were formed into states over the past century or two included peoples who were set apart geographically (like East and West Pakistan, or Great Britain and Northern Ireland), historically (like the United States or Czechoslovakia), linguistically (like Switzerland or Belgium), racially (like the Soviet Union or Algeria). Half of the aforesaid countries undertook to form the national consensus within the framework of a unitary state; the other half found it expedient to develop a system of government called federalism. The process of consensus-formation is not the same in both cases.

It is obviously impossible, as well as undesirable, to reach unanimity on all things. Even unitary states find it wise to respect elements of diversity, for instance by administrative decentralization as in Great Britain,[1] or by language guarantees as in Belgium; but such limited securities having been given, a consensus is obtained which recognizes the state as the sole source of coercive authority within the national boundaries. The federal state proceeds differently; it deliberately reduces the national consensus to the greatest common denominator between the various groups composing the nation. Coercive authority over the entire territory remains a monopoly of the (central) state, but this authority is limited to certain subjects of jurisdiction; on other subjects, and within well-defined territorial regions, other coercive authorities exist. In other words, the exercise of sovereignty is divided between a central government and regional ones.

Federalism is by its very essence a compromise and a pact. It is a compromise in the sense that when national consensus on *all* things is not desirable or cannot readily obtain, the area of consensus is reduced in order that consensus on *some* things be reached. It is a pact or quasi-treaty in the sense that the terms of that compromise cannot be changed unilaterally. That is not to say that the terms are fixed forever; but only that in changing them, every effort must be made not to destroy the consensus on which the federated nation rests. For what Ernest Renan said about the nation is even truer about the

[1] Since the Government of Ireland Act, 1920, it might be more exact to think of Great Britain and Northern Ireland as forming a quasi-unitary state.

federated nation: "L' existence d'une nation est . . . un plébiscite de tous les jours."[2] This obviously did not mean that such a plebiscite could or should be held every day, the result of which could only be total anarchy; the real implication is clear: the nation is based on a social contract, the terms of which each new generation of citizens is free to accept tacitly, or to reject openly.

Federalism was an inescapable product of an age which recognized the principle of self-determination. For on the one hand, a sense of national identity and singularity was bound to be generated in a great many groups of people, who would insist on their right to distinct statehood. But on the other hand, the insuperable difficulties of living alone and the practical necessity of sharing the state with neighbouring groups were in many cases such as to make distinct statehood unattractive or unattainable. For those who recognized that the first law of politics is to start from the facts rather than from historical "might-have-been's," the federal compromise thus became imperative.

But by a paradox I have already noted in regard to the nation-state, the principle of self-determination which makes federalism necessary makes it also rather unstable. If the heavy paste of nationalism is relied upon to keep a unitary nation-state together, much more nationalism would appear to be required in the case of a federal nation-state. Yet if nationalism is encouraged as a rightful doctrine and noble passion, what is to prevent it from being used by some group, region, or province within the nation? If "*nation algérienne*" was a valid battle cry against France, how can the Algerian Arabs object to the cry of "*nation kabyle*" now being used against them?

The answer, of course, is that no amount of logic can prevent such an escalation. The only way out of the dilemma is to render what is logically defensible actually undesirable. The advantages *to the minority group* of staying integrated in the whole must on balance be greater than the gain to be reaped from separating. This can easily be the case when there is no real alternative for the separatists, either because they are met with force (as in the case of the U.S. Civil War), or because they are met with laughter (as in the case of the *Bretons bretonnisants*). But when there is a real alternative, it is not so easy. And the greater the advantages and possibilities of separatism, the more difficult it is to maintain an unwavering consensus within the whole state.

One way of offsetting the appeal of separatism is by investing tremendous amounts of time, energy, and money in nationalism, *at the federal level.* A national image must be created that will have such an appeal as to make any image of a separatist group unattractive. Resources must be diverted into such things as national flags, anthems, education, arts councils, broadcasting corporations, film boards; the territory must be bound together by a network of railways, highways, airlines; the national culture and the national economy must be protected by taxes and tariffs; ownership of resources and industry by nationals must be made a matter of policy. In short, the whole of the

[2] Ernest Renan, *Discours et conférences* (Paris, 1887), p. 307—also p. 299.

citizenry must be made to feel that it is only within the framework of the federal state that their language, culture, institutions, sacred traditions, and standard of living can be protected from external attack and internal strife.

It is, of course, obvious that a national consensus will be developed in this way only if the nationalism is emotionally acceptable to all important groups within the nation. Only blind men could expect a consensus to be lasting if the national flag or the national image is merely the reflection of one part of the nation, if the sum of values to be protected is not defined so as to include the language or the cultural heritage of some very large and tightly knit minority, if the identity to be arrived at is shattered by a colour-bar. The advantage as well as the peril of federalism is that it permits the development of a regional consensus based on regional values; so federalism is ultimately bound to fail if the nationalism it cultivates is unable to generate a national image which has immensely more appeal than the regional ones.

Moreover, this national consensus—to be lasting—must be a living thing. There is no greater pitfall for federal nations than to take the consensus for granted, as though it were reached once and for all. The compromise of federalism is generally reached under a very particular set of circumstances. As time goes by these circumstances change; the external menace recedes, the economy flourishes, mobility increases, industrialization and urbanization proceed; and also the federated groups grow, sometimes at uneven paces, their cultures mature, sometimes in divergent directions. To meet these changes, the terms of the federative pact must be altered, and this is done as smoothly as possible by administrative practice, by judicial decision, and by constitutional amendment, giving a little more regional autonomy here, a bit more centralization there, but at all times taking great care to preserve the delicate balance upon which the national consensus rests.

Such care must increase in direct proportion to the strength of the alternatives which present themselves to the federated groups. Thus, when a large cohesive minority believes it can transfer its allegiance to a neighbouring state, or make a go of total independence, it will be inclined to dissociate itself from a consensus the terms of which have been altered in its disfavour. On the other hand, such a minority may be tempted to use its bargaining strength to obtain advantages which are so costly to the majority as to reduce to naught the advantages to the latter of remaining federated. Thus, a critical point can be reached in either direction beyond which separatism takes place, or a civil war is fought.

When such a critical point has been reached or is in sight, no amount, however great, of nationalism can save the federation. Any expenditure of emotional appeal (flags, professions of faith, calls to dignity, expressions of brotherly love) at the national level will only serve to justify similar appeals at the regional level, where they are just as likely to be effective. Thus the great moment of truth arrives when it is realized that *in the last resort* the mainspring of federalism cannot be emotion but must be reason.

To be sure, federalism found its greatest development in the time of the nation-states, founded on the principle of self-determination, and cemented together by the emotion of nationalism. Federal states have themselves made use of this nationalism over periods long enough to make its inner contradictions go unnoticed. Thus, in a neighbouring country, Manifest Destiny, the Monroe Doctrine, the Hun, the Red Scourge, the Yellow Peril, and Senator McCarthy have all provided glue for the American Way of Life; but it is apparent that the Cuban "menace" has not been able to prevent the American Negro from obtaining a renegotiation of the terms of the American national consensus. The Black Muslims were the answer to the argument of the Cuban menace; the only answer to both is the voice of reason.

It is now becoming obvious that federalism has all along been a product of reason in politics. It was born of a decision by pragmatic politicians to face facts as they are, particularly the fact of the heterogeneity of the world's population. It is an attempt to find a rational compromise between the divergent interest-groups which history has thrown together; but it is a compromise based on the will of the people.

Looking at events in retrospect, it would seem that the French Revolution attempted to delineate national territories according to the will of the people, without reference to rationality; the Congress of Vienna claimed to draw state boundaries according to reason, without reference to the will of the people; and federalism arose as an empirical effort to base a country's frontiers on both reason and the will of the people.

I am not heralding the impending advent of reason as the prime mover in politics, for nationalism is too cheap and too powerful a tool to be soon discarded by politicians of all countries; the rising *bourgeoisies* in particular have too large a vested interest in nationalism to let it die out unattended.[3] Nor am I arguing that as important an area of human conduct as politics could or should be governed without any reference to human emotions. But I would like to see emotionalism channelled into a less sterile direction than nationalism. And I am saying that within sufficiently advanced federal countries, the auto-destructiveness of nationalism is bound to become more and more apparent, and reason may yet reveal itself even to ambitious politicians as the more assured road to success. This may also be the trend in unitary states, since they all have to deal with some kind of regionalism or other. Simultaneously in the world of international relations, it is becoming more obvious that the Austinian concept of sovereignty could only be thoroughly applied in a world crippled by the ideology of the nation-state and sustained by the heady stimulant of nationalism. In the world of today, when whole groups of so-called sovereign states are experimenting with rational forms of integration, the exercise of sovereignty will not only be divided within federal states; it will have to be further divided between the states and the communities of states. If this tendency is accentuated the very idea of national sovereignty will recede and, with it, the need for an emotional

[3] On the use of nationalism by the middle classes, see Cobban, *Dictatorship*, p. 140. And for a striking and original approach, see Albert Breton, "The Economics of Nationalism," *Journal of Political Economy*, August 1964.

justification such as nationalism. International law will no longer be explained away as so much "positive international morality," it will be recognized as true law, a "coercive order . . . for the promotion of peace."[4]

Thus there is some hope that in advanced societies, the glue of nationalism will become as obsolete as the divine right of kings; the title of the state to govern and the extent of its authority will be conditional upon rational justification; a people's consensus based on reason will supply the cohesive force that societies require; and politics both within and without the state will follow a much more functional approach to the problems of government. If politicians must bring emotions into the act, let them get emotional about functionalism!

The rise of reason in politics is an advance of law; for is not law an attempt to regulate the conduct of men in society rationally rather than emotionally? It appears then that a political order based on federalism is an order based on law. And there will flow more good than evil from the present tribulations of federalism if they serve to equip lawyers, social scientists, and politicians with the tools required to build societies of men ordered by reason.

Who knows? humanity may yet be spared the ignominy of seeing its destinies guided by some new and broader emotion based, for example, on continentalism.

[4] Hans Kelsen, *Law and Peace* (Cambridge, 1948), pp. 1 and 7.

V

The Contemporary Debates: Federal Citizenship in Culturally Diverse Democracies

21

Editors' Introduction

Without lapsing into the federalism-as-a-panacea view, most recent writings on federalism emphasize the particular relevance of this form of political arrangement for the challenges faced by many states today. It is now common among political thinkers to observe that, in the words of Ronald Watts, "we appear to be in the midst of a paradigm shift which is taking us from a world of sovereign nation-states to a world of diminished state sovereignty and increased interstate linkages of a constitutionally federal character."[1] In short, 65 years after Laski wrote his famous piece, any talk of the "obsolescence of federalism" would itself sound distinctly obsolete.

As we mentioned in the general introduction of this volume, the period from the mid-1960s to the late 1980s was not a golden age for federalism in either theory or practice. European integration proceeded at slow pace, newly created postcolonial federations were unstable and often short-lived, and academic political theorists generally did not consider federalism as a major issue or analytical tool. This would change by the early 1990s with the creation of several new federations and federal-like arrangements in Eastern, Central, Southern, and Western Europe, as well as in South Africa. During this same period, significant steps toward European integration have led to open debates about the possibility of a European federation. As a result, today federalism is increasingly considered—sometimes imprudently—as a potential solution for the management of ethno-national conflicts within states. And in political theory, the federal idea appears now in the major debates about cultural diversity, nationalism, liberalism, citizenship, justice, and stability. In this last section of the volume we cannot hope to do justice to the tremendous range of topics and debates about federalism in our day. In particular, we cannot possibly examine the way these debates are being played out within specific countries and regions around the world. Instead, after a survey of the range of federalist options in the world today by Ronald Watts, we focus primarily on a set of issues that arise within states shared by more than one national community. The authors in this section bring different philosophical and political perspectives to bear on a similar range of problems and challenges for democratic multinational states and superstates.

Ronald Watts's "Comparing Forms of Federal Partnerships" (1998) provides an excellent survey of the language and comparative practice of federalism. Indeed, it could serve as an excellent introduction for any student of federal systems and federalist studies. Apart from defining the main concepts, it classifies the various types of federal (and quasi-federal) systems as forms of partnerships, describes their differences and similarities, and compares them in terms of formation and stability. Alfred Stepan's "Federalism and Democracy: Beyond the U.S. Model" (1999) has a narrower focus. This article raises the question of the potential of federalism for newly democratizing multinational countries. Stepan argues that answering such a difficult question requires going beyond the U.S. model of federalism that dominates political science. He systematically criticizes the principal characteristics of this model—involving what he dubs "coming-together," "demos-constraining," and symmetrical federalism—for providing "a misleading picture of federalism" and for narrowing the range of options offered by the federal tradition. He concludes by suggesting that federations like Belgium, Canada, India, and Spain are much more likely to provide fruitful lessons for newly democratizing multinational states.

Will Kymlicka, who is perhaps the most important contemporary political philosopher to address the challenge of multinational federalism, arrives at similar conclusions from rather different premises and arguments in his article, "Federalism, Nationalism and Multiculturalism" (2004). In many ways, Kymlicka is ambivalent about the virtues of federalism. For some kinds of disadvantaged minority groups, such as immigrants, it may be largely irrelevant. It is, however, highly relevant for territorially concentrated national minorities; in fact, they will legitimately demand the special forms of autonomy and self-government that federalism facilitates. Like Stepan, and also Requejo, Kymlicka is skeptical about the ability of the U.S.-inspired "territorial" model of federalism to provide a sufficient degree of autonomy for such groups. Instead, Kymlicka makes a strong normative case for a "multinational" federal partnership with more significant forms of autonomy and recognition for minority nations. But this solution gives rise to an apparent paradox: the most appropriate form of federalism for multinational states may ultimately lead to the disintegration of these same states if national minorities are likely to use their federal autonomy to prepare the way for their own eventual secession.

The next selection addresses the highly controversial question of the nature of the European Union (EU), the boldest (con)federal experiment of the last two centuries. In "Building the Union: The Nature of Sovereignty in the Political Architecture of Europe" (1997), Richard Bellamy and Dario Castiglione compare three normative and institutional views of the EU. While the *cosmopolitan* view recognizes the variety and plurality of allegiances and favors the sharing of sovereignty through two different versions of federalism, *communitarians* believe that the nation-state is still the main locus of identity and that the EU should at best be confederal. Bellamy and Castiglione favor a third and more complex position, one inspired by a mixture of cosmopolitan and communitarian arguments. According to them, "[w]hat distinguishes this third position is a certain support both for the open, piecemeal nature of the constitutionalization process and for a constitutional structure that mixes national and federal elements." Perceptive readers will notice that the contemporary debate over the nature of the EU both integrates and reformulates many of the key issues of the history of federal thought.

We finish with an interesting argument that seems to draw on the perspectives of the four preceding texts. Ferran Requejo is one of Spain's leading political theorists, and is an active advocate of greater political autonomy for Catalonia within Spain and the EU. His text, "Federalism in Plurinational Societies: Rethinking the Ties between Catalonia, Spain and the European Union" (1999) is an excellent example of the kinds of arguments advanced by liberal-democratic minority nationalists within what he calls "plurinational" states. In effect, whether or not it is ultimately persuasive, it is the kind of argument for asymmetrical federalism that the four preceding texts have tried in their various ways to make room for.

NOTE

1. Ronald Watts, *Comparing Federal Systems,* 2nd edition (Kingston, Ontario: Queen's University, 1999), p. 4.

22

Comparing Forms of Federal Partnerships

Ronald L. Watts

Introduction

This chapter draws upon the field of comparative politics to identify examples of alternative forms of political partnership. This will include an examination of the tradeoffs involved in these various alternatives, and an exploration of the differences between federation, confederation and functional intergovernmental organization as models of political partnership.

The Value and Limitation of International Comparisons

Comparisons may help in several ways. They may help to identify options that might otherwise be overlooked. They may identify consequences, including unforeseen ones, that are likely to flow from particular arrangements that are advocated. Through identifying similarities and contrasts they may draw attention to certain features whose significance might otherwise be underestimated. Furthermore, we can learn not only from the successes but also from the failures of solutions attempted elsewhere.

But some cautions must also be kept in mind. Models cannot be just picked off a shelf. Even where similar institutions are established, different circumstances may make them operate quite differently. A classic illustration of this is the operation of the similar formal procedures in Switzerland and Australia for constitutional amendment involving ratification by referendum requiring a double majority in the federation as a whole and in a majority of the constituent units. This requirement has produced over 110 constitutional amendments in the former since 1891 and only eight out of 42 attempts in the latter since 1901. Each political partnership involves its own unique blend of societal, economic, cultural and political factors; the dynamic interaction of these with the institutions for political partnership will always be distinctive to a degree. In the process of comparison, therefore, the recognition not only of similarities but also of differences is important.

Federalism as One Form of Political Partnership

The term "federal political system" is in much of the contemporary comparative literature now taken to refer to a broad category of political systems in which there are two or more levels of government which combine *self-rule* for the governments of the constituent units with elements of *shared-rule* through common institutions. This broad genus encompasses a whole spectrum of species represented by constitutionally decentralized unions, federations, confederations, federacies, associated statehood, condominiums, leagues and joint functional authorities.[1] All of these involve some element of political and/or economic partnership. Thus, there is an enormous range of possible federal partnership relationships.

Within the genus of "federal political systems," "federations" represent a particular species in which neither the federal nor the constituent units of government are constitutionally or politically subordinate to the other, that is, each having sovereign powers derived from the constitution rather than another level of government, each empowered to deal directly with its citizens in the exercise of its legislative, executive and taxing powers, and each directly elected by its citizens. Even within this species there is enormous scope for variation, as the twenty-three currently existing federations in the world illustrate. There can be and are significant variations in the number and relative size, population and wealth of the constituent units, in the form and scope of the distribution of legislative and executive authority between arenas of government; in the allocation of financial resources to governments, in the degree of centralization or decentralization; the degree of symmetry or asymmetry in the allocation of powers to constituent units; in the structures and processes relating to intergovernmental relations; in the form of the common federative institutions including the provisions for representation of distinct regions or groups in those institutions; in the selection, composition, powers and roles of federal second chambers; in the processes for constitutional adjudication and review including the role of the courts; and in the procedures for constitutional adjustment and amendment.

Furthermore, each of the other species within the broad genus of federal political systems, for instance confederations, federacies, associate statehood and joint functional organizations may itself encompass a variety of arrangements.

Thus, one major theme of this chapter is that federal political systems generally, and even the more specific form represented by federations, provide an enormous array of ways in which partnership can be expressed through political institutions and processes. In examining examples of political partnership elsewhere, attention will be given to three aspects: (1) the forms of partnership, (2) the partners involved, and (3) processes for establishing partnerships.

FORMS OF PARTNERSHIP

The Spectrum of Political Partnerships

The spectrum of political systems embodying political partnerships among distinct political units is extremely broad[2]

Unions

These are polities established in such a way that the constituent units preserve their respective integrities primarily or exclusively through the common organs of the general government rather than through dual government structures. New Zealand and Lebanon are examples. Belgium prior to becoming a federation in 1993 was an example (when central legislators served also with a dual mandate as regional and community councillors).

Constitutionally Decentralized Unions

These are basically unitary in form in the sense that ultimate authority rests with the central government, but they incorporate constitutionally protected sub-national units of government which have functional autonomy. An example is Japan. See table 22.1 for other examples of this and other embodiments of partnership.

Federations

These are compound polities, combining strong constituent units and a strong general government, each possessing powers delegated to it by the people through a constitution, each empowered to deal directly with the citizens in the exercise of its legislative, administrative and taxing powers, and each directly elected by the citizens. There are currently 23 federations in the world.

Confederations

These occur where several pre-existing polities join together to form a common government for certain limited purposes (for foreign affairs, defence or economic purposes) but the common government is dependent upon the constituent governments, being composed of delegates from the constituent governments and therefore having only an indirect electoral and fiscal base. Among historical examples have been Switzerland for most of the period 1291–1847, and the United States 1776–1789. In the contemporary world, the European Union is primarily a confederation although it has increasingly incorporated some features of a federation.

Federacies

These are political arrangements where a large unit is linked to a smaller unit or units, where the smaller unit retains considerably more autonomy than other segments but has a smaller role in the government of the larger and where the relationship can be dissolved only by mutual agreement. These represent a radically asymmetrical form of federal relationship and usually

Table 22.1 Examples of varieties of federal political partnerships

a. Decentralized unions	b. Federations	c. Confederations	d. Federacies	e. Associated states	f. Condominium	g. Leagues
Antigua-Barbuda	Argentina	Benelux Economic Union	Denmark–Faroes	France–Monaco	Andorra–France and Spain (until 1993)	Arab League
China	Australia	Caribbean Community	Finland–Aaland	India–Bhutan		Assoc. of SE Asian Nations (ASEAN)
Colombia	Austria	Commonwealth of Independent States	India–Kashmir	Italy–San Marino		Baltic Assembly
Italy	Belgium	European Union	Portugal–Azores	Netherlands–Netherlands Antilles		Commonwealth of Nations
Japan	Brazil		Portugal–Madeira	New Zealand–Cook Islands		North Atlantic Treaty Organization (NATO)
Netherlands	Canada		UK–Guernsey	New Zealand–Niue Island		Nordic Council
Papua/New Guinea	Comoros		UK–Jersey	Switzerland–Liechtenstein		South Asian Assoc. for Regional Cooperation (SAARC)
Solomon Islands	Ethiopía		UK–Man			
Sudan	Germany		US–Northern Marianas			
Tanzania	India		US–Puerto Rico			
United Kingdom	Malaysia					
Vanuatu	Mexico					
	Nigeria					
	Pakistan					
	Russia					
	South Africa					
	Spain					
	St. Kitts-Nevis					
	Switzerland					
	United Arab Emirates					
	United States					
	Venezuela					
	Yugoslavia (Serbia and Montenegro)					

relate to peripheral or remote territories or islands. Examples are the relationship of Puerto Rico to the United States and of the Faroe Islands to Denmark.

Associated States

These relationships are similar to federacies, but can be dissolved by either of the units acting alone on prearranged terms. Consequently, associated states usually have even less of a role in the governance of the associated power. Examples are the relationships between New Zealand and the Cook Islands and between Italy and San Marino.

Condominiums

These are political units which function under the joint rule of two or more external states in such a way that the inhabitants have substantial internal self-rule. An example was Andorra which functioned under the joint rule of France and Spain for 700 years until 1993.

Leagues

These are linkages of politically independent polities for specific purposes that function through a common secretariat rather than a government and from which members may unilaterally withdraw. See table 22.1 for examples.

Joint Functional Intergovernmental Organizations

These are organizations or agencies established by two or more polities for the joint implementation of a particular task or tasks. There are numerous examples such as the North Atlantic Fisheries Organization (NAFO), the International Atomic Energy Agency (IAEA), the World Trade Organization (WTO) and the International Labor Organization (ILO). First developed in the nineteenth century, there are now more than a hundred functional intergovernmental organizations. Joint functional authorities may also take the form of transborder organizations established by adjoining sub-national governments, for example, the interstate grouping for economic development involving four regions in Italy, four Austrian *Länder*, two Yugoslav republics and one West German *Land* established in 1978, and the interstate *Regio Basiliensis* involving Swiss, German and French cooperation in the Basle area.

Hybrids

Some political systems have combined characteristics of different forms of political partnership. Examples are Canada initially in 1867, which was basically a federation but contained some quasi-unitary elements; more recently South Africa (1996), which is a federation retaining some quasi-unitary features; and the European Union after Maastricht, which is basically a confederation but has some features of a federation. Hybrids occur because statesmen are often more interested in pragmatic political solutions than in theoretical purity.

Examples of the variety of forms of partnership within the broad genus of federal systems are set out in table 22.1.

Categories of Economic Integration and Social Integration and Their Relationship to Different Forms of Political Integration

The literature on economic integration has traditionally identified five categories in ascending order of economic integration.[3]

1. *Free trade area* which involves the removal of customs tariffs and of quantitative restrictions, such as quotas, on trade between member states, but with each of them retaining its own distinct barriers against non-members (e.g., EFTA and NAFTA).
2. *Customs union* which, in addition to (1), standardizes customs barriers by member-states against non-members (e.g., the German Zollverein 1834–1867).
3. *Common market* which, in addition to (2), removes the restrictions on the movement of labor, services and capital between member-states (e.g., the European Economic Community before the Single European Act and Maastricht).
4. *Economic union* which, in addition to (3), involves varying degrees of harmonization of state economic policies in order to remove discrimination that would be due to disparities in these policies (e.g., European Union following Single European Act and Maastricht).
5. *Monetary union* which adds a single currency and monetary policy (e.g., West African Monetary Union and proposal for EMU as part of EU).

More recent developments in Europe and North America have suggested the need for a radical reformulation of this typology. Rather than depicting a set of stages of economic integration, the reformulation would identify various aspects of integration that may be pursued in different degrees in different settings. Furthermore, these would involve not just issues of tariffs and removal of barriers to trade but policies for removal of non-tariff barriers to trade and to movement of services, capital and labor. Peter Leslie, for instance, has suggested listing forms of economic association in terms of the following aspects: a *free trade area* liberalizing the movement of goods, services and capital among participating states; a *labor market union* guaranteeing free movement of workers and their families; a *trade policy union* whereby the participating states (whether joined together by a federal constitution or more loosely linked by international treaty) act as a single entity in international trade negotiations; a *monetary union* where participating states adopt a common currency, or at least fixed and irrevocable parities among their currencies; and a *structural and development union* in which common institutions have the powers and effective policy capacity to engage in sectoral policies and policies affecting the location of industry, implying a policy role in the distribution and redistribution of resources and wealth.[4]

An important aspect that the traditional literature on economic integration commented little upon but that has attracted particular attention during the past decade in both Canada and the European Union is the notion of a *social union.* This relates to policies directed at enhancing the level of social welfare and social programs within the participating territories, not only through economic development but through joint action (either federal or intergovernmental) including the redistribution of finances and resources. Its implementation has some relation to the idea of a structural and development union. In the European Union context the social union has been closely linked to the notion of a labor market union referred to above.

An important consideration is what forms of political institutions are required to sustain each of these levels or aspects of economic association effectively. Given that economic outcomes are shaped not only by market forces but also by political decisions, the framework for political decision making has a very real bearing on the kind and degree of economic integration that may be achieved. For example, it is noteworthy that as the European Economic Community has progressed closer and closer to economic integration, its political institutions have progressed from a purely confederal political structure to one after Maastricht that involves some elements more typical of federations. These include voting by qualified majority rather than unanimity in the Council on a wide range of matters, and a co-decision role for the European Parliament on a range of matters rather than a purely advisory role, thus significantly adding to the real powers of the European Parliament.

The relative effectiveness of confederations or federations as structures to sustain economic association has often been debated. Few confederations have sustained all five levels of the traditional categories of economic integration, usually going no further than the level of a common market. The European Union has gone further, having already achieved an economic union and is now undergoing the process of moving toward a monetary union, but while still primarily confederal in character it has had to establish political institutions and processes that in certain respects approximate those in federations. Most federations, on the other hand, have encompassed all five levels of the traditional categories of economic partnership, although in some cases, most notably Canada, the common market has not been fully implemented.

But a comparison between federations and confederations as forms of political partnership facilitating economic association is more complex than that. It depends not just on the general form but also on the specific powers and processes for common decision making embodied in the particular federation or confederation.

The Distinction between Federations and Confederations as Political Partnerships

The traditional arguments about the relative effectiveness of confederations and federations as forms of political partnership were first elaborated in *The Federalist*, where confederations were strongly denigrated both in terms of

American and comparative historical experience.[5] The relative success of the European Community has revived this discussion during the past two decades, not the least within Europe between those who believe that the current structure should be only a way-station on the path to full federation and those who believe that political integration within the European Union has already gone far enough or even too far. What is significant is that the European Union in its current form is very different from traditional concepts or examples of confederation. Historically confederations like Switzerland (1291–1798, 1815–1848), the United Netherlands (1579–1795), the United States (1781–1789), and Germany (1815–1866) were political partnerships for limited purposes focusing primarily, although not exclusively, on foreign affairs and defence. The European Community and the subsequent European Union have had a very different focus, primarily on economic integration.[6]

Both federations and confederations belong to the broad genus of federal political systems in that they involve elements of shared-rule for certain purposes and self-rule of the constituent units for others. What distinguishes them from each other as forms of political partnership are two characteristics. First, in federations the structures and powers of the federative institutions and of the federated constituent units are derived from a supreme constitution not unilaterally amendable, so that neither order of government is constitutionally or politically subordinate to the other. Each derives its own assigned sovereign powers from the constitution. In a confederation, which is essentially a union of states, the federative institutions derive their powers from a treaty involving the agreement of the constituent units who in effect retain ultimate sovereignty. Thus the federative institutions are dependent upon the consent of the constituent governments and act only on behalf of those constituent units in those respects in which they agree by a treaty to pool their sovereignty. Second, the federative institutions in federations and confederations consequently differ. In federations, the federative institutions are representative bodies directly elected by the citizens and deal directly with the citizens in the exercise of their legislative, administrative and taxing powers. In confederations, the federative institutions that make binding decisions on their members are instead intergovernmental in character, composed of delegates from the constituent governments; in terms of legislation, administration and taxation, the shared institutions act on the citizens indirectly through those constituent governments.

What are the relative advantages and disadvantages of these two forms of federal political partnership?[7] The confederal form often appeals to advocates of regional distinctiveness because it usually provides a veto to each constituent government over all major common policies undertaken by the institutions of shared-rule. In this respect it maximizes the protection of regional interests. A disadvantage is that arriving at agreed policies for common action is dependent on the agreement of the constituent units, and the difficulty of reaching such agreement often means that effective resolution is not achieved or at least is much delayed. Policies requiring the redistribution of resources are particularly difficult to achieve where agreement upon their differential impact is required on the part of all the constituent governments. Furthermore, historically such systems have tended in the long term to be politically unstable. In the end, the confederal systems in te United States and Switzerland, and ultimately Germany, were replaced by federations and in the Netherlands by a consociational unitary system. In the contemporary world they have often not lasted for long (e.g., the East African Common Services Organization and the Central American Common Market). The European Union as an economic confederation has been the most successful contemporary example, but it has gone beyond a simple confederation by incorporating some (although not yet all) of the features of a federation.

Federations have the advantage that in the specific areas of authority assigned by the constitution to institutions exercising shared-rule, they are not dependent upon the consent of all the constituent governments and can, therefore, act more decisively. Furthermore, federations have typically been able to implement more extensive policies relating to the redistribution of resources among territories. On the other hand, a constituent unit is in a position to guarantee the protection of its particular interests only in those fields where the constitution of the federation has assigned to the constituent units exclusive responsibility. Federations are also complicated systems of government involving the division of legislative and administrative responsibilities, complex financial arrangements, and intricate cooperative machinery for coordinating the activities of the two orders of government. Critics sometimes have argued that federations have an inherent tendency to progressive centralization, but although this may be true of many examples, such as the United States and Australia, it is not the universal experience of federations.[8]

One difference between confederations and federations as forms of political partnership that was not raised in traditional comparisons, but has been brought to the fore by concerns within the European Union, is the so-called "democratic deficit" inherent in the essentially intergovernmental character of the federative institutions of confederations. In federations where federal and provincial or state governments each have a direct democratic relationship with their citizens, federal decision making in the areas of shared-rule would appear to be more fully democratic than in confederations where decision making related to shared-rule is primarily intergovernmental in character and thus is only indirectly democratic. The concerns about the "democratic deficit" in the European Union and the resultant increasing questioning by citizens of the legitimacy and bureaucratic remoteness of decisions taken in its confederal bodies illustrate the problems that can arise in confederal structures in an age when there is such a strong emphasis upon democratic processes and accountability. Even some federations where "executive federalism" as a characteristic of intergovernmental relations has become prominent (e.g., Australia and Canada) have experienced similar reactions to the development of such confederal processes.

Supporters of confederation as opposed to federation as a form of political partnership have criticized the latter as simply a more complicated form of nation-state based on the notion of single nationhood. They argue that a confederal partnership better recognizes the multinational diversity among its constituent members.[9] This is an important consideration in contemplating appropriate forms of political partnership. It assumes that the sovereign nation-state remains the ultimate political unit and that therefore any partnership of nations must be intergovernmental. Countering this must be the recognition that an increasingly global economy has itself unleashed economic and political forces strengthening both international *and* local pressures at the expense of the sovereign nation-state. The effective sovereignty of the nation-state has become increasingly perforated and unattainable. This had led to pressures for pooling sovereignty, particularly in economic matters. This pooling of sovereignty in a multinational partnership may take a variety of forms including not only confederations but federations. There is nothing in the concept of federation that inherently precludes a multinational federation. Indeed it could be argued that Spain, Belgium and India are evolving in this direction. It is also certainly the conception envisaged by those in the European Union who advocate its progressive evolution into an eventually full-fledged multinational federation.

The Range of Variations

The possible options for partnership are not limited simply to the choice between a federation, a confederation or an intergovernmental functional organization. Indeed, within each of these categories and within each of the other forms described earlier and listed in table 22.1, there is room for a wide variation.

Among federations, for example, there is a great variety. These include highly differing allocations of specific legislative, administrative and fiscal powers to the federal government and to the provincial or state governments, and in the powers shared between them.[10] As a result, federal government expenditures after intergovernmental transfers (as a percentage of total federal-state-local expenditures) ranged (in 1991) between 82.2 percent (in Malaysia), and 27.4 percent (in Switzerland), with Canada near the lower end at 40.8 percent.[11] This illustrates what a high degree of variation there can be among federations in the general level of centralization or decentralization.

The degree of constitutional symmetry and asymmetry in the relative powers and relationships of the constituent units to the federation has also varied. Some federations have been marked by virtually complete symmetry, such as the United States and Australia, while others have exhibited a considerable degree of asymmetry, such as Malaysia, Belgium, India, and Spain.[12] Furthermore, the degree of asymmetry does not necessarily correspond to the general degree of decentralization. Malaysia, for example, is one of the most centralized federations in terms of the general federal government powers but has a higher degree of asymmetry than most federations. There are variations too among federations in their federative institutions and the degree to which these are, as in Canada, largely majoritarian in their character and processes, or where consociational processes predominate, as in Switzerland or Belgium.[13] Some federations even embody significant elements of confederal processes, either in the federal second chambers (e.g., the German *Bundesrat*) or in intergovernmental processes that take on the character of "executive federalism." Many federations may be described as mono-national but others encompass multilingual and indeed multinational peoples (e.g., India). The degree to which these variations facilitate economic integration and competitiveness, security from external domination and protection of the interests of major federal minorities depends significantly therefore on the particular arrangements adopted or developed in each federation. Thus, even within the category of federations a wide range of differing partnership arrangements is possible. Federation as a form of partnership is by no means limited to that represented by the current Canadian status quo.

Confederations, too, exhibit a wide variation. Particularly significant is what functions or purposes are assigned to the shared institutions and the specific processes and checks applied to the decision-making processes for shared-rule. Thus, for instance, the European Union, which in its current form represents a highly developed economic confederation but is only embryonic in the development of its two other pillars relating to non-economic aspects (i.e., foreign and security policy, and justice and home affairs) represents just one variant and is not necessarily the only possible confederal arrangement.

Variations in the Role of Constituent Units in International Affairs

An issue that illustrates the variety among both federations and confederations is the role played by their constituent units in the arena of international affairs. There are two aspects to this issue: (1) the degree to which the constituent units themselves play a direct role on the international stage, and (2) the role of the constituent units in the collective decision making of the federation or confederation in relation to foreign policy.

Regarding the first aspect, the traditional view in confederations and certainly federations has been that a major purpose of such political partnerships is the creation of an international entity in the interests of improved security and diplomatic influence. Hence it has usually been regarded as normal that there should be a transfer of control over foreign affairs to the governing councils of the confederation or federation as a whole. Among confederations typical examples were the earlier Swiss, Dutch, United States, and German confederations formed with security and defence as primary motives. This was also typical of the earlier modern federations such as the United States in 1789 (Constitution, article 1, sections 8, 10, and article 2, section 2), Switzerland (1848) and Australia (1901) which transferred exclusive control over foreign relations to their federal governments.

But this has not in fact been the universal pattern in either confederations or federations. For example, among confederations the European Union stands out by its emphasis upon economic objectives rather than upon defence or foreign policy. In relation to the economic sphere, the treaties establishing the European Union did, nevertheless, express a political commitment to act as a single entity in external economic relations in order to establish a strong trade policy union. This thrust has been exemplified in a wide range of international trade negotiations by the European Union acting collectively, including those relating to the World Trade Organization (WTO). But in areas outside external economic relations the situation has been different. Although one of the three pillars of the European Union relates to the objective of a common foreign policy, as yet little has in practice been achieved beyond the statement of that objective.

Among federations there are in fact significant variations in the constitutional basis for the roles of the federal and constituent unit governments on the international scene. In a number of federations including the United States, Switzerland, Australia, and Spain, treaty-making powers are exclusively assigned to the federal government.[14] In others the federal government is assigned the treaty-making power but treaties require provincial or state implementation or consent insofar as they impinge on the normal legislative jurisdiction of the constituent units. Examples are Canada (as a result of judicial review) and Germany and Austria (by constitutional stipulation). In yet other federations such as India, Malaysia and Pakistan (1962) the federal government has been required by the constitution to consult the states or provinces, although their consent has not been required.

There are two federations, Germany and Belgium, where the constituent units themselves have been assigned some treaty-making powers of their own. The German Basic Law granted to the *Länder* an original right to conclude treaties with foreign states and international organizations in areas in which the *Länder* have exclusive or concurrent legislative powers, although *Länder* treaties in the area of concurrent jurisdiction require the consent of the federal government.[15] The treaties concluded so far by the *Länder* have not been particularly numerous or complicated, mainly addressing regional cross-frontier concerns or cultural conventions with a range of other countries. The process of European integration has also raised the issue of the role of the *Länder* both in relation to the transfer of powers to the European Union and to their representation in the decision-making processes of the Union, most notably in terms of the liaison offices which the *Länder* have individually set up in Brussels and the participation of the *Länder* in the European Union's Committee of Regions.[16]

The Belgian federal constitution of 1993 went even further. It extended the authority of the federated entities in the international arena for all matters otherwise under their jurisdiction. It did, however, attempt to retain the coherence of Belgian foreign policy by requiring a process of consultation and negotiations with the federal cabinet.[17]

The above examples indicate that among both confederations and federations there is a great variety of arrangements, often complex, governing the relative roles of the different orders of government in the international arena.

Some bear a similarity to the current Canadian arrangements, but many vary significantly.

No Single Continuum in the Range of Variations

One misconception to be avoided is the notion that there is a single continuum from federations to confederations, and on to federacies, associated states, leagues, and joint functional authorities. While in a loose sense these represent a spectrum of partnership arrangements ranging from the more to the less integrated, as in a spectrum, the colors may at the margins shade into each other. Furthermore, these categories refer to the form of the partnership and not to the scope of shared decision making. Thus, it is quite possible that the powers or purposes assigned to the common institutions in a relatively centralized confederation may be greater than those in more decentralized federations. The highly decentralized West Indies Federation and the more centralized East African Common Services Organization, both now defunct, illustrate this possibility. Another example is the way in which in some respects the European Union is more centralized with regard to bureaucratic regulation of the internal economic union than is the Canadian federation. In considering possible forms of future partnership for the relationship of Quebec to Canada, federation and confederation each encompass a wide range of possibilities, but some possible variants of federation may be more decentralized than some of confederation. It is necessary, therefore, to consider the relative implications both for effective autonomy and for effective shared policy making of particular variants and not just the general form.

THE PARTNERS

The Issues

In addition to forms of partnership, consideration must be given to the nature of the constituent partners. Here attention needs to be given to four issues: (1) the equality of partners; (2) the number of partners; (3) multiple levels of partners; (4) partners representing territories or communities.

The Equality of Partners

Does a partnership require that the partners be equal in status and powers? There may be good grounds to argue for equality of partners, but such a notion is not conceptually inherent in partnership. Indeed, in many business or professional partnerships it is not at all unusual to have clearly distinguished "senior" and "junior" partners.

In the realm of political partnerships there are many examples of asymmetry, either *de facto* or *de jure* (specified by a constitution or treaty), in the status and powers of the constituent partners. The most obvious examples are those of the many federacies and associated states listed previously in table 22.1 where smaller or peripheral political units are joined to larger unions or federations in a clearly asymmetrical relationship.[18] In most confederations and federations all the full-fledged constituent units are constitutionally symmetrical in their powers and relationships as constituent members, but there is a significant number of instances where that is not the case. For example, within the European Union since Maastricht special exemptions apply to the United Kingdom and Denmark, and the plan to proceed with the European Monetary Union has led to the notions of a Europe with "variable geometry" and integration at "varying speeds." Among federations, examples of significant constitutional asymmetry in the powers and relationships of the constituent units include Spain, Belgium, Germany, Malaysia, and India. Thus, the Canadian Constitution Act, 1867 is by no means unique in this respect nor is Canada the most asymmetrical federation in character.[19]

The Number of Partners

Most federations, confederations and leagues are composed of multiple partners. Some, however, are composed of only two. The particular difficulties of dyadic confederations or federations have long been recognized.[20] Of fifteen bicommunal polities considered by Ivo Duchacek in a 1988 study (Belgium, Burundi, Canada, Cyprus, Czechoslovakia, Fiji, Finland, Guyana, Northern Ireland, Israel, Malaysia, Sri Lanka, Suriname, Pakistan and Tanzania), he noted that in the previous two decades at least half of them had provided the first pages of the world press with dramatic stories of intercommunal tensions and violence. Bipolar federations have invariably experienced serious tensions, instability and a high failure rate. The splitting of Pakistan, Czechoslovakia (each composed of two partners) and of the bipolar Malaysia–Singapore relationship together with the intensifying bipolarity within Belgium provide cautionary examples.[21] In multi-member political partnerships, including multiethnic ones, there is an opportunity for flexibility and accommodation through shifting alliances and coalitions on different issues so that all groups in the end gain some satisfaction. Bipolar situations in practice have proven harder to resolve than multi-group ones because the former invariably take on the characteristics of a zero-sum game.

In a confederation, where each partner government possesses a veto on all major policy decisions, the problem is accentuated. The existence of mutual vetoes where there are only two units is likely to be a recipe for repeated impasses and deadlocks, contributing to a cumulative sharpening of frustrations on both sides. Indeed, it is largely for this reason that Peter Leslie has concluded that the Maastricht model of the European Union would be unworkable in a two-unit confederation of Quebec and Canada.[22] Furthermore, in the Canadian case, where the disparity in population and GNP of the proposed two units (three to one) is greater than that in any of the bipolar federations referred to above, it is likely that obtaining agreement in the first place upon the stipulation of a mutual veto for all major policy decisions would be extremely difficult to achieve.[23]

Tripartite political partnerships have also tended to experience particular difficulties. Among this category have been the federations of Nigeria (when it was composed of three Regions during the period 1954–1963) and Rhodesia and Nyasaland (1953–1963 composed of three Territories), the unfulfilled proposals in 1963 for a Federation of East Africa (composed of Kenya, Uganda, and Tanganyika), the confederations of Benelux (Belgium, the Netherlands and Luxembourg) and the East African Common Services Organization (EACSO, composed of Kenya, Uganda, and Tanzania), and among leagues the North American Free Trade Area (NAFTA, composed of Canada, the United States, and Mexico). Typically most of these have suffered difficulties either from the fears of each partner that it would be vulnerable to a permanent alliance of the other two (e.g., Nigeria and the 1963 proposal for an East African Federation), or the hegemony of one of the three partners (e.g., Northern Nigeria, Southern Rhodesia, or within NAFTA the United States). These tensions were resolved by the further subdivision of Nigeria into four constituent units in 1963 and then progressively to the point where there are now 30 states and one territory, the disintegration of the Federation of Rhodesia and Nyasaland and of the confederal EACSO, and the effective absorption of the confederal Benelux within the wider European Union. The proposals for the expansion of membership in NAFTA would similarly counter the current tripartite dynamics of that association.

Multiple Levels of Partners

A notable feature in the contemporary world is the membership of a number of federations within wider federal organizations. An example is the membership of Belgium, Germany, Spain and now Austria in the European Union, creating a compound set of political partnerships.

Membership in the European Union, itself a hybrid that is predominantly confederal in character but with some characteristics of a federation, has had implications for the internal relationships within those member states of the European Union that are themselves federations. Among the issues that have arisen has been the appropriate role of the regional units within each of these federations in negotiations within the institutions of the European Union. This has led to the establishment by these regional units of offices in the European Union capital in Brussels and to their direct representation in the Committee of Regions of the European Union. Consequently, a new element of complexity has been introduced into intergovernmental relations in these federations. The impact upon the federal-regional balance within each federation of the transfer of powers to Brussels has also on occasion become a contentious issue, most notably in Germany where it led to an important recent case before the German Constitutional Court.

Another illustration of federations within a wider supra-federation partnership is the membership of Canada, the United States and Mexico, all three themselves federations, within the North American Free Trade Agreement (NAFTA). Elsewhere Malaysia is a member of the Association of South East Asian Nations (ASEAN) and India and Pakistan (both currently federations) are participants in the South Asian Association for Regional Cooperation (SAARC). In each of these cases membership in the wider organization has had implications for the internal organization and balance within the member federations.

Traditionally, the analysis of federations and confederations has centred upon relations between their federative and state governments. But increasingly in the contemporary world, federal arrangements have taken on the multi-tiered character of a compound system of partners. It has been the effort to maximize citizens' preferences and reduce their frustrations that has led to the establishment of multiple levels of federal organization, each operating at a different scale for performing most effectively their particular functions.[24] At the same time the resulting multi-tiered systems have created a more complicated context for the operation of the individual federations participating in these wider forms of federal organization. These considerations have implications for such proposals as that of Philip Resnick for a Canada-Quebec Union composed of a federation of English Canada on the one hand and Quebec on the other, and for the relationship of any such union to NAFTA.[25]

Partners Representing Territories or Communities

In the various forms of political partnerships outlined earlier and in table 22.1, the partners have usually consisted of territorial units. But while most federal partnerships have been based on territorial components, sometimes where communities overlap territorial delineations it has been proposed that communities rather than territories should be the constituent units in the partnership.

Belgium in fact combines the two kinds of partners. The current federal structure is composed of three Regions (the Flanders, Walloon, and Brussels Regions) with Councils responsible predominantly for economic matters and three Communities (the Flemish-speaking, French-speaking, and German-speaking) responsible primarily for cultural affairs, education, personalized services and use of languages in certain matters. Each of the six constitute distinct legal entities with their own constitutionally allocated jurisdiction. The Regions represent a *territorial* jurisdiction but overlapping them are the Communities which represent a *personal* jurisdiction. Although the emergent Belgian federation (1993) is too recent to allow firm conclusion to be drawn from its operation, this example points to at least the possibility of other forms of partners than those delineated solely by territorial boundaries.

Processes for Establishing Political Partnerships

The Significance of Different Processes for Establishing Political Partnerships

In the consideration of revised arrangements for political partnership, four different processes may be identified: (1) the aggregation of partners, (2) the creation of new partners by devolution, (3) the combination of the processes of aggregation and devolution, and (4) the break-up of an existing union or federation, followed by the joining together in a new partnership of the separated units. Examples of all four processes have occurred, although the fourth would appear to involve the greatest difficulties.

Establishing Political Partnerships by Aggregation

One common pattern for the creation of federal partnerships (both confederations and federations) has been the aggregation of formally distinct political units. In both the United States and Switzerland this took the form first of aggregation into confederation but, following the failure of that confederation, conversion into a federation. In the case of Australia the process of aggregation led directly to the establishment of a federation. The European Union, both in terms of its original six members and its subsequent progressive enlargement, has been the result of aggregation and continues to espouse as an objective of its basic treaties the achievement of a closer union. NAFTA too has been the product of a process of aggregation. Indeed, most confederations, leagues and functional agencies have been the product of a process of aggregation.

Establishing Political Partnerships by Devolution

Some federations and also some federacies have been created by a process of devolution within previously unitary systems. In these cases, either existing regional units have been given increased powers and autonomy or new regional units have been created. Notable examples are Belgium and Nigeria, and also Spain which is well along the path. The devolution of a federation into a confederation has been much rarer. The Commonwealth of Independent States (CIS), established immediately as a successor to the USSR, does provide an example, but its character as a confederation has been somewhat compromised by the efforts of the Russian federation to assert military and economic hegemony within the CIS.

Establishing Political Partnership by a Combination of Aggregation and Devolution

Some federations have been the product of a combination of aggregation and devolution. The Canadian federation in 1867 involved not only the bringing together of colonies but also the division of the single province established by the Act of Union, 1840, into two new provinces, Quebec and Ontario. Other examples of federations that have involved a combination of aggregation and devolution have been India and Malaysia.[26] There is no logical reason why such a combination of processes might not be employed in the evolution into a confederation, and the history of the Swiss Confederation provides an example, although there aggregation was the predominant process.

Break-Up of an Existing Union or Federation Followed by a New Partnership

There would seem to be a certain logic to the argument that before the creation of a new political partnership the preceding one should be dismantled, thus leaving the individual sovereign partners to negotiate freely the terms of a new partnership in a process of aggregation. Such a process might be used to avoid the full effects of balkanization induced by a secession. This solution has often appealed to the advocates of political independence or sovereignty as a way of retaining some of the benefits of continued economic association.

But such a solution is not as simple as it appears at first sight.[27] Almost invariably the process of secession where it has occurred elsewhere has created a situation that has presented enormous barriers to the creation of a subsequent partnership, even when that was avowed as an objective at the time of separation. Not uncommonly, once the complete independence of one partner in a federation has been conceded, other units have raised similar demands which have led to further fragmentation or disintegration (e.g., the break-ups of the West Indies Federation, the Federation of Rhodesia and Nyasaland, and of the USSR). Moreover, resentments aroused at the time of separation or dissolution have tended to persist and to discourage for a considerable period of time any subsequent creation of a looser form of partnership between the territories concerned, even where that was a declared objective at the time of separation.

Whenever secession has occurred, it has inevitably been accompanied by sharp political controversies and acrimony which are not easily forgotten.[28] The unscrambling of a federation raises many controversial issues such as the allocation of debts and assets, relocation of members of the federal public service and armed forces, the maintenance or not of a single currency and monetary policy, citizenship entitlements, the place of minorities in the successor states and the appropriate boundaries. These have added to the resentments felt by both sides, and this has made the negotiation of a new partnership that much more difficult. This has been apparent in the continued hostility between India and Pakistan ever since partition in 1947 (despite Jawarlahal Nehru's original expectation that Pakistan would eventually return to the fold), and the failure in the early years after the demise of the federations in the West Indies, Rhodesia, Nyasaland, and Czechoslovakia, and the separation of Singapore from Malaysia, to develop alternative forms of post-federal interterritorial economic association. Eventually, some ten years after the dismantling of the West Indies Federation a confederal Caribbean Community and Common Market (CARICOM) did emerge in 1973 and some functional economic linkages between Malaysia and Singapore have occurred, but the length of time before these developed gives some insight into the impact that secession and separation can have on public attitudes and on the prospect for negotiating an alternative form of economic or political partnership immediately following such events.

The Modification of Existing Partnerships

Experience in many federations elsewhere such as Switzerland, Australia, the United States and Germany has indicated that attempts at major comprehensive constitutional reform have always proved difficult and have usually failed.

Generally, in most federations substantial change and even transformation have been effected not by radical constitutional amendment but rather by incremental piecemeal constitutional adjustment and even more by pragmatic non-constitutional political adaptation.[29] To effect such changes it has been necessary to avoid having these changes interpreted in terms of winners and losers. Where constitutional referendums have been employed almost always their impact has been divisive rather than helpful.[30] Experience elsewhere also indicates, however, that despite the difficulties of effecting significant change, the persistent failure to resolve fundamental problems can have a cumulatively corrosive impact upon an existing political partnership and is likely to contribute eventually at some point to its total breakdown. Incremental but significant and responsive adjustment seems to be the most effective mode for maintaining long-run stability within federations and confederations.

NOTES

1. These various species are distinguished later in this chapter.
2. This categorization has been derived from Daniel J. Elazar (ed.), *Federal Systems of the World: A Handbook of Federal, Confederal and Autonomy Arrangements*, 2nd ed. (Harlow, Essex: Longman Group Limited, 1994), pp. xvi–xviii. See also Watts, *Comparing Federal Systems*, table 1, pp. 8–9.
3. See, for instance, A.E. Safarian, *Canadian Federalism and Economic Integration* (Ottawa: Information Canada, 1973), p. 2. See also Bela Balassa, *The Theory of Economic Integration* (Homewood, Illinois: Irwin, 1961), p. 2.
4. See Peter Leslie, "Governing the Economy within Economic Unions: Canada, the EU, and the NAFTA," paper delivered at the European Consortium on Political Research Workshop on *Multi Level Governance and Regional Integration*, Bern, Switzerland, March 1997.
5. Alexander Hamilton, James Madison and John Jay, *The Federalist Papers*, originally published in 1787–1788, and republished by various publishers including the New American Library, New York, 1961. See especially Papers 15–23.
6. Murray Forsyth, *Unions of States: The Theory and Practice of Confederation* (Leicester: Leicester University Press, 1981), pp. 4–6, 160–187. See also Frederick K. Lister, *The European Union, the United Nations, and the Revival of Confederal Governance* (Westport, Connecticut: Greenwood Press, 1996), pp. 11–13, 22–26, 55–109.
7. For an advocacy of the advantages of confederation see Lister, *The European Union*, pp. 32–47.
8. See, for instance, Elazar, *Exploring Federalism* (Tuscaloosa: University of Alabama Press, 1987), pp. 201–203; Lister, *The European Union*, pp. 20–22.
9. See, for instance, Philip Resnick, *Toward a Canada-Quebec Union* (Montreal and Kingston: McGill-Queen's University Press, 1991).

10. For a fuller discussion see Watts, *Comparing Federal Systems in the 1990s* (Kingston and Montreal: Institute of Intergovernmental Relations, Queen's University and McGill-Queen's University Press, 1997), pp. 65–74.
11. Watts, *Comparing Federal Systems*, table 8, p. 43.
12. Watts, *Comparing Federal Systems*, pp. 60–62.
13. Watts, *Comparing Federal Systems*, pp. 75–89.
14. But note that in Australia the Adelaide Federation Centenary Conference held on April 20–23, 1997 included in its draft principles for consideration at the conference that to "equip Australia to take its place in the international community of the 21st century" the constitutional system should be modified so that "both national and sub-national governments are able to participate in international relations and international economic activity."
15. Klaus Otto Nass, "The Foreign and European Policy of the German Länder," *Publius: The Journal of Federalism*, Vol. 19, no. 4 (Fall 1989), pp. 165–84, 166–67; Uwe Leonardy, "Federation and Länder in German Foreign Relations: Power-Sharing in Treaty-Making and European Affairs," in Charlie Jefferey and Roland Sturm (eds.), *German Politics*, Vol. 1, no. 3 (December 1992), "Special Issue on Federalism, Unification and European Integration," pp. 119–135, 120–124. The relevant section of the constitution is Article 32.
16. Leonardy, "Federation and Länder in German Foreign Relations," pp. 121–122, 123–124, 127–129, 130–133.
17. André Alen and Rusen Ergec, *Federal Belgium After the Fourth State Reform of 1993* (Brussels: Ministry of Foreign Affairs, 1994), pp. 29–33.
18. See the earlier part of this chapter for a definition of federacies and associated states.
19. R. Watts, "Asymmetrical Federalism," in Richard Simeon and Mary Janigan (eds.), *Toolkits and Building Blocks: Constructing a New Canada* (Toronto: C.D. Howe Institute, 1991), pp. 133–138.
20. See the special issue devoted to "Bicommunal Societies and Polities," *Publius: The Journal of Federalism*, Vol. 18, no. 2 (Spring 1988); and especially the article in that issue by Ivo Duchacek, "Dyadic Federations and Confederations," pp. 5–31.
21. The Belgian Federation is actually composed of six entities (three Regions and three Communities) but its politics have been predominantly bipolar. See André Alen, *Bipolar and Centrifugal Federalism* (Brussels: Ministry of Foreign Affairs, 1990).
22. Peter M. Leslie, *The Maastricht Model: A Canadian Perspective on Economic Union* (Kingston: Institute of Intergovernmental Relations, Queen's University, 1995), pp. 74–75.
23. This difficulty would be accentuated by the fact that one province within one of the two partners, Ontario, with a larger population and GNP than Quebec would have no veto on major policy decisions affecting it.
24. See, for instance, J.R. Pennock, "Federal and Unitary Government—Disharmony and Reliability," *Behavioural Science*, Vol. 4, no. 2 (1959), pp. 147–157.
25. Resnick, *Toward a Canada–Quebec Union*, pp. 112–119.
26. The process in Malaysia involved first the conversion of the Malayan Union into the Federation of Malaya (1948 and 1957), the addition of the Borneo states, Sabah and Sarawak, and Singapore in the wider Federation of Malaysia, 1963, and then the expulsion of Singapore in 1965.

27. Ronald L. Watts, "Survival or Disintegration," in Richard Simeon (ed.), *Must Canada Fail?* (Montreal and Kingston: McGill-Queen's University Press, 1977), pp. 42–60, especially pp. 53–59. See also Robert Young, *The Secession of Quebec and the Future of Canada* (Montreal and Kingston: McGill-Queen's University Press, 1995), pp. 127–167, 208–244; Ursula K. Hicks, *Federalism: Failure and Success* (London: Macmillan, 1978); Thomas Franck, *Why Federations Fail: An Inquiry into the Requisites for a Successful Federation* (New York: New York University Press, 1966); Milica Zarbovic Bookman, *The Economics of Secession* (New York: St. Martin's Press, 1993).
28. Watts, *Comparing Federal Systems*, pp. 106–107 considers the processes and consequences of the disintegration of federations.
29. This was a major theme that emerged from the international conference on *Redesigning the State: The Politics of Mega Constitutional Change* held at the Australian National University in Canberra, July 27–29, 1994.
30. For this reason Belgium has studiously avoided resorting to constitutional referendums from a fear of their explosive and divisive impact on the fragile Belgian unity.

23

Federalism and Democracy: Beyond the U.S. Model

Alfred Stepan

For those of us interested in the spread and consolidation of democracy, whether as policy makers, human rights activists, political analysts, or democratic theorists, there is a greater need than ever to reconsider the potential risks and benefits of federalism. The greatest risk is that federal arrangements can offer opportunities for ethnic nationalists to mobilize their resources. This risk is especially grave when elections are introduced in the subunits of a formerly nondemocratic federal polity prior to democratic countrywide elections and in the absence of democratic countrywide parties. Of the nine states that once made up communist Europe, six were unitary and three were federal. The six unitary states are now five states (East Germany has reunited with the Federal Republic), while the three federal states—Yugoslavia, the USSR, and Czechoslovakia—are now 22 independent states. Most of postcommunist Europe's ethnocracies and ethnic bloodshed have occurred within these postfederal states.

Yet in spite of these potential problems, federal rather than unitary states are the form most often associated with multinational democracies. Federal states are also associated with large populations, extensive territories, and democracies with territorially based linguistic fragmentation. In fact, every single longstanding democracy in a territorially based multilingual and multinational polity is a federal state.

Although there are many multinational polities in the world, few of them are democracies. Those multinational democracies that do exist, however (Switzerland, Canada, Belgium, Spain, and India), are *all* federal. Although all these democracies, except for Switzerland, have had problems managing their multinational polities (and even Switzerland had the Sonderbund War, the secession of the Catholic cantons in 1848), they remain reasonably stable. By contrast, Sri Lanka, a territorially based multilingual and multinational unitary state that feared the "slippery slope" of federalism, could not cope with its ethnic divisions and plunged headlong into a bloody civil war that has lasted more than 15 years.

In addition to the strong association between multinational democracies and federalism, the six longstanding democracies that score highest on an index of linguistic and ethnic diversity—India, Canada, Belgium, Switzerland, Spain, and the United States—are all federal states. The fact that these nations chose to adopt a federal system does not *prove* anything; it does, however, suggest that federalism may help these countries manage the problems that come with ethnic and linguistic diversity. In fact, in my judgment, if countries such as Indonesia, Russia, Nigeria, China, and Burma are ever to become stable democracies, they will have to craft workable federal systems that allow cultural diversity, a robust capacity for socioeconomic development, and a general standard of equality among their citizens.

Consider the case of Indonesia, for example. It seems to meet all the indicators for a federal state. It has a population of over 200 million, and its territory is spread across more than 2,000 inhabited islands. It has great linguistic and ethnic fragmentation and many religions. Thus it is near the top in virtually all the categories associated with federalism. If Indonesia is to become a democracy, one would think that it would have to address the question of federalism or decentralization. Yet at a meeting of Indonesian political, military, religious, and intellectual leaders that I attended after the fall of Suharto, most of the participants (especially those from the military) rejected federalism out of hand because of secessionist conflicts at the end of Dutch colonial rule. Indonesia should at least consider what I call a *federacy* to deal with special jurisdictions like Aceh or Irian Jaya. A federacy is the only variation *between* unitary states and federal states. It is a political system in which an otherwise unitary state develops a federal relationship with a territorially, ethnically, or culturally distinct community while all the other parts of the state remain under unitary rule. Denmark has such a relationship with Greenland, and Finland with the Aaland Islands.

A Misleading Picture of Federalism

In seeking to understand why some countries are reluctant to adopt federal systems, it is helpful to examine what political science has had to say about federalism. Unfortunately, some of the most influential works in political science today offer incomplete or insufficiently broad definitions of federalism and thereby suggest that the range of choices facing newly democratizing states is narrower than it actually is. In large part, this stems from their focusing too exclusively on the model offered by the United States, the oldest and certainly one of the most successful federal democracies.

One of the most influential political scientists to write about federalism in the last half-century, the late William H. Riker, stresses three factors present in the U.S. form of federalism that he claims to be true for federalism in general.[1] First, Riker assumes that every longstanding federation, democratic or not, is the result of a bargain whereby previously sovereign polities agree to give up part of their sovereignty in order to pool their resources to increase their collective security and to achieve other goals, including economic ones.

I call this type of federalism *coming-together federalism*. For Riker, it is the only type of federalism in the world.

Second, Riker and many other U.S. scholars assume that one of the goals of federalism is to protect individual rights against encroachments on the part of the central government (or even against the "tyranny of the majority") by a number of institutional devices, such as a bicameral legislature in which one house is elected on the basis of population, while in the other house the subunits are represented equally. In addition, many competences are permanently granted to the subunits instead of to the center. If we can call all of the citizens in the polity taken as a whole the *demos*, we may say that these devices, although democratic, are "*demos-constraining*."

Third, as a result of the federal bargain that created the United States, each of the states was accorded the *same* constitutional competences. U.S. federalism is thus considered to be constitutionally *symmetrical*. By contrast, *asymmetrical* arrangements that grant different competencies and group-specific rights to some states, which are not now part of the U.S. model of federalism, are seen as incompatible with the principled equality of the states and with equality of citizens' rights in the post-segregation era.

Yet although these three points are a reasonably accurate depiction of the political structures and normative values associated with U.S. federalism, most democratic countries that have adopted federal systems have chosen not to follow the U.S. model. Indeed, American-style federalism embodies some values that would be very inappropriate for many democratizing countries, especially multinational polities. To explain what I mean by this, let me review each of these three points in turn.

"Coming-Together" vs. "Holding-Together"

First of all, we need to ask: How are democratic federal systems actually formed? Riker has to engage in some "concept-stretching" to include all the federal systems in the world in one model. For example, he contends that the Soviet Union meets his definition of a federal system that came about as the result of a "federal bargain." Yet it is clearly a distortion of history, language, and theory to call what happened in Georgia, Azerbaijan, and Armenia, for example, a "federal bargain." These three previously independent countries were conquered by the 11th Red Army. In Azerbaijan, the former nationalist prime minister and the former head of the army were executed just one week after accepting the "bargain."

Many democratic federations, however, emerge from a completely different historical and political logic, which I call *holding-together federalism*. India in late 1948, Belgium in 1969, and Spain in 1975 were all political systems with strong unitary features. Nevertheless, political leaders in these three multicultural polities came to the decision that the best way—indeed, the only way—to hold their countries together in a democracy would be to devolve power constitutionally and turn their threatened polities into federations. The 1950 Indian Constitution, the 1978 Spanish Constitution, and the 1993 Belgian Constitution are all federal.

Let us briefly examine the "holding-together" characteristics of the creation of federalism in India to show how they differ from the "coming-together" characteristics correctly associated with the creation of American-style federalism. When he presented India's draft constitution for the consideration of the members of the constituent assembly, the chairman of the drafting committee, B.R. Ambedkar, said explicitly that it was designed to maintain the unity of India—in short, to hold it together. He argued that the constitution was guided by principles and mechanisms that were fundamentally different from those found in the United States, in that the Indian subunits had much less prior sovereignty than did the American states. Since they had less sovereignty, they therefore had much less bargaining power. Ambedkar told the assembly that although India was to be a federation, this federation was created not as the result of an agreement among the states, but by an act of the constituent assembly.[2] As Mohit Bhattacharya, in a careful review of the constituent assembly, points out, by the time Ambedkar had presented the draft in November 1948, both the partition between Pakistan and India and the somewhat reluctant and occasionally even coerced integration of virtually all of the 568 princely states had already occurred.[3] Therefore, bargaining conditions between relatively sovereign units, crucial to Riker's view of how and why enduring federations are created, in essence no longer existed.

Thus one may see the formation of democratic federal systems as fitting into a sort of continuum. On one end, closest to the pure model of a largely voluntary bargain, are the relatively autonomous units that "come together" to pool their sovereignty while retaining their individual identities. The United States, Switzerland, and Australia are examples of such states. At the other end of the democratic continuum, we have India, Belgium, and Spain as examples of "holding-together" federalism. And then there is what I call "putting-together" federalism, a heavily coercive effort by a nondemocratic centralizing power to put together a multinational state, some of the components of which had previously been independent states. The USSR was an example of this type of federalism. Since federal systems have been formed for different reasons and to achieve different goals, it is no surprise that their founders created fundamentally different structures. This leads us to our next point.

"*DEMOS*-CONSTRAINING" VS. "*DEMOS*-ENABLING"

Earlier, I described American-style federalism as "*demos*-constraining." In some respects, all democratic federations are more "*demos*-constraining" than unitary democracies. There are three reasons for this. First, unitary democracies have an open agenda, as Adam Przeworski points out, while in a federal democracy the agenda of the *demos* is somewhat restricted because many policy areas have been constitutionally assigned to the exclusive competence of the states.[4] Second, even at the center there are two legislative chambers, one (in theory) representing the one person-one vote principle, and the other representing the territorial principle. Third, because jurisdictional disputes are a more difficult and persistent issue in federal than in unitary systems, the judiciary, which is not responsible to the *demos*, is necessarily more salient and powerful.

Riker sees the *demos*-constraining aspect of federalism (and the weak politywide political parties normally associated with federalism) as basically good, because it can help protect individual rights from being infringed by the central government's potential for producing populist majorities.[5] But when examined from the point of view of equality and efficacy, both of which are as important to the consolidation of democracy as is liberty, the picture becomes more complicated. The deviation from the one citizen-one vote principle that federalism necessarily implies may be seen as a violation of the principle of equality. Overrepresentation in the upper house, combined with constitutional provisions requiring a supermajority to pass certain kinds of legislation, could, in certain extreme cases, lead to a situation in which legislators representing less than 10 percent of the electorate are able to thwart the wishes of the vast majority. This raises serious questions for the efficacious and legitimate functioning of democracy. If one were interested only in creating a system that best reflects the *demos* and that functions as an effective democracy, a case could be made that the democratic values of participation, decentralization, and equality would be better addressed in a unitary system that has decentralized participation than in a federal system. But if a polity has great linguistic diversity, is multinational, and is very large, its chances of being a democracy are much better if it adopts a federal system.

If federal systems were forced to adhere to the Rikerian model, multinational democracies would be faced with a stark choice: If they wished to adopt a federal system to reduce ethnic, religious, or linguistic tensions, they could do so only at the risk of severely constraining majority rule. But if we look at the federal systems that actually exist in the world, we see that not all federal systems are *demos*-constraining to the same degree. American-style federalism is *demos*-constraining, and Brazil is the most *demos*-constraining federation in the world. Yet the German federal system is much more *demos*-enabling than that of the United States, and India's is even more *demos*-enabling than Germany's. We can, in fact, construct a continuum, ranging from federal systems that are *demos*-constraining to those that are *demos*-enabling. Where a particular federal system lies on this continuum is largely determined by the nature of the party system, which I discuss elsewhere, and by three constitutionally embedded variables: (1) the degree of overrepresentation in the upper chamber; (2) the policy scope of the territorial chamber; and (3) the sorts of policy issues that are off the policy agenda of the *demos* because they have been allocated to the states or subunits.

(1) Overrepresentation in the Territorial Chamber

I think it is fair to argue that the greater the representation of the less populous states (and therefore the underrepresentation of the more populous states), the greater the *demos*-constraining potential of the upper house will be. The United States and Brazil follow the same format: In both countries, each state gets the same number of senators. Since Wyoming had a population of 453,000 and California had a population of 30 million in 1990, this meant that one vote for a senator in Wyoming was worth 66 votes in California. In Brazil, the overrepresentation is even more extreme. One vote cast for senator in Roraima has 144 times as much weight as a vote for senator in São Paulo. Moreover, Brazil and Argentina are the only democratic federations in the world that replicate a version of this overrepresentation in the lower house. With perfect proportional representation, São Paulo should have 114 seats. It actually has 70. With perfect representation, Roraima should have one seat. It actually has eight. The Brazilian Constitution, inspired by the ideology of territorial representation, specifies that no state can have more than 70 seats in the lower house (thereby partially disenfranchising São Paulo) and that no state can have fewer than eight.

Yet the principle of equal representation of each state in the upper house is not democratically necessary and may even prove to be a disincentive to multinational polities that contemplate adopting a federal system. Many democratic federations have quite different formulas for constructing their upper houses. In Germany, the most populous states (or *Länder*) get six votes in the upper chamber, those of intermediate size get four, and the least populous get three. Austria, Belgium, and India are still closer to the one person-one vote end of the continuum. If multilingual India had followed the U.S. pattern, it would not have been able to do some things that were absolutely crucial for political stability. Between 1962 and 1987. India created six new culturally distinctive states in the northeast, mostly carved out of Assam, a conflict-ridden region bordering Burma and China. If India had followed the U.S. model, these new states, containing barely one percent of India's population, would have had to be given 25 percent of all the votes in the upper chamber. The other Indian states would never have allowed this. Thus something democratically useful—the creation of new states, some of which were demanding independence by violent means—would have been difficult or impossible under the U.S. principle of representing each state equally.

The range of variation among the world's federal democracies can be seen in table 23.1 on the following page. This table also illustrates what I said above about most federal democracies choosing not to follow the U.S. model. The United States, along with Brazil and Argentina, which follow the same model, is an outlier on this continuum. The first line measures the degree of inequality of representation according to the Gini index. The values range from 0, which indicates perfect one person one vote representation, to 1, which indicates that one subunit has all of the votes in the upper house. Belgium's upper house has a Gini-index value of close to 0. Austria's is not much higher. India's is 0.10. Spain's is 0.31. The U.S. Gini-index value is almost 0.50, and Brazil's is 0.52. This means that the best-represented decile in the United States has 39 percent of the votes in the Senate; in Brazil, the best-represented decile has 43 percent of the votes. In India, it only has

Table 23.1 A continuum of the degree of overrepresentation in the upper houses of 12 modern federal democracies[a]

Gini index of inequality[b]	*Belgium* *0.015*	Austria 0.05	*India* *0.10*	Spain 0.31	*Germany* *0.32*	Canada 0.34	*Australia* *0.36*	Russia[c] 0.43	*Switzerland* *0.45*	U.S.A. 0.49	*Brazil* *0.52*	Argentina 0.61
Ratio of best-represented to worst-represented federal unit (on basis of population)	*Austria* *1.5/1*	Belgium 2/1	*Spain* *10/1*	India 11/1	*Germany* *13/1*	Australia 13/1	*Canada* *21/1*	Switzerland 40/1	*U.S.A.* *66/1*	Argentina 85/1	*Brazil* *144/1*	Russia 370/1
Percentage of seats of best-represented decile	*Belgium* *10.8*	Austria 11.9	*India* *15.4*	Spain 23.7	*Germany* *24.0*	Australia 28.7	*Canada* *33.4*	Russia 35.0	*Switzerland* *38.4*	U.S.A. 39.7	*Brazil* *41.3*	Argentina 44.8

[a] Complete information on all federal countries is contained in the Alfred Stepan–Wilfrid Swenden federal data-bank. We are grateful to Cindy Skach and Jeff Kahn for having provided us with the data on India and Russia, respectively. Other data were taken from *Whitakers Almanac* (London: J. Whitaker, 1977); *The Europa World Year Book* (London: Europa, 1995); and Daniel J. Elazar, ed., *Federal Systems of the World*. For the constitutional provisions on second chambers, see S.E. Finer, Vernon Bogdanor, and Bernard Rudden, *Comparing Constitutions* and A.P. Blaustein and G.H. Flanz, *Constitutions of the Countries of the World* (Dobbs Ferry, New York: Oceana, 1991).

[b] The Gini coefficient equals zero if the composition of the upper chamber is fully proportional and equals one if one subunit has all the votes in the second chamber. Arend Lijphart was among the first authors to use the Gini coefficient as a measure of inequality for the composition of second chambers. See Arend Lijphart, *Democracies: Patterns of Majoritarian and Consensus Government in Twenty-one Countries* (New Haven, Conn.: Yale University Press, 1984), 174.

[c] The status of Russia as a democracy is the most questionable of the 12 countries in the table. The data are included for comparative purposes.

15 percent. The variations are immense. On this indicator, the United States is clearly on the *demos*-constraining end of the continuum.

(2) Policy Scope of the Territorial Chamber

Now let us turn to our second variable, the competences of the territorially based chamber. My proposition is that the greater the competences of the territorial house. the more the *demos*—which is represented on a one person-one vote basis in the lower house—is constrained. In the United States, the lower house has a somewhat more important role than the Senate in budget initiation, but if one takes into account the Senate's constitutionally exclusive prerogatives to advise and consent on judicial, ambassadorial, and major administrative appointments, the two houses come fairly close to policy-making parity. On this variable, Brazil has the most *demos*-constraining system in the world. There is no area that the Brazilian Senate does not vote on, and there are 12 areas where it has exclusive competence, including authority to set limits on how much states can borrow.

As we can see in Table 23.2 on the following page, however, other federal democracies do not give the upper house as much policy scope as they give the lower house. The German, Spanish, and Indian systems are less *demos*-constraining, because their upper houses are less unrepresentative and less powerful. While in Brazil senators representing 13 percent of the total electorate can block ordinary legislation (and in the United States, a committee chairman alone can at times block important nominations), in Germany important bills are seldom vetoed by the upper chamber. How can we account for such a difference? First of all, the upper chamber cannot participate in the two most important legislative votes, those for government formation and government termination. This power is the exclusive competence of the lower chamber. Second, the upper chamber can delay, but not veto, bills that do not directly involve the *Länder*. Third, on the approximately 50 percent of the bills that the upper chamber can theoretically veto because they do relate directly to the *Länder*, it seldom does so after closed-door reconciliation meetings are held in the joint committee representing both houses.

In Spain, Belgium, India, and Austria, as well as in Germany, only the lower house participates in no-confidence votes. In many countries, the upper house is largely a revisionary chamber, although it has a major role in anything having to do with federal intervention. In Spain, for example, if the government wishes to take action against a regional government that is in contempt of the constitution, the decision must be approved by two-thirds of the upper house. This, in my view, is entirely appropriate.

(3) The Degree to which Policy-Making Authority is Constitutionally Allocated to Subunits

The third constitutionally embedded variable on which democratic federations differ greatly is the powers that are given to the *demos* at the

Table 23.2 A continuum of the upper chamber's constitutional prerogatives to constrain a majority at the center

Least constraining	←	→		*Most constraining*
India	Spain	Germany	United States	Brazil
The territorial chamber has no constitutional powers to protect subunit autonomy against a 60-day central intervention. Upper chamber has capacity to review or deny "President's Rule" only after 60 days. Largely a revisionary chamber.	Major power is granted by Article 155 of the Constitution, which precludes intervention by the center unless it has received approval by an absolute majority of the upper house. Plays no role in constructive vote of no confidence or normal legislation. Largely a revisionary chamber.	Plays no role in constructive vote of no confidence. Can play a potential veto role only in that part of the legislative agenda that directly relates to center-subunit issues. Power has grown somewhat over the last 20 years. Conflicts between the two chambers are resolved in closed-door meetings.	Extensive capacity to block a democratic majority. Senate has the same voting rights on all legislation as the "one person-one vote" chamber. Has exclusive competence to confirm or deny all major judicial and administrative appointments. A committee chairman alone can at times block important nominations.	Excessive for the efficacious and legitimate functioning of democratic government. The extremely disproportional upper chamber must approve all legislation. The Senate has 12 areas of exclusive lawmaking prerogatives. Senators representing 13 percent of the total electorate can block ordinary legislation supported by senators representing 87 percent of the population.

center versus the powers that are constitutionally allocated to the states. The 1988 Brazilian Constitution is so extensively detailed that a great deal of ordinary legislation can be passed only by a supermajority. In Brazil, many specific provisions on state and municipal pensions, state banks (all the states have banks), and the right of states to tax exports were constitutionally embedded. This is extremely *demos*-constraining. When too many issues are constitutionally embedded, the result is profoundly undemocratic, because these issues cannot be decided by a normal majority. Almost everything of importance in Brazil is constitutionally embedded. In order to change the constitution, 60 percent of the members of both houses (both those present and those absent) must vote in favor of an amendment *twice*. In a country the size of a continent, with bad transportation, it is hard even to get 60 percent of the legislature to show up.

At the opposite end of the continuum (see table 23.3 on the following page), India has a very *demos*-enabling constitution. At the time of its drafting, its authors were painfully aware that there were more than 15 languages spoken in the country that at least 20 million people could claim as their mother tongue. The boundaries of the states did not correspond with linguistic boundaries. To get the government closer to the people, the framers of the Indian Constitution had to respect the linguistic principle, so they decided (Article 3) that the lower house, by a simple majority vote, could eliminate any state, carve new states out of existing ones, or change their names. That is the sort of provision that a "holding-together" federation can write. In a "states' rights" federation like the United States, such a provision would be absolutely impossible. But if it had not been possible in India, the failure to realize the "imagined communities" of the country's hundreds of millions of non-Hindi speakers might have led to secession in a number of places.

The U.S. Constitution is even more difficult to amend than the Brazilian Constitution, but it is parsimonious, so the vast majority of legislation can be passed by ordinary majorities. In Spain, the main constraint on the majority at the center derives from the statutes of autonomy, which deal primarily with questions of culture and language. In Germany, many federal programs are administered by the *Länder*, but lawmaking and policy oversight remain the prerogative of the center.

CONSTITUTIONALLY SYMMETRICAL VS. ASYMMETRICAL

Let us now turn to a final point concerning the U.S. model. The U.S. Constitution, as discussed above, establishes a form of symmetrical federalism, which is bolstered by a certain normative disinclination on the part of Americans to accept the concept of collective rights. With the exception of Switzerland (where none of the political parties strictly represents any one linguistic or religious group), all of the multinational democracies are constitutionally asymmetrical: In order to hold the multinational polity together, they assign different linguistic, cultural, and legal competences to different

Table 23.3 The degree to which policy making is constitutionally allocated to subunits of the federation

Least	←——	———	——→	*Most*
India	Germany	Spain	United States	Brazil
Does not constrain *demos*. Capacity to respond to minority desires by redrawing the boundaries of states. Probably should constrain the ease with which the majority can intervene in states. Since 1994 Supreme Court decisions give somewhat more protection to subunits from imposition of "President's Rule" from the center.	Federal Law explicitly given precedent over Land Law. Wide areas where lawmaking powers are either explicitly given to the center or are concurrent responsibilities. More tax money is spent by the *Länder* than by the center. Many federal programs are decentralized so as to be administered by the *Länder*, while lawmaking and policy oversight remains the prerogative of the center.	Major constraints on majority at the center derives from the statutes of autonomy. Occasional bargaining process if center needs votes of regional party during process of government formation.	Constitution is extremely difficult to amend but is parsimonious, so the vast majority of legislation can be passed as ordinary legislation. Power is horizontally shared at the center between three branches. Power is vertically devolved and shared in "marble-cake" federalism between the federal and the state governments.	1988 Constitution is so detailed about states' rights that much ordinary legislation can only be passed by exceptional majorities. States and municipalities had such extreme control over export taxes and banking that central government's fiscal and trade policy in 1989–1996 was impeded. Some centralization of tax and bank policies in 1996–1997 but extremely costly to the center.
Residual power with center.	Most powers are concurrent.	Residual power with center.	Residual power with states.	Residual power with states.

states. Under the symmetrical American model, many of the things that are most essential in a multinational context cannot be accomplished. With the possible exception of the special case of Switzerland, *all* federations that are constitutionally symmetrical—Austria, Germany, Australia, the United States, Argentina, and Brazil—are mononational. India, Belgium, Canada, and Spain are multinational and their federations are all asymmetrical. (The Russian Federation is also asymmetrical, but, constitutionally, it does not yet work as a democratic federation.)

The concept of collective rights is in tension with the traditional American way of thinking about such matters, which is based on individual rights. It is true that a polity cannot be a democracy unless the individual rights of all citizens are enshrined in the constitution and a countrywide system of horizontal and vertical controls is credibly established to support these rights. Whatever rights the national subunits may posses, they cannot constitutionally or politically violate the rights of individual citizens. The enforcement of individual rights can be an obligation of both the center and the subunits, but the center cannot completely delegate responsibility for the establishment and maintenance of democratic rights and continue to be a democracy. Alexis de Tocqueville is very clear on this point. He admired the robust local associationalism of U.S. democracy but pointed out that the rule of law in the entire polity had to be guaranteed and enforced by the center.

In multinational polities, however, some groups may be able to participate fully as individual citizens only if they acquire, as a group, the right to have schooling, mass media, and religious or even legal structures that correspond to their language and culture. Some of these rights may be described as group-specific collective rights. Many thinkers in the liberal tradition assume that all rights are individual and universal and view any deviation from individualism and universalism with suspicion, but this assumption is open to question.

Let me conclude with four observations, partly drawn from studies of the historical development of democracy, about democratic group-specific rights (to use a term coined by the Canadian political philosopher Will Kymlicka).[6] First, individuals are indeed the primary bearers of rights, and no group rights should violate individual rights in a democratic polity. In democratic multinational federal states, this means that something like a bill of individual rights should be promulgated by the federal center, and any laws and social policies that violate it must fall outside the constitutionally guaranteed policy scope of the subunits.

Second, while individual rights are universal, it is simply bad history to argue that in actual democracies all rights have been universal. Frequently, the struggle to reconcile the imperatives of political integration with the legitimate imperatives of cultural difference has led countries to award certain minorities group-specific rights, such as those given to French-speaking Quebec in Canada, to cultural councils in Belgium, and to Muslim family courts in India. The key point is that it is the obligation of the democratic state to ensure that no group-specific right violates individual or universal rights.

Third, while individuals are the bearers of rights, there may well be concrete circumstances in which individuals cannot develop or exercise their full rights unless they are active members of a group that struggles for some collective goods common to most of its members. If, for example, the Catalans had not been given certain group-specific rights involving the public status of their own language, I doubt whether as individuals they could have become full democratic citizens of Spain. Similarly, I do not think Kurds will become full democratic citizens of Turkey unless they are granted certain group-specific rights (such as the right to Kurdish newspapers and radio stations in the southeast of Turkey, where Kurds are a majority).

Finally, although such group-specific rights may not be consistent with some nineteenth-century tenets of Anglo-Saxon liberal democracy or with the French idea of citizenship in a nation-state, they are consistent with a polity in which group rights do not violate individual rights, and they permit effective democratic citizenship and loyalty to be extended throughout the polity. They offer, in fact, one of the few ways to craft democracy successfully in the difficult and populous world of multinational states.

The Limits of the U.S. Model

The U.S. model of federalism, in terms of the analytical categories developed in this article, is "coming-together" in its origin, "constitutionally symmetrical" in its structure, and "*demos-constraining*" in its political consequences. Despite the prestige of this U.S. model of federalism, it would seem to hold greater historical interest than contemporary attraction for other democracies.

Since the emergence of nation-states on the world stage in the aftermath of the French Revolution, *no* sovereign democratic nation-states have ever "come together" in an enduring federation. Three largely unitary states, however (Belgium, Spain, and India) have constructed "holding-together" federations. In contrast to the United States, these federations are constitutionally asymmetrical and more "*demos-enabling*" than "*demos-constraining.*" Should the United Kingdom ever become a federation, it would also be "holding-together" in origin. Since it is extremely unlikely that Wales, Scotland, or Northern Ireland would have the same number of seats as England in the upper chamber of the new federation, or that the new upper chamber of the federation would be nearly equal in power to the lower chamber, the new federation would not be "*demos-constraining*" as I have defined that term. Finally, it would obviously defeat the purpose of such a new federation if it were constitutionally symmetrical. A U.K. federation, then, would not follow the U.S. model.

The fact that since the French Revolution no fully independent nation-states have come together to pool their sovereignty in a new and more powerful polity constructed in the form of a federation would seem to have implications for the future evolution of the European Union. The European Union is composed of independent states, most of which are nation-states. These states are indeed increasingly becoming "functionally federal." Were there to be a prolonged recession (or a depression), however, and were some EU member states to experience very high unemployment rates in comparison to others, member states could vote to dismantle some of the economic federal structures of the federation that were perceived as being "politically dysfunctional." Unlike most classic federations, such as the United States, the European Union will most likely continue to be marked by the presumption of freedom of exit.

Finally, many of the new federations that could emerge from the currently non-democratic parts of the world would probably be territorially based, multilingual, and multinational. For the reasons spelled out in this article, very few, if any, such polities would attempt to consolidate democracy using the U.S. model of "coming-together," "*demos-constraining*," symmetrical federalism.[7]

NOTES

1. See William H. Riker, "Federalism," in Fred Greenstein and Nelson W. Polsby, eds., *Handbook of Political Science* (Reading, Mass.: Addison-Wesley, 1975) vol. 5: 93–172.
2. Ambedkar's speech is found in its entirety in: India. Constituent Assembly. *Debates: Official Report* (New Delhi: Manager of Publications, 1951) vol. II: 31–44.
3. Mohit Bhattacharya, "The Mind of the Founding Fathers," in Nirmal Mukarji and Balveer Arora, eds., *Federalism in India: Origins and Development* (New Delhi: Vikas, 1992), 81–102.
4. Adam Przeworski, "Some Problems in the Study of the Transition to Democracy," in Guillermo O'Donnell, Philippe C. Schmitter, and Laurence Whitehead, eds., *Transitions from Authoritarian Rule: Comparative Perspectives* (Baltimore: Johns Hopkins University Press, 1986), 47–63.
5. See William H. Riker, *Liberalism Against Populism: A Confrontation Between the Theory of Democracy and the Theory of Social Choice* (San Francisco: W.II. Freeman, 1982), 247–253. As Riker acknowledges, however, federalism may also give the majority in the subunits the power to limit the freedom of some of the citizens (as the history of the southern United States shows), making it difficult for the federal government to protect them.
6. See Will Kymlicka, *Multicultural Citizenship: A Liberal Theory of Minority-Rights* (Oxford: Clarendon, 1995). For a powerful argument by a distinguished legal theorist that group rights are often a precondition of individual rights, see Joseph Raz, *The Morality of Freedom* (Oxford: Clarendon, 1986), 193–216. For a political and philosophically acute discussion of these issues in India, see Rajeev Bhargava, "Secularism. Democracy, and Rights," in Mehdi Arslan and Jannaki Rajan, eds., *Communalism in India: Challenge and Response* (New Delhi: Manohar, 1994), 61–73.
7. The tentative arguments made in these concluding paragraphs will be developed analytically and empirically in much greater depth in *Federalism, Democracy and Nation*, a book being written by Juan J. Linz and myself.

24

Federalism, Nationalism, and Multiculturalism

Will Kymlicka

Many commentators argue that federalism provides the most appropriate mechanism for accommodating the increasingly "multicultural" nature of modern societies. Federalism, it is said, respects the desire of groups to remain autonomous, and to retain their cultural distinctiveness, while nonetheless acknowledging the fact that these groups are not self-contained and isolated, but rather are increasingly and inextricably bound to each other in relations of economic and political interdependence. Moreover, since federalism is a notoriously flexible system, it can accommodate the fact that different groups desire different levels or forms of self-government.[1]

I think there is much truth in this picture of the value of federalism in accommodating national minorities. On any reasonable criteria, democratic federations (as opposed to Communist federations) have been surprisingly successful in accommodating minority nationalisms. Both historic multination federations, like Switzerland and Canada, and more recent multination federations, like Belgium and Spain, have not only managed the conflicts arising from their competing national identities in a peaceful and democratic way, but have also secured a high degree of economic prosperity and individual freedom for their citizens. This is truly remarkable when one considers the immense power of nationalism in this century. Nationalism has torn apart colonial empires and Communist dictatorships, and redefined boundaries all over the world. Yet democratic multination federations have succeeded in taming the force of nationalism. Democratic federalism has domesticated and pacified nationalism, while respecting individual rights and freedoms. It is difficult to imagine any other political system that can make the same claim.

Of course, many federal systems were not designed as a response to ethnocultural pluralism—for example United States or Australia. In these federal systems, the federal units do not correspond in any way with distinct ethnocultural groups who desire to retain their self-government and cultural distinctiveness. These sorts of federal systems can be quite stable. I will discuss the American model of federalism in the next section, but my focus in this paper is on countries that have adopted federalism in order to accommodate ethnocultural pluralism in general, and national minorities in particular.

FEDERALISM AND THE ACCOMMODATION OF ETHNOCULTURAL GROUPS

Immigration and the incorporation of national minorities are the two most common sources of ethnocultural diversity in modern states. Most (though not all) ethnocultural groups can be located within one or other of these broad categories.[2] Virtually all liberal democracies are either multinational[3] or polyethnic,[4] or both. The "challenge of multiculturalism" is to accommodate these national and ethnic differences in a stable and morally defensible way. In this section, I will discuss whether federalism provides a feasible or desirable mechanism for responding to the demands of national minorities and ethnic groups.

There is no universally accepted definition of "federalism." For the purposes of this paper, I take federalism to refer to a political system which includes a constitutionally entrenched division of powers between a central government and two or more subunits (provinces/lander/states/cantons), defined on a territorial basis, such that each level of government has sovereign authority over certain issues. This distinguishes federalism from both (a) administrative decentralization, where a central government establishes basic policy in all areas, but then devolves the power to administer these policies to lower levels of government, typically regional or municipal governments; and (b) confederation, where two or more sovereign countries agree to coordinate economic or military policy, and so each devolves the power to administer these policies to a supranational body composed of delegates of each country.[5]

(a) Immigrant Groups

As a general rule, federalism is not relevant to immigrant groups. This is partly because immigrant groups are rarely territorially concentrated, and hence it would be difficult if not impossible to draw federal boundaries in such a way that these groups form a majority within a federal subunit. In principle this obstacle could be overcome either by encouraging territorial concentration, or by adopting a non-territorial form of self-rule, such as the millet system of the Ottoman Empire, or the Cultural Councils in pre-war Estonia.[6] But the fact is that immigrant groups within the major immigrant countries historically have not sought the sort of institutional separateness and political self-government which federalism provides. Italian Americans or Japanese Canadians do not seek to form separate and self-governing societies based on their mother-tongue, alongside the mainstream anglophone society. They seek to integrate within the mainstream anglophone society.

To be sure, many immigrant groups—particularly since the "ethnic revival" in the 1970s—have demanded greater accommodation of their ethnocultural differences. For example, there have been demands for: recognition of Jewish and Muslim religious holidays in school schedules; exemptions from school or government dress-codes so that Muslim girls can wear headscarves and Sikh and Jewish men can wear turbans or yarmulkes; greater recognition of the role of ethnic groups in school history textbooks; and proportional representation of ethnic groups in the police, or judiciary, or the legislature. But none of these demands involves the desire to establish a separate and self-governing society alongside the mainstream society. On the contrary, they aim to reform mainstream institutions so as to make immigrant groups feel more at home within them. These measures—which I elsewhere call "polyethnic rights"—are consistent with, and indeed often promote, the integration of immigrants into the public institutions of the mainstream society, including its political structures.[7]

I should emphasize that I am speaking here of immigrant groups within those liberal democratic countries where there is a tradition of welcoming immigrants, and where it is easy for immigrants to become full citizens regardless of their race, religion or ethnic origin. Under these circumstances, immigrant groups have not demanded the sort of group self-government provided by federalism. Of course, in many parts of the world—including some Western democracies—immigrants are much less welcome, and it is far more difficult for them to acquire equal citizenship. Where immigrants are subject to severe prejudice and legal discrimination—and hence where full equality within the mainstream society is unachievable—it is more likely that immigrants will seek to create a separate and self-governing society, alongside the mainstream society. For example, if the German government persists in refusing to grant citizenship to long-term Turkish residents (and their children and grandchildren), one would expect Turks to press for greater powers of self-government—perhaps through some quasi-federal or consociational form of devolution—so that they can create and perpetuate a separate and self-governing society alongside the German society to which they are denied entry. But this is not the preference of the Turks, whose main goal, like immigrants in other liberal democracies, is to become full and equal participants in German society. And while I cannot argue the point here, I believe that any plausible account of liberal justice will insist that long-term immigrants should be able to acquire citizenship.[8] In short, the historical record suggests that quasi-federal forms of self-government will only be sought by immigrant groups within liberal democracies if they face unjust barriers to their full integration and participation in the mainstream society.

(b) National Minorities

The situation of national minorities is very different. In most multination states, the component nations are inclined to demand some form of political autonomy or territorial jurisdiction, so as to ensure the full and free development of their cultures, and to promote the interests of their people. They demand certain powers of self-government which they say were not relinquished by their (often involuntary) incorporation into a larger state. At the extreme, nations may wish to secede, if they think their self-determination is impossible within the larger state.

One possible mechanism for recognizing claims to self-government is federalism. Where national minorities are regionally concentrated, the boundaries of federal subunits can be drawn so that the national minority forms a majority in one of the subunits. Under these circumstances, federalism can provide extensive self-government for a national minority, guaranteeing its ability to make decisions in certain areas without being outvoted by the larger society.

For example, under the federal division of powers in Canada, the province of Quebec (which is 80 percent francophone) has extensive jurisdiction over issues that are crucial to the survival of the francophone society, including control over education, language, culture, as well as significant input into immigration policy. The other nine provinces also have these powers, but the major impetus behind the existing division of powers, and indeed behind the entire federal system, is the need to accommodate the Québécois. At the time when Canada was created in 1867, most English-Canadian leaders were in favour of a unitary state, like England, and agreed to a federal system primarily to accommodate French Canadians. Had Quebec not been guaranteed these substantial powers—and hence protected from the possibility of being outvoted on key issues by the larger anglophone population—it is certain that Quebec either would not have joined Canada in 1867, or would have seceded sometime thereafter.

Historically, the most prominent examples of federalism being used in this way to accommodate national minorities are Canada and Switzerland. The apparent stability and prosperity of these countries has led other multination countries to adopt federal systems in the post-war period (e.g., Yugoslavia), or upon decolonization (e.g., India, Malaysia, Nigeria). Even though many of these federations are facing serious difficulties, we are currently witnessing yet another burst of interest in federalism in multination countries, with some countries having recently adopted, or in the process of adopting, federal arrangements (e.g., Belgium, South Africa, Russia, and Spain).

This widespread interest in federalism reflects a welcome, if belated, acknowledgement that the desire of national minorities to retain their distinct cultures should be accommodated, not suppressed. For too long, academic theorists and political elites assumed that modernization would inevitably involve the assimilation of minority nationalities, and the withering away of their national identity. Central governments around the world have tried to dissolve the sense amongst national minorities that they constitute distinct peoples or nations, by eliminating their previously self-governing political and educational institutions, and/or by insisting that the majority language be used in all public forums. However, it is increasingly recognized that these efforts were both unjust and ineffective, and that the desire of national minorities to maintain themselves as culturally distinct and political autonomous societies must be accommodated.[9]

Federalism is one of the few mechanisms available for this purpose. Indeed, it is quite natural that multination countries should adopt federal systems—one would expect countries which are formed through a federation of peoples to adopt some form of political federation. But while the desire to satisfy the aspirations of national minorities is welcome, we should be aware of the pitfalls involved. Federalism is no panacea for the stresses and conflicts of multination states. In the rest of the paper, I will discuss a number of qualifications regarding the potential value of federalism in multination states.

I will separate my concerns into three areas. First, the mere fact of federalism is not sufficient for accommodating national minorities—it all depends on how federal boundaries are drawn, and how powers are shared. Indeed, federalism can and has been used by majority groups as a tool for disempowering national minorities, by rigging federal units so as to *reduce* the power of national minorities. We need therefore to distinguish genuinely multinational federations which seek to accommodate national minorities from merely territorial federations which do not (section 2). Second, federalism is not as flexible as its proponents often claim. Where the subunits of a federal system vary in their territory, population, and their desire for autonomy, as is often the case, developing an "asymmetric" form of federalism has proven to be very complicated (section 3). Finally, even where federalism is successfully working to accommodate the aspirations of national minorities, its very success may simply lead minorities to seek even greater autonomy, through secession or confederation (section 4).

MULTINATIONAL VS. TERRITORIAL FEDERALISM

While federalism is increasingly being considered as a solution to the problems of multination states, it is important to note that many federal systems arose for reasons unrelated to ethnocultural diversity. In fact, the most famous and widely studied federation—the American system—makes no effort to respond to the aspiration of national minorities for self-government.

Anglo-Saxon settlers dominated all of the original 13 colonies which formed the United States. As John Jay put it in *The Federalist*, "Providence has been pleased to give this one connected country to one united people—a people descended from the same ancestors, speaking the same language, professing the same religion, attached to the same principles of government, very similar in their manners and customs." Jay was exaggerating the ethnocultural homogeneity of the colonial population—most obviously in ignoring Blacks[10]—but it was true that none of the thirteen colonies were controlled by a national minority, and that the original division of powers within the federal system was not defined with a view to the accommodation of ethnocultural divisions.

The status of national minorities became more of an issue as the American government began its territorial expansion to the south and west, and eventually into the Pacific. At each step of this expansion, the American government was incorporating the homelands of already-settled, ethnoculturally distinct peoples—including American Indian tribes, Chicanos, Alaskan Eskimos, native Hawaiians, Puerto Ricans, and Chamoros. And at each step, the question arose whether the American system of federalism should be used to accommodate the desire of these groups for self-government.

It would have been quite possible in the nineteenth century to create states dominated by the Navaho, for example, or by Chicanos, Puerto Ricans, and native Hawaiians. At the time these groups were incorporated into the United States, they formed majorities in their homelands. However, a deliberate decision was made *not* to use federalism to accommodate the self-government rights of national minorities. Instead, it was decided that no territory would be accepted as a state unless these national groups were outnumbered within that state. In some cases, this was achieved by drawing boundaries so that Indian tribes or Hispanic groups were outnumbered (Florida). In other cases, it was achieved by delaying statehood until anglophone settlers swamped the older inhabitants (e.g., Hawaii; the Southwest).[11] As a result, none of the 50 states can be seen as ensuring self-government for a national minority, the way that Quebec ensures self-government for the Québécois.

Indeed, far from helping national minorities, there is reason to believe that American federalism has made them worse off. Throughout most of American history, Chicanos, American Indian tribes and native Hawaiians have received better treatment from the federal government than from state governments. State governments, controlled by colonizing settlers, have often seen national minorities as an obstacle to greater settlement and resource development, and so have pushed to strip minorities of their traditional political institutions, undermine their treaty rights, and dispossess them of their historic homelands. While the federal government has of course been complicit in much of the mistreatment, it has often at least attempted to prevent the most severe abuses. We can see the same dynamic in Brazil, where the federal government is fighting to protect the rights of Indians in Amazonia against the predations of local state governments.

In short, American-style territorial federalism, far from serving to accommodate national minorities, has made things worse. This should be no surprise, since the people who devised American federalism had no interest in accommodating these groups. In deciding how to arrange their federal system—from the drawing of boundaries, to the division of powers and the role of the judiciary—their aim was to consolidate and then expand a new country, and to protect the equal rights of individuals within a common national community, not to recognize the rights of national minorities to self-government. As I discuss below, insofar as national minorities in the US have achieved self-government, it has been outside of—and to some extent, in spite of—the federal system, through non-federal units such as the "commonwealth" of Puerto Rico, the "protectorate" of Guam, or the "domestic dependent nations" status of American Indian tribes.

Since American federalism was not intended to accommodate ethnocultural groups, why then was it adopted? There are several reasons why the original colonists, who shared a common language and ethnicity, nonetheless adopted federalism—reasons which are famously explored in *The Federalist*. Above all, federalism was seen as a way to prevent a liberal democracy from degenerating into tyranny. As Madison put it, federalism helped to prevent "factions"—particularly an economic class or business interest—from imposing its will through legislation to the detriment of "the rights of other citizens, or to the permanent and aggregate interests of the community." Federalism makes it more difficult for those who "have a common motive to invade the rights of other citizens" to "act in unison with each other." The "influence of factious leaders may kindle a flame within their particular States, but will be unable to spread a general conflagration through the other States."[12] Conversely, the existence of strong, independent state governments provided a bulwark for individual liberties against any possible encroachment by a federal government which is captured by sinister factions.

Federalism was just one of several mechanisms for reducing the chance of tyranny. An equal emphasis was placed on ensuring a separation of powers *within* each level of government—for example separating the executive, judicial and legislative powers at both the state and federal levels. This too helped minimize the amount of power that any particular faction could command, as did the later adoption of a Bill of Rights. The adoption of federalism in the United States should be seen in the context of this pervasive belief that the power of government must be limited and divided so as to minimize the threat to individual rights.

It is important to note that Madison was not thinking of ethnocultural groups when talking about "factions." Rather, he was concerned with the sorts of conflicts of interest which arise amongst "a people descended from the same ancestors, speaking the same language." These include, above all else, economic divisions between rich and poor, or between agricultural, mercantile and industrial interests. Madison's preoccupations are reflected in his list of the "improper or wicked projects" which federalism will help prevent—namely, "A rage for paper money, for an abolition of debts, for an equal division of property."[13]

The subsequent history of the United States suggests that federalism offers other, more positive, benefits. For example, it has helped provide room for policy experimentation and innovation. Faced with new issues and problems, each state adopted differing policies, and those policies which proved most successful were then adopted more widely. Moreover, as the United States expanded westward and incorporated vast expanses of territory with very different natural resources and forms of economic development, it became increasingly difficult to conceive how a single, centralized unitary government would be workable. Some form of territorial devolution was clearly necessary, and the system of federalism adopted by the original 13 colonies on the Atlantic coast served this purpose very well.

So there are many reasons, unrelated to ethnocultural diversity, why a country would adopt federalism. Indeed, any liberal democracy which contains a large and diverse territory will surely be pushed in the direction of adopting some form of federalism, regardless of its ethnocultural composition. The virtues of federalism for large-scale democracies are manifested, not only in the United States, but also in Australia, Brazil, and Germany. In each of these cases, federalism is firmly entrenched, and widely endorsed, even though none of the federal units are intended to enable ethnocultural groups to be self-governing.

In some countries, then, federalism is adopted, not because it accommodates the desire of national minorities for self-government, but rather because it provides a means by which a single national community can divide and diffuse power. Following Philip Resnick, I will call this "territorial federalism," as distinct from "multinational federalism."[14]

My concern in this chapter is with multinational federations. Most scholarly discussions of federalism, however, have focused on territorial federalism. This is partly due to the historical influence of American federalism. Perhaps because it was the first truly democratic federation, American federalism has become the model, not just of territorial federalism, but of federalism *tout court*, or at least of "mature" or "classic" federalism. Similarly, *The Federalist* is often taken to be the paradigm expression of "the federalist principle." Other federal systems are then categorized on the basis of how closely they conform to the basic attributes of the American system. Thus, for example, Australia is typically seen as a more truly federal system than Canada or India, since the latter deviate significantly from the American model.

Yet if our concern is with multinational federalism, then we cannot use the United States as our model. The American federal system, and *The Federalist*, offer us no guidance on how to accommodate ethnocultural groups. On the contrary, as I noted earlier, federal subunits were deliberately manipulated to ensure that national minorities could not achieve self-government through federalism. More generally, territorial federalism, in and of itself, is no guarantee that ethnocultural groups will be accommodated. Whether the allocation of powers to territorial subunits promotes the interests of national minorities depends on how the boundaries of those subunits are drawn, and on which powers are allocated to which level of government. If these decisions about boundaries and powers are not made with the conscious intention of empowering national minorities, then federalism may well serve to worsen the position of national minorities, as has occurred in the United States, Brazil, and other territorial federalisms.

How Flexible is Multinational Federalism?

For a federal system to qualify as genuinely multinational, decisions about boundaries and powers must consciously reflect the needs and aspirations of minority groups.[15] But to what extent can the boundaries and powers of federal units be defined so as to accommodate these groups? As I noted earlier, many theorists argue that federalism is appropriate precisely because it has great flexibility in answering these questions. Even a cursory survey of federal systems shows that there is a great variety in how boundaries are drawn, and powers distributed. There seem to be few if any *a priori* rules regarding the size, shape, or powers of federal subunits.

I believe, however, that federalism is less flexible than many people suppose. There are significant limitations on how powers can be divided, and on how boundaries can be drawn. I will discuss these two problems in turn.

(a) Dividing Powers in a Multinational Federation

Let us assume that boundaries can be drawn in such a way that national minorities form a majority in their federal subunit, as with Quebec or Catalonia. This provides a starting-point for self-government, but whether the resulting federal system is satisfactory to national minorities will depend on how powers are distributed between the federal and provincial levels. The historical record suggests that this issue may lead to intractable conflicts, because different units may seek different powers, and it is difficult for federalism to accommodate these divergent aspirations.

This is particularly true if only one or two of the federal units are vehicles for self-governing national minorities, while the rest are simply regional divisions within the majority national group. This is the case in Canada, for example, where the province of Quebec secures self-government for the Québécois, but the nine remaining provinces reflect regional divisions within English-Canada. A similar situation exists in Spain, where the Autonomous Communities of Catalonia, the Basque Country and Galicia secure self-government for national minorities, while most of the other 14 Autonomous Communities, such as La Mancha or Extremadura, reflect regional divisions within the majority Spanish national group.[16] In both countries, then, some units embody the desire of national minorities to remain as culturally distinct and politically self-governing societies (what I will call "nationality-based units"), while others reflect the decision of a single national community to diffuse powers on a regional basis (what I will call "regional-based units").

It is likely that nationality-based units will seek different and more extensive powers than regional-based units. As a general rule, we can expect nationality-based units to seek greater and greater powers, while regional-based units are less likely do so, and may indeed accept a gradual weakening of their powers. This is reflected in the way the American and Canadian federal systems have developed. It has often been pointed out that the United States, which began as a strongly decentralized federation, with all residual powers attributed to the states, has gradually become one of the most centralized; whereas Canada, which began as a strongly centralized federation, with all residual powers attributed to the federal government, has gradually become one of the most decentralized. This is often said to be paradoxical, but is understandable when we remember that the United States is a territorial federation, composed entirely of regional-based units. Because none of the 50 states in the United States are nationality-based, centralization has not been seen as a threat to anyone's national identity. While many Americans object to centralization as inefficient or undemocratic, it is not seen as a threat to the very survival of anyone's national group. By contrast, centralization in Canada is often seen as a threat to the very survival of the Québécois nation, insofar as it makes French-Canadians more vulnerable to being outvoted by anglophones on issues central to the reproduction of their culture, such as education, language, telecommunications, and immigration policy.

This difference has had a profound effect on how the U.S. and Canada have responded to the pressures for centralization in the twentieth century. In both countries, there have been many occasions—most notably the Depression and the two world wars—where there were great pressures to strengthen the federal government, at least temporarily. In Canada, these pressures were counterbalanced by the unyielding insistence of French-Canadians that the self-governing powers of Quebec be protected, so that any temporary centralization would ultimately be reversed. In the United States, however, there was no similar countervailing pressure, and the various forces for greater centralization have gradually and cumulatively won out.

The fact that regional-based and nationality-based units typically desire different levels of power is also reflected within both Canada and the United States. For example, while most Québécois want an even more decentralized division of powers, most English Canadians favour retaining a strong central government. Indeed, were it not for Quebec, there is good reason to believe that Canadian federalism would have succumbed to the same forces of centralization which won out in the United States. And while the regional-based American states have gradually lost power, we find a very different story if we look at the quasi-federal units used to accommodate national minorities—for example, the Commonwealth of Puerto Rico, Indian tribes, or the Protectorate of Guam. In these cases of nationality-based units, we see a clear trend toward greater powers of self-government, in order to sustain their culturally distinct societies.

We find the same pattern throughout Europe as well. For example, Catalonia and the Basque Country have expressed a desire for greater autonomy than is sought by other regional-based units in Spain. Corsica seeks greater autonomy than other regional-based units in France. While many European countries are engaging in forms of regional decentralization, particularly if they had previously been highly centralized states, this process is going much farther in countries where the resulting units are nationality-based (e.g., Belgium) than regional-based (e.g., Italy). And of course the most extreme assertion of self-government—namely, secession—has only been made by nationality-based units, whether it be in the former Czechoslovakia, Yugoslavia or the Soviet Union, not regional-based units.

In a federal system which contains both regional-based and nationality-based units, therefore, it seems likely that demands will arise for some form of *asymmetrical federalism*—that is, for a system in which some federal units have greater self-governing powers than others. Unfortunately, it has proven extraordinarily difficult to negotiate such an asymmetrical model. There seems to be great resistance, particularly on the part of majority groups, to accepting the idea that federal units can differ in their rights and powers. As a result, national minorities have found it very difficult to secure the rights and recognition that they seek.

The difficulty in negotiating asymmetry is, in one sense, quite puzzling. If English Canadians want a strong federal government, and the Québécois want a strong provincial government, asymmetry would seem to give both groups what they want. It seems perverse to insist that all subunits have the same powers, if it means that English Canadians have to accept a more decentralized federation than they want, while French Canadians have to accept a more centralized federation than they want.

Yet most English Canadians overwhelmingly reject the idea of "special status" for Quebec. To grant special rights to one province on the grounds that it is nationality-based, they argue, is somehow to denigrate the other provinces, and to create two classes of citizens.[17] Similar sentiments have been expressed in Spain about the demand for asymmetrical status by the Basques and Catalans.[18] Some commentators—such as Charles Taylor—argue that this simply reflects confused moral thinking.[19] Liberal democracies are deeply committed to the principle of the moral equality of persons, and equal concern and respect for their interests. But equality for individual citizens does not require equal powers for federal units. On the contrary, special status for nationality-based units can be seen as promoting this underlying moral equality, since it ensures that the national identity of minorities receives the same concern and respect as the majority nation. Insofar as English Canadians view the federal government as their "national" government, respecting their national identity requires upholding a strong federal government; insofar as Québécois view Quebec as their national government, respecting their national identity requires upholding a strong provincial government. Accommodating these differing identities through asymmetrical federalism does not involve any disrespect or invidious discrimination.

It is difficult to avoid the conclusion that much of the opposition to asymmetry amongst the majority national group is rooted in a latent ethnocentrism—that is, a refusal to recognize that the minority has a distinct national identity that is worthy of respect. This fits into the long history of neglecting or denigrating the desire of national minorities to remain culturally distinct societies, which I discussed earlier.

Another factor underlying the opposition to asymmetry is the profound influence of the American model of federalism. As I noted earlier, many people have supposed that American federalism is the model of federalism *tout court*, and that all federalisms should aim to be purely territorial. On this view, any special accommodations for nationality-based units are seen as merely transient measures which are not appropriate in a "mature" territorial federalism.

The problem is not simply that regional and nationality-based units happen to desire different powers. These variations in desired powers reflect an even deeper difference in the very conception of the nature and aims of political federation. For national minorities, federalism is, first and foremost, a federation of *peoples*, and decisions regarding the powers of federal subunits should recognize and affirm the equal status of the founding peoples. On this view, to grant equal powers to regional-based units and nationality-based units is in fact to deny equality to the minority nation, by reducing its status to that of a regional division within the majority nation. By contrast, for members of the national majority, federalism is, first and foremost, a federation of *territorial units*, and decisions regarding the division of powers should affirm and reflect the equality of the constituent units. On this view, to grant unequal powers to nationality-based units is to treat some of the federated units as less important than others.

This difference in the conception of federalism can lead to conflicts even when there is little variation in the actual powers demanded by regional-based and nationality-based units. For example, some people have proposed a radical across-the-board decentralization in Canada, so that all provinces would have the same powers currently demanded by Quebec. This is intended to avoid the need to grant "special status" to Quebec. The response by many Quebec nationalists, however, was that this missed the point. The demand for special status was a demand, not just for this or that power, but also for *national recognition*. As Resnick puts it, "They want to see Quebec recognized as a nation, not a mere province; this very symbolic demand cannot be finessed through some decentralizing formula applied to all provinces."[20] Quebec nationalists want asymmetry, not just to gain this or that additional power, but also for its own sake, as a symbolic recognition that Quebec alone is a nationality-based unit within Canada.

This may seem like a petty concern with symbols rather than the substance of political power. But we find the same response in other multinational federations. For example, prior to the breakup of Czechoslovakia, some people proposed a decentralized federation composed of three units with equal powers—Slovakia and two Czech regions (Moravia and Bohemia). This would enable Slovak national self-government, while also accommodating Moravia's historical status as a distinct region within the Czech nation. However, Slovak nationalists dismissed this proposal, since "it would have meant equivalence between the Slovak nation and Moravian cultural and historical specificity, thus lessening the relevance of Slovak nationhood."[21]

Or consider the response of Catalan and Basque nationalists to the proposal to make the same maximal level of autonomy exercised by their nationality-based units available to all federal units in Spain, including the regional-based units (i.e., to "generalize" autonomy):

> . . . the 1978 Constitution assumed the principle of autonomy because it was absolutely essential to resolve the claims to self-government made by Catalonia and the Basque country if indeed a democratic system was to be installed which aimed not just at the freedom and rights of citizens but also of peoples. When the attack began via what has been called the generalization of autonomies, the politicians tried to forget what was originally intended.[22]

We can now see why disputes about the division of powers within a multinational federalism are so difficult to resolve. The problem is not simply that units differ in their preferences regarding the extent of autonomy. That problem can often be resolved by reasonable people of good will. And indeed many English Canadians are willing to accept a more decentralized federation than they would ideally like in order to accommodate Quebec; while many Québécois are willing to accept a less decentralized federation than they would ideally like in order to accommodate English Canada. Reasonable people are willing to compromise, within limits, on the precise powers they seek for their federal units.

Unfortunately, the problem goes deeper than this. While the majority may be willing to compromise on the precise degree of decentralization, they are unwilling to compromise on what they take to be a basic principle of federalism—namely, that all federal units should be equal in their rights and powers. Conversely, while the national minority may be willing to compromise on its demands for autonomy, it is not willing to compromise on what it takes to be a basic principle of federalism—namely, that its status as one of the founding peoples must be symbolically recognized through some form of asymmetry between nationality-based and region-based units. As a result, even if both regional-based and nationality-based units happen to desire a roughly similar set of powers, serious conflicts are likely to remain. For each side rejects on principle what the other side views as part of the very nature and purpose of federalism. For the majority nation, federalism is a compact between equal territorial units, which therefore precludes asymmetry; for the national minority, federalism is a compact between peoples, which therefore requires asymmetry between nationality-based units and regional-based units.

This helps explain why asymmetry has been so difficult to negotiate within multinational federations. But there are other problems which further reduce the flexibility of federalism in adopting asymmetry. Let's assume that the conflicts I have just been discussing are somehow solved, and there is a widespread acceptance of the need for some form of asymmetry for nationality-based units. There remain some practical problems to be solved, particularly regarding the representation of the nationality-based unit in the federal government. These problems are, I believe, formidable, and we have very few models around the world of how to resolve them.

Let's imagine, then, that an asymmetrical transfer of powers from the federal government to Quebec occurs, so that the federal government would be passing laws that would apply to all provinces except Quebec. Under these circumstances, it seems only fair that Quebecers not have a vote on such legislation (particularly if they could cast the deciding vote). For example, it would seem unfair for Quebec's elected representatives at the federal level to vote on federal legislation regarding immigration if the legislation does not apply to Quebec. In short, insofar as the jurisdiction of the federal government over a national minority is reduced, compared to other regional-based units, this seems to entail that the minority group should have reduced influence (at least on certain issues) at the federal level.

Some national minorities do have this sort of reduced influence at the federal level. For example, because residents of Puerto Rico have special self-governing powers which exempt them from certain federal legislation, they have reduced representation in Washington. They help select presidential candidates in party primaries, but do not vote in presidential elections. And they have only one representative in Congress, a "commissioner" who has a voice but no vote, except in committees. This reduced representation is seen by some as evidence that Puerto Rico is "colonized" by the United States. But while the details of the existing arrangement are subject to criticism, the existence of reduced representation can be seen as a corollary of Puerto Rican self-government, not just its colonial subjugation. The less that a group is governed by the federal government, the less of a right it has to representation in that government. An asymmetry in powers entails an asymmetry in representation.

But how exactly should an asymmetry in the powers of subunits be reflected in terms of representation at the federal level? If a particular subunit has greater powers, one would expect its representatives to be fewer in number, and/or restricted in their voting power. Both of these apply to Puerto Rico. But the Puerto Rican model has obvious weaknesses. While Puerto Rico has very limited federal representation, it is still very much subject to Congressional authority in some areas. It would seem preferable, therefore, to reduce their influence in a more issue-specific way—for example, by allowing their Congressional representative to have a full vote on legislation which applies to Puerto Rico, but no vote on legislation from which Puerto Rico is exempt. Unfortunately, this is easier said than done. Many pieces of legislation deal with areas of jurisdiction that Puerto Rico is partly exempt from, and partly subject to. There is no way to divide up the business of government into such clear-cut groupings. Moreover, this leaves unanswered the question of how many representatives a nationality-based unit should have at the federal unit. A strong asymmetry in powers for federal subunits suggests that there should be a compensating reduction in the number of representatives, but what is a fair trade-off here?

This has been a serious stumbling-block in developing a workable model of asymmetrical federalism in Canada. It is increasingly accepted that a strongly asymmetrical status for Quebec will require reducing the influence of Quebec's elected representatives in the federal legislature. However, there is no available model which tells us how to do this. And of course this problem links up with the previous problem of differing conceptions of federalism. Since members of the majority are already inclined to view any form of asymmetry as an unfair privileging of the minority, they will be keenly sensitive to any evidence that the minority is exercising undue power at the federal level (e.g., by voting on legislation from which they are themselves exempt).

Yet we can expect the national minority to resist any serious reduction of their representation at the federal level. After all, they are already, by definition, a minority at the federal level, and to reduce their influence even further will just make the federal government seem more remote, and indeed more of a threat. It will seem increasingly like an "alien" government. The more Quebec's influence is reduced at the federal level, the more tempting it will be for Quebecers to decide to simply go it alone, and seek secession. Why stay within the federation if their influence on federal policy is gradually eroding? The danger that asymmetry will eventually lead to secession is a serious one, I believe, since there are other factors pulling in the direction of secession, which I discuss in the next section.

So there are many reasons why federal systems have difficulty adopting asymmetrical arrangements. Indeed, these problems are so severe that some people have claimed that a federal system cannot survive for long if it adopts asymmetry. This is an overstatement, but there are greater limits on the flexibility of federalism than many proponents of federalism admit.[23]

The inability of federalism to accommodate asymmetry is exacerbated by the fact that the procedure for amending the constitution in a federal system is so cumbersome. For example, to amend the constitution in the United States requires the consent of 35 states, and two-thirds of the members of Congress. In Canada, depending on the nature of the proposed change, a constitutional amendment requires the consent of both federal houses, plus either 7 provinces containing 50 percent of population, or all 10 provinces. Recent experience with the Equal Rights Amendment in U.S., or the Meech Lake and Charlottetown Accords in Canada, suggests that achieving this level of agreement is very difficult. If implementing asymmetrical federalism requires amending the powers of federal subunits, or the system of federal representation, the obstacles are enormous. Whereas a unitary state can typically amend its constitution by a single majority or super-majority vote, federalism requires the consent of concurrent majorities—that is, majorities in the country as a whole, plus in all of its constituent units. This sets the threshold so high that even a widely supported proposal for asymmetry may fall short.

(b) Drawing Boundaries in a Multinational Federation

One limitation on federalism's ability to accommodate national minorities, then, is that it may be difficult to achieve the desired division of powers. But in addition to dividing powers, we must also draw boundaries, and this raises another limit on the flexibility of multinational federalism. For federalism to serve as a mechanism for self-government, it must be possible to draw federal subunits in such a way that the national minority forms a majority within a particular subunit, as the Québécois do in Quebec. This is simply not possible for some national minorities, including most indigenous peoples in the United States or Canada, who are fewer in number, and who have been dispossessed of much of their historic lands, so that their communities are often dispersed, even across state/provincial lines. With few exceptions, indigenous peoples currently form a small minority within existing federal units, and no redrawing of the boundaries of these federal subunits would create a state, province or territory with an indigenous majority.[24] It would have been possible to create a state or province dominated by an Indian tribe in the nineteenth century, but given the massive influx of settlers since then, it is now virtually inconceivable.

For most indigenous peoples in the U.S. or Canada, therefore, self-government can only be achieved outside the federal system. Self-government has been primarily tied to the system of reserved lands (known as tribal "reservations" in the United States, and band "reserves" in Canada). Substantial powers are exercised by the tribal/band councils which govern each reserve. Indian tribes/bands have been acquiring increasing control over health, education, family law, policing, criminal justice and resource development. (Or, more accurately, they have been reacquiring these powers, since of course they governed themselves in all these areas before their involuntary incorporation into the larger Canadian or American polity.) They are becoming, in effect, a kind of "federacy," to use Daniel Elazar's term, with a collection of powers that is carved out of both federal and state/provincial jurisdictions.[25]

One could, in principle, define each of these reserved lands as a new state or province within the federal system. But that is impractical, given that there are so many separate tribes/bands in the United States and Canada (over 600 in Canada alone), and that many of these groups are very small both in population and territory, and that they are located within existing federal subunits. Moreover, Indian peoples do not want to be treated as federal subunits, since the sort of self-government they seek involves a very different set of powers from that exercised by provinces. They would only accept the status of a federal subunit if this was a strongly asymmetrical status, which included powers typically exercised by both the federal and provincial levels. Furthermore, Indian tribes/bands differ enormously amongst themselves in the sorts of powers they desire. They seek not only asymmetry, but varying degrees of asymmetry. Yet, for the reasons I've just discussed, it is extremely difficult to achieve that sort of flexibility within a federal system. Hence Indians have pursued self-government through a sort of "federacy" relationship that exists outside the normal federal system.

As the term suggests, a "federacy" has important analogies with federalism—for example, both involve a territorial division of powers. But because most Indian tribes now form a minority even within their historic homelands, and so are territorially located within existing states or provinces, their self-government occurs outside of, and to some extent in opposition to, the federal system. Rather than possessing the standard rights and powers held by federal subunits, and governing under the same rules which apply to federal subunits, they instead possess a set of group-specific powers and exemptions which partially removes them from the federal process, by reducing the jurisdiction of both the federal and state/provincial governments over them. As I noted earlier, federalism in the United States and Canada, far from empowering Indian peoples, has in fact simply increased their vulnerability, by making their self-governance subject to encroachment from both federal and state/provincial governments. The achievement of Aboriginal self-government through "federacy," therefore, involves protection against the federal system.

The fact that Indians in the United States do not control state governments has tended to make them more vulnerable, since their self-government powers do not have the same constitutional protection as states' rights. They are therefore more subject to the "plenary power" of Congress, which has often been exercised to suit the needs and prejudices of the dominant society, not of the national minority. However, the fact that they lie outside the federal structure has compensating advantages. In particular, it has provided much greater flexibility in redefining those powers to suit the needs and interests of the minority. Whereas there is pressure within federal systems to make all subunits equal in their powers and federal representation, "federacy" arrangements allow for greater variations. Moreover, it is much easier to negotiate new self-government provisions for the Navaho than to amend the powers of individual states.

The same applies to other national minorities in the United States. For example, because Puerto Rico is a "Commonwealth" not a state, it has been easier to amend its self-governing powers, and to negotiate an asymmetrical status in terms of both powers and federal representation. This might have proved impossible had Puerto Rico been granted statehood when it was incorporated by the United States in 1898.

For a variety of reasons, then, federalism may lack the flexibility needed to accommodate national minorities. It may be impossible for a small national minority to form a majority in one of the federal subunits. For such groups, self-government can only be achieved outside the federal system, through some special non-federal or quasi-federal political status. And even if the boundaries can be drawn in such a way that the national minority forms a majority within a federal subunit, it may be impossible to negotiate a satisfactory division of powers, particularly if the federation includes both nationality-based and regional-based subunits.

Therefore, in many cases, the aspirations of national minorities may best be achieved through political institutions which operate outside the federal system—as "commonwealths," "federacies," "protectorates," or "associated states"—rather than by controlling a standard federal subunit. Standard models of federalism, with their implicit assumptions of equal powers and regional-based units, and their complex amendment procedures, may not be capable of responding to the distinctive interests and desires of nationality-based units.

FEDERALISM, SECESSION, AND SOCIAL UNITY

So far, I have been discussing limits on the ability of federalism to accommodate the needs of national minorities. Let's imagine, however, that these problems have been overcome. Let's assume that national minorities are satisfied with the boundaries of their subunit, that they possess sufficient self-governing powers to maintain themselves as culturally distinct societies, and that some form of asymmetry has either been accepted or proven unnecessary. In short, let's assume that federalism is working as its proponents envisage to combine shared rule with respect for ethnocultural differences. There is one further problem that is worth considering. The very success of federalism in accommodating self-government may simply encourage national minorities to seek secession. The more that federalism succeeds in meeting the desire for self-government, the more it recognizes and affirms the sense of national identity amongst the minority group, and strengthens their political confidence. Where national minorities become politically mobilized in this way, secession becomes more feasible, even with the best-designed federal institutions.

One way to describe the problem is to say that there is a disjunction between the legal form of multinational federalism and its underlying political foundations. *Legally speaking*, as I noted earlier, federalism views both levels of government as possessing inherent sovereign authority. This distinguishes it from a confederation, where sovereign states delegate certain powers to a supranational body, powers which they can reclaim. In a federal system, however, the general government has inherent, not just delegated, power to govern its citizens. Just as the province of Quebec has the inherent authority to govern all Quebecers—an authority which the federal government did not delegate and cannot unilaterally revoke—so the federal government of Canada has the inherent authority to govern all Canadians (including Quebecers), an authority which the provincial governments did not delegate, and cannot unilaterally revoke.

This is the legal form of federalism. But *political perceptions* of it are likely to be rather different. Multinational federations are often viewed by national minorities as if they were confederations. National minorities typically view themselves as distinct "peoples," whose existence predates that of the country they currently belong to. As separate "peoples," they possess inherent rights of self-government. While they are currently part of a larger country, this is not seen as a renunciation of their original right of self-government. Rather it is seen as a matter of transferring some aspects of their powers of self-government to the larger polity, on the condition that other powers remain in their own hands. In countries that are formed from the federation of two or more national groups, the (morally legitimate) authority of the central government is limited to the powers which each constituent nation agreed to transfer to it. And these national groups often see themselves as having the (moral) right to take back these powers, and withdraw from the federation, if they feel threatened by the larger community.

Legally speaking, of course, nationality-based federal units do not have the right to reclaim the powers exercised by the federal government. Legally, these powers are inherently vested in the federal government, and the subunits cannot "reclaim" what was never theirs. But the political perceptions of national minorities are unlikely to match these legal niceties. For them, the larger country feels more like a confederation than a federation, in the sense that the larger country's existence is seen as morally dependent on the revocable consent of the constituent national units. As a result, the larger political community has a more conditional existence than a unitary state, or a territorial federalism.

In short, the basic claim made by national minorities is not simply that the political community is culturally diverse (as immigrants, e.g., typically claim). Instead, the claim is that there is more than one political community, and that the authority of the larger state cannot be assumed to take precedence over the authority of the constituent national communities. If democracy is the rule of "the people," national minorities claim that there is more than one people, each with the right to rule themselves. Multinational federalism divides the people into separate "peoples," each with its own historic rights, territories, and powers of self-government; and each, therefore with its own political community. They may view their own political community as primary, and the value and authority of the larger federation as derivative.[26]

The reason why multinational federalisms are likely to be contested should now be obvious. The more a federal system is genuinely multinational—that is, the more it recognizes and affirms the demand for self-government—the more it will strengthen the perception amongst national minorities that the federal system is *de facto* a confederal system. That is, the more successful a multinational federal system is in accommodating national minorities, the more it will strengthen the sense that these minorities are separate peoples with inherent rights of self-government, whose participation in the larger country is conditional and revocable. And if the attachment of national minorities to the larger state is conditional, then sooner or later one can expect conditions to change so that staying within the federation no longer seems beneficial. The members of the minority are likely to disagree about this, and many of them may conclude that the federation remains the best option. But it will always be a salient question, and a source of lively debate within the national minority.

Federalism also provides national minorities with the experience of self-government, so that they will feel more confident of their ability to go it alone, and with an already recognized territory over which they are assumed to have some *prima facie* historical claim.

Moreover, if secession can be achieved peacefully, then the costs of secession have dramatically fallen. In the past, national minorities needed to join larger countries in order to gain access to economic markets, and/or to ensure military security. But these benefits of federalism can now be achieved through confederal arrangements (like the European Union, or the North American Free Trade Agreement), and through the gradual strengthening of international law. If Quebec or Catalonia seceded, they would still be able to participate in continental or international free trade and security arrangements.

In any event, the option of secession will always be present. Indeed, in a sense, it becomes the default position, or the baseline against which participation in the federation is measured. Amongst national minorities, the starting point will not be "Why should we seek greater autonomy?," but rather "Why should we continue to accept these limits on our inherent self-government?" After all, there seems to be no natural stopping point to the demands for increasing self-government. If limited autonomy is granted, this may simply fuel the ambitions of nationalist leaders who will be satisfied with nothing short of their own nation-state. Any restrictions on self-government— anything short of an independent state—will need justification.

For all these reasons, it seems likely that multinational federalism will contain secessionist movements pushing for confederation or simply break up. And yet, despite all these tendencies towards secession, the remarkable fact is that no multination federation in the West has yet fallen apart. While secessionist parties have been competing freely and actively in several Western democracies for decades, they have never received a democratic mandate for secession, and no referendum on secession has succeeded. Paradoxically, multination federations appear to combine a weak sort of unity with a surprising degree of resilience.

In thinking about social unity, therefore, we must be modest in our aims. The sort of unity that we can achieve in a multination federation is different from that which uni-national states often possess. We cannot expect the Québécois to express unconditional allegiance to Canada, or to put "Canada first." The only sort of unity we can achieve is one which allows national minorities to give equal standing, or even primacy, to their national identity, and to give conditional allegiance to Canada. The only sort of unity we can hope to achieve, therefore, is one which co-exists with the firm belief amongst national minorities that they have the right to secede, and with ongoing debate about the conditions under which it would be appropriate to exercise that right.

Yet if we lower our sights in this way, there are grounds for cautious optimism. There is no reason to take the ever-present possibility of secession as proof that multination federations will fail, and that secession must occur. On the contrary, the experience to date in the West suggests that democratic multination federations are remarkably resilient. This suggests that weak bonds of social unity may nonetheless be enduring bonds, and that conditional allegiances may nonetheless be powerful allegiances.

What then can keep a multination federation together? Since the main instrumental arguments for federation (economic markets and military security) have lost much of their force, it seems that we need to focus more on the intrinsic benefits of belonging to a federation—that is, the value of belonging to a country which contains national diversity. In some circumstances, I think this can be a very powerful argument. For example, Petr Pithart, the former Prime Minister of Czechoslovakia, reflecting on its dissolution, stated that:

> In the last 55 years, the Czechs have lost—as co-tenants in their common house—Germans, Jews, Ruthenians, Hungarians and Slovaks. They are now, in effect, an ethnically cleansed country, even if it was not by their own will. It is a great intellectual, cultural, and spiritual loss. This is particularly true if we consider central Europe, which is a kind of mosaic. We are still living touristically

> from the glory of Prague, which was a Czech-German-Jewish city and a light that reached to the stars. But you cannot win elections with that kind of argument.[27]

It seems to me that there often is a "great intellectual, cultural and spiritual loss" when multination states dissolve. And, contrary to Pithard, I think you can sometimes win elections with those kinds of arguments. As I noted earlier, no referendum on secession from a democratic multination federation has succeeded in the West.[28] It may not be easy to explain the benefits of living in a multination state, or to articulate the losses when it dissolves, which would in any event vary tremendously from country to country, depending on its history and demography. But average citizens are capable of seeing the benefits of living in a multination federation, and of comparing it with the alternatives, most (all?) of which have a much worse track record in dealing with ethnonational diversity.

NOTES

1. See, for example, Daniel Elazar's *Federalism and the Way to Peace* (Kingston, Ontario: Institute of Intergovernmental Affairs, Queen's University, 1994); and his *Exploring Federalism* (Tuscaloosa: University of Alabama, 1987).
2. African-Americans are an important example of an ethnocultural group which does not fit these categories. They do not fit the voluntary immigrant pattern, not only because most were brought to America involuntarily as slaves, but also because when they arrived they were prevented (rather than encouraged) from integrating into the institutions of the majority culture (e.g., racial segregation; laws against miscegenation and the teaching of literacy). Nor do they fit the national minority pattern, since they do not have a homeland in America or a common historical language. They came from a variety of African cultures, with different languages, and no attempt was made to keep together those with a common ethnic background. For further discussion of this case as well as other atypical minority groups, see Will Kymlicka and Wayne Norman, eds., *Citizenship in Diverse Societies* (Oxford: Oxford University Press, 2000), pp. 18–24. A recent survey of ethnocultural conflicts around the world suggests that the two broad categories I have outlined do cover most groups involved in these conflicts—see Ted Gurr, *Minorities at Risk: A Global View of Ethnopolitical Conflict* (Washington, D.C.: Institute of Peace Press, 1993).
3. By "nation" I mean a historical community, more or less institutionally complete, occupying a given territory or homeland, sharing a distinct language and culture. A country which contains more than one nation is, therefore, not a nation-state but a multination state, and the smaller cultures form "national minorities." The incorporation of different nations into a single state may be involuntary, as occurs when one cultural community is invaded and conquered by another, or is ceded from one imperial power to another, or when its homeland is overrun by colonizing settlers. But the formation of a multination state may also arise voluntarily, when different cultures agree to form a federation for their mutual benefit. Many Western democracies are multinational.
4. A state is "polyethnic" if it contains numerous ethnic groups that have arisen from individual and familial immigration.

5. Other characteristic features of federalism include the existence of a bicameral legislature at the federal level, with the second chamber intended to ensure effective representation for the federal subunits in the central government. Thus, each federal subunit is guaranteed representation in the second chamber, and smaller subunits tend to be overrepresented. Moreover, each subunit has a right to be involved in the process of amending the federal constitution, but can unilaterally amend its own constitution. In defining federalism in this manner, I am following Wheare's classic account (K.C. Wheare, *Federal Government*, 4th Edition (New York: Oxford University Press, 1964), chapters 1–2; cf. Jonathan Lemco, *Political Stability in Federal Governments* (New York: Praeger, 1991), chapter 1. For a typology of various "federal-type" arrangements—which distinguishes federations from confederations, consociations, federacies, legislative unions, associated states, and condominiums—see Elazar, *Exploring Federalism*, chapter 2, and Ronald Watts, "Comparing Forms of Federal Partnerships" [reprinted in this volume].
6. On non-territorial forms of minority rights, see J.A. Laponce, "The Government of Dispersed Minorities: From Constantinople to Ottawa," in *Divided Nations*, ed. Tamas Kozma and Peter Drahos (Budapest: Educatio Publishing, 1993). On the millet system, see my "Two Models of Pluralism and Tolerance," *Analyse & Kritik*, vol. 14/1, 1992, pp. 33–56.
7. I develop this at length (and discuss the few exceptions) in *Multicultural Citizenship* (Oxford: Oxford University Press, 1995, chapter 5). Exceptions to this generalization include certain immigrant-based religious sects which seek to disassociate from the mainstream society.
8. For a defense of this claim, see Joseph Carens, "Membership and Morality: Admission to Citizenship in Liberal Democratic States," in William Brubaker (ed.), *Immigration and the Politics of Citizenship in Europe and North America* (Lanham, MD: University Press of America, 1989), pp. 31–49.
9. For a discussion of why national identity has been so enduring, and why national minorities differ in this respect from immigrants, see *Multicultural Citizenship*, chapters 5–6.
10. [See "Federal Theory in *The Federalist*" reprinted in this volume]. Jay not only ignores the sizeable black population, but also pockets of non-English immigrants (particularly Germans), and the remnants of Indian tribes who had been dispossessed of their lands.
11. Hence Nathan Glazer is quite wrong when he says that the division of the United States into federal units preceded its ethnic diversity—see N. Glazer, *Ethnic Dilemmas: 1964–1982* (Cambridge, Mass.: Harvard University Press, 1983), pp. 276–277. This is true of the original thirteen colonies, but decisions about the admission and boundaries of new states were made after the incorporation of national minorities, and these decisions were deliberately made so as to avoid creating states dominated by national minorities.
12. Madison, *Federalist* no. 10, pp. 54, 61. The belief that federalism helps prevent tyranny was one reason why federalism was imposed by the Allies on Germany after World War II. It was supposed to help prevent the re-emergence of nationalist or authoritarian movements. For a critique of the claim that federalism is inherently more protective of individual liberty, see Martha Minow, "Putting Up and Putting Down: Tolerance Reconsidered," in Mark Tushnet (ed.), *Comparative Constitutional Federalism: Europe and America* (Greenwood, New York, 1990), pp. 77–113; Franz Neumann, "Federalism and Freedom: A Critique" [reprinted in this volume].

13. As he put it, "the most common and durable source of factions has been the various and unequal distribution of property." A lesser concern was the periodic schisms within the Protestant churches, which often gave rise to upsurges of religious conflict.
14. Philip Resnick, "Toward a Multination Federalism," in Leslie Seidle (ed.), *Seeking a New Canadian Partnership: Asymmetrical and Confederal Options* (Montreal: Institute for Research on Public Policy, 1994), p. 71.
15. If the United States is the paradigm of territorial federalism, what is the prototype of multinational federalism? Elazar argues that Switzerland is "the first modern federation built upon indigenous ethnic and linguistic differences that were considered permanent and worth accommodating," in D. Elazar, "The Role of Federalism in Political Integration," in D. Elazar (ed.), *Federalism and Political Integration* (Turtledove Publishing, Ramat Gan, 1987), p. 20. Yet, as Murray Forsyth notes, the old Swiss confederation, which existed for almost 500 years, was composed entirely of Germanic cantons, in terms of ethnic origin and language. While French and Italian-speaking cantons were added in 1815, the decision to adopt a federal structure was not primarily taken to accommodate these ethnolinguistic differences. According to Forsyth, the Canadian federation of 1867 was the first case where a federal structure was adopted to accommodate ethnocultural differences. This is reflected in the fact that the 1867 Constitution not only united a number of separate provinces into one country, it also divided the largest province into two separate political units—English-speaking Ontario and French-speaking Quebec—to accommodate ethnocultural divisions (see Murray Forsyth, "Introduction," in M. Forsyth (ed.), *Federalism and Nationalism* (Leicester: Leicester University Press, 1989), pp. 3–4.
16. Some of the remaining 14 Communities are not simply regional divisions, but form culturally distinct societies, even if they are not self-identified as distinct "nations." This is true, for example, of the Balearic Islands, Valencia and Asturias, where distinct languages or dialects are spoken. But many of the Autonomous Communities do not reflect distinct ethnocultural or linguistic groups. For a discussion of Spain's Autonomous Communities, and their varying levels of ethnocultural distinctiveness, see Audrey Brassloff, "Spain: The State of the Autonomies," in Forsyth (ed.), *Federalism and Nationalism*, pp. 24–50.
17. On English-Canadian opposition to special status, see Alan Cairns, "Constitutional Change and the Three Equalities," in Ronald Watts and Douglas Brown, eds, *Options for a New Canada* (Toronto: University of Toronto Press, 1991), pp. 77–110; David Milne, "Equality or Asymmetry: Why Choose?" in *ibid*, pp. 285–307; Andrew Stark, "English-Canadian Opposition to Quebec Nationalism," in R. Kent Weaver (ed.), *The Collapse of Canada?* (Washington, D.C.: Brookings Institute, 1992), pp. 123–158; Stephane Dion, "La fédéralisme fortement asymétrique," in Seidle (ed.), *Seeking a New Canadian Partnership*, pp. 133–152, who cites a poll showing 83% opposition to special status.
18. Brassloff, p. 44.
19. Charles Taylor, "Shared and Divergent Values," in Ronald Watts and Douglas Brown, eds, *Options for a New Canada*, pp. 53–76.
20. Resnick, p. 77.
21. Petr Pithard, "Czechoslovakia: The Loss of the Old Partnership," in *Seeking a New Canadian Partnership*, p. 164.
22. M. Fernandez, quoted in Brassloff, p. 35.
23. For a survey of various forms of asymmetrical federalism, see Elazar, *Exploring Federalism*, pp. 54–57; and Dion, "La fédéralisme fortement asymétrique."

24. Two exceptions would be the Navaho in the American Southwest, and the Inuit in the Canadian Northwest. The boundaries of the Northwest Territories in Canada were redrawn in 1999 so as to create an Inuit-majority territory within the federation called Nunavut.
25. Elazar, *Exploring Federalism*, p. 229. For the relation of Indian self-government to federalism, see Frank Cassidy and Robert Bish, *Indian Government: Its Meaning in Practice* (Halifax, Nova Scotia: Institute for Research on Public Policy, 1989); J.A. Long, "Federalism and Ethnic Self-Determination: Native Indians in Canada," *Journal of Commonwealth and Comparative Politics* 29/2 (1991): 192–211.
26. To reduce this danger, federal governments have encouraged national minorities to identify with, and feel loyalty towards, the federal government. This new identification, it is hoped, would then compete, and possibly even supersede, their original national identity. However, the historical record suggests that these efforts have limited success. See, on this, Kenneth Wheare, "Federalism and the Making of Nations," in A. MacMahon (ed.), *Federalism Mature and Emergent*, pp. 28–43; Robert Howse and Karen Knop, "Federalism, Secession, and the Limits of Ethnic Accommodation: A Canadian Perspective," *New Europe Law Review* (1993) vol. 1/2, pp. 269–320; Wayne Norman, "Towards a Normative Theory of Federalism," in Judith Baker (ed.), *Group Rights* (Toronto: University of Toronto Press, 1994); and my *Multicultural Citizenship*, chapter 9.
27. Pithard, "Czechoslovakia," p. 198.
28. It's worth noting that even in the case of Czechoslovakia there was no referendum in Slovakia on secession, and many observers argue that had a referendum been held, it would not have passed. Meciar avoided a referendum precisely because he worried that secessionists would lose to the federalists in a free and fair referendum.

25

Building the Union: The Nature of Sovereignty in the Political Architecture of Europe*

Richard Bellamy and Dario Castiglione

Is national sovereignty dead? Many writers on Europe appear to believe so. This thesis draws on a number of increasingly familiar arguments. The related processes of globalisation and social differentiation have undermined the state's claims to sovereignty. It neither controls the most important decisions in the economy or defense, nor expresses a common identity capable of sustaining a shared sense of justice and a commitment to the collective good. The future lies with new forms of political and social order that take us below and beyond the sovereign nation-state, to regional and global blocs regulated by a cosmopolitan legal system based on individual human rights. So far as Europe is concerned, imperatives of both a functional and a normative nature impel the creation of an ever closer Union.

This article takes a different tack. We believe these reports of the nation-state's demise to be exaggerated. The impact of global forces and the associated pressures towards greater social individuation have been far from uniform, and the normative claims of national cultures and group identities show few signs of diminishing. The capacity of the nation-state to act as the primary locus of administrative, legal and political power and authority may have been weakened but not in ways that necessarily point in a cosmopolitan direction. Rather, both the allegiances of citizens and their forms of economic, social and political interaction, cooperation and organisation have become a complex mixture of the subnational, national and supranational. Instead of convergence on a common normative framework and a single set of institutions, such a highly differentiated social system is characterised by numerous subsystems each governed by its own rules and practices.

* Research for this paper was supported by an ESRC research grant awarded for a project on "Languages and Principles for the Constitution of Europe" (R000221170). We are grateful to Neil MacCormick and the participants in the ESRC funded research seminar series on "The Legal Theory of the European Union" for their comments on and discussion of earlier versions.

Sovereignty does not lose its relevance in such a situation. If anything, the need for authoritative mechanisms capable of mediating between diverse values and interests increases rather than diminishes. However, sovereignty does need to be reconfigurated to reflect the competing attachments and norms emanating from the various spheres of people's lives, and the complexities of the relationships that exist between them. If politics is defined by the questions of who gets what, when, where and how, then the answers increasingly must be in the plural—different people, in different ways and employing different criteria according to the context and the good concerned. That suggests that sovereignty will also be plural, because more dispersed, with different persons or bodies having the power to decide in different circumstances, without there necessarily being any single, hierarchical system of decision-making.

In what follows, we shall pursue this notion of a pluralist conception of sovereignty as a way of conceiving the interaction between the various actors within the European Union. On this understanding, the Member States, citizens, regions, the various Community institutions and so on each represents a semi-autonomous component of a far from homogenous political system. They interact in different ways, respond to different sorts of problem and represent different constituencies. Drawing on our earlier work in this field,[1] we shall characterise the resulting mixed polity in terms of a combination of the normative and empirical elements to be found in cosmopolitan and communitarian political moralities. Each of these broad schools of thought offers a particular model of the political architecture for Europe, involving different understandings of sovereignty and legitimacy. Whereas the first favors federal arrangements of various kinds, the second emphasises the centrality of the component nation-states. Sections one and two examine each of these schools respectively, noting that both contain a range of positions some of which are more compatible with those from the alternative camp than others. Section three presents a view of Europe as a mixed commonwealth which draws on those more complementary elements in a manner we dub cosmopolitan communitarianism. The resulting amalgam may be more bricolage than grand architectonic design, but none the worse for that.

FEDERAL ARCHITECTURE

Supporters of various federal arrangements share the fundamental intuition that material and ideal developments since the Second World War have

[1] "The Communitarian Ghost in the Cosmopolitan Machine: Constitutionalism, Democracy and the Reconfiguration of Politics in the New Europe," in R. Bellamy (ed.), *Constitutionalism, Democracy and Sovereignty: American and European Perspectives* (Aldershot: Avebury, 1996); "The normative challenge of a European polity: Cosmopolitan and communitarian models compared, criticised and combined," in A. Follesdal and P. Koslowski, (eds.), *Democracy and the EU* (Berlin: Springer Verlag, 1997); "Between Cosmopolis and Community: Three Models of Rights and Democracy within the European Union," in D. Archibugi, D. Held, and M. Koehler, *Transnational Democracy* (Cambridge: Polity, 1998).

severed the historical connection between political legitimacy and collective self-determination on the one hand, and identification with a unitary state, defined by its territorial borders and a high degree of cultural and linguistic homogeneity, on the other. To differing degrees, they accept that national and state units will, and should, retain some capacity for autonomous self-organisation. But they believe that the political and legal structure of the new European polity must rest on a number of key centralised institutions and be based on principles of rights, justice and the rule of law of a fairly universalistic nature. It is this two-level structure of the polity that makes it a federation, even though the fundamental legitimacy of this arrangement lies in the values and efficacy of the centralised level.

There are two versions of federalism: a more conventional view centered on a federal state, and a more philosophical position that sees federalism in terms of a set of legal principles that take us beyond notions of the state. The more traditional understanding takes federalism to be both a form and a principle of state organisation. The nation-state (even in the idiosyncratic form of the United Kingdom) traditionally developed as a unitary and highly centralised polity, where powers remained under the strict control of the central authorities and were only devolved for administrative and functional reasons. Federal states, by contrast, offered a more divided model of sovereignty and the representation of interests, expressed in the idea of dual citizenship. The federal model seemed better adapted to conditions of cultural and linguistic diversity, or situations where for either historical or geographical reasons there was no great homogeneity within the state. Historically, federalism was also conceived as a vertical form of checks and balances, which by dividing the legislature against itself would ensure the balanced and diffuse representation of views and interests as well as the reciprocal control and limitation of local and centralised powers. Because of its essentially dual nature, the political significance of federalism has varied according to historical circumstances. Demands for state federalism have played an important part in processes of state consolidation, as in the formation of the United States and in present day Europe; but have also been instrumental to the disaggregation of more unitarian polities, as with the introduction of federal structures in Germany and Spain, and demands for devolution in Britain and Italy.

This view of federalism does not imply a denial of the centrality of state formations in contemporary politics (i.e., a congruence of territory and competences, supported by a monopoly of force in the hands of legally established authorities). Nor does it doubt that sovereignty is an important attribute of political states. It questions instead whether—given the increasingly interconnected nature of economies and, in the present nuclear age, of defense—single European nation-states retain sufficient power and authority to act effectively as sovereign states. As Herman Heller suggested in the 1920s,[2] a federal Europe does not mean the abolition of state sovereignty

[2] Herman Heller, *Die Souveränität. Ein Beitrag zur Theorie des Staats- und Völkerrechts* (Berlin & Leipzig: W. de Gruyter, 1927), ch. 10.

itself, but its partial or total transference to a different level, deemed more capable of exercising it with efficacy.

In contemporary Europe, state federalism of this kind need not be justified on the purely negative ground of the nation-state's loss of effective sovereignty. Less immediately instrumental reasons have also been advanced. After all, the ideals of peace and prosperity motivated the originators of the European movement, and continue to inspire many of the current proponents of a federal Europe.[3] There is no denying that during the last two hundred years nationalist ideologies have greatly contributed to support and justify discrimination, oppression and power politics, within and outside Europe, with appalling human consequences. Supranationalism, on this view, promotes peace by breaking down the barriers between peoples and strengthening communication and reciprocal understanding between them. It builds on the more idealistic and universally oriented features of a common European culture (rationality, tolerance, diversity, civility, etc.), and treats national ties as atavistic throwbacks of less civilised times.

Parallel considerations link federalism to prosperity. Jean Monnet's functionalist method and strategy may be construed as an administrative and institutional response to the spontaneous development of a European civil society, characterised by the rapid increase in transnational exchanges and economic and cultural cooperation that have been instrumental in sustaining high levels of productivity and welfare distribution. According to this view, the piecemeal construction of the administrative and legal machinery (even more than the political structure) of a still-in-the-making European federal state has put into place the institutional framework needed to support the autonomous development of a European economy and society.[4] This position involves a conception of the European Union as an inherently dynamic system, whose constitution, unlike those of fully established states, must both mirror and promote a process of continuous change and integration.[5]

This model of Europe involves a new kind of co-operative federalism.[6] This does not rest on a constitutionally fixed division of competences between the various levels of the federal structure, but encourages the setting up of new formal and informal structures of co-operation both between the component states and between them and the federal state. This functionalist conception of federalism and its evolution envisages a more technocratic

[3] On the role of ideals in the construction of the European Union, cf. J.H.H. Weiler, "Idéaux et construction européenne," in M. Telò (ed.), *Democratie et Construction Européenne* (Bruxelles: Université de Bruxelles, 1995).

[4] P.C. Schmitter, "If the Nation-State were to Wither Away in Europe, What Might Replace It?" in S. Gustavsson and L. Lewin (eds.), *The Future of the Nation-State: Essays on Cultural Pluralism and Political Integration* (Stockholm: Nerenius & Santérus, 1996), pp. 228–229.

[5] G. Folke Schuppert, "The Evolution of a European State: Reflections on the Conditions of and the Prospects for a European Constitution," in J.J. Hesse and N. Johnson (eds.), *Constitutional Policy and Change in Europe* (Oxford: Oxford University Press, 1995), p. 331.

[6] W. Heun, "The Evolution of Federalism," in C. Starck (ed.), *Studies in German Constitutionalism* (Baden-Baden: Nomos Verlagsgesellschaft, 1995), pp. 185–187.

model of the state as a kind of enterprise association. It rests on an a-political vision of civil society as consisting primarily of economic and social activities that can be regulated and harmonised using legal and administrative procedures alone.[7]

There remains a fundamental ambiguity in the project of a European federal state. Its underlying ideals of peace and prosperity are presented as having universal value, making the European Union a model for others to imitate; but the very means by which peace and prosperity can be ensured—from economic competitiveness to border control—may in some cases imply the exclusion of others (poor nations and economic migrants) from their benefits. Indeed, state federalism in Europe may need the construction of a European identity with both its encompassing and exclusionary features. These particularist implications are rejected by the second, more cosmopolitan, interpretation of a federal Europe.

This version equates federalism with a radical criticism of state sovereignty. The principles underlying this position are the recognition of the dignity and basic liberties of the individual, and the fact that these fundamental rights apply generally and universally. According to the individualist understanding of these principles adopted by most cosmopolitans, obligations are either self-chosen or dependent on one's (interactional and/or institutional) relationships with other individuals.[8] No nation, or any other ascriptive community, has moral worth apart from that attaching to its individual members. All particular political allegiances are dissolved in a world community of human beings, with legitimate sovereignty meaning no more than the power to enact the principles of cosmopolitan justice. Most cosmopolitans contend, however, that it does not follow that the only legitimate political unit is a world state. Such a polity is as impracticable as it is inadvisable because of the threat that such a concentration of power might pose to individual liberty and rights.[9] The world society advocated by cosmopolitans does not necessarily imply a concentration of sovereignty. On the contrary, it may best be served by a dispersion of sovereignty (hence their advocacy of federalism) beyond the traditional unit of the (nation-) state, and by its dissolution as a form of ultimately personalized collective agency. Cosmopolitan federalism represents a challenge both to the nation-state and to the idea of sovereignty itself.

The cosmopolitan view understands federalism not as a form of state, but mainly in juridical terms as "law without a state."[10] This position harks back

[7] On the anti-political conception of civil society, cf. C. Taylor, "Invoking Civil Society," in *Philosophical Arguments* (Cambridge MA & London: Harvard University Press, 1995), pp. 215–220.

[8] On various understandings of cosmopolitanism, cf. T.W. Pogge, "Cosmopolitanism and Sovereignty," in C. Brown (ed.), *Political Restructuring in Europe: Ethical Perspectives* (London & New York: Routledge, 1994), pp. 89–98.

[9] Cf. Pogge, "Cosmopolitanism and Sovereignty" and D. Archibugi, "Immanuel Kant, Cosmopolitan Law and Peace," *European Journal of International Relations* 1 (1995), pp. 429–456.

[10] T. Koopmans, "Federalism: The Wrong Debate," *Common Market Law Review* 29 (1992), pp. 1047–1052, at p. 1051.

to medieval constitutional theories, which distinguished jurisdiction (*jurisdictio*) from governance (*gubernaculum*).[11] Fundamental laws, rights and privileges, and the whole juridical apparatus were considered as the main brakes on the power of the political ruler. In international law, this line of argument was carried into the modern world by the jurisprudential tradition that understands the law of the nations (*jus gentium*) to be not the product of agreements between sovereign states, but the legal framework of an ideal *civitas maxima* within which sovereign states operate.[12] Such a conception implies that the juridical order of the state is not a closed unit, and that its sovereignty is therefore subject to important limitations both in its internal and external dealings. From a cosmopolitan perspective, the problem has often been that the validity of the superior law lacked practical application. This lacuna has now been partly addressed by the positivisation of human rights via various international conventions and declarations and the establishment of international organisations, such as the UN and the International Court of Justice, with the function of implementing them, even if their capacity to do so remains highly limited in practice.[13] These mechanisms go some way towards fulfilling the cosmopolitan ideal, as expressed by Kant, of law-governed relationships both within the state, when this gives itself a "civil constitution," and between states, when they accept to be united in a "lawful *federation* under a commonly accepted international right."[14] As a result, in a cosmopolitan federation, sovereignty—in its absolute sense, as the authority to make the ultimate decision—is dissolved in the impersonality of the law.

Our reference to the medieval lineage of the modern cosmopolitan view of the dissolution of state sovereignty has perhaps more than historical significance. Some of the institutional models favored by cosmopolitans have something in common with medieval pluralist structures of power, such as the Holy Roman Empire. This entity was a "political body constituted around a juridical organization,"[15] where the issue of *plenitudo potestatis* was a deeply contested one. The European Union may be considered the primary example of the "return" of this model of federal Empire. Its constitutionalisation mainly through the jurisprudence of the European Court of Justice, the apparent dispersion of sovereignty because of the overlapping competences at national and European level, and the ambiguous nature (international or

[11] Cf. C.H. MacIlwain, *Constitutionalism: Ancient and Modern* (Ithaca NY: Cornell University Press, 1958), ch. 4.

[12] Cf. Hans Kelsen, *Das Problem der Souveränität und die Theorie des Völkerrechts. Beitrag zu einer Reiner Rechtslehre* (Tübingen: Mohr, 1920), ch. 9; and L. Ferrajoli, *La Sovranità nel Mondo Moderno. Nascita e Crisi dello Stato Nazionale* (Milano: Anabasi, 1995).

[13] Cf. D. Held, *Democracy and the Global Order: From the Modern State to Cosmopolitan Governance* (Cambridge: Polity Press, 1995), chs. 5 and 6; and L. Ferrajoli, "Beyond Sovereignty and Citizenship: A Global Constitutionalism," in Bellamy (ed.), *Constitutionalism, Democracy and Sovereignty.*

[14] I. Kant, "On the Common Saying: "This May Be True in Theory But Not in Practice," in *Kant Political Writings* (ed.), by H. Reiss and transl. by H.B. Nisbet (Cambridge: Cambridge University Press, 1991), p. 90.

[15] A. Winckler, "L'Empire revient," *Commentaire* 15 (1992), pp. 17–25, at p. 19.

federal?) of the treaties that have given rise to the Union and the Community; all these factors taken together have produced a complex polity with an elaborate structure of administrative and legal powers, with no single hierarchy and no overarching authority to which all other powers are clearly accountable. Similarities with the pre-modern structure of the federal Empire may end here, however, for cosmopolitans argue for the dissolution of state sovereignty on normative grounds that reflect post-national, rather than supranational, developments.[16] It is not just globalisation and social differentiation that make the difference. Cosmopolitans see these processes as providing the opportunities rather than the reasons for rejecting the moral value of communitarian attachments. The crisis of the nation-state has opened up a whole number of other issues on which cosmopolitans contest traditional conceptions of legal and political sovereignty.

The main cosmopolitan challenges concern ideas of democracy and political identity in the nation-state. The post-national challenge to democracy has two aspects to it. First, it rejects the idea that democracy is, in essence, "people rule"; pointing out that democratic sovereignty cannot be absolute, since this would risk allowing a democracy to abolish itself. Democracy must rest on self-standing rights, which need constitutional entrenchment in order to be protected against even democratic majorities. On the face of it, this seems a criticism of the majority principle as the main rule of democracy. In fact, it strikes at the core of democratic theory by questioning the legitimating role of the Demos as both the constituent power and the basic unit on which the boundedness of the democratic community ultimately rests. By displacing the Demos from its central position, cosmopolitans also undermine the idea of popular sovereignty. They substitute the former with the "civil multitude,"[17] and the latter with the more impersonal sovereignty of the law, which becomes the proper object of a cosmopolitan patriotism. From this point of view, the integration of Europe and the redistribution of popular sovereignty is theoretically unproblematic. Since cultural, national and similar ties are deemed morally insignificant, setting the boundaries and scope of political and administrative units are matters of practical convenience alone. Territorial contiguity and economic viability rather than a sense of belonging are the decisive factors.[18]

The second aspect of the cosmopolitan challenge to traditional ideas of democracy is based on the recognition that in complex societies there is a disjunction between the political-administrative sphere, where decisions are taken, and the public sphere—in the Habermasian sense of those private and semi-private associations that act in the public realm—where opinions are formed and debated.[19] In modern national democracies, representative

[16] Cf. J-M. Ferry, "Une 'philosophié' de la communauté," in: J-M. Ferry and P. Thibaud, *Discussion sur l'Europe* (Paris: Calmann-Levy, 1992), pp. 169–189.

[17] In Kantian terms, a "civil multitude" is composed of cosmopolitan citizens—those, that is, that are bound by both the civil constitution and the idea of cosmopolitan right: I. Kant, "Perpetual Peace: A Philosophical Sketch," in *Kant Political Writings*.

[18] Cf. Pogge, "Cosmopolitanism and sovereignty."

[19] Cf. Ferry, "Une 'philosophie' de la communauté," pp. 148–166.

institutions are meant to link the two spheres by rendering the executive power publicly accountable through the formal mechanisms of a parliamentary regime. This procedure has now become both technically difficult, due to the complexity of the issues and the number of decision-making levels involved, and politically problematic, because of the apparent inability of the political machinery to give expression to a common will in highly differentiated societies. Cosmopolitans maintain that this enervation of political representation can be offset by the diversification of the technical and the critical functions of the state. The latter is increasingly found in the informal institutions comprising the public sphere, such as the media, professional associations, charities and similar bodies. These are located in civil society and are said to exercise a constant control over the political and administrative process. Together with the judicial power, they assume the dual function of legitimating political and administrative decisions, by exposing them to the test of public reason more than that of popular consent, and of limiting the power of the political and technocratic apparatuses by giving publicity to their actions. As a consequence, the main democratic deficit in the European Union, as presently structured, does not lie in the limited powers vested in the institutions of direct representation, but in the lack of a fully developed and integrated European society and public sphere.

The other main cosmopolitan challenge to nation-state sovereignty concerns the idea of political identity. Its questioning follows directly from the deconstruction of the Demos into a "civil multitude," with important consequences for citizenship and territoriality. In modern societies, the law already recognises that there are rights of the person, to which all are entitled irrespective of their affiliation to a particular political community. Citizenship rights, however, still have an exclusionary character. In increasingly globalised societies, so it is argued, such a distinction is not warranted.[20] Obligations towards others' negative and positive rights should not be restricted by community or national boundaries. The globalisation of responsibility implies that state sovereignty be both broadened, by requiring the state to intervene beyond the confines of the immediate interests of its citizenry (as in, for example, the Bosnian crisis), and narrowed, by sanctioning a general and universal right to free movement and to take up residence. In a very limited sense, European citizenship, as imperfectly introduced by the Maastricht Treaty, goes some way towards bridging the gap between human and citizenship rights, which seems integral to the idea of communal identity, and which the emergence of nation-states widened further.

On the basis of this criticism of the privileged status normally associated with membership of a political community, the very idea of political unity and the right of self-determination that goes with it may only be justified on

[20] Cf. B.S. Turner, "Citizenship Studies: A General Theory," *Citizenship Studies* 1 (1997), pp. 15–18, especially pp. 15–17; and L. Ferrajoli, "Dai diritti del cittadino ai diritti della persona," in D. Zolo, *La Cittadinanza. Appartenenza, Identità, Diritti* (Roma & Bari: Laterza, 1994).

instrumental grounds,[21] and be strictly within the legal framework of a cosmopolitan federation. This makes an entitlement to political self-determination for both ascriptive and voluntary groups conditional on a number of factors concerning, on the one hand, their relevance and encompassing nature, and on the other, the effects that self-determination may have on both groups' members and non-members. The territorial boundaries of these units cannot be assumed on simply historical or allegedly "natural" grounds, they may need to be continuously negotiated and re-negotiated. Cosmopolitan federalism, therefore, has no privileged place for national sovereignty in the political architecture of the European Union. Nor does it regard issues of national sovereignty as carrying special weight in the process of constitutionalization of the European Union, thus denying that the nation-states are (or should be) the *Herren der Verträge*.

This radical criticism of national sovereignty does not exclude that there may still be a place for nation-states. According to at least one version of cosmopolitan federalism, a certain socio-political homogeneity between the political units comprising the federation is needed to prevent its transformation into a federal state.[22] In other words, states may remain relatively independent so long as they are sufficiently similar for centralised schemes of redistribution or mechanisms for mediating conflicts of legal norms to be unnecessary. In the European Union, however, that requirement could be met by autonomous regions, which may be better equipped to address local needs and demands, as much as by existing national states.

Cosmopolitan federalism may also support more radical solutions to the political architecture of the European Union by advocating either a vertical or a horizontal dispersion of sovereignty. The former solution[23] insists that what matters is the best level at which a decision-making unit can satisfy the conditions of maximum decentralisation (units that are as small as possible) and optimal centralisation (units that include as equals all persons significantly and legitimately affected by the relevant decisions). This vertical dispersion of sovereignty would have the added benefits of creating a multi-layered structure, strengthening the vertical system of checks and balances and of the division of powers, and encouraging a cosmopolitan culture that favors multiple identifications. The horizontal dispersion of sovereignty[24] addresses a different aspect of the crisis of the nation-state, by suggesting a

[21] Cf. A. Margalit and J. Raz, "National Self-Determination," *Journal of Philosophy* 87 (1990), pp. 439–461; and C.R. Beitz, "Cosmopolitan Liberalism and the States System," in Brown (ed.), *Political Restructuring in Europe*, pp. 131–135.

[22] On the condition of "political homogeneity," cf. O. Beaud, "La Fédération entre l'état et l'empire," in B. Théret (ed.), *L'État, la finance et le sociale* (Paris: La Decouverte, 1995), pp. 299–302.

[23] Cf. Held, *Democracy and the Global Order* and Pogge, "Cosmopolitanism and Sovereignty."

[24] On social federalism in Europe, cf. M. Telò, "L'intégration sociale en tant que réponse du modèle européen à l'interdépendance globale? Les chances, les obstacles et les scénarios," in Ibid. (ed.), *Quelle Union Sociale Europeenne?* (Bruxelles: Université de Bruxelles, 1994).

model of social federalism that shifts the focus of decision-making processes from a territorially-based to a socially-based representation of interests. This is not as far fetched a proposal as it may perhaps seem, for some features of European integration have *de facto* anticipated such a move. There is an obvious danger of corporatism, which could perhaps be offset by guaranteeing both a diffuse system of representation and a centralised dialogue based on strong normative criteria. This may have costs in terms of both political democracy and formal legitimacy, but would be aimed mainly at increasing social legitimacy in the European Union. The proposals for either a vertical or a horizontal dispersion of sovereignty, however, seem to be particularly vulnerable to the kind of criticisms more generally directed against the cosmopolitan position. Namely, that they are too abstract and disregard the open-textured nature of discussions about the substantive legitimacy of decision-making units.[25] To imagine the political architecture of the European Union without taking questions of political identity seriously may court serious danger. This, by contrast, is the starting point for models of political architecture based on a communitarian mode of argument.

NATION-BASED ARCHITECTURE

Current defenses of nation-states and of their sovereignty within the political architecture of the European Union rest on a belief in the importance and justifiability of collective forms of self-determination that are not simply seen as instrumental to individualist values and interests. Defenders of these positions place great weight on the communitarian argument that there are no disembedded selves. Individuals need communities with which to identify, in order both to make sense of their lives and to give substance to their autonomy of judgment and action. Communal self-determination is an important part of this autonomy; but the kind of community needed and the form that self-rule should take are still open questions to which many different answers can be given. National sovereignty in Europe requires some arguing, therefore, even from a communitarian perspective.

A first set of arguments contests the claim that national sovereignty has been eroded by globalization.[26] Three main ripostes are offered. The first suggests that globalists fail to recognize the important conceptual distinction between the limitation and the transferal of sovereignty. The nation-state's incapacity to control economic and environmental dynamics, for instance, results in a *de facto* limitation of the state's external sovereignty, without this having any major legal or political implications that signify the transferal of

[25] On the relationship between substantive legitimacy and the boundedness of the democratic community, cf. A. Weale, "Democratic Legitimacy and the Constitution of Europe," in R. Bellamy, V. Bufacchi, and D. Castiglione (eds.), *Democracy and Constitutional Culture in the Union of Europe* (London: Lothian Foundation Press, 1995), pp. 86–89.

[26] This paragraph essentially summarises arguments found in P. Hirst and G. Thompson, *Globalisation in Question: The International Economy and the Possibilities of Governance* (Cambridge: Polity Press, 1996).

sovereignty to some other body. The second suggestion is that globalists overrate the impact that globalization has on the capacity of the nation-state to control socio-economic processes. The development of inter-national and inter-governmental—more than supranational—institutions should be seen as attempts by nation states to keep their power, rather than as revealing a loss of sovereignty. Nation-statists, for example, can defend monetary unification for much the same reasons that state federalists do, by suggesting that this is the only way in which political communities can keep financial markets under control. The all important difference, which has significant implications for institutional design, is that while federalists consider a central European bank as part of a broadly federal structure, supporters of nation-state sovereignty look on it as an inter-state institution. The third criticism questions the globalists' view that the state has lost control over its territory. It suggests that, although this may be the case in a number of areas involving economic regulation, capital circulation, information and technological developments, it is not so in the crucial area of human mobility. Indeed, if anything, states in the late twentieth century have a firmer grip over the great majority of their own population; while there are no longer opportunities for mass migrations on the scale of those that took place in the past up until the First World War.

The second set of arguments in support of the nation-state suggest that at present the nation-state is still the main collective entity capable of offering a stable, encompassing and relevant identity to its members; of guaranteeing recognition by other such collective bodies; and of providing the basic unity necessary for the exercise of political self-determination.[27] The privileging of the national dimension can be argued on strongly organic grounds, emphasizing ethnic and racial identity, a narrow conception of past history, and a commonality of language and culture. This clearly can give rise to extremely unpleasant forms of nationalism. But some of the same elements can also be integrated into a civic understanding of national identity that constructs it in broadly voluntary terms and is respectful of the person as separate from the community.[28]

Civic communitarians, however, may find it difficult to demonstrate that nations should be privileged over other communities. In principle, there seems to be no particular reason why identity, recognition and self-determination should be better served by nations than by any other group or corporate body. This difficulty is not greatly different from that encountered by cosmopolitans in establishing the optimal level for the vertical distribution of sovereignty. Cosmopolitans argue for it in purely instrumental terms, so

[27] A discussion of the distinction between identity, recognition and self-determination is found in C. Taylor, "Why do nations have to become states?" in *Reconciling the Solitudes: Essays on Canadian Federalism and Nationalism*, ed. by G. Laforest (Montreal & Kingston: McGill-Queen's University Press, 1994).

[28] On a possible distinction between ethnic and liberal nationalism, cf. N. MacCormick, "Liberalism, Nationalism and the Post-Sovereign State," in R. Bellamy and D. Castiglione, *Constitutionalism in Transformation: European and Theoretical Perspectives* (Oxford: Blackwell, 1996).

that there is always the possibility that a group within the political community may argue for sovereignty on certain matters to be moved either upwards or downwards. Similarly, civic communitarianism allows all kinds of groups to claim recognition, without there being any substantive principle on the basis of which to match processes of contextual identification with the allocation of sovereignty.[29] It would seem to follow that "tribalism," as the universal attribute of human beings to join in groups, requires that self-determination be attached to any group claiming to have a common identity and demanding to be recognized by others. But the primacy of identity, though maintained in principle, is denied by civic communitarians in practice. Indeed most of them accept that political self-determination is an important precondition for sustaining identity itself and for guaranteeing its recognition. They conclude, therefore, that political personality should be granted only to those "tribes" that are politically viable. In the modern world, this implies a number of conditions: territorial contiguity, to facilitate decision making and its application; mutual trust, to guarantee social dealings with the minimum of force; the sense of being an active and lasting community, where everyone feels some direct or indirect involvement in its affairs; some shared belief and common identification, but neither too fixed nor based on ascriptive characteristics, so that they are congruent with social differentiation and do not undermine the territoriality condition; and a capacity to mix particular attachments with consideration for the community as a whole, both of which may be needed to sustain a sense of justice and solidarity. Of the many communities we inhabit, nations seem to approach such conditions best, and so are commonly regarded as the natural focus of political sovereignty.[30]

A number of other arguments are often given in support of maintaining national sovereignty as a central feature of the European Union. First, it is suggested that political and administrative uniformity bring with them social and cultural homogeneization. This would undermine the pluralism of traditions, institutional settings and styles of life for which Europe is often praised, and which is considered to be a vital ingredient in sustaining an autonomous civil society. Historically, this pluralism has been fostered by the multiplicity of nations that comprise Europe, and by a fundamental balance of power between them. This circumstance has prevented the establishment of a single empire on the European continent, maintaining instead a "concert of nations." Federal structures at the European level and a diminution of national self-rule would have a negative impact on social and cultural pluralism, posing a threat to individual and collective liberties.[31]

[29] The indeterminacy of the communitarian argument on the natural unit for self-determination is evident in M. Walzer, "Notes on the New Tribalism," in Brown (ed.), *Political Restructuring in Europe*.

[30] The arguments suggested at the end of this paragraph are based on D. Miller, "The Nation-State: A Modest Defence," in Brown (ed.), *Political Restructuring in Europe*; cf. also D. Miller, *On Nationality* (Oxford: Clarendon Press, 1995).

[31] Cf. P. Thibaud, "L'Europe par les nations (et réciproquement)" in Ferry and Thibaud, *Discussion sur l'Europe*, pp. 101–117.

Secondly, communitarians insist that democracy—which everyone agrees is one of the fundamental values on which the European Union ought to rest—needs to foster a sense of unity and a minimum of common identity in the people, so that everyone is prepared to accept the democratic game of majorities and minorities. Without this background assumption, there is no fundamental bond on which to rely, and no trust between the citizens that the rules of the game will be kept. Deep and irreconcilable divisions may set in, driving the democratic community apart and making democratic rules and institutions irrelevant.[32] As with arguments on nationality, so conceptions of the "people" can be based on either organic (ethnic-historical-cultural) or artificial (civic-voluntary) constructions. However, the kinds of criticism of federal projects that these conceptions imply amount to the same thing. These projects are considered either unrealistic (state federalism), because there is no European Demos; or anti-democratic (cosmopolitan federalism), because it would undermine democratic forms of legitimacy. It is also added that projects to construct a European Demos contradict the original, and often repeated, aim of an "ever closer Union of the *peoples* of Europe."[33] Federalists seem to advocate a melting-pot strategy, something which was never intended, and which may turn out to be either impracticable or counterproductive for democracy both at a European and, indirectly, at the national level.

Thirdly, communitarians regard the idea of European citizenship with a certain suspicion. At one level, they consider the introduction of European citizenship alongside national citizenship as deeply problematic because of the conflict of allegiances that this may give rise to. In a fully integrated federal system, dual citizenship expresses the participation of the citizen in two different sets of institutions—one at the national and the other at the local level. Those conflicts that emerge from this vertical dispersion of sovereignty are conflicts between institutions. They do not concern the citizen directly, and do not test his or her allegiance to the political community, except in the extreme case of secession. But in a less integrated system, a plurality of citizenships would seem unworkable.[34] This reason for the communitarians' rejection of multiple citizenship is compounded by a more fundamental objection they raise against cosmopolitanism. Communitarians emphasize that citizenship implies both rights and obligations and that the disjunction of the idea of citizenship from a community-based sense of solidarity and reciprocity would render citizenship highly problematic. A sense of commonalty and a minimum degree of homogeneity seem to be required for citizenship, therefore, as they were for the definition of the Demos.

[32] On the relationship between democracy and Demos, cf. D. Grimm, *Braucht Europa eine Verfassung?* (Berlin: Carl Friedrich von Siemens Stiftung, 1995), pp. 36–47; and G.E. Rusconi, "La cittadinanza europea non crea il 'popolo europeo'," *Il Mulino* 45 (1996), 831–841.

[33] On this contradiction, cf. J.H.H. Weiler, "European Neo-Constitutionalism: In Search of Foundations for the European Constitutional order," in Bellamy and Castiglione, *Constitutionalism in Transformation*, pp. 110–113.

[34] Cf. R. Aron, "Une citoyenneté multinationale est-elle possible?" *Commentaire* 14 (1991–1992), pp. 695–704.

What all these arguments amount to is that political self-determination requires a community of fate. The European Union in its present form is at most an individualist based form of state. There do not seem to be the conditions for Europe itself to become a community of fate capable of sustaining democratic forms of government and principles of social citizenship. Such a development is both highly problematic and detrimental to social and cultural pluralism. Recent attempts at forging a European identity to sustain and justify greater integration have resulted in the shallow symbolism of self-celebration. The celebration of Europe *per se*, rather than its various national cultures and values, tends to be strikingly contentless.[35] The famous fantasy bridges of the ill-fated new European banknotes are a good illustration of this phenomenon.

Communitarian models of the European Union agree that nation-states are the *Herren der Verträge* and that the Union can at most be regarded as an "association of states" (*Staatenverbund*), retaining full external sovereignty, but willing to pool it together in order either to co-ordinate their actions in matters of common interest or to increase their influence and bargaining power in international affairs. The transference of sovereignty from the states to the Union is limited and conditional and has no implications for internal sovereignty therefore; nor does it envisage a vertical dispersion of sovereignty. These sorts of considerations, for instance, motivated the German Constitutional Court's Maastricht judgment reaffirming its competence at the national level.[36]

But there are other aspects of the political architecture of the Union on which communitarians diverge. On the whole, three main positions can be identified, arising out of different conceptions of the nature of the national community and of politics. The first is based on strongly organic conceptions of the nation and the people harking back to nationalist values and aspirations and demanding the scaling down of all federal-like institutions of the Union. At the core of this position is a deep suspicion of external influence and the conviction that any form of organic co-operation risks jeopardizing the sovereignty of the nation. The second model, usually associated with British Eurosceptics and their "hostility" to things European, mixes a traditional defense of national sovereignty on broadly nationalist grounds with the neoliberal conviction that economic matters escape politics and so should not be subject to state intervention but left to market mechanisms. In this scheme, the European Union is a form of technical-administrative association (*Zweckverband*),[37] whose power is narrowly limited to guaranteeing the existence and the functioning of a European-wide free market. There may be

[35] Cf. Thibaud, "L'Europe par les nations," p. 50.

[36] For discussions of the judgment of the Federal Constitutional Court of Germany on Maastricht, cf. N. MacCormick, "The Maastricht-Urteil: Sovereignty Now," *European Law Journal* 1 (1995), pp. 255–262; and M. Herdegen, "Maastricht and the German Constitutional Court: Constitutional Restraints for an 'Ever Closer Union'," *Common Market Law Review* 31 (1994), pp. 235–249.

[37] On this form of association in Europe, cf. G. Winter's "Introduction" to *Reforming the Sources and Categories of EC Legal Acts*, Report for the General Secretariat of the European Consortium (March 1995), pp. 7–9.

spillovers into other areas, but these should remain strictly subordinate to the primary technical and economic objective of the formation of a common market. The individualist "universalism" of this position clashes with the rhetoric on the strengthening of the national economy, so that, echoing nineteenth-century traditions, economic individualism is harnessed to a would-be politics of national supremacy. In European terms, this means the acceptance of those supra-national institutions and established co-operative procedures which ensure open and competitive markets, but the preservation of national sovereignty by limiting the functional expansion of supra-national institutions and by keeping the veto power of the nation-states.

While the previous two models appeal to a more nationalistic oriented communitarianism, the third is based on a civic-democratic (as opposed to a national) idea of sovereignty, which needs preserving both because it is crucial for self-determination and because of its formative and civilizing role. As was suggested earlier, from such a perspective post- and supra-national developments are seen as jeopardizing the way in which democracy itself works—either because the new polity would lack the social pre-conditions for democratic decision making, or because it would not need democratic processes of will formation. Supporters of this position, however, accept that a "natural" move towards a larger European polity is possible, and indeed to a certain degree auspicable, in so far as this is functional to propping up the "civic" aspects of the nations of Europe. Ideas of civicness and civility are bridges to more universalist considerations, suggesting an alternative model to the "individualist" European Union as it has so far been constructed. It substitutes "voice" for "exit" mechanisms, for example, and tries to preserve difference where homogeneity seems to set in.[38] Civic nationalists are critical of those moves that expropriate nations of their external sovereignty, which in their view also undermine internal sovereignty and self-determination. But, in principle, it is not averse to a pulling together of external sovereignty in forms that preserve the democratic configuration of internal sovereignty itself.[39] They also depart from the nationalist version of communitarianism by accepting that the construction of the European Union is a two-way process of preserving national identities in Europe, but also of making the nations of Europe more European. In their view, both processes need to be seen as contributing to keeping alive civic and democratic values and practices.

A Mixed Commonwealth

Models of the European Union inspired by a mixture of communitarian and cosmopolitan arguments give a more positive gloss to the two-way

[38] Cf. Thibaud, "L'Europe par les nations," p. 41.

[39] In a state, or a political unit, *external* sovereignty is the power to act autonomously, while *internal* sovereignty means "who" has the authority to make decision. On this distinction, cf. N. MacCormick, "Sovereignty, Democracy and Subsidiarity," in Bellamy, Bufacchi, and Castiglione (eds.), *Democracy and Constitutional Culture in the Union of Europe*, pp. 98–100; and Ferrajoli, *La sovranità nel Mondo Moderno*, ch. 2.

transformation of national politics acknowledged by civic communitarians. They tend to combine a communitarian appreciation of the importance of identity politics within a civic and democratic setting, with the recognition that globalization and supra- and post-national processes have already altered the structure of state sovereignty beyond what communitarians are prepared both to admit and to allow. In other words, communitarianism has to be modified to take into account cosmopolitan concerns arising out of the increasing interaction between states and peoples brought on by the processes of globalisation. This cosmopolitan communitarianism, however, needs to be distinguished from a communitarian cosmopolitanism that seeks simply to flesh out cosmopolitan sentiments. It works out from existing identities and attachments and acknowledges that global forces have modified these to different degrees and in diverse ways.[40]

In many respects, the gradual constitutionalisation of Europe that has so far occurred confirms the intuition at the root of this third group of models, that there is something fundamentally new, or, as is often said, *sui generis*, in the constitutional structure of the European Union, and that such novelty is captured by neither federal nor nation-based forms of political architecture. What distinguishes this third position is a certain support both for the open, piecemeal nature of the constitutionalisation process and for a constitutional structure that mixes national and federal elements. But, given the post-Maastricht crisis of confidence, supporters of this position have felt compelled to distance themselves from a purely functionalist justification of the piecemeal process and from the vacuity of the *sui generis* formula, both of which tend to ignore questions of legitimacy.[41] Thus, there have recently been a number of attempts to give theoretical and institutional substance to the re-configuration of sovereignty that comes with the construction of the European Union as a new form of polity.

A first consideration, captured by Duverger's suggestion that a neo-federalist structure is in the making in Europe,[42] follows from the simple observation that the basic units of the new polity are fully formed nation-states, commanding strong allegiances from their citizenries and with long established histories, well developed identities and rooted institutional traditions. The development of a federation-like structure at the European level cannot avoid confronting and accommodating the demands that come from these national dimensions of politics. In recognition of all this, Joseph Weiler has proposed a dual form of citizenship, as in traditional federal structures, but based on different sources of allegiance and identification.[43] This, he believes, can be achieved by decoupling the idea of citizenship at the European level from its elements of nationhood. The European Demos, formed on the basis of

[40] See Bellamy and Castiglione, "The Normative Challenge of the European Polity," and Ibid, "Between Cosmopolis and Community," for further elaboration of this distinction.

[41] Cf. P.C. Schmitter, "Is It Really Possible to Democratize the Euro-Polity?" (Stanford, March 1996, mimeo), pp. 21–22.

[42] M. Duverger, *L'Europe dans tous ses Etats* (Paris: Presses Universitaires de France, 1995).

[43] Weiler, "European Neo-Constitutionalism," pp. 113–116.

universalistic values and principles, as implicit, for instance, in Habermas' idea of constitutional patriotism, should not supplant the national Demoi, but only act as a civilizing force keeping under control the emotional drive and particularist focus of national citizenship. Such a dual form of citizenship and legitimacy would not simply require a vertical dispersion of sovereignty, but its more nuanced articulation, by giving to representation at national and European levels different functions, as perhaps suggested by a post-national vision of the European polity. It may also imply, as Neil MacCormick has argued, a vision of internal sovereignty in the European Union as dependent on distinct legal and political systems, the validity of whose actions is a function of co-ordination and cross-referencing, both between centre and periphery and between individual states.[44] This takes us beyond the sovereign state, into a pluralist, and implicitly contested vision of sovereignty.

The polycentric polity that is therefore emerging is a definite departure from the nation-state, mainly because it implies a dissociation of the traditional elements that come with state sovereignty: a unified system of authority and representation controlling all functions of governance over a given territory. The personalised character of traditional sovereignty, associated with the idea of a *government*, is substituted by a more diffuse, and hence impersonal, idea of multi-layered *governance*.[45] The underlying logic of such a system of governance is nonetheless unclear. Domenico Majone has argued that while national institutions still maintain a semblance of unified control over the territory, they are complemented by European institutions, whose character is mainly regulatory, and which concern areas with increasing problems of externalities in decision making (e.g., the economy and the environment).[46] Philippe Schmitter has noticed, however, that although the European level of governance is increasingly affecting all areas of policy making, a multiplicity of institutional and semi-institutional arrangements between different partners are encouraged.[47] This institutional flexibility tends to blur the lines of identity and jurisdiction and, according to Schmitter, may develop either towards a form of *consortium*, with nation-states still in control of the areas and forms of cooperation, or towards a *condominium*, which implies a "variation in both territorial and functional constituencies."[48]

In spite of the many differences of analysis, we wish to suggest that all these attempts agree on the basic intuition that the polity that is gradually

[44] Cf. N. MacCormick, "Beyond the Sovereign State," *Modern Law Review* 56 (1993), pp. 1–23; and "Liberalism, Nationalism and the Post-Sovereign state," pp. 143–150.

[45] On this, cf. Hirst and Thompson, *Globalisation in Question*.

[46] For a discussion of the European polity as a "regulatory state," cf. G. Majone, "The Rise of the Regulatory State in Europe," *West European Politics* 17 (1994), pp. 77–101; and "La communauté européenne comme état régulateur," in Théret (ed.), *L'État, la finance et le social*. For a discussion of regulation and economic models in Europe, cf. S. Wilks, "Regulatory Compliance and Capitalist Diversity in Europe," *Journal of European Public Policy* 3 (1996), pp. 536–559.

[47] P.C. Schmitter, "Imagining the Future of the Euro-Polity with the help of New Concepts," in G. Marks et al., *Governance in the European Union* (London: Sage, 1996).

[48] Schmitter, "Imagining the future," p. 136.

emerging is a "mixed commonwealth":[49] that is, a polity where the subjects of the constitution are not homogeneous, but a mixture of political agents sharing in the sovereignty of the polity under different titles. In practical terms, this thesis implies that neither the nation-states nor the citizens of the European Union are the sole, exclusive subjects of the constitution; but that they both, together with other new socio-political agents, may contribute to the democratic construction of a democratic Europe. It also requires that political practices of mediation and reconciliation have a primary role, to which legal means and institutions need to be subordinated. For democratic deliberation has a capacity that legal mechanisms lack to build new allegiances and identities, and to negotiate workable compromises when a consensus on new forms of common life cannot be achieved.[50]

Proponents of the "mixed commonwealth" hypothesis also demonstrate a certain scepticism towards traditional views of political architecture. Both federal and nation-state versions presuppose a unified and systematic vision of the principles that should guide the construction of the European polity.[51] But the political architecture of a mixed commonwealth clearly implies a mixture of principles, which must in part reflect the willingness of the political agents to re-define their identities and practices. Such a mixture is more likely to emerge and be accepted as legitimate as the result of time and as part of a process of selection of procedures and institutions by trial and error. What distinguishes this position from traditional functionalist justifications is the appreciation of the element of design, which is central to constitution-making processes that take on board the need for both formal and social legitimacy. It is this conception of the open-ended nature of the constituent process, which may look more like bricolage than political architecture, that for the time being unifies those who favor the construction of a mixed commonwealth.

The result may not have the symmetry and proportionality that come with the principles of classical architecture. It may perhaps lack the dynamism and sense of material, surfaces and space typical of modernism. But it is not necessarily going to be a hotchpotch of half-digested architectural idioms, like many post-modern buildings. Perhaps, more than structural architecture—whose image is conjured up by the "pillars" of the Maastricht Treaty—urban development is a better metaphor for the construction of a mixed commonwealth. This may not involve as much careful planning, precise engineering and unity of conception as is thought necessary in creating a single building or a group of buildings. It may rather require that mixture of design and spontaneous development that is so much part of successful urban environments, where a plurality of groups and individuals dwell, and in which they pursue their different needs and aspirations.

[49] We owe this concept to Neil MacCormick.

[50] See R. Bellamy, "The Constitution of Europe: Rights or Democracy," in Bellamy, Bufacchi and Castiglione (eds.), *Democracy and Constitutional Culture in the Union of Europe*, pp. 153–175

[51] For a defense of a fully coherent and cohesive system, cf. D. Curtin, "The Constitutional Structure of the Union: A Europe of Bits and Pieces," *Common Market Law Review* 30 (1993), pp. 17–69.

26

Federalism in Plurinational Societies: Rethinking the Ties between Catalonia, Spain, and the European Union

Ferran Requejo

Is the federal state a good model to regulate democratic citizenship in plurinational societies (i.e., in political communities containing more than one group with a national identity)? I believe that the possible answers to this question are to be found somewhere between "no" and a hesitant or reluctant "maybe."

In the words of one of its best known analysts, classic liberal federalism "is designed to prevent tyranny without preventing governance," on the one hand and, on the other hand, it "has to do with the need of people and polities to unite for common purposes yet remain separate to preserve their respective integrities. It is rather like wanting to have one's cake and eat it too."[1] It is a model that in principle is unrelated, historically or normatively, to any regulation of cultural pluralism. Any discussion about federalism is irrelevant to many forms of cultural pluralism; for example, those related to feminist or immigrant movements.[2] It may be relevant, however, in the case of cultural pluralism movements characterized by territoriality and self-government (nationalist and indigenous movements).

Both institutional and normative analyses of federalism have been dominated, moreover, by the historical example of the USA. This is an empirical case historically not linked to cultural pluralism.[3] If we remain within the orbit of American federalism, the answer to the question about the possibilities of regulating democratic citizenship in plurinational societies is basically a negative one. The reasons are both historical and organizational.

Federalism is fundamentally a *territorial* model[4] and one that is governed by homogenizing interpretations of the democratic concept of "popular sovereignty"—thereby avoiding the basic question, unanswered in democratic theory, about who the people are, and who decides who they are—as well as ideas about equality of citizenship and equality between the federated units. In my view, it is practically impossible from these presuppositions to include the idea of *citizenship as identity* in the constitutional rules of the game of plurinational societies.[5] However, starting from strictly liberal premises there are other federal models with greater potential to include the cultural pluralism of a variety of national identities within the same state. In what follows, I will defend *asymmetrical federalism* as a better model for this kind of cultural pluralism.

After a period of relative neglect within academic circles, over the past few years interest in the possibilities and limitations of "asymmetrical federalism" has increased. In 1965, Charles D. Tarlton published an article in which he identified a number of deficiencies in the usual analyses of federalism, especially those of a judicial nature, that often presupposed symmetrical relations between member states and the federation. In general terms, federal *asymmetry* refers to the degree of heterogeneity that exists in the relations between each member state and the federation, and between the member states themselves. Tarlton's suggestion was that in order to understand the true logic of federal states, the analyses should not be so focused on the judicial and constitutional considerations of "sovereignties" or on the distribution of powers, but on the different political links that each member state establishes with the central government and with the other member states, whether these links were constitutionally regulated or not.[6]

A constitutional solution for different national realities is not only a question of distribution of powers, which may be solved, once and for all, by a "closed" constitutional model. It is a question that also affects the symbolic, institutional and procedural framework of the state in a social and technological context characterized by its dynamism. A constitutional model that is suitable for plurinational societies should be flexible and "open," and offer the different national realities it regulates stability and good future prospects. According to historical and comparative analysis, these requirements are very difficult to achieve from the premises of a regional state that decentralizes itself, or from those of territorial or symmetrical federalism.[7] If the "politics of recognition" for national realities should be based on the liberal-democratic organizational principles, it seems slightly out of place to insist on equality between "regions" or between the federated units of the territorial federalism model. These politics imply that equality between nations should be integrated into a revised concept of equality of citizenship, beyond the implicit statism of traditional liberalism. To equate national minority communities with mere regions, or to treat them exactly the same as federal subunits that are controlled by members of the national majority, is intrinsically inegalitarian, both in substantive and procedural terms. And it is also inegalitarian in the individual and universalist terms of a concept of citizenship based on the liberal view of identity, and not only, as is common in liberal tradition, from the point of view of *status* of a group that is uniform in rights and duties.

It is in this sense that I believe that the model of federal asymmetry is more able to integrate plurinationalism into the concept of citizenship and the liberal-democratic rules of the game. Or, put in negative terms, without asymmetrical mechanisms it would be very difficult to achieve *recognition* of the plurinationality of a state. This does not mean that certain issues cannot, or even must not, be regulated in symmetrical or "comparative" terms. From the standpoint of traditional liberalism, asymmetrical federalism is normally seen as merely an intermediate step towards the establishment of confederal agreements, or towards the complete independence of the different nationalities involved. However, to maintain the inevitability of this process is, I believe, an out-of-date attitude, at least in Western Europe. In the context of the European Union, the processes of integration and regionalization have ceased to be contradictory aspects and have become complementary aspects of the same process.

PLURINATIONALISM AND FEDERALISM

The internal logic of the Spanish *Estado de las Autonomías* is fundamentally based on an approach in which decentralization prevails over the permanent regulation of the national asymmetries of the state.[8] It is a model that finds it difficult to regulate a "liberal politics of recognition" and a revised concept of democratic citizenship that would be suitable for Spain's internal national pluralism. In my opinion, any discussion nowadays of territorial organization should concentrate more on the future than on settling past scores. The discussion about Catalonia's symbols, institutions, and responsibilities should focus more on the second half of the twenty-first century than on the largely essentialist concepts and approaches derived from the nineteenth century. In this sense, any modern perspective about how national realities like Catalonia fit into the political organizations of other territories must take into account the process of European integration. The existence of the EU changes the grounds of the federalizing discussion within the states of the Union. In the first instance, the future of all nationalisms, including those of nation-states, is inextricably linked to "European regionalism." So, from the perspective of present-day Catalan nationalism, it is no longer a question of achieving the highest number of instrumental "state" competences as possible, as this is clearly obsolete in view of the current process of economic and technological internationalization. It is more important to achieve the highest possible level of democratic self-government (symbolic, institutional and functional/financial presence) in those areas that reinforce and develop Catalonia's national personality as far beyond its borders as possible.

The aim of the following points is only to illustrate some aspects of a possible federalizing reform in Spain in order to give the national realities a more comfortable and operative fit than the one that the current constitutional model of the *Estado de las Autonomias* permits. A reform that, in my view, would have to include bold asymmetrical regulations as a feasible way to establish real *recognition* and *self-government* for the different nations that make up the Spanish state. Thus, the aim here is not to establish a detailed "party" programme, but to show a set of illustrative elements of a federalizing model to regulate Spain's plurinational character with the focus on the future and on the EU.

The Symbolic and Linguistic Spheres

The regulation of symbolic and linguistic aspects is a key issue in order to ensure that the nations "fit comfortably" into the state and into Europe. In Catalonia an asymmetrical federalizing regulation would have to include the following.

Symbols

Symbols of national character are very important elements as far as individual identity is concerned, that is, with respect to how individuals understand themselves and their own dignity in relation to the groups they live in. The representative symbols of the Spanish state continue to be a source of problems as far as their use and legitimization is concerned, especially in the Basque Country and Catalonia. Therefore, the use of the national group's own symbols (flag, anthem, etc.) should be regulated on an optionally preferential basis by the institutions of the Catalan Government (the *Generalitat*), in relation to the symbols of other levels of political organization (the Spanish state, the European Union). At present, neither the Spanish symbols nor their use reflects the plurinational character of the state.[9]

Languages

Although this is a neglected issue in liberal-democratic theory, language has never been a *neutral* issue in liberal politics. This is a fundamental subject for a liberal recognition of national entities. Official languages have usually been important in nation-building processes, and the language of the majority has often been imposed by liberal institutions regardless of the plurilinguistic and plurinational reality of the state. In Spain, plurilingualism is a fundamental feature of state plurinationality, and as such should be part of the policies of the state institutions (education, culture, etc.) and not only those of the autonomous communities with their own languages.[10] The present linguistic regulation is asymmetrical as far as the territories of some autonomous communities are concerned, but the formal and practical symmetrical prevalence of only one language (Spanish) is established throughout the state's territory. This should be changed in favour of the prevalence of the Catalan language (defined as the autochthonous language by the Catalan Constitutional Law) in the Catalan territory, while Spanish would also remain as an "official" language. I have called this "the regulation of asymmetrical bilingualism."

The Institutional Sphere

The Second Chamber

Nowadays, hardly anybody in Spain denies that the second chamber should be closely linked to the autonomous communities and not to the administrative "provinces" inherited from the nineteenth century. Two questions stand out in the discussion about the reform of the Senate: its composition, and its competences. From a "minimalist" point of view, I believe that the senators should be chosen through the institutions of the autonomous communities in secondary elections, and not directly by the citizens. This is because it is inadvisable for possible malfunctions to exist between the senators and the autonomous community they represent. It is debatable whether the senators should be chosen by the executive of the autonomous communities or by its parliament (or by both). There are arguments for both methods. What seems institutionally out of place, both from a representative and from a functional point of view, is for the senators to be chosen directly by the electorate.

A federal structure, especially if it includes elements of asymmetrical federalism, requires a certain degree of "symmetrical bicameralism." If the *Estado de las Autonomías* is to live up to its name, the Senate cannot be a lesser chamber, more "second division" than second reading, as it is now. Its power should be similar to that of the lower chamber, although not in the same spheres. Hence, it would be necessary to establish special competences for the two chambers of the central parliament, in the same way as in other federations (including symmetrical ones). The Senate must have precedence in the creation, handling and final decision-making of issues relating to autonomic policy, both for issues at state level and at European level. In order to guarantee a regulation that openly includes national asymmetries, the representatives of the historical nationalities in the Senate should have power of veto over issues that affect their national characteristics (language, culture, representation and aspects of foreign policy, etc). Here the mere distribution of competences is clearly insufficient.

Judicial Power

Another institutional element is the integration of the plurinational character of the state in the composition of the Constitutional Court and in the structure of the judiciary. The Constitutional Court is not an institution of the central power of the state, but an institution of the state itself. As such, it would be better if its composition reflected the state's plurinational character. Moreover, the present structure of the judiciary continues to be that of a centralized state. The *Estado de las Autonomías* has not altered this fact, unlike the structure of the executive and the legislature. The federalization of the judiciary is another unresolved matter for Spanish institutional reform, at least in the territories of the nationalities (the Catalans, the Basques and the Galicians). So, the main Catalan Court, the *Tribunal Superior de Justícia,* should become the Supreme Court in cultural and linguistic matters, as well as in those which are related to Catalan self-government.

Federated Units

The increased size of the model to include 17 subunits, and starting from a basically symmetrical approach, means that the content of the national groups has almost inevitably been watered down. And this is a problem not only for these collectives, but for the whole system. Therefore, I believe it is necessary to create executive cooperation mechanisms between the autonomous communities and the central government as well as between the different autonomous communities. At present these mechanisms are insufficient, and some of them are even blocked constitutionally (those that affect the relations between autonomous communities). I am referring to mechanisms that for specific reasons would develop only between a few communities (this would be the case of Mediterranean, linguistic, migration, cultural policies, etc.), depending also on the degree of self-government enjoyed by each community. The homogenization of the current *Estado de las Autonomías* makes it difficult to achieve a kind of integration that minimizes the reservations the national groups have of being part of a state when they are treated like any other of the 17 Spanish autonomous communities (plus two towns on the coast of North Africa, Ceuta and Melilla, which also have their own "statute of autonomy").

Administrative Rationalization

Functionally speaking, only two basic administrative levels would be necessary: the national (Catalan) and the municipal. Central power and, in the future, that of the European Union can operate through the Catalan administration, as is the case of other federations (Germany). This decreases the need to maintain the "provinces" as an administrative unit of the state (or as electoral districts).

The Sphere of Competences

Linguistic and Cultural Policies

Territories endowed with a national character should be able to dictate cultural and linguistic policies without the interference of other territorial powers. These policies are fundamental to achieve a real politics of recognition of the national entities in different arenas. Regarding these issues, they should be able to act as independent states, that is, with a "cultural sovereignty" that includes the international dimension of these policies.

Internal Competences

Real self-government of national entities implies a broad regulation of a set of specific competences such as health care and social security services, civil law, public order, local power, infrastructures, education, and universities, among others. In practical terms this objective requires the adoption of asymmetrical regulations in order to guarantee that nations will not simply be treated as Spanish regions in these areas.

European and International Spheres

Any politics of national recognition should include the presence of nationalities within the EU and other institutions and international decision-making processes (e.g. UNESCO). The presence in these spheres constitutes one of the most important elements for the recognition and self-government of any national unity, apart from its symbolic effects, which are also important.

Constitutional Laws and Territoriality

A radical change is necessary in relation to the treatment of two questions that suppose a restrictive interpretation of political self-government: the meaning of the Spanish constitutional laws and the intervention of the central government when an autonomous community's exclusive competence is exercised beyond its own borders. Both suppositions imply a deformation of the contents of self-government, even from the barely pluralist point of view of the current Spanish constitutional model. Firstly, the content of some of the constitutional laws passed in the last decade proved to be centralizing instruments in matters of point responsibility (local government, universities, civil servants, etc.). This content should, in my opinion, permit, and even in some cases encourage, a series of optionally asymmetrical regulations by the autonomous communities. Secondly, the supra-autonomic "taking back" by the central government of competences exclusive to the autonomous communities when the scope of the matter goes beyond the autonomous territory constitutes a constant threat to these communities of being relegated to a subordinate role. This affects different matters (transport, insurance, etc.) over which the central government does not in principle have exclusive competence, but only the right to dictate basic legislation. At times this point has been interpreted not symmetrically, but simply from a centralist standpoint.

Taxes

The *Generalitat* should have exclusive rights to collect taxes in its own territory, use them for its own government, and hand over a previously agreed amount to the central Spanish government and to the institutions of the European Union.[11] In practical terms, this is a central element of self-government, regardless of whether it is regulated on a symmetrical or asymmetrical basis. Solidarity or subsidiarity cannot be principles used against national self-government. It is rather more coherent, for example, to invoke the principle of solidarity when the self-government of national realities is fully developed. We could say that, in order to regulate solidarity well, it is necessary to distinguish between the differences that must be corrected and the differences that must be maintained and consolidated. National differences may belong to the second group.

SUMMARY AND CONCLUSIONS

The aim of this article has been to focus on liberal non-state nationalism as a new way of approaching liberal democracies. A way that focuses on some conceptual limits of classical liberalism, as well as a way of improving the normative and institutional premises of liberal democracies in the increasingly culturally pluralistic societies of the end of twentieth century. I have tried to show that traditional "territorial" federalism is a bad model to regulte a concept of democratic citizenship based on the liberal politics of recognition of plurinational states. I have pointed out the need to establish asymmetrical regulations, and have given a number of specific examples for the case of the plurinational Spanish state. The concept of asymmetrical federalism has traditionally been controversial from the perspective of classical liberalism. Different authors have pointed out a lack of limits in the concept of asymmetry, focusing on the likely continuity between federal asymmetrical regulations and the final secession from the federation of the asymmetrical member-state. Different images have been suggested to clarify this process towards the final constitution of an independent state: a "slippery slope" or a "stepping stone" towards independence. However, I think that these images are misleading at least in the European context. They still reflect an excessively statist approach. The process towards a European Union goes some way to dilute the importance of the state as an organization, and the bipolarity that always characterizes competition between the processes of *nation-building* and *state-building* within plurinational states. On the one hand, this new multi-polar context will probably introduce asymmetrical regulations among the states' members. On the other hand, in contrast to past agreements, the Maastricht Treaty (1992) included the political role of the regions within the EU. That is, Maastricht has begun to consider the "regions" as legitimate political actors, in contrast to the previous community laws that stem from the Treaty of Rome, in which they were looked on merely as the objects of policies while playing no part in the decision-making process. The fact that a process of gradual unification is taking place within the EU may mean that not only the member states but also the "regions" will find their place in the institutions and collective decision-making processes of the Union. In fact, Maastricht has begun to recognize that European integration and regionalization are two features of the same process. And the "regions" which are also nations such as Catalonia have added reasons to show their support for the process of European integration. I believe that to reduce the states monopolistic role as a political actor, as well as the dualism between the different forms of nationalism, are necessary conditions for the institutional expression of a future "liberal politics of recognition" within the concept of European citizenship. To live in increasingly plural societies is one of the essential *values* of democratic organizations, and some asymmetrical regulations will be needed in order to link European (state and non-state) national pluralism in the decades to come. Without any doubt, the dilution of statism that characterizes the European order since Westphalia will be a slow process full of obstacles, but I believe that it is very likely that, at the end of the coming century, European regulation of different kinds of national pluralism and an effective European citizenship will be two parts of the same process.

And if not, "We'll always have Paris" (or Brussels–New York).

ACKNOWLEDGMENTS

This article is a part of a revised version of the paper awarded the "*Rudolf Wildenmann Prize*" (Bern, March 1997) for the best workshop paper presented at the Oslo Joint Sessions of the *European Consortium for Political Research*. I am grateful for the comments of the participants at the ECPR workshop, as well as those received at the presentations at The Johns Hopkins University (Baltimore, USA), at the Political and Social Sciences Institute, and at Pompeu Fabra University (Barcelona).

NOTES

1. D. Elazar, *Exploring Federalism* (Tuscaloosa: The University of Alabama, 1987), pp. 129 and 33.
2. See the chapter by Kymlicka in this volume.
3. In contrast to those federal states which embrace their plurinational character, such as Canada Belgium, and to a lesser extent, Switzerland see Bakvis & Chandler, eds., *Federalism and the Role of the State* (Toronto: University of Toronto Press, 1987). In the analytical field, traditional studies of federalism have often committed the fallacy of taking a part, the USA, to represent the whole. For a current general overview of federalism see R. Watts, "Contemporary Views on Federalism" in B. de Villiers, ed., *Evaluating Federal Systems* (Cape Town/Dordrecht: Juta/Martinus Nijhoff, 1994), pp. 1–29. For a general empirical perspective of federalism see D. Elazar, *Federal Systems of the World* (Essex: Longman, 1991).
4. P. Resnick, "Toward a Multinational Federalism" in L. Seidle, ed., *Seeking a New Canadian Partnership: Asymmetrical and Confederal Options* (Montreal: Institute for Research on Public Policy, 1994). I maintain Resnick's duality between territorial and plurinational federalism because it has become a common point of reference. I think, however, that it is not very accurate: all federalisms are territorial. Perhaps it would be better simply to talk about uninational and plurinational federalisms (R. Pelletier, "Les arrangements institutionels d'un partenariat Canadien," unpublished paper). For the latest trend in Canada, see K. McRoberts, *Misconceiving Canada* (Toronto: Oxford, 1997).
5. I focus here on plurinational states which have failed to develop a strong and fundamentally uncontroversial sense of nation-state building compatible with the maintenance of non-state national identities (like Belgium, Canada, or Spain). Clearly, there are other plurinational states that have been successful in combining both aspects (like Switzerland). In this last case classical federalism offers a better way to relate national pluralism with the *republican* unity of the "demos."
6. This is a model that is able to draw together the perspectives that Elazar calls *workable* polity and *just* polity, in contrast to other territorial models that are more "comprehensive" in the constitutional sphere.
7. It should not be forgotten that federalism is not based on decentralization, but on noncentralization. For a consideration of asymmetrical arrangements for recognition see J. Webber, *Reimagining Canada* (Montreal: McGill-Queens University Press, 1994); and D.J. Lenihan, G. Robertson & Tassé, *Canada: Reclaiming the Middle Ground* (Montreal: Institute for Research on Public Policy, 1994). From a European perspective see N. MacCormick, "Liberalism, Nationalism and the Post-Sovereign State," *Political Studies* 44 (1996), pp. 553–567.
8. The current Spanish Constitution (1978) does not recognize the plurinational character of the Spanish State. After recognizing the existence of "nationalities and regions" (art. 2), it treats these two entities in fundamentally egalitarian terms referring to them as "autonomous communities" in the rest of the text. The differences between those autonomous communities, which the constitutional text considers to be more or less asymmetrical, are largely transitory in character

(differences in institutions, competences, and procedures for achieving autonomy). Only the reference to tax policies in the Basque Country and Navarre, and the reference, not without its ambiguities, to linguistic and cultural differences are related to asymmetrical considerations. The perspective of a homogenizing symmetry was reinforced in the 1980s by the post-constitutional political pacts of 1981. The current Spanish constitutional model is not based on a "liberal politics of recognitions" of the plurinational reality which it tries to regulate. In this section, I will concentrate on the case of Catalonia.

9. Another issue is Catalonia's representation in international sporting events (world and European championships, Olympic Games, etc.). This is another aspect of symbolic representation that should not be ruled out in future asymmetrical political regulations. Another sphere which has barely been explored by the Spanish plurinational reality is the education system. Outside the territories of the historical nationalities, knowledge of non-Castilian culture is still very poor. This encourages impoverished attitudes of homogenization–separation on both sides. For example, the standard of analysis of the history, literature and culture of the Catalan, Basque, and Galician nationalities in some textbooks is very low.
10. Banknotes and coins, stamps, personal documents (passport, identity cards, etc.), or the name of the state itself should also reflect the plurilinguistic character of the state. The euro, for example, is a currency which speaks only one language, Spanish; in contrast to other European currencies (Belgium, Switzerland, Norway, Finland, Ireland).
11. This is already the current situation in the Basque Country and Navarre. The recent controversies surrounding the transfer of 15%, and later of 30%, of personal income tax is simply ridiculous in federal terms, even in terms of symmetrical federalism.

Further Readings

Allen, Barbara, "Alexis de Tocqueville on the Covenantal Tradition of American Federal Democracy," *Publius* 28:2 (1998), pp. 1–23.

Baker, J. Wayne, "Faces of federalism: From Bullinger to Jefferson," *Publius* 30:4 (2000), pp. 25–41.

Baubock, Rainer, "Why Stay Together? A Pluralist Approach to Secession and Federation," in W. Kymlicka and W. Norman, eds., *Citizenship in Diverse Societies* (Oxford: Oxford University Press, 2000), pp. 366–394.

Bauer, Otto, *The Question of Nationalities and Social Democracy* (Minneapolis: University of Minnesota Press, [1907] 2000).

Beer, Samuel H., *To Make a Nation: The Rediscovery of American Federalism* (Cambridge, Mass.: Harvard University Press, 1993).

Benson, Georges C.S., ed., *Essays in Federalism* (Claremont: Claremont Men's College, 1961).

Braybrooke, David, "Can Democracy Be Combined With Federalism or With Liberalism?" in *Liberal Democracy*, NOMOS XXV, ed. J. Roland Pennock and John W. Chapman (New York: New York University Press, 1983), pp. 109–118.

Bryce, James, *The American Commonwealth* (Indianapolis: Liberty Fund, [1888] 1995).

Burgess, Michael, *Federalism and European Union: Political Ideas, Influences and Strategies in the European Community, 1972–1987* (London: Routledge, 1989).

——— and Alain-G. Gagnon, eds., *Comparative Federalism and Federation: Competing Traditions and Future Directions* (Toronto: University of Toronto Press, 1993).

———, *The British Federal Tradition* (London: Leicester University Press, 1995).

———, *Federalism and European Union: The Building of Europe, 1950–2000* (London: Routledge, 2000).

Calhoun, John, *Union and Liberty: The Political Philosophy of John C. Calhoun* (Indianapolis: Liberty Fund, 1992).

Dahl, Robert A., "Federalism and the Democratic Process," in *Liberal Democracy*, NOMOS XXV, ed. J. Roland Pennock and John W. Chapman (New York: New York University Press, 1983), pp. 95–108.

Davis, Solomon Rufus, *The Federal Principle: A Journey through Time in Quest of a Meaning* (Berkeley: University of California Press, 1978).

———, *Theory and Reality: Federal Ideas in Australia, England and Europe* (University of Queensland Press, 1995).

De Villiers, Bertus, ed., *Evaluating Federal Systems* (Cape Town/Dordrecht: Juta/Martinus Nijhoff, 1994).

Dicey, A.V., *Introduction to the Study of the Law of the Constitution* (London: Macmillan & Co, [1885] 1908).

Elazar, Daniel J., *Exploring Federalism* (Tuscaloosa, Al.: University of Alabama Press, 1987).
———, ed., *Federalism as Grand Design: Political Philosophers and the Federal Principle* (Lanham, Md.: University Press of America and Center for the Study of Federalism, 1987).
———, ed., *Constitutional Design and Power-Sharing in the Post-Modern Epoch* (Lanham, Md.: University Press of America, 1991).
———, *Federalism and the Way to Peace* (Kingston, Ont.: Institute of Intergovernmental Relations, Queen's University, 1994).
———, *Constitutionalizing Globalization: The Postmodern Revival of Confederal Arrangements* (Lanham, Md.: Rowan & Littlefield, 1998).
Føllesdal, Andreas, "Subsidiarity," *Journal of Political Philosophy* 6:2 (1998), pp. 190–218.
Forsyth, Murray, *Union of States: The Theory and Practice of Confederation* (London: Leicester University Press, 1981).
———, ed., *Federalism and Nationalism* (London: Leicester University Press, 1989).
Friedrich, Carl J., *Trends of Federalism in Theory and Practice* (New York: Praeger, 1968).
Gagnon, Alain-G. and James Tully, eds., *Multinational Democracies* (Cambridge: Cambridge University Press, 2001).
Gierke, Otto von, *The Development of Political Theory* (New York: W.W. Norton, 1939).
———, *Community in Historical Perspective* (Cambridge: Cambridge University Press, 2002).
Goldwin, Robert A., ed., *A Nation of States: Essays on the American Federal System* (Chicago: Rand McNally, 1961).
Hesse, Joachim Jens and Vincent Wright, eds., *Federalizing Europe? The Costs, Benefits, and Preconditions of Federal Political Systems* (Oxford: Oxford University Press, 1996).
Hueglin, Thomas, *Early Modern Concepts for a Late Modern World: Althusius on Community and Federalism* (Waterloo, Ont.: Wilfrid Laurier University Press, 1999).
———, "From Constitutional to Treaty Federalism: A Comparative Perspective," *Publius* 30:4 (2000), pp. 137–153.
———, "Federalism at the Crossroads: Old Meanings, New Significance," *Canadian Journal of Political Science/Revue canadienne de science politique* 36:2 (2003), pp. 275–294.
Karmis, Dimitrios, "Fédéralisme et relations intercommunautaires chez Tocqueville: entre prudence et négation des possibles," *Politique et sociétés* 17:3 (1998), pp. 59–91.
———, "Pourquoi lire Proudhon aujourd'hui? Le fédéralisme et le défi de la solidarité dans les sociétés divisées," *Politique et sociétés* 21:1 (2002), pp. 43–65.
——— and Jocelyn Maclure, "Two Escape Routes from the Paradigm of Monistic Authenticity: Post-Imperialist and Federal Perspectives on Plural and Complex Identities," *Ethnic and Racial Studies* 24:3 (2001), pp. 361–385.
King, Preston, *Federalism and Federation* (London: Croom Helm, 1982).
Kinsky, Ferdinand, "Personalism and Federalism," *Publius* 9:4 (1979), pp. 131–155.
Knop, Karen, Sylvia Ostry, Richard Simeon, and Katherine Swinton, eds., *Rethinking Federalism: Citizens, Markets, and Governments in a Changing World* (Vancouver: UBC Press, 1995).

Kymlicka, Will, "Is Federalism a Viable Alternative to Secession?" in *Theories of Secession*, ed. Percy Lehning (London: Routledge, 1998), pp. 111–150.
———, "Minority Nationalism and Multination Federalism," in Will Kymlicka, *Politics in the Vernacular: Nationalism, Multiculturalism, and Citizenship* (Oxford: Oxford University Press, 2001), pp. 91–119.
LaSelva, Samuel, *The Moral Foundations of Canadian Federalism: Paradoxes, Achievements, and Tragedies of Nationhood* (Montreal & Kingston: McGill-Queen's University Press, 1996).
Le Fur, Louis, *État fédéral et confédération d'États* (Paris: Panthéon-Assas, [1896] 2000).
Lister, Frederick K., *The Early Security Confederations: From the Ancient Greeks to the United Colonies of New England* (Westport, Conn.: Greenwood Press, 1999).
Livingston, William S., *Federalism and Constitutional Change* (Westport: Greenwood Press, 1956).
Lutz, Donald S., "The Iroquois Confederation Constitution: An Analysis," *Publius* 28:2 (1998), pp. 99–127.
Marhold, Hartmut, ed., *Le nouveau débat sur l'Europe* (Nice: Presses d'Europe, 2002).
McCoy, Charles S., "Federalism: The Lost Tradition?" *Publius* 31:2 (2001), pp. 1–14.
McKay, David, *Designing Europe: Comparative Lessons from the Federal Experience* (Oxford: Oxford University Press, 2001).
Mogi, Sobei, *The Problem of Federalism: A Study in the History of Political Theory* (London: Allen & Unwin, 1931), 2 volumes.
Monnet, Jean, "Memorandum of 3 May 1950," ed. Giovanni Vigo, *The Federalist: A Political Review* XXX:3 ([1950] 1988), pp. 232–236.
———, *Les États-Unis d'Europe ont commencé* (Paris: Laffont, 1955).
———, *Memoirs* (Garden City, N.Y.: Doubleday, 1978).
Mouvement fédéraliste européen (M.F.E.), "Charte fédéraliste," in *La révolution fédéraliste*, ed. Alexandre Marc (Paris: Presses d'Europe, 1969).
Nelson, Ralph, "The Federal Idea in French Political Thought," *Publius* 5:3 (1975), pp. 7–62.
Nicolaidis, Kalypso and Robert Howse, eds., *The Federal Vision: Legitimacy and Levels of Governance in the United States and the European Union* (Oxford: Oxford University Press, 2001).
Norman, Wayne, "Towards a Philosophy of Federalism," in *Group Rights* ed. Judith Baker (Toronto: University of Toronto Press, 1994), pp. 79–100.
———, "The Morality of Federalism and the European Union," *Archiv für Rechts- und Sozialphilosophie*, v. 59, 1995, pp. 202–211.
———, "Federalism and Confederalism," in *Routledge Encyclopedia of Philosophy*, ed. Edward Craig, London: Routledge, 1998, v. 3, pp. 572–574.
———, "The Ethics of Secession as the Regulation of Secessionist Politics," in *Self-Determination and Secession*, ed. M. Moore (Oxford: Oxford University Press, 1998), pp. 34–61.
———, "Domesticating Secession," in *Secession and Self-Determination*, ed. Stephen Macedo and Allen Buchanan, NOMOS XLV (New York: New York University Press, 2003), pp. 193–237.
Pagden, Anthony, ed., *The Idea of Europe: From Antiquity to the European Union* (Cambridge: Cambridge University Press, 2002).
Pinder, John, ed., *Altiero Spinelli and the British Federalists: Writings by Beveridge, Robbins and Spinelli* (London: Federal Trust, 1998).

Proudhon, Pierre-Joseph, *Oeuvres complètes de P.-J. Proudhon,* volume 14: *Du principe fédératif et oeuvres diverses sur les problèmes politiques européens* (Paris: Marcel Rivière, 1959).

Randall, Stephen J. and Roger Gibbins, eds., *Federalism and the New World Order* (Calgary: University of Calgary Press, 1994).

Riker, William, *Federalism: Origin, Operation, Significance* (Boston: Little, Brown and Company, 1964).

———, "Federalism," in *A Companion to Contemporary Political Philosophy,* ed. Robert E. Goodin and Philip Pettit (Oxford: Blackwell, 1993), pp. 508–514.

Riley, Patrick, "Rousseau As a Theorist of National and International Federalism," *Publius* 3:1 (1973), pp. 5–18.

———, "Three 17th Century German Theorists of Federalism: Althusius, Hugo and Leibniz," *Publius* 6:3 (1976), pp. 7–41.

———, "Federalism in Kant's Political Philosophy," *Publius* 9:4 (1979), pp. 43–64.

Rougement, Denis de, "Toward a New Definition of Federalism," *The Atlantic Community Quarterly* (Summer 1970), pp. 224–233.

———, ed., *Dictionnaire international du fédéralisme* (Brussels: Bruylant, 1994).

Saint-Pierre, Abbé Charles de, *Projet pour rendre la paix perpétuelle en Europe* (Paris: Fayard, [1712] 1986).

Schuman, Robert, *Pour l'Europe* (Paris: Nagel & Guillaume Briquet, [1963] 2000).

Smith, Graham, ed., *Federalism: The Multiethnic Challenge* (London: Longman, 1995).

———, "Sustainable Federalism, Democratization, and Distributive Justice," in *Citizenship in Diverse Societies,* ed. W. Kymlicka and W. Norman (Oxford: Oxford University Press, 2000), pp. 345–365.

Spinelli, Altiero, *The Eurocrats: Conflicts and Crisis in the European Community* (Baltimore: The Johns Hopkins Press, 1966).

——— and Ernesto Rossi, "The Ventotene Manifesto: Towards a Free and United Europe—A Draft Manifesto," 1944 (http://www.federalunion.uklinux.net/archives/ventotene.htm).

Storing, Herbert and Murray Dry, eds., *The Anti-Federalist* (Chicago: University of Chicago Press, 1985).

Taylor, Charles, *Reconciling the Solitudes: Essays on Canadian Federalism and Nationalism* (Montreal & Kingston: McGill-Queen's Press, 1993).

Tocqueville, Alexis de, "Voyage en Suisse" (1836) and "Rapport sur 'La démocratie en Suisse' de Cherbuliez" (1848), in Alexis de Tocqueville, *Œuvres,* ed. André Jardin (Paris: Gallimard, 1991), volume 1, pp. 615–632 and 635–654.

Tully, James, *Strange Multiplicity: Constitutionalism in an Age of Diversity* (Cambridge: Cambridge University Press, 1995).

Vernon, Richard, "The Federal Citizen," in *Perspectives on Canadian Federalism,* ed. R.D. Olling and M.W. Westmacott (Scarborough, Ontario: Prentice-Hall, 1988), pp. 3–15.

Vipond, Robert C., *Liberty and Community: Canadian Federalism and the Failure of the Constitution* (Albany: State University of New York Press, 1991).

Voyenne, Bernard, *Histoire de l'idée fédéraliste* (Paris: Presses d'Europe, 1973–1981), 3 volumes.

Weinstock, Daniel, "Towards a Normative Theory of Federalism," *International Social Science Journal* (2001), pp. 75–83.

Wheare, Kenneth C., *Federal Government* (Oxford: Oxford University Press, 1946).

———, "Federalism and the Making of Nations," in *Federalism: Mature and Emergent*, ed. Arthur W. Macmahon (Garden City, New York: Doubleday & Company, 1955), pp. 28–43.

Whitaker, Reg, "Federalism and Democratic Theory," in *A Sovereign Idea: Essays on Canada as a Democratic Community*, ed. Reg Whitaker (Montreal & Kingston: McGill-Queen's University Press, 1992), pp. 165–204.

Index

CPSIA information can be obtained at www.ICGtesting.com
Printed in the USA
LVOW081438080313
323401LV00002B/8/A

9 780312 295813